melbourne
ARCHITECTURE

First published in 1999 by
The Watermark Press
Sydney, Australia

The publishers would like to acknowledge the support and encouragement
of The Hon Robert Maclellan, MLA, Minister for Planning and Local
Government, Victoria, in making this publication possible.

*This publication is supported by
Heritage Victoria*

Advisory Group: Neil Clerehan, Conrad Hamann, Bryce Raworth,
George Tibbits, Ray Tonkin, Bruce Trethowan, Meg Bartel

Editor: Simon Blackall
Copy Editor: Leith Hillard
Production Editor: Siobhan O'Connor
Assistant Editor: Elly Bloom
DTP: Alex Stafford

Text copyright © Philip Goad 1999
   except where otherwise credited
Photographs copyright © Patrick Bingham-Hall 1999
   except where otherwise credited

Maps: Cartodraft
Contributing Writers: Neil Clerehan, Conrad Hamann,
Bryce Raworth, Bruce Trethowan, George Tibbits

National Library of Australia
Cataloguing-in-Publication data

Goad, Philip.
    A guide to Melbourne architecture.

    Includes index.
    ISBN 0 949284 36 X.

    1. Architecture — Victoria — Melbourne. 2. Buildings — Victoria —
    Melbourne — Guidebooks. 3. Historic buildings — Victoria — Melbourne
    — Guidebooks. 4. Melbourne (Vic.) — Buildings, structures, etc. —
    Guidebooks. 5. Melbourne (Vic) - Guidebooks.
    I. Bingham-Hall, Patrick. II. Title.

720.99451

Original Design by IKON Graphic Design
Typeset in Rotis Sans Serif Light
Printed in Australia by Southwood Press

melbourne ARCHITECTURE

PHILIP GOAD

The Watermark Press

St Patrick's Cathedral, East Melbourne

CONTENTS

INTRODUCTION

At the head of the flat basin of Port Phillip Bay, Melbourne's settlement in 1835 was a shrewd, if not entirely legal, piece of real estate speculation, not at all like Sydney and Hobart which began as penal colonies. Surveyor Robert Hoddle's grid plan grew over the next 160 years, and Melbourne developed from a hick pastoral outpost to an urbane city. Today, that grid remains, housing a dense concentration of skyscrapers studded with elegant Victorian public buildings, surrounded by graceful public gardens to the north, east, and south; serviced until recently by docks to the west; and approached by the tree-lined boulevards of St Kilda and Flemington roads and Royal and Victoria parades.

Named after British Prime Minister Viscount Melbourne (1779–1848), the township was to balloon in size with the discovery of gold at Ballarat in 1851. The Renaissance Revival style flourished — for banks, shops and even warehouses. Grand statements were reserved for the Treasury, Public Library and Parliament House.

By the 1880s, Melbourne was thoroughly Victorian — rich and booming. A fashion for coffee palaces went hand in hand with rampant property speculation. Just as Marvellous Melbourne rose to dizzy heights with Queen Anne skyscrapers and Venetian Gothic office blocks, it fell into deep recession with the economic bust of 1893.

Red brick, turned timber and terracotta tiles marked a dramatic shift in architectural tastes between 1890 and 1920. Federation architecture was thoroughly original, as architects talked of a definable 'Australian style'. American Romanesque influences brought tall arcading to warehouses and commercial buildings, while Edwardian Baroque was favoured for government architecture, a suitably grand style, as Melbourne was temporarily the nation's capital from 1901 until 1927.

The Great War (1914–18) resulted in Melbourne's most enduring monument, its Shrine of Remembrance, and ushered in a conservative street architecture. In the suburbs, the speculative house success of the interwar years was the Californian bungalow. By 1934, the centenary year, Melbourne could claim examples of revolutionary functionalist architecture as well as the streamlined Moderne. Hospitals and schools were the harbingers of new stripped forms. During World War II, city building came to a standstill. Postwar shortages engendered a new resourcefulness and central city building was given further tonic by the 1956 Olympic Games.

During the 1950s and 1960s, Melbourne sprawled outwards unhindered. Freeways began to radiate from the city's core and Melbourne's planners grappled with a city torn between love for its trams, its high streets, the emergence of a heritage movement and a sprawl which matched Los Angeles. Today, in Melbourne, the Yarra's south bank has been developed, the architecture of streets has returned and the carpet of suburbs, from the city to the bush, has new threads of density which increase its richness as a modern metropolis.

HOW TO USE THIS BOOK

The sample page below is typical of those found in the listings throughout the book. Each period of architecture has its own chapter and is colour-coded for easy reference. Individual numbered entries contain standard information and symbols, as well as text outlining details about the building itself.

Colour-coded chapter tabs for quick and easy reference

Building name, which may be either present or former name, or both

Address or location, including opening hours

Condition, Visibility and Accessibility of the building or site

Timeline of important historical and social events

Picture number cross-references to the building number

Map reference taken from the *Melway Street Directory*

Architect or architects, including any subsequent renovations

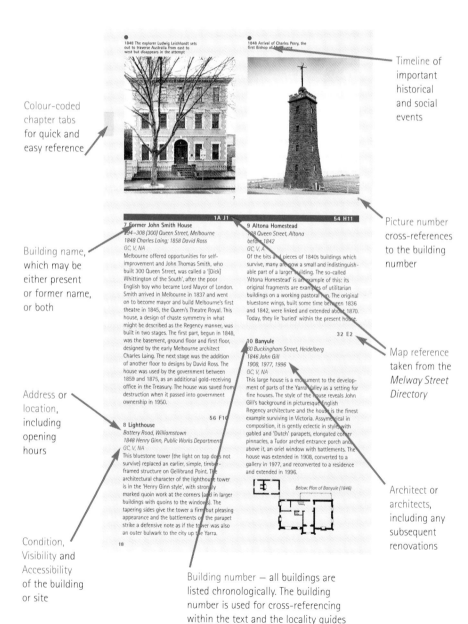

1848 The explorer Ludwig Leichhardt sets out to traverse Australia from east to west but disappears in the attempt

1848 Arrival of Charles Perry, the first Bishop of Melbourne

1A J1

7 Former John Smith House
294–308 (300) Queen Street, Melbourne
1848 Charles Laing; 1858 David Ross
GC, V, NA
Melbourne offered opportunities for self-improvement and John Thomas Smith, who built 300 Queen Street, was called a '[Dick] Whittington of the South', after the poor English boy who became Lord Mayor of London. Smith arrived in Melbourne in 1837 and went on to become mayor and build Melbourne's first theatre in 1845, the Queen's Theatre Royal. This house, a design of chaste symmetry in what might be described as the Regency manner, was built in two stages. The first part, begun in 1848, was the basement, ground floor and first floor, designed by the early Melbourne architect Charles Laing. The next stage was the addition of another floor to designs by David Ross. The house was used by the government between 1859 and 1875, as an additional gold-receiving office in the Treasury. The house was saved from destruction when it passed into government ownership in 1950.

56 F10

8 Lighthouse
Battery Road, Williamstown
1848 Henry Ginn, Public Works Department
GC, V, NA
This bluestone tower (the light on top does not survive) replaced an earlier, simple, timber-framed structure on Gellibrand Point. The architectural character of the lighthouse tower is in the 'Henry Ginn style', with strongly marked quoin work at the corners (and in larger buildings with quoins to the windows). The tapering sides give the tower a firm but pleasing appearance and the battlements of the parapet strike a defensive note as if the tower was also an outer bulwark to the city up the Yarra.

18

54 H11

9 Altona Homestead
128 Queen Street, Altona
before 1842
GC, V, A
Of the bits and pieces of 1840s buildings which survive, many are now a small and indistinguishable part of a larger building. The so-called 'Altona Homestead' is an example of this: its original fragments are examples of utilitarian buildings on a working pastoral run. The original bluestone wings, built some time between 1836 and 1842, were linked and extended about 1870. Today, they lie 'buried' within the present house.

32 E2

10 Banyule
60 Buckingham Street, Heidelberg
1846 John Gill
1908, 1977, 1996
GC, V, NA
This large house is a monument to the development of parts of the Yarra Valley as a setting for fine houses. The style of the house reveals John Gill's background in picturesque English Regency architecture and the house is the finest example surviving in Victoria. Assymetrical in composition, it is gently eclectic in style with gabled and 'Dutch' parapets, elongated corner pinnacles, a Tudor arched entrance porch and, above it, an oriel window with battlements. The house was extended in 1908, converted to a gallery in 1977, and reconverted to a residence and extended in 1996.

Below: Plan of Banyule (1846)

Building number — all buildings are listed chronologically. The building number is used for cross-referencing within the text and the locality guides

8

HOW TO USE THIS BOOK

Buildings are listed chronologically so that it is possible to trace the history of the city through the architecture. A timeline runs along the top of each page relating current events in Australia.

The listings are divided into ten periods: 'Settlement' (1835–1851); 'The Victorian City' (1851–1880); 'Marvellous Melbourne' (1880–1890); 'The Federation City' (1890–1920); 'Between the Wars' (1920–1932); 'The Moderne City' (1930–1945); 'Postwar Recovery' (1945–1955); 'The Contemporary City' (1955–1970); 'The City and the Bush' (1970–1980); 'Modern Metropolis' (1980–1998). The buildings are numbered so that the first digit relates to the section in which they are found. Each section is preceded by an introduction, some of which have been written by guest authors, providing an overview of the period relating to the architecture in the pages following. Brief explanations of styles and movements are provided alongside the entries, approximately where a change of style has occurred.

Each entry in the listings is located by a *Melway Street Directory* map reference and an indication of its condition, visibility from the street and accessibility.

Condition/Visibility/Accessibility

GC — Good Condition
AC — Average Condition
BC — Bad Condition
V — Visible
NV — Not Visible
A — Accessible
NA — Not Accessible

Abbreviations

HCV — Housing Commission of Victoria
PWD — Public Works Department
RAIA — Royal Australian Institute of Architects
RVIA — Royal Victorian Institute of Architects

Where possible, an indication of opening times is provided, although it is important that these be confirmed before visiting.

Tours of areas of concentrated architectural interest are provided at the end of the book. Entries are cross-referenced to the listings.

Settlement
1835–1851

1835–1851

'Early Melbourne' is a ghostly presence within the city.

A scattered few of the earliest buildings survive, in various states of addition and alteration. These survivors prompt questions from the visitor and the expert as to whether what is there today can be called 'original'. A less obvious, but more tangible, reminder of Melbourne from the 1830s and 1840s lies not in its buildings, but in survey lines: the rectangular grid dividing the public domain of streets in central Melbourne, and the main streets and roads of suburban Melbourne, from the domain of private property. Also, from the myths and realities of the early years of settlement there emerged a belief that enterprise and buildings would eventually create a great city that would vie with London and Paris.

Melbourne began as an illegal settlement in 1835. Indeed, the entire pastoral occupation of Victoria was forbidden by the colonial administration in Sydney, from where the area was called the Port Phillip District of New South Wales. During the 1840s, that name became a yoke of bondage until it was removed in 1851, when the separate Colony of Victoria was created. Government buildings came to be seen as a representation of the separateness of the polity of Victoria and Melbourne from New South Wales and Sydney. The great public buildings from the 1850s and later, made possible by the discovery of gold in 1850, were to be the fruits of Separation.

From the 1840s, political independence sharpened the sense of purpose that Melbourne would become a city of international significance. While enormous changes after 1851 overwhelmed the old Melbourne, they nevertheless have not entirely displaced the pre-gold rush city.

As an illegal settlement of private individuals, Melbourne had become established before there was official recognition of its existence. Only after that recognition came – and it had to come from London to Governor Richard Bourke in Sydney – was government authority introduced. The result was the dispatch of a small civil and military contingent, under Captain William Lonsdale, which arrived at the start of October 1836. Among the consequences of the assertion of government authority was the survey of the area, the laying out of the town plan and all the surrounding agricultural land, and the sale of land to individual bidders for the highest price.

For the town, the government surveyors established a large reserve within which the small Melbourne township was laid out. Outside the town reserve, they marked out large rectangular groups of agricultural allotments bordered by roads one chain wide, which soon became suburbs outside the town reserve. Even today, the boundaries of the reserve of 1837 remain strongly defined: by the east–west Victoria Street, the north–south Hoddle Street and the course of the Yarra River. Within that open area, 24 ten-acre square blocks, in three rows of eight, were laid out, each block bounded by major streets that were 99 feet (1.5 chain; 30.84 metres) wide and bisected in an east–west direction by narrow streets only 33 feet (0.5 chain; 10.25 m) wide, the 'little' streets of central Melbourne, the whole being bounded by Flinders, Spring, Lonsdale and Spencer streets.

The town grid was aligned by natural features and was at a 28° angle to the boundary of the town reserve: the river and its flood plain positioned Flinders Street, an escarpment on the western edge that of Spencer Street, and a sharp drop where the Rialto building stands today (and which can still be seen) positioned the south side of the west end of Collins Street. The line of a creek may also have influenced the position of the streets and the angle of the grid, such that the creek would drain down Elizabeth Street (the creek is still there today, but runs under Elizabeth Street in large barrel drains). Much of the town was on the sloping ground of two hills—an eastern and western hill—and the eastern edge of the town at Spring Street coincides with the crown of its hill. The grid therefore seems to have been 'juggled' into a best-fit position.

Because of the rapidly increasing population, more town blocks north of Lonsdale Street were then surveyed and sold, taking the town towards the edge of the town reserve boundary at Victoria Street. Later, at the time of the gold rushes and after the reserve had been extended to Park Street, the suburbs of East Melbourne, Carlton and North Melbourne were laid out and sold. The result is that within the area of the town reserve there is a regular layout of wide streets. Outside the town reserve, things turned out quite differently as a result of a different process. The large agricultural allotments began to be subdivided by their owners such that an irregular patchwork of contrasting narrow streets was created. The old suburbs of Fitzroy, Collingwood, Richmond and Brunswick came into being as a result of private subdivision, which created the streets as well as the allotments. In Brunswick, for example, the only road surveyed and marked out by the government surveyors was the Sydney Road, a straight road one chain (10.5 m) wide, which was flanked on either side by large agricultural allotments of nearly 100 acres (40.5 hectares) running eastwards or westwards down to creeks in the valleys. Today, the street pattern in Brunswick is the result of myriad private subdivisions and the streets run mainly in an east–west direction. The differences between suburbs within the town reserve and those outside it are a legacy of the earliest years of settlement.

There was never the same government presence in early

Melbourne that there was in Sydney. The large, and often architecturally designed, barracks for convicts and the military were not part of the early Melbourne scene. Only late in the 1840s did government buildings of any size appear, such as the beginnings of the Melbourne Gaol in Russell Street (though none of the 1840s work survives) and the Government Offices in William Street (where the Supreme Court now is). Officials in Melbourne mediated between local interests and the colonial government in Sydney, an increasingly difficult situation for the Superintendent Charles Joseph La Trobe, who arrived in October 1839. For private sector interests, government buildings became a symbol of the importance of Melbourne, whereas in Sydney government buildings represented government power independent of the private sector. Only one government building survives from this early period, the recently restored bluestone **Lighthouse** at Gellibrand Point, Williamstown.

In the rapidly growing town of Melbourne, the principal building materials were brick and timber. It seems that most brick buildings were not initially rendered with stucco, as became the fashion later. The use of bluestone, sources of which were soon discovered for quarrying, was slow to be implemented; however, by the late 1840s, bluestone was being used for government buildings, commercial buildings and residences. In modern times, bluestone came to be regarded as a quintessential building material of 'old Melbourne'. Imported building materials, sandstones, bricks and timber, slates and glass, were also used and, by the 1850s, this was an accepted practice for some significant buildings. Timber shingles were widely used and, under later galvanised iron sheeting, examples survive to this day. Some prefabricated buildings were sent from Sydney, while others came from Britain such as **La Trobe's Cottage**, which was prefabricated by John Manning and survives re-created on a site by the Royal Botanic Gardens.

The early architects of Melbourne are still known today. Of the small group, Robert Russell (1808–1900) is the most puzzling. Before arriving in Sydney in 1833, he worked in three important architectural offices in Britain and also had surveying experience in Ireland. He came to Melbourne in September 1835 from Sydney, as a member of the government's survey team. He failed as a government surveyor and left, but returned in March 1838 as Clerk of Works, representing the Colonial Architect's Office. He failed again and went into private practice, but with no more success. The work he is now known for, **St James' Old Cathedral**, may have been secured for him by his father-in-law, James Smith. Russell's legacy was not in architecture, but in his watercolour views of the early years of the settlement. Another early figure was Samuel Jackson (1807–1876), who arrived in August 1835 from

Launceston. He was an architect–builder, designed **St Francis Catholic Church**, and left one of the most important relics of early Melbourne—a panorama of the town in 30 July 1841, which is now in the La Trobe Collection of the State Library of Victoria.

On a higher architectural level was Charles Laing (1809–1857), who arrived in 1840 from Manchester, England. Between 1845 and 1850, Laing was both city surveyor and a private architect. His practice included houses, churches, and commercial and institutional buildings. In the city, the nave and tower of **St Peter's Eastern Hill** survives, and an interesting house, Coryule, outside Geelong. Another early architect was John Gill (c. 1797–1866), who arrived in August 1842. Gill's house in Spring Street (long since demolished) became a social centre for architects, poets and artists. Like Laing, Gill had a broad practice and attracted influential clients, and a number of his houses survive, such as **Banyule**, **The Hawthorns** and Burwood (now **Invergowrie**). In the public sphere, two resident architects were also successive clerks of works in the Colonial Architect's Office. Nothing by James Rattenbury survives in Melbourne. Henry Ginn (1818–1892) became the Colonial Architect in the Victorian administration. His Williamstown **Lighthouse** and the **Under Gardener's Cottage** in the Royal Botanic Gardens survive.

Parish map showing Hoddle grid.

By the late 1840s, Melbourne and its suburbs had established characteristics which still pervade the city. The lower river area had developed into an industrial and shipping area. The western hill had become the administrative centre of government, around the Government Offices built in 1845, where the Supreme Court now stands. The valley of Elizabeth Street was becoming a retail and business area, while to the east, along Collins Street, fashionable houses were built. There was industry along the river banks at Richmond and Collingwood; further upstream, from South Yarra out to Heidelberg, estates of fine houses, such as **Como** in South Yarra were in evidence.

The population of Melbourne grew to about 23 000 people when the Port Phillip District was separated from New South Wales and became the Colony of Victoria. Despite a serious depression in 1842, the town had developed into an impressive settlement. Its size, scale, vitality and wealth, however, was almost negligible in comparison with the metropolis which developed after gold was discovered.

GEORGE TIBBITS

1

2L A1

1 Jolimont, La Trobe's Cottage
Dallas Brooks Drive, South Yarra
1839
GC, V, A

Superintendent Charles Joseph La Trobe arrived in Melbourne in 1839, bringing with him a small prefabricated cottage, a prized example of the John Manning (London) system of prefabrication. It used evenly spaced slotted posts, between which uniform panels for standard doors, windows and wall sections were fixed. La Trobe's Cottage (with its dining room addition), called 'Jolimont', was moved from land near the Melbourne Cricket Ground and reconstructed in 1963 on the edge of the Botanic Gardens, with new components made to match missing or deteriorated ones. The National Trust, in a bold move for its time, was responsible for Jolimont's relocation and commissioned its restoration by John and Phyllis Murphy, pioneers of restoration architecture in Melbourne. It has recently been moved again to a site in Dallas Brooks Drive.

1B L2
2 St Francis's (Catholic) Church
Elizabeth and Lonsdale Streets, Melbourne
1841–45, 1849 Samuel Jackson; 1856 George & Schneider; 1878 Reed & Barnes
GC, V, A

Though altered and extended, this is the oldest Roman Catholic church in Victoria and has been in continuous service since the early 1840s. The main vessel of the church, the nave, with wooden shingles on the roof, was built first. The cement-rendered walls of the exterior are modelled in the manner of the late 18th-century Georgian Gothick idiom practised in England before the Gothic Revival proper set in after the 1830s, a movement pioneered by the Catholic architectural radical AWN Pugin. The first additions to Jackson's simple nave were

designed by David Ross: a porch (1855, demolished) and a Lady Chapel (1858). Internally, the chapel is in the manner of Pugin, with the decoration carried out by claimed pupils of his, Le Gould & Souter. Externally, however, the idiom was never achieved and the extensions of the porch, the Lady Chapel, the sanctuary (1878) and a recent narthex (1956) follow the cement rendering of the earliest part of the church. In 1988–89, the church was repaired and restored by the conservation architects Allom Lovell & Associates and Kosinova Thorne as well as Falkinger Andronas P/L (1990–97).

2F K1
3 St Peter's (Anglican) Eastern Hill
Gisborne and Albert Streets, Melbourne
1846–48 Charles Laing; 1853 Charles Vickers; 1876 Terry & Oakden; 1896 Inskip & Butler
GC, V, A

St Peter's was begun in 1846 and is the oldest Anglican church in the city, with a continuous history of service. The early services emphasised the liturgy in the manner advocated by the Tractarian Movement in England, begun in 1833 with the ideal of restoring pre-Reformation English Catholicism to the Church of England. Such a liturgical orientation gradually affected the layout and appearance of the church. Charles Laing designed the nave in a simple Gothic style, with lancet windows, buttresses with pinnacles, and with the walls and ornament in stucco – a pre-Gothic Revival Gothic. The nave was extended in 1853 by the addition of transepts and galleries designed by Charles Vickers, while the chancel was extended in 1876, with a vestry and organ loft gallery to the design of Terry & Oakden. In 1896, further changes were made by the architects Inskip & Butler. The pinnacles and transept galleries were removed and the buttresses of the old Laing nave altered.

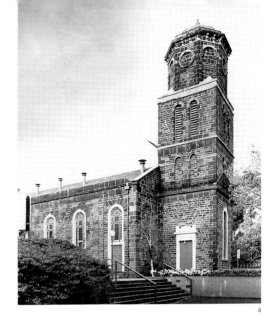

4

2E K1

4 St James's (Anglican) Old Cathedral

419-435 King Street, Melbourne
(originally in Collins Street west)
1839-51 Robert Russell; 1841 Charles Laing;
1913 relocated to King Street
GC, V, A

St James's Anglican Church originally stood in Collins Street, on a large site bounded by William and Little Collins streets. The church's popularity waned as the Gothic Revival progressed and, whether from ecclesiastical prejudice or structural uncertainty, was deemed unsafe. When it was closed in 1912, pioneers rallied to save the church by having it moved and rebuilt on its present site. It is the first Anglican church and the only surviving example of a once much-used local sandstone quarried from the south side of the Yarra, and an example of inter-colonial architectural influence—Robert Russell, the designer, drew on the work of Francis Greenway in Sydney. Russell was succeeded by Charles Laing, who added the side porches, a tall octagonal tower above Russell's square tower and the remarkable 'east' end (now the north end, as the church was turned 90° when it was relocated), which has been claimed to be based on the entrance to Robert Adam's Edinburgh University. The antique character of Old St James's was maintained after its rebuilding with some significant changes: the two-stage square tower has been raised to three stages and the blind windows changed from two to three; of the tall, two-stage octagonal tower, only the upper part was reproduced.

2C A11

5 Former Devonshire Arms Hotel

Now part of the Sisters of Charity
St Vincent's Hospital, 38 Fitzroy Street, Fitzroy
1842–43
AC, V, NA

This is the oldest known hotel building to survive in Melbourne and its inner suburbs. It is assumed that building started in 1843, being built on a bluestone base on which brick walls were raised (although they may not have been rendered originally), and with a roof covered with timber shingles. The timber was pit-sawn and the nails were handmade. The present-day surroundings not only emphasise how small and somewhat primitive the building was, but also how slight was the distinction in scale between houses, shops and hotels in the early years of Melbourne settlement. A stable and kitchen were added in about 1849. In 1988, it was refurbished (which involved replacing the floors and introducing fire sprinklers) for St Vincent's alcohol and drugs rehabilitation unit—an ironic and touching use for the city's oldest hotel building.

1B N2

6 Brooks Building

305–325 Swanston Street, Melbourne
c. 1850
AC, V, A

This is the longest row of 19th-century two-storey shops to survive in central Melbourne and it is remarkable that they should date from just before Separation and the discovery of gold in 1851. Their diminutive scale is their most interesting feature, as they provide a glimpse of the size of many early buildings and the scale of the streetscape. Nothing is known of their origin other than that the original owner was a W Hawkins. Their original appearance, whether plain brick or stuccoed, is also not known.

7

8

1A J1

7 Former John Smith House

294–308 (300) Queen Street, Melbourne
1848 Charles Laing; 1858 David Ross
GC, V, NA

Melbourne offered opportunities for self-improvement and John Thomas Smith, who built 300 Queen Street, was called a '[Dick] Whittington of the South', after the poor English boy who became Lord Mayor of London. Smith arrived in Melbourne in 1837 and went on to become mayor and build Melbourne's first theatre in 1845, the Queen's Theatre Royal. This house, a design of chaste symmetry in what might be described as the Regency manner, was built in two stages. The first part, begun in 1848, was the basement, ground floor and first floor, designed by the early Melbourne architect Charles Laing. The next stage was the addition of another floor to designs by David Ross. The house was used by the government between 1859 and 1875, as an additional gold-receiving office in the Treasury. The house was saved from destruction when it passed into government ownership in 1950.

56 F10

8 Lighthouse (Time Ball Tower)

Battery Road, Williamstown
1848 Henry Ginn, Public Works Department
GC, V, NA

This bluestone tower (the light on top does not survive) replaced an earlier, simple, timber-framed structure on Gellibrand Point. The architectural character of the lighthouse tower is in the 'Henry Ginn style', with strongly marked quoin work at the corners (and in larger buildings with quoins to the windows). The tapering sides give the tower a firm but pleasing appearance and the battlements on the parapet strike a defensive note as if the tower was also an outer bulwark to the city up the Yarra.

54 H11

9 Altona Homestead

128 Queen Street, Altona
before 1842
GC, V, A

Of the bits and pieces of 1840s buildings which survive, many are now a small and indistinguishable part of a larger building. The so-called 'Altona Homestead' is an example of this: its original fragments are examples of utilitarian buildings on a working pastoral run. The original bluestone wings, built some time between 1836 and 1842, were linked and extended about 1870. Today, they lie 'buried' within the present house.

32 E2

10 Banyule

60 Buckingham Street, Heidelberg
1846 John Gill
1908, 1977, 1996
GC, V, NA

This large house is a monument to the development of parts of the Yarra Valley as a setting for fine houses. The style of the house reveals John Gill's background in picturesque English Regency architecture and the house is the finest example surviving in Victoria. Assymetrical in composition, it is gently eclectic in style, with gabled and 'Dutch' parapets, elongated corner pinnacles, a Tudor arched entrance porch and, above it, an oriel window with battlements. The house was extended in 1908, converted to a gallery in 1977, and reconverted to a residence and extended in 1996.

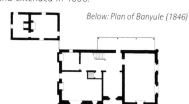

Below: Plan of Banyule (1846)

11

2M C4

11 Como
Como Avenue, South Yarra
1846; 1854
1874 AE Johnson
GC, V, A

Of all the estates created to the east of Melbourne in proximity of the Yarra, Como is the best known. It became the high profile 'home' of the National Trust after the property passed to the Trust in 1959. The Como estate has been greatly reduced by subdivision, but an open playing field below it permits one to appreciate the sweep of the land, once part of its garden, down to the river. The land was acquired in 1846 by E. E. Williams who built the first parts of the present house up on the slope running down to a billabong and the river. It is claimed the billabong reminded him of Lake Como in the north of Italy, after which he named his house. In 1854, Como was acquired by John Brown, who transformed Williams' house into the fine elegant Regency house that survives today, adding slightly later the veranda of iron posts, palisaded iron railing and gates, imported from Scotland. In the early 1870s, AE Johnson was engaged by the Armytage family (owners from 1864 until 1959) to design a ballroom, making Como a social centre for the elite of Melbourne. It is also possible to appreciate the workings

Right: Plan of Como (1846)

and hierarchical social relationships from the variety of the parts of the house and the outbuildings which survive, pristine as all the parts are now. As a notable scholar has said, 'It [is] Melbourne's most complete monument to the social life of the mid-Victorian era.'

1B U5

12 Crossley's Building
54–62 Bourke Street, Melbourne
1848–49
AC, V, A

Crossley's Building is the only commercial building from the pre-Separation and pre-gold decade which conveys something of the plain character and modest scale of that period, and is just decrepit enough today to show its age, altered though it has been in unknown ways. Nothing is known of who designed it, but its early occupant was butcher William Crossley. This part of east Bourke Street was a trade area for small business and the building remained connected with the meat trade, being leased in 1900 by William Angliss, a name now renowned as a famous Melbourne butcher and pioneer of the frozen meat export industry. There were also modest residences and studios here. In 1857–58, the artist Eugene von Guérard lived in No. 56.

2H J5

13 The Hawthorns
5 Creswick Street, Hawthorn
1846–47 John Gill
GC, V, NA

This two-storey out-of-town house is striking for its plain though solid character and is built entirely of bluestone. Designed originally for prominent public servant JP Pinnock, the house was also associated with HCE Childers, who played a crucial role in establishing the University of Melbourne.

14

2M K5

14 The Swedish Church
Former Toorak House
21 St Georges Road, Toorak
1849–51; 1854 and later
GC, NV, NA

Toorak House, which gave Toorak Road its name, has undergone a sequence of additions and alterations. Its pre-gold rush origin as a picturesque Italianate house was given social significance, and therefore architectural influence, by its early incarnation as Government House. All the additions, while consistent with the classical vernacular Italianate idiom — even the first-floor Victorian-style cast-iron balcony — mimicked the social elevation of its occupants by transforming it to a higher architectural species, a more formal Renaissance Revival model. The original house stood in an estate of nearly 60 hectares which ran down to the Yarra River from Toorak Road.

2G B11

15 Under Gardener's Cottage,
Royal Botanic Gardens
Alexandra Avenue, South Yarra
1850 Henry Ginn
AC, V, A

The Under Gardener's Cottage is near gate H in the north-west section of the gardens. When the township of Melbourne was laid out there were no reserves for parks and gardens. A site reserved in early 1846 was soon to develop into the Royal Botanic Gardens. This cottage is the only surviving example of Henry Ginn's domestic architecture, the other example in Melbourne having been the long-demolished Powder Magazine Keeper's House which stood on the corner of Spencer and Bourke streets. The Under Gardener's Cottage, despite later alterations and additions, still conveys the miniature scale and idealist formality of the original design.

2H J8

16 Invergowrie (formerly Burwood)
21 Coppin Grove, Hawthorn
1846 Attrib. John Gill; 1869; 1855; 1869
GC, V, NA

The original bluestone house, which survives as part of a much larger house in which the extensions are also in bluestone, was built by a leading early settler, Dr (later Sir) James Palmer. Its design is attributed to architect John Gill, who is also credited with the design of Banyule (10). The house, with its Gothick overtones, has a ground floor and an attic first floor, the windows of which form graceful gables projecting from the transverse gabled roof. The axis is marked by a gabled, two-storey projecting frontispiece in which there is the pointed arched entrance (now a window) and above it an oriel window to the first floor. The symmetry of the plan is obscured by later additions which were made c. 1855. The gate lodge to the progressively subdivided estate is now 8 Burwood Road.

391 D1

17 Bear's Castle
Yan Yean Reservoir Reservation,
Cades Lane, Yan Yean
c. 1848
BC, NV, NA

This two-storey building is a reminder of the variety of early construction techniques which often reflected local practices from the 'home country'. In the case of Bear's Castle, it seems to be built of cob, a mixture of moist clay and straw built up in layers and with planks of timber used as ties within each layer. Some years ago, the walls were re-surfaced to protect them from further damage, thereby covering the interesting cob construction. The square building with thick walls and round towers at its corners, one being a stair and the other a fireplace, is believed to have had a thatched roof.

18 St John's Anglican Church
1 Burgundy Street, Heidelberg
1849–1851 John Gill; 1858 Purchas & Swyer;
1963–65 (entrance porch and side chapel)
GC, V, A

This small church is one of Melbourne's earliest and retains a character appropriate to its original rural and semi-suburban community. At first the church was an undecorated brick building and it was not until 1858 that it received its present embellishments. The architects Purchas & Swyer were responsible for the work, which included rebuilding the roof and parapets, and its stuccoed detail.

19 Gulf Station (homestead and outbuildings)
Melba Highway, Yarra Glen
1851 and later
GC, V, A

This property is one of the most remarkable survivals from the early years of settlement. The timber slab buildings and other primitive aspects of construction display what photographs from other pastoral properties of that mostly disappeared past attest—that materials at hand were fashioned by crude but ingenious methods to create the different types of buildings needed. What now seems unique at Gulf Station must have been universal. It has been restored and protected by the National Trust since 1976. There are ten buildings, including the homestead, built in timber slab construction, with vertical and horizontal slabs used for the walls, logs used for the structure and timber shingles (now covered with corrugated galvanised iron) for the roofs. The homestead building has been added to and altered, and five stages of change between 1851 and 1913 have been identified.

20 Bishopscourt
120 Clarendon Street, East Melbourne
1849–53 Newson & Blackburn;
1903 Walter Butler
GC, V, NA

Bishopscourt was built for the first Anglican bishop to Melbourne and has been the residence for all the Anglican bishops and archbishops to the present day, although between 1874 and 1876 it was also used as Victoria's Government House. Both the building and its site represent the Anglican power and influence in colonial affairs. The 1849 design of Bishopscourt is of significance in the development of the picturesque tower and loggia Italianate style. Its lineage is through the work of James Blackburn Snr, whose son was the partner of Arthur Newson of Newson & Blackburn. While admired for the bald expression of its bluestone walls, the hiatus caused by the gold rushes may have resulted in them not having been stuccoed, as was the tradition in Italianate designs. In 1903, a substantial half-timbered and red-brick addition, designed by Walter Butler, replaced the bluestone north wing.

Italianate
Melbourne's most popular 19th-century domestic style, the Italianate arose from an amalgam of romantic associations with the Italian rural vernacular, the Renaissance Revival and design principles gleaned from the land-scape painters and gardens of the Picturesque. Asymmetrical massing (produced by projecting window bays, a tower, and offset building masses), low hipped roofs, eaves elaborated by classical detail and Renaissance-derived window surrounds set within plain stuccoed walls characterised the Italianate house.

Victorian City
1–1880

1851–1880

It is hard to imagine the chaos that the gold rush brought to Melbourne.

The year 1851 was an important one. This was when Victoria separated from New South Wales to become an independent colony and it was also the year gold was discovered at Ballarat, heralding a period of exceptional growth and prosperity for the newly established colony. In 1851, the population of Victoria was 23 000. Ten years later, it had grown to 540 000 and, in that period, more than £75 000 000 worth of gold passed through Melbourne. Gold also attracted ambitious and visionary men and women ready to seek their fortune and make their reputation in the New World.

It is hard to imagine the chaos that the gold rush brought to Melbourne. Residents left for the goldfields only to be supplemented by more fortune seekers from the groaning decks of every ship that entered port. These ill-equipped adventurers would then set out, usually on foot, into the wilderness. Some were destitute. Others would return laden with new-found wealth that was initially lavished on entertainment and goods, but it was eventually invested in property, industry, commerce and construction.

The Melbourne of 1852, claimed Archibald Michie in 1860, 'then but a very inferior English town, unpaved, unlighted, muddy, miserable, dangerous, has become transformed into a great city, as comfortable, as elegant, as luxurious (it is hardly an exaggeration to say it), as any place out of London or Paris.' William Kelly had seen the rebuilding of San Francisco and regarded it 'as a miracle—the event of a lifetime—not to be again equalled in an age ... I lived to see this northern queen city eclipsed by the superior radiance of a southern metropolis ... Melbourne, young as she is, is, without doubt, the overtopping wonder of the world.' While these exclamations are infused with Victorian exaggeration, there can be little doubt that writers were surprised by the presence of Melbourne as it prospered through the 1870s. Many photographs of the period show a dramatic skyline punctuated by spires and domes with substantial warehouses and grand public buildings. By 1876, this was complemented by the tower of **Government House** and the substantial forms of **St Patrick's Cathedral** and the **Law Courts**.

Two-, three- and four-storey buildings lined the principal thoroughfares such as Collins Street and Bourke Street, which were terminated at their eastern end by the **Treasury Building** and **Parliament House**, respectively. The width of the streets still dominated the scale of their flanking buildings, but the consistency and quality of these buildings were commensurate with most English or American cities. Modest homes lined the intermediate lanes and alleyways, which always gave on to the ubiquitous corner pub. The consistent classicism of these minor buildings and several banks complemented grander edifices such as the **Melbourne Town Hall**, the **Public Library**, the **General Post Office** and the **Treasury Building**. These buildings show a consistent allegiance to the classicism of Rome, Venice or Florence. They were soon matched by a rich collection of churches – nineteenth-century interpretations of the Gothic Revival.

Collectively, these buildings demonstrate a vision attributable not only to the architects who emigrated, but also to significant public figures including Charles Joseph La Trobe, Redmond Barry, Samuel Wilson and Francis Ormond. Their vision was to give Melbourne the presence of a great nineteenth-century city.

The popularity of Italian classicism can be attributed to its similar popularity in England at the time and the direct parallels with the Italian climate. Houses, offices, banks, clubs, public buildings and even churches were designed as skilful reinterpretations of temples, palazzi and villas. Joseph Reed's Bank of New South Wales in Collins Street, constructed in 1856 and retained today as a remnant façade in the grounds of the University of Melbourne, has direct parallels with Sansovino's Library in Venice. Sansovino's Villa Garzoni can also be seen in JJ Clark's **Treasury Building**. The palazzi of Bramante and Palladio are echoed in Clark's **Royal Mint** (1872), Smith and Johnson's Bank of Victoria in Collins Street (1862, now demolished) and other banks by Leonard Terry and Lloyd Tayler.

The rolling hills or bayside location of the city's environs provided the perfect setting for newly wealthy citizens to construct villas with names that often reflected the Arcadian ideals of writers such as Pliny and Cicero – Como, Mentone, Leura, Norla. These villas generally adopted a picturesque Italianate style with bay windows, arcades and a tower, the latter invariably required as a status symbol. Suburbs such as Malvern, Toorak, Kew and Brighton, must have once echoed the environs of Renaissance Rome with Italianate towers dotting a horizon of wooded hillsides and the sweep of bayside beaches. The apotheosis of this style and its social focus was **Government House**. Its main block adopts a strict Victorian Renaissance Revival vocabulary, with wings grouped around a magnificent tower.

Melbourne's suburbs also provided the setting for a series of fine gardens, both private and public. It was during this period that James Sinclair and William Guilfoyle planted the seeds of today's Fitzroy Gardens and the Royal Botanic Gardens, respectively. Melbourne's private gardens were equally impressive. Remnants of some of these landscapes survive at Como (planted by William Sangster) and Rippon Lea (said to be the work of Fredrick Sargood, the owner of the property).

Allotment sizes were generally smaller in the suburbs surrounding the central city. This did not preclude the design and construction of interesting individual townhouses and terraces, including **Royal Terrace** in Fitzroy, **Rochester Terrace** in South Melbourne and Canterbury Terrace and Burlington Terrace in East Melbourne. These buildings often relied on tiers of colonnades, arcades and verandas for their decorative effect and saw the popular introduction of cast iron for veranda posts and valances, fences and gateposts.

Substantial amounts of government expenditure were directed to public institutions during this period. From 1857 to 1864, this included the construction of twelve gaols throughout the state, the most substantial being the forbidding **(Old) Melbourne Goal** and **Pentridge**. The government then embarked on the construction of three vast lunatic asylums at Beechworth, Ararat and Kew. In plan, the **Kew Asylum** (1868-72) resembles similar institutions in England; its hilltop setting and picturesque grouping of towers, however, give the sense of a giant palace overlooking the Yarra Valley.

Melbourne's architectural scene during this period was dominated by Joseph Reed (1823–1890). He arrived from England in 1852 and, although his architectural education was obscure, his talent was soon recognised when he won the competition for the **Melbourne Public Library**. In time, Joseph Reed and his partner Frederick Barnes headed Melbourne's largest and most prolific architectural practice, designing in any number of styles depending on the function and location, and the dignity, of the opportunity at hand.

After a trip to England and Europe in 1863, Reed declared the architecture of Lombardy ideal for the climate of Victoria and there followed his greatest work, the former **Independent Church** in Collins Street, with its distinctive brick campanile and arcaded windows. Reed's pioneering use of polychrome brickwork, derived no doubt from current architecture in England and Italy, set a trend that was to continue until the end of the century. His ability to adapt the principles of a particular style to the requirements at hand was extraordinary, evinced in his Reading Room (Queens Hall) at the **Public Library**, the Great Hall (Wilson Hall, 1878–82; now demolished) at the University of Melbourne, and his church interiors.

Perhaps the only other architectural office that could rival that of Reed and Barnes was the Public Works Department, a government office dealing with the construction of everything from **Parliament House** to the most humble lock-up. Many of

Australia's most talented architects were employed here, including AL Smith, AE Johnson, JG Knight and, most importantly, Peter Kerr, JJ Clark and WW Wardell. Peter Kerr's life work was **Parliament House**, a tour-de-force in Roman Revivalism. JJ Clark joined the Public Works Department in 1851 at the age of thirteen and designed the **Treasury Building** five years later. William Wardell (1823–1899) was a rising star of the Gothic Revival when he arrived from England in 1858. He was immediately employed as Inspector General of Public Works and headed the department for twenty years. Wardell believed that public buildings should be as simple as possible, and this principle can be viewed in the diverse range of buildings undertaken by the department during this period. Wardell's government appointment was unique and controversial in that he was allowed the right to private practice. In parallel therefore with his significant involvement in Victoria's public buildings, his private practice generated an important series of churches from **St Patrick's Cathedral** to parish churches such as St John's, Toorak (1860–62), St Mary's, East St Kilda (1871), and **St Ignatius**, Richmond (1867–83). Wardell's purist Gothic Revival style contrasts with Reed's freer adaptations at **Scots Church** (1873–74), with its raked floor, and **Wesley Church** (1857), with its encircling galleries—innovations that reflect Reed's preaching house background.

Melbourne's ordered vision and restrained character are perhaps its greatest legacy from this period of extraordinary growth and development. This vision as expressed in architecture gave the city a dignity which enabled it to develop from a gold rush phenomenon into a financial and trading metropolis – a metropolis which evoked the idealism of the Victorian Age.

BRUCE TRETHOWAN

21

21 Corrugated iron houses

399 Coventry Street, South Melbourne
1853, 1854
GC, V, A

Extremely rare and evidence of humble beginnings to housing in Melbourne and gold-rush Victoria, the three portable and prefabricated corrugated iron-clad houses in Coventry Street are owned by the National Trust of Australia (Victoria). The six-room attic cottage directly facing the street is original to the site and is constructed of T-section wrought angles and clad in 5-inch (130-mm) pitch corrugated iron. Internally, the house is partitioned and lined with horizontal boards. The second house (1854), first erected in Fitzroy and moved to South Melbourne in the 1970s, was made according to a system patented by Edward Bellhouse of Manchester and may be the only such identified example surviving in the world. Clad with horizontal corrugated iron sheeting, which was fixed to shaped flanges on a cast-iron staunchion frame, it rested on timber ground sleepers and internally was also lined with horizontal boards. The third house, Abercrombie House, was transported to its current site in 1980.

•••

Other portable prefabricated houses can be found in Melbourne. The 'Singapore House', 136 Sackville Street, Collingwood (1853) was originally located in Hoddle Street, East Melbourne. Timber framed with part corrugated iron and part timber linings, the house was imported from Singapore, evidence of which is given by Chinese characters incised onto some of the timbers. There is also a group of four corrugated iron houses that can be seen in Brunswick Road, Brunswick.

22 Shop and Residence

328–330 King Street, Melbourne
1850–51
GC, V, A

This Lilliputian building evokes the humble scale of pre-gold rush Melbourne and still functions as a shop and dwelling. Another diminutive residence still surviving in the CBD is 72–74 Collins Street (1855), a Georgian townhouse.

23 Glass Terrace

64–78 Gertrude Street, Fitzroy
1854 David Ross
1856 Charles Webb
GC, V, NA

Located in what was originally known as Newtown, Melbourne's first suburb, Glass Terrace is Georgian in character and one of the city's oldest terraces. The bluestone-faced terrace was built in two stages and developed by Hugh Glass, who, by 1862, was reputed to be the richest man in Victoria. The first two houses were designed by architect David Ross, the remaining six by architect Charles Webb. Distinctive aspects of this austere terrace are the double French doors on the ground floor and the six-pane casement windows on the first floor. Glass also developed the terrace next door at 39–49 Brunswick Street (1857–58) and used local architect Charles Laing. Comprising six rendered brick houses with the two end houses being three storeys rather than two, the corner terrace at Gertrude Street is a particularly fine composition. The two-storeyed iron lace verandas were added in 1881, replacing the original single-storey verandas.

24

24 Royal Terrace
Nicholson and Gertrude Streets, Fitzroy
1853–58 attributed to John Gill
GC, V, NA

Built largely of bluestone (Victorian basalt), a local material that distinguishes Melbourne from its interstate neighbours, Royal Terrace is one of the city's oldest and largest terraces. The planning for each house was standardised, with living and service areas on the ground floor and bedrooms on the first and second floors. Yet, from the street, the architectural impression was of a large and single building. Royal Terrace was built for an upper–middle-class clientele indicative of the street's then fashionable address and John O'Shanassy, three times premier of Victoria, lived here. The ground floor has a continuous veranda of striped corrugated iron, painted to resemble drooping canvas awnings and shaped in a gracious Regency curve. The first- and second-floor windows have elegant Italianate aedicules and a flat cornice parapet is broken only by urns and a raised block showing the building's name and date. The telescoping forms of each terrace, which enable natural light and access to the linear garden/service plots behind, are visible from the rear service lane.

25 Young and Jackson's Hotel
210-220 Flinders Street, Melbourne
1853; 1860; 1875; 1922
GC, V, A

Melbourne's best-known corner hotel sits on a block of land purchased for £100 by John Batman, the city's founder, at the first land sales. The building erected in 1853 was a hotel by 1861 and the licence was procured by Young and Jackson in 1875, two young miners who had made a fortune in New Zealand. Their hotel gained notoriety when Young bought 'Chloe', the nude painting which had scandalised Melbourne in 1883 for its apparent indecency. The painting still hangs in the hotel. Over the years, Young and Jackson's was extended along Swanston and Flinders streets.

26 Manse
Formerly Stanhope
42 Barkly Street, St Kilda
1875
AC, V, NA

Originally called Stanhope and built for merchant Alexander Sutherland, this double-storey house with its imposing central classical portico of Doric surmounted by Ionic Orders and flanking arcade of cast-iron is a grand variation on a typical free-standing Victorian house. The Presbyterian Church acquired the house for use as a manse in 1919.

●●●

From the mid-1850s to mid-1880s, St Kilda was regarded as one of Melbourne's better suburbs. Its virtual resort location away from the grime of the inner city, good access by train and tram, situation within a short carriage ride of the sea and the elevation of St Kilda Hill were all seen as advantageous. Mansions such as Oberwyl at 33 Burnett Street (1856, 1878), built for John Gomes Silva; Berkeley Court, 48 Burnett Street (1877), built for lawyer John Barker; Berkeley Hall, 11 Princess Street (1854, colonnaded veranda added c. 1910), built by Henry Field Gurner and designed by Albert Purchas; and Linden, 26 Acland Street (1870), built for German-born entrepreneur and philanthropist Moritz Michaelis, and designed by Alfred Kursteiner, architect for the workers' cottages in Greeves Street, Fitzroy (49) all evoke an ambience of gracious suburban living.

27

2G D1

1B P7

27 Clarendon Terrace
208–212 Clarendon Street, East Melbourne
1856–57 Osgood Pritchard
GC, V, NA

A most unusual solution in Melbourne to the problem of a terrace, these three houses are given the grandest of fronts, a giant order Corinthian portico rising through two storeys. Architect Osgood Pritchard also designed the neighbouring Italianate house at 206 Clarendon Street (1856, 1859, 1862). Both these houses indicate the gracious nature of East Melbourne in the late 1850s. It was one of the city's most sought after residential locations.

1B S3

28 Wesley Church
128–148 Lonsdale Street, Melbourne
1857–58 Joseph Reed; 1914 sexton's cottage
GC, V, A

Wesley Church was the first Gothic church designed by architect Joseph Reed (1823–90), and the first sophisticated expression of the Gothic designed for the Wesleyans who had previously considered such a style to be Popish. Their tradition of social welfare and reform was given great physical presence with the construction of this bluestone church with freestone mouldings, adjacent manse and Sunday school all designed by Reed. Wesley Church became 'the focus of Victorian Wesleyanism' on its completion.

29 Collins Street Baptist Church
170–174 Collins Street, Melbourne
1845 John Gill; 1861-62 Reed & Barnes
GC, V, A

Behind Reed and Barnes's Roman temple facade is John Gill's original brick structure that comprises the oldest Baptist church in Victoria. The grand portico with its giant Corinthian columns was added when the church was expanded to seat 1000 people. Another grand Corinthian front to another old Melbourne Baptist church can be seen at the former Baptist Church (now offices), 486 Albert Street, East Melbourne (1859) by Thomas Watts and later modified by Smith and Watts (1863). Next door at 488 Albert Street is Victoria's largest 19th-century synagogue, the Mickva Yisrael Synagogue (1877) **(73)** designed by Crouch and Wilson.

1A F5

30 Former Goldsborough Mort Woolstore
514–528 Bourke Street,
152–162 William Street, Melbourne
1862 John Gill; 1882 additions
GC, V, A

Part of a huge complex of woolstores that once sat on this site, the survival of the remaining portion of the Goldsborough Mort Building is remarkable given its neighbouring 1960s high-rise office towers. Like the warehouses nearby in King and Lonsdale streets, such a building remains as evidence of Melbourne's successful commercial past. Designed by John Gill, this bluestone building, the largest stone warehouse in Melbourne, was part of Richard Goldsborough's wool empire and is the only surviving relic of what was once the largest wool and trading company in Australia.

31

31 Old Treasury Building

Spring Street, Melbourne,
1858-62 Public Works Department (JJ Clark)
1867 Public Works Department (bluestone terrace and lamps)
1994-95 Bates Smart & McCutcheon and Office of Building, Department of Planning & Development (restoration and refurbishment)
GC, V, A

Situated on an open site and on axis with Collins Street, the Treasury Building has long been regarded as Melbourne's most elegant 19th-century edifice. Remarkably, the designer of this Renaisssance Revival masterpiece, John James Clark (1838–1915), was a 19-year-old draughtsman in the Public Works Department. It was his first major work in a long career that included many substantial buildings in other Australian states and New Zealand. In Melbourne alone, Clark's name is associated with the design of the Royal Mint **(54)**, former Melbourne (later Queen Victoria) Hospital **(154)** and the Melbourne City Baths **(142)**.

Strategically located as close as possible to Parliament House **(36)**, the building was designed to house offices and, in its barrel-vaulted basement, strongrooms for gold bullion brought from the mining towns and quarters for the messengers, servants and guards. The floor above was a metre thick.

The exterior of the building was faced in Bacchus Marsh sandstone and its styling, derived from 16th-century Italian palazzi, was to become immensely popular in Melbourne for residential and institutional design. The unusual aspect of the exterior treatment is the scholarly virtuosity of the central portion of the Spring Street facade. The building appears to be a palazzo cut in half to reveal its arcaded cortile,

a gesture that an architect such as Englishman CR Cockerell might have attempted.

The Treasury Building, in fact, has no inner court, but is a rectangular slab with three main entrances off Spring Street. Today, the Old Treasury Building houses a museum focusing on the history of Melbourne and, in the basement, for those interested in gold-rush history and its links to government, a gold museum.

•••

Behind the Treasury Building, the government erected the State Government Offices, 2 Treasury Place (footings, 1859; building, 1874–76; additions, 1993. 1949). Another major Renaissance Revival office building, it was designed by Michael Egan (PWD). The complex was restored and refurbished in 1997 by Peter Elliott Architects Pty Ltd with Curnow Freiverts Glover and the Building Services Agency.

2L A2

32 Melbourne Church of England Boys' Grammar School

Domain Road, South Yarra
1856-58 Webb and Taylor (gate lodge, quadrangle west wing); 1861-91 (north and south wings); 1892 AE Johnson (chapel); 1908 gymnasium; 1928 War Memorial Hall
GC, V, A

A distinguished work from the firm of prolific architect Charles Webb, the original building for Melbourne Grammar School is a handsome essay in castellated Tudor Gothic style. This boys school was established in 1854 and is the oldest denominational school in Victoria. Over the years, numerous additions have been made and post–World War II structures by Mockridge Stahle and Mitchell **(303)** are sympathetic additions to a remarkably cohesive precinct of buildings.

33

1B P1

33 State Library of Victoria
304-328 Swanston Street, Melbourne
1854 Joseph Reed; 1870 Reed and Barnes;
1906-11 Bates Peebles and Smart; 1951 Percy
Everett, Public Works Department
1990-98 Ancher Mortlock and Woolley
GC, V, A

Begun in 1853, the State Library of Victoria has also been home to the National Museum and National Gallery. Joseph Reed's competition-winning Roman Revival design was extended many times by his successors. The barrel-vaulted reading room that is Queen's Hall houses one of Melbourne's grandest 19th-century interiors. The library's founder, Sir Redmond Barry (who envisioned Melbourne as the Rome of the South), stands proudly before one of Victoria's most loved public institutions. The domed Reading Room (1906-11), designed by Bates Peebles and Smart, was for a short time the world's largest reinforced concrete dome. The dome, which was constructed using the system of steel bar (Kahn bar) reinforcing developed by American Albert W Kahn in 1902, covers a panoptic layout of reading tables and an overseeing librarian, and sits on a classically composed polygonal drum which rises over four levels and is punctuated by arched openings. In recent years, under the guidance of architect Ken Woolley, the main orientation and inquiry spaces have been refurbished, new wings added on Russell Street and La Trobe Street, the neoclassical modern La Trobe Library (1951) gutted and refitted, and plans are in place to return the clear glass to the domed Reading Room and recover spaces such as McCoy Hall, once occupied by the Museum of Victoria's dinosaurs and a stuffed Phar Lap.

58 F10

34 Glenfern
Cnr Hotham and Inkerman Streets, Balaclava
1857 attributed to Charles Laing
AC, V, NA

One of Melbourne's best-known domestic Gothick or picturesque medieval-inspired house designs, Glenfern is a steep gable-roofed house with elaborately carved timber barge boards and finials, and clusters of chimneys. It was once the residence of Captain John TT Boyd (1825-91), founder of the famous line of influential Australian artists that has included painters Penleigh Boyd and his nephew Arthur Boyd, writer Martin Boyd and architect Robin Boyd.

1A F9

35 Immigration Museum, Old Customs House
424 Flinders Street, Melbourne
1856-59 Knight Kemp and Kerr
1873-76 Public Works Department (JJ Clark)

Located on a site which since 1835 had been allocated as a customs reserve, the Old Customs House is an amalgam of two major building programs. The first resulted in a three-storey building, while the second brought the building to its current form. The building's most important internal space, the Long Room, corresponds externally to the northern location of the beautifully proportioned set of Ionic columns. Its serene yet sober Renaissance Revival was much favoured as an official building style in Melbourne during the 1860s and 1870s under William Wardell's two-decade tenure as Victoria's Chief Architect. The Customs House was strategically located directly opposite Queen's Wharf, where ships could berth in what was once known as The Pool.

36

36 Parliament House

Spring Street, Melbourne
1856 Knight and Kerr (Legislative Assembly)
1856 Knight and Kerr (Legislative Council)
1859–61 Knight and Kerr (library)
1877–79 Peter Kerr (Queen's Hall)
1879–92 Peter Kerr (west facade)
GC, V, A

A building which epitomises the lofty ideals of 19th-century civic architecture with its symbolic stylism drawn from Imperial Rome, Parliament House also contains some of the finest mid-19th-century interior spaces in Australia. At its inception, the design of the new parliament for the recently created Colony of Victoria was controversial and building progress over the decades was discontinuous. In theory, the building still remains unfinished. The grand Roman Revival facade, with its massive Roman Doric columns, seems to suggest otherwise. But in 1877, for example, in his new scheme for the building's exterior, architect Peter Kerr proposed a grand dome supported above a massive drum that was to sit on top of the entry lobby. As historian George Tibbits has observed, however, Parliament House was built 'from the inside out'. Each of the major interior spaces preceded the completion of the exterior facade. The two Upper and Lower houses were built first and the lavish Corinthian-style Legislative Council Chamber remains the most ornate interior. Each of the Corinthian columns is a single piece of Tasmanian freestone and there are sculptured figures in ceiling spandrels, a coffered barrel vault, a Stranger's Gallery, a Ladies' Gallery and a richly decorated Royal Canopy behind the Speaker's Chair. Another distinguished interior space is the Library (1859–61), with its columns with gilded capitals over two levels. In the 1860s, these spaces were realised externally as a series of forbidding bluestone boxes. By 1879, with the completion of Queen's Hall and the Vestibule with its tiled floor by Minton's of England, the major interior spaces were complete. The new facade designed by Kerr in 1877 was intended to wrap and complete the building, but progress was hampered by the difficulty of finding a suitable finishing stone. The west facade was finished in 1892 after a parliamentary inquiry and several defective stone consignments. The dome was never built. Between 1901 and 1927, the Commonwealth Government became tenants of Parliament House and added extensive refreshment rooms. Since that time, Parliament House has remained an unfinished masterpiece.

•••

The sculptures by Bertram McKennal on the west facade of Parliament House reveal an interest in allegorical tableaux. For example, in the attic storey of the northern pavilion on Spring Street is represented a seated draped figure of 'Australia' receiving 'Commerce' (Mercury) and 'Agriculture' (Ceres), while Australia's arm rests protectively on a small boy who represents the industrial youth of Victoria.

Below: Proposed facade and dome (1877), Parliament House

37

37 St Patrick's Roman Catholic Cathedral
5 Gisborne Street, Melbourne
1858–1869 William Wardell (nave and aisles);
1860–97 William Wardell (transepts, sanctuary,
chapels and sacristy); 1936–40 WP Connolly
and GW Vanheems (three spires & west porch
remodelling); 1989-96 Falkinger Andronas P/L
(restoration)
GC, V, A

One of the world's largest Gothic Revival churches, St Patrick's Cathedral is also the finest work of architect William Wilkinson Wardell (1823–1899) and one of his earliest commissions on arrival in Australia in 1858. Having sold his practice and emigrated to Australia's warmer climate for health reasons, Wardell had quickly gained two prestigious commissions: St Patrick's Cathedral and St John's College, Sydney (1859–1935). At the same time, he won the position of Inspector-Clerk of Public Works in 1859, and then the next year was promoted to Inspector-General with rights to private practice.

London-born, Wardell, a Roman Catholic since 1843, had already completed 30 churches in England between 1846 and 1858, and it is almost certain that he would have come under the sway of Augustus Welby Northmore Pugin, the great Catholic promoter of Gothic Revival architecture in England. It is not surprising that he should have been encouraged by James Goold, Roman Catholic Archbishop of Melbourne, to propose colossal plans for the third St Patrick's Church on its elevated site in East Melbourne.

St Patrick's Cathedral was completed over 80 years from 1858 until 1940. It is the largest church building in Victoria and the centre of the Roman Catholic Church in the state. The nave and aisles followed an English Gothic idiom, while the transepts, sanctuary, chapels and sacristy were based on 14th-century French

models such as Amiens and Rouen cathedrals. It is this latter influence which gives the cathedral its dramatic east end of apsidal chevet chapels, while internally the spatial flow of the ambulatory, chapels and sanctuary is masterful. Outside, flying buttresses and large windows with geometric tracery relieve the mighty walls of Footscray bluestone. Almost all the stained glass was supplied by Hardman of Birmingham. The three reinforced concrete spires faced in stone (revisions of Wardell's original designs and taller by 27 m) were added between 1936 and 1940, rising above Parliament House **(36)** in Bourke Street and terminating the axis of Brunswick Street, Fitzroy.

St Patrick's Cathedral is a testament to the words of the very Reverend James O'Neal, Canon of Westminster, who wrote to Wardell:

> *As an architect I have no hesitation in attesting that you rank second to no other gentleman in that profession. The monuments of your genius and talents are most numerous throughout this Empire and will proclaim the name of Mr Wardell to the admirers of ecclesiastical architecture for future generations.*

•••

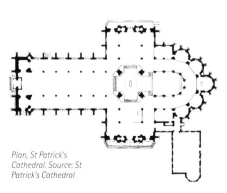

Plan, St Patrick's Cathedral. Source: St Patrick's Cathedral

38

38 Melbourne General Post Office

Cnr Elizabeth and Bourke Streets, Melbourne
1859–67 PWD (Smith and Johnson)
1885–90 PWD (addition of third storey & tower)
1906–07 PWD (additions, Elizabeth Street)
GC, V, A

Situated in the heart of Melbourne's retail centre, the GPO has so far resisted attempts to transform it into yet another shopping centre. The current building was built following the designs of AE Johnson (1821–95) of Smith and Johnson, architects of the Supreme Court **(74)**. It is an outstanding essay in the super-imposition of the trabeated classical orders of architecture onto an arcuated structure. The vaulted arcade along Elizabeth and Bourke streets is one of the city's authentic Renaissance spaces.

39 Seabrook House

573–577 Lonsdale Street, Melbourne
1858 Leonard Terry
GC, V, NA

Seabrook House is a distinguished Renaissance Revival-style bluestone warehouse, one of the more elegant of the many which appeared in this part of Melbourne in the late 1850s. Leonard Terry also designed the Grain Store Tavern (former warehouse and office), 46–52 King Street (1859), and the three-storey store at 234–238 King Street (1858). Other bluestone warehouses nearby include the former F Blight & Co. Store, 240–244 King Street (1854–58); former Zanders No. 3 Store, 2–24 King Street (1872–73); and the former York Butter Factory, 62–66 King Street (1854, 1855).

40 Melbourne Club

36–50 Collins Street, Melbourne
1858–59 Leonard Terry; 1883 Terry and Oakden
GC, V, NA

The Melbourne Club is the city's oldest institution. Established in 1838, the Renaissance Revival, three-storey, brick and stucco design became the club's third home. The large bay-windowed extension (1883) at the west end indicates the great space of the members' dining room. Inside, meticulously restored smoking rooms, library and lounge spaces continue to evoke the conservative air of class and privilege. The club also conceals one of the most beautiful outdoor spaces in central Melbourne. The north-facing garden at the building's rear contains massive plane trees and an arcaded veranda of cast-iron brackets moulded to resemble timber lattice.

•••

Renaissance Revival
Popular in Melbourne between the 1850s and 1880s, especially for banks, commercial and civic buildings such as JJ Clark's Royal Mint and Old Treasury, this style was inspired by the urban palazzi of the Italian Renaissance. Rusticated ground floors, a piano nobile (generally the grandly scaled first floor) and then an attic story of smaller scaled windows beneath an elaborate classical cornice supporting the eaves to a low hipped roof were the pure examples of the style. In England, the Renaissance Revival in the hands of architect Sir Charles Barry, was the favoured idiom for the gentleman's club. The Melbourne Club followed suit with its premises designed by the city's most talented exponent, Leonard Terry.

41

42

2B D7

41 Cloisters, Law School,

South Lawn, University of Melbourne, Parkville
1854–55 FM White (east and west wings)
1856–57 FM White (north wing)
1930 Gawler and Drummond
(east and west wing terminations)
1970 Rae Featherstone, Berg and
Alexandra (south wing)
GC, V, A

The series of Tudor Gothic buildings, their cloisters and stone flagged pavements that surround the quadrangle at the north of South Lawn are the first buildings constructed for the University of Melbourne. In 1853, a large site north of the CBD was granted to the new institution and the building design, won in competition by FM White, followed Cambridge and Oxford university models with its quadrangle plan. White's original scheme had a turreted tower on the main south facade, but a shortage of funds meant that only the east and west wings were built initially. These housed lecture rooms and accommodation for the founding professors and their families. The north wing housed a library, museum (the beginnings of the Museum of Victoria) and further lecture rooms. The quadrangle was finally enclosed with the building of the south wing (1970).

2B F12

42 Old Melbourne Gaol

Russell Street, Franklin Street, Melbourne
1841–64
GC, V, A

Old Melbourne Gaol grew from the need to house the increasing population of criminals after the 1851 discovery of gold. Demand for prison space was such that, by 1853, in addition to stockades at Richmond, Collingwood, and Pentridge, hulks moored off Williamstown were used as floating prisons. With its design based on the universal specifications laid down by British prison engineer Joshua Jebb, the gaol also appeared to follow London's Pentonville Model Prison. The Cell Block which exists today held about 170 prisoners in relatively sanitary conditions. The walls, 600 mm thick, were laid in an offset pattern so that, if a keen prisoner removed a stone from one side, he could not dig all the way through. The scene of 104 hangings (the last in 1919), the gaol's most infamous tenant was bushranger Ned Kelly, executed there at 10 a.m. on 11 November 1880. The Melbourne Gaol closed in 1929 and the existing buildings were among the first to be classified (1957) by the National Trust of Australia (Victoria).

45 B5

43 D'Estaville

7 Barry Street, Kew
1858 Knight and Kerr
GC, V, N A

A substantial two-storeyed, fourteen-roomed, Italianate-style mansion constructed in exposed Footscray basalt, D'Estaville compares in style with Newson & Blackburn's Bishopscourt **(20)**. Although it lacks a signature Italianate tower, it remains a rare example in Melbourne of this style applied to a bluestone house.

1861 Unification of Italy by
Giuseppe Garibaldi

44

46

44 Former Clement Hodgkinson House

157 Hotham Street, East Melbourne
1861 Joseph Reed
GC, V, NA

This two-storey bluestone house, built for
Deputy Surveyor-General Clement Hodgkinson,
is designed in a picturesque Gothic Revival style,
an unusual idiom for an inner suburban townhouse. The house is remarkable for its decorative
timberwork featuring quatrefoil cut-outs to the
balustrades, doubled turned timber veranda
columns and its romantic cottage silhouette
roof, with the veranda eaves folding up to form
picturesque gablets.

45 Victoria Barracks

St Kilda Road, Melbourne
1860-67 PWD (Gustav Joachimi)
1914-20 John Smith Murdoch (five-storey
northern extension)
GC, V, NA

The Victoria Barracks houses one of the most
impressive collections of bluestone structures in
Victoria. The three-storey A Block (1860-67)
facing St Kilda Road is a Renaissance Revival
design with two flanking dormitories. During
World War II, it housed the conference room
used by the War Cabinet. F Block (c. 1860) was
built as an ordnance store and is severe in its
utilitarian stripped formality. G Block (1860) was
originally a barracks, while J Block (1860) was
designed as a hospital and had verandas added
later. There is even a crenellated keep built c. 1860
after the apparent threat of a Russian invasion.

46 Little Parndon

159 Gipps Street, East Melbourne
1862
GC, V, NA

Little Parndon was the home built by Austrian
painter-emigrant Eugene Von Guérard (1811–
1901), who was to become one of Australia's
best known early landscape painters. A later
occupier of this modest home was Lord Casey,
Governor General of Australia (1965–69).
His wife Maie Casey's book *Early Melbourne
Architecture* (1953) is an invaluable record
of many 19th-century Melbourne houses long
since demolished.

•••

*Across the street from Little Parndon, Nepean
Terrace, 128–132 Gipps Street, East Melbourne
(1863–65), is a typical early set of terraces with
Hawthorn bricks, flat timber veranda arches and
doubled posts. Numerous early Melbourne houses
remain in East Melbourne and as a precinct it is
one of the richest in terms of variety.*

47 Num Pon Soon Chinese Club

200–202 Little Bourke Street, Melbourne
1861 Peter Kerr
AC, V, NA

Evidence of the strong presence of the Chinese
in Little Bourke Street since the 1860s, this clubhouse was part of an effort to provide support
for Chinese emigrants from Canton. The owner
of the building was Lowe Kong Meng (1831–
1888), president of the Sam Yup society later
known as Num Pon Soon, referring to a district
in Canton province. The building represents a
fascinating blend of formal classicism with
Chinese detail and function. The club is still
owned by the society and, while the ground
floor operates as a grocery shop, the upper floor
continues to be used as a meeting house.

48

50

17 J11

48 Her Majesty's Prison, Pentridge

Sydney Road and Champ Street, Coburg
1858–64 PWD (Gustav Joachimi)
GC, V, A

Recently closed after a long and infamous history, Her Majesty's Prison, Pentridge, still looks like a forbidding bluestone castle of incarceration, with its crenellated battlements and macchicolated round towers. The entrance gates, towers and flanking buildings were part of a major redevelopment of an earlier timber stockade. Additions were made to Pentridge over the years, often reflecting changes in prison design philosophy and correctional psychology. At the time of writing, the future use of Pentridge is unknown.

2C A8

49 Workers' Cottages

1–30 Greeves Street, four corner buildings,
310–313 Fitzroy Street,
12, 14 Mahony Street, Fitzroy
1871–74 Alfred Kursteiner
GC, V, NA

A significant example of intact 19th-century speculative housing in Melbourne, the Greeves Street precinct was developed by Daniel Mahony and designed by architect Alfred Kursteiner. Thirty-three single-storey cottages flank both sides of the street; at the Fitzroy Street intersection, there are four double-storey corner houses and, at Mahony Street (Nos 12 and 14), another two double-storey corner houses which complete a remarkably formal piece of urban design. The original cast-iron brackets, veranda floor tiles and cast-iron fences, the door handles, knockers and narrow door panels can still be seen in many of the houses.

29 G8

50 Christ Church

10 Glenlyon Road, Brunswick
1857 Purchas and Swyer (nave)
1863–64 Smith and Watts (transepts,
chancel & vestry)
1870–71 Smith and Watts (campanile)
1874–75 Frederick Wyatt (apse)
GC, V, A

Christ Church, built in four stages, is a rare example of a church designed according to the idea of Italian country villa architecture, which had been popularised through pattern books such as Charles Parker's *Villa Rustica* (1835) and the application of which was more generally applied to the detached villa. The picturesque grouping of cruciform planned church, detached campanile and the adjoining parsonage and parish hall (1926, 1985) contribute to the sense of a series of farm buildings and a village-like atmosphere.

104 H8

51 Beleura

42–44 Kalimna Drive, Mornington
1863–65
GC, V, NA

A lavish brick and stucco villa with its veranda designed as a Corinthian colonnade, Beleura is unusual for its elaborate Italianate design predating the classical flamboyance of the 1880s. It was built as a country seat for James Butchart, who, by the time he was 40, could retire after just ten years in the station and stock market. For later owner John Tallis, painter Wesley Penberthy undertook a series of Tiepolo- and Veronese-inspired ceiling frescoes between 1951 and 1954 in the entrance hall and drawing and dining rooms. Beleura possesses spacious gardens developed over the decades by each owner and includes a fountain designed by society architect Harold Desbrowe-Annear.

52

54

52 See Yup Temple
76 Raglan Street, South Melbourne
1866 George Wharton
1901 Harold Desbrowe-Annear (meeting hall)
GC, V, A

The See Yup Temple was the main centre of worship and death registry of the Cantonese in Victoria. Chinese migrants arrived in great numbers during the Victorian gold rush (1851–61), many coming via South Australia having walked overland to the Bendigo and Ballarat goldfields. The See Yup Society was founded in the 1850s as a democratic mutual self-help organisation. The temple is a substantial Classical Revival building which includes Chinese-inspired detail, with fragrant durable camphor wood used throughout the interior. Adjoining halls contain tiers of memorial tablets on which are inscribed the names and home districts of See Yup Society members who have died in Australia. The red-brick meeting hall, designed by Desbrowe-Annear in a fluid Free Style, is complemented internally by exquisite curving timber, Chinese-inspired arched openings.

53 Former Kew Asylum, now Willsmere
Wiltshire Drive, Kew
1864–1880s Public Works Department
1995 Span Group (conversion to housing)
GC, V, A

One of the largest collections of institutional buildings erected in 19th century Victoria, the former Kew Asylum complex included walled gardens, fever tents and seemingly endless stretches of ward blocks with attached cast-iron verandas planned around courtyards. Now recently developed as medium-density housing, the asylum followed contemporary English models of asylum planning and adopted similar systems of institutional control and observation. It had the same plan form as asylums at Ararat and Beechworth, but was considerably larger.

54 Marriage Registry Office
Former Royal Mint
280–318 William Street, Melbourne
1869–72 Public Works Department (JJ Clark)
GC, V, A

Another of Melbourne's public buildings whose architectural pedigree lies with the palazzi of the Italian Renaissance, the former Royal Mint was built to mint the gold from Victoria's goldfields. The complex included a two-storey office block and guardhouses, garden and perimeter wall, as well as buildings which have been removed from the site—a coining hall and melting and assaying departments. Designed by brilliant young architect JJ Clark from within the Public Works Department, the design of the central administration wing, with its gracious piano nobile, is believed to have been based on Raphael's Palazzo Vidoni-Caffarelli, Rome (1515). Clark's design was a modification of plans developed by officials of the Royal Mint in London and followed Inspector-General of Public Works William Wardell's instruction that the new design for the central administration block be carried out in 'the plainest possible character, without any ornamentation'. Despite this requirement, Clark's design achieved considerable elegance, particularly in the decorative treatment of the aedicules surrounding the first-floor windows. In 1968, the Royal Mint closed its operations and a number of buildings were demolished.

1865 First bicycle with cranks and pedals invented in France

55

55 Melbourne Town Hall and Offices

90-130 Swanston Street, Melbourne
1867-70 Reed and Barnes; 1869 Reed and
Barnes (Prince Alfred Tower); 1887 Reed and
Barnes (portico); 1925-28 Stephenson and
Meldrum, A & K Henderson
GC, V, A

Another distinguished work by Reed and Barnes that celebrates its corner site with a campanile (this time in grand French Renaissance style), this is a resoundingly picturesque urban composition. The progressive additions of the Prince Alfred Tower (1869), temple-like portico (1887), the subsequent enlargement of the hall itself and the creation of the lower hall and extension along Collins Street (1925) have contributed to the building's scenographic form. The exterior Tasmanian freestone facades sitting above a rusticated bluestone plinth are modulated by giant order Corinthian pilasters and attached Corinthian columns overlaid onto a richly modelled composition. The clock tower with its mansard roof and stacked classical composition houses clocks donated by the son of Melbourne's first mayor. A magnificent collection of classically composed pavilions, the Melbourne Town Hall was to be the protoype for numerous suburban town halls that would be built in the late 1870s and 1880s.

56 Queen Victoria Markets

Cnr Elizabeth and Victoria Streets, Melbourne
1868, 1887-1936; 1884 William Salway (Meat
Market & Elizabeth Street shops)
GC, V, A

A extensive complex of open market structures and enclosed halls, the Queen Victoria Market is the only surviving market of four such facilities that once existed in 19th-century central Melbourne. A wholesale meat market was the first structure built in 1868 and, after the Melbourne City Council acquired part of the old Melbourne General Cemetery in 1877 which had originally occupied a large portion of the rear of the site, the market gained fruit and vegetable sheds. In 1884, the Elizabeth Street buildings that include the Meat Market with its Diocletian windows and arched tympanum containing a sculptural relief of various edible livestock were added. In recent years, the Melbourne City Council has restored, upgraded and added to the market complex, which continues to be a thriving centre for buying (and consuming) food. The council's inclusion of street furniture, monuments, public toilets and carefully designed hard landscaping has contributed to the market's ongoing popularity.

57 Royal Arcade

331-339 Bourke Street, Melbourne
1869-70 Charles Webb (original north-south
arcade); 1901-23 Hyndman and Bates (east-west
addition to Elizabeth Street)
GC, V, A

One of the new forms of retail space of the 19th century, Royal Arcade, with its glazed ceiling and fanlight windows, is Melbourne's oldest arcade. It is the first of many shopping arcades such as the Block Arcade (111) and Centreway Arcade (163) that would provide a complex network of covered shopping pedestrian streets as an intimate alternative to Melbourne's street grid and act as forerunners to the modern day shopping mall. A much-loved feature of the Royal Arcade are the two mechanised sculptural figures of Gog and Magog (1892), who flank the magnificent Gaunt and Sons Clock at the southern end of the arcade and move to chime each hour.

58

59

58 St Michael's Church
Former Independent Church
122-125 Collins Street, Melbourne
1866–67 Reed and Barnes
GC, V, A

The first church in Victoria to be designed in a Lombardic Romanesque style, St Michael's, or the Independent Church, is one of Joseph Reed's most innovative church designs. It is one of the first major buildings to introduce polychrome brickwork to Melbourne, a design tendency finding some popularity in England at the time amongst architects such as GE Street and William Butterfield, who were influenced by the writings of John Ruskin. The Romanesque style interior was designed to maximise the church's acoustic properties. It has an amphitheatre-like plan, with surrounding upper galleries and sloped auditorium seating that focus on the pulpit, choir and organ. Externally, the Independent Church's campanile is a fine rendition of the round-arched Romanesque idiom, but it is worth noting that Reed had also submitted a polychrome design in Gothic style to his clients. Reed's eclectic design is strictly non-conforming; an experimental contrast to his very proper Scots Church **(75)** across the street. The Independent Church site was also the site of Melbourne's first permanent church, built in 1839.

●●●

*Other notable polychrome brickwork designs by Reed and Barnes include the Gothic Revival St Jude's Church of England, 351–357 Lygon Street, Carlton (1866–67, 1869–70); and his Lombardic Romanesque 'Xanadu' for Frederick Sargood, Rippon Lea **(61)**.*

59 St Ignatius Roman Catholic Church
326 Church Street, Richmond
1867–83 WW Wardell; 1927 GW Vanheems
GC, V, A

Dramatically sited on Richmond Hill, St Ignatius is one of Melbourne's most substantial suburban bluestone churches and an accomplished example of the Gothic Revival by church specialist William Wardell. With its long aisled nave and apse with an ambulatory and series of chevet chapels, the overall design has a French character. Completed by Wardell's sons after his removal to Sydney, the enormously tall spire (1927) was a later addition by GW Vanheems.

60 Heronswood
105 La Trobe Parade, Dromana
1870 Edward La Trobe Bateman, Reed and Barnes
GC, V, A

Designed by Edward La Trobe Bateman, artist, book designer, landscape designer, architect, friend and correspondent with some of England's Pre-Raphaelite artists, Heronswood is a picturesque Medieval-style house designed as a summer retreat on the slopes of Arthurs Seat, Dromana, on Port Phillip Bay. Bateman also designed the original garden, although little evidence of it remains. The house, constructed of bluestone with limestone dressings, is asymmetrically composed as a series of wings, each having the distinctive Bateman bell-cast slate roof which gives the house its romantic repose and also a vaguely Oriental flavour. Bateman was also involved in the design of Barragunda at Cape Schanck (c.1866); the System Garden, University of Melbourne (1856) and the original layout for the Fitzroy Gardens (1857).

61

61 Rippon Lea

192 Hotham Street, Elsternwick
1868, 1879–80, 1887 Reed and Barnes
GC, V, A

In 1868, Frederick Sargood, junior partner in his father's hugely successful retail draper's firm, decided to build a 15-room mansion for his family. The property was named in honour of his mother, Emma Rippon. The original house was designed in a Lombardic Romanesque style: architect Joseph Reed had just returned from northern Italy and was taken with the style's eminent suitability as a domestic and institutional building style appropriate to Melbourne's climate and plentiful clay pits for brickmaking.

Over the ensuing decades, Reed and Barnes made additions and alterations, each time consolidating the Romanesque theme with elements such as the Romanesque campanile, more arcaded loggias and window sets and even a Romanesque style glazed cast iron porte-cochère. In 1887, a ballroom was added, the location for concerts, balls and parties for up to 500 people. By the late 1880s, the house had grown to 33 rooms. In 1901, Sargood, already knighted and a long-serving member of Victorian State Parliament, became a senator in the first Parliament of the Commonwealth of Australia.

By 1903, the year of Sargood's death, the grounds spread over 43 acres and included an elaborate complex of gardens and orchards, ferneries (one of which, with an arched roof and walls of wooden battens, represented a natural fern gully), glasshouses and conservatories, ornamental lake (its water drawn from an underground river), aviary, stables and six carriage houses, croquet lawn, archery house and range, stock paddocks, a picturesque man-made hill of earth and rocks and a lookout tower with views of Port Phillip Bay and the distant skyline of central Melbourne. Sargood also installed an extraordinarily complex and extensive system of drainage and irrigation for gardens which, in design and layout, could have been a satellite to Melbourne's Royal Botanic Gardens in the Kings Domain.

Rippon Lea became a centre of Melbourne's social life, the location of grand charitable occasions and garden parties. When Sargood died, his estate was sold to Sir Thomas Bent, Premier and Treasurer of Victoria, who did not live there, but proceeded to subdivide and sell off 35 building allotments at the property's southern tip. In 1909, Rippon Lea was sold again, to Benjamin Nathan, founder of the Maples furniture chain, who continued to maintain the property. On his death in 1935, it passed into the hands of his daughter, Mrs Louisa Jones, who entertained in grand style.

During the 1930s, she removed the original ballroom, put in the Hollywood-style swimming pool and change rooms, and converted the billiard room/museum to a new ballroom. Further land was sold off in 1954 to ABC Television for their Elsternwick studios. In 1972, on Louisa Jones's death, the house and its remaining 10 acres of gardens were given to the National Trust of Australia (Victoria). Today, a complete range of high-style interiors from the 1860s to the 1930s can be seen at Rippon Lea, all evidence of the continued occupation of a much-loved home for living and entertaining.

The gardens at Rippon Lea continue to be one of Australia's best examples of 19th-century landscape design.

62

64

2K B5

62 Rochester Terrace

33–51 St Vincent Place, South Melbourne
1869–79 Charles Boykett and Charles Bolton
Boykett
GC, V, NA

Rochester Terrace is the finest terrace in one
of Melbourne's most elegant 19th-century subdivisions. Laid out in 1858 in the tradition of
residential squares in British cities, the first six
terrace houses (Nos 33–43) of Rochester Terrace
were erected in 1869. Developed by local estate
agent and auctioneer William Parton Buckhurst,
the symmetrical composition of Rochester
Terrace is remarkable for its projecting central
block and end pavilions. These dominant
elements each include a ground floor arcaded
loggia and a generous first-floor loggia created
by a Corinthian colonnade. Rochester Terrace
was designed by little-known architect Charles
Boykett, whose son Charles Bolton Boykett
completed the terrace after his father's death.

1B V8

63 House for Hon. William Campbell

61 Spring Street, Melbourne
1871 Leonard Terry
1983 Robert Peck YFHK Pty Ltd and Denton
Corker Marshall Pty Ltd (restoration)
GC, V, NA

Designed by Renaissance Revival specialist
Leonard Terry, this corner townhouse is a reminder
of the once dominant and urbane Italianate
character of the upper end of Collins Street by
1880, some of which still remains. Nearby are
Terry's Melbourne Club **(40)**, opposite is Lloyd
Tayler's Portland House, 8–10 Collins Street
(1873), built for Henry 'Money' Miller for his
daughter Jane and her oculist husband
Dr Aubrey Brown. At 70 Collins Street (1867) is
the Renaissance palazzo-styled residence and
consulting rooms for the surgeon John Wilkins.

2M G6

64 Trawalla

22 Lascelles Avenue, Toorak
1867–68 Levi Powell
1885 Powell and Whittaker (additions)
GC, V, NA

A two-storey stucco-rendered brick mansion
now sitting on a much reduced block from its
initial 8-hectare site, Trawalla was built
originally as a 20-room Italianate-style home
for Melbourne merchant George Stevenson. In
1885, the house was enlarged to become a
50-room mansion for retired pastoralist John
Simson of Trawalla in Victoria's Western District.
A distinctive feature of the house is its west
elevation, which features a beautiful Regency
styled bow front with Ionic colonnade at ground
level and cast-iron Corinthian columns above.

1B P4

65 Methodist Mission Church

196 Little Bourke Street, Melbourne
1872 Crouch and Wilson
GC, V, A

Crouch and Wilson's modest warehouse-like
design for the Methodist Mission Church had
two halls—one for women meeting upstairs and
one for men downstairs. An early polychromatic
brick church design built soon after Reed and
Barnes's Independent Church **(58)**, it had other
polychrome neighbours with religious functions.
At 108–110 Little Bourke Street (1894), a mission
hall and training centre for Chinese evangelists
of the Church of England was designed by
Charles Webb and Sons. The Church of England
Mission Church, 119–125 Little Bourke Street
(1902), was designed by Nahum Barnet. Both
these buildings were built as a result of the
fundraising efforts of Cheong Cheok Hon, a
prominent Chinese missionary and social
reformer.

66

66 Government House
Government House Drive,
The Kings Domain, Melbourne
1872–76 Public Works Department
(William Wardell)
GC, V, NA

With its serene, classically detailed tower rising above the picturesque English landscape of Melbourne's Royal Botanic Gardens, Government House has long been one of the most important landmarks of the city's skyline south of the Yarra River. Thought to have been inspired by (rather than modelled on) Prince Albert and Thomas Cubitt's design for Osborne House, Isle of Wight (1845-51), Government House is one of the largest, most beautiful and most elaborate Italianate houses in Australia. Since 1876, it has been a vice-regal residence, the third (some would argue fourth, the first being a wattle-and-daub hut) in Melbourne after La Trobe's Cottage, Jolimont **(1)** and Toorak House **(14)**. Between 1901 and 1926, it was home to Australia's governors-general during Canberra's establishment.

The architect of Government House was William Wardell (1823–1899), then Inspector-General within the Public Works Department. He was ably assisted by JJ Clark and Peter Kerr within his department. Located within 11 hectares of grounds and designed as a palatial residence for entertaining, state occasions and temporary residence for visiting royalty, Government House also houses the offices of the Governor.

Government House is comprised essentially of three simple rectangular volumes, with entry to each marked by a Tuscan Doric porte-cochère: the State Ballroom; the State rooms; and the vice-regal apartments. The State Ballroom occupies the entire south wing and is a magnificent and vast double-height space with elaborate stencilling and gilding to its ceiling. The State apartments contain a grand staircase hall, resplendent with Ionic columns at ground level beneath an open well. Above, Corinthian pilasters and columns support a vaulted ceiling. Also on the ground floor are the State Dining and Drawing rooms. The dining table seats 42 people comfortably. The vice-regal apartments for the Governor are similarly sumptuous in decoration and accommodation. Coach houses, stables and staff quarters complete the complex.

While criticised at the time of its construction for its lavish detail and cost, Government House is an Italianate masterpiece. Seen up close by very few people (such as those receiving awards for bravery, Orders of Australia or those lucky enough to tour the house on one of the annual Government House Open Days), the glimpsed romantic view of the belvedere rising above the trees remains as compelling evidence of the wealth and aspirations of 19th-century Victorian Melbourne.

1B T5

67 Former ES&A Bank
88-90 Bourke Street, Melbourne
1870-72 Leonard Terry
GC, V, A

A typically restrained Renaissance Revival bank by the designer of the similarly styled Melbourne Club **(40)**, the former English Scottish and Australian Chartered Bank follows the Italian palazzo model to the letter, with rusticated base, gracious piano nobile and attic storey above. Terry and Oakden's similarly fine design for the former London Chartered Bank, 170 Elgin Street, Carlton (1876), is another three-storey bank located on a corner in order to show off its prismatic form and finely detailed cornice.

68

67 E7

68 Kamesburgh

78 North Road, Brighton
1872–74 Lloyd Tayler
1884 Lloyd Tayler
GC, V, A

Kamesburgh was a vast two-storey villa with
a three-storey tower set on 10 acres of land,
with two of those set aside as gardens. Its main
feature is its two-storeyed parapetted and
classically styled veranda, which extends around
three sides of the house. Tuscan Doric on the
ground floor with Ionic columns on the first
floor, the west elevation faces the garden and is
developed with projecting bays and a silhouette
of ornamental urns lining the parapet. Tayler
designed two other important towered villa
mansions in Brighton during the early 1870s:
Chevy Chase, 203 Were Street, Brighton (1881);
and Blair Athol, 5 Leslie Grove, Brighton (1872).
Kamesburgh was purchased by the Repatriation
Department in 1918: nurses quarters were
added, the billiard room and dairy were
converted to a dining room and some verandas
were glazed in. Known as the Anzac Hostel,
Kamesburgh was a home for permanently
incapacitated servicemen from World War I and
other conflicts until 1996. The gardens are now
open to the public.

2B F11
69 Trades Hall

Cnr Lygon and Victoria Streets, Carlton
1873 Reed & Barnes
1882–84, 1888, 1890, 1917,1922–26, 1961
GC, V, A

Trades Hall is, like Joseph Reed's nearby State
Library of Victoria **(33)**, a pavilioned, classically
derived design with a giant order portico (1917)
and walls modulated by giant order Corinthian
pilasters. It is the result of an extended building
program lasting more than 50 years, with

additions at the rear dating from 1961.
Located diagonally opposite the Eight Hour Day
Memorial **(140)**, Trades Hall is also next door
to the Brutalist-style Plumbers and Gasfitters'
Union Headquarters **(375)**. Flags, banners and
honour boards testify to the ongoing traditions
of the trade union movement, who have been
continuous occupiers of this building since
1873. Trades Hall has considerable social significance for its links not only with the trade union
movement, but also as the birthplace of the
Labor Party. Another classically-derived Reed
& Barnes design and also close by is the Royal
Society Building, 9 Victoria Street (1858,
1867–69, 1880).

2K B2
70 State School No. 1253

286 Dorcas Street, South Melbourne
1878-80 Charles Webb
GC, V, NA

Designed by the architect of the grandly
classical South Melbourne Town Hall **(82)**, State
School No. 1253 came about through the 1873
amalgamation of two Emerald Hill schools. The
resulting symmetrical pavilion-ended double-
storey composition was built in tuckpointed
polychromatic brickwork. The style was a form
of modernised Tudor Gothic, extremely popular
for schools throughout Melbourne during the
late 1870s and early 1880s, with hood moulds
over the square headed multi-paned windows
and gothic-style entry arches. Favoured because
of the traditional associations between church
and education, the style allowed generous
daylighting of classrooms from the large
Tudor/Elizabethan scaled windows. Although the
classroom galleries were removed in 1906 and
minor alterations made to the rear in 1924, the
building is substantially intact.

71

71 Werribee Park

South Drive, Werribee
1873–78 James Henry Fox
1923
GC, V, A

Built for pastoralist brothers Thomas and Andrew Chirnside, Werribee Park is an imposing Italianate homestead–mansion erected as the showpiece of a grazing estate that, in 1888, had grown to 82 000 acres of freehold land. Designed by London-born architect James Henry Fox, the 50-room, symmetrically composed house is crowned by a four-level tower directly above its entry. At ground level, a stone arcaded loggia surrounds three sides of the house, a gesture described as the 'monumentalisation of the traditional veranda'. The house is constructed of bluestone and faced with a honey-coloured freestone. An opulent, classically detailed hall runs the width of the house, terminated by a monumental return staircase. The ground floor comprises gracious reception rooms, including a billiard room, conservatory, picture gallery and library. On the first floor, bedrooms open onto a tiled terrace above the loggia. Extensive additions (complete with tower) were made in 1923 by then owners, the Roman Catholic Church, to enlarge the house to become Corpus Christi College, a religious seminary. In the 1870s, a 25-acre garden/park was laid out by William Guilfoyle, Curator of Melbourne's Royal Botanic Gardens, and populated with red deer, pheasant, hares, rabbits and foxes. Thomas Chirnside was a keen hunter. In the hallway at Werribee Park, the Chirnside coat of arms can be seen, with its motto: *Fac aut morere* (Do or die). Tragically, that was the case. Despite so much wealth and obvious accomplishment, in 1887, Thomas Chirnside became a melancholic and killed himself. Today, the house and gardens can be visited. The latter feature a zoo and many of the original greenhouses, gates and lodge.

72 Customs House

Nelson Place, Williamstown
1873 Public Works Department (Peter Kerr)
GC, V, A

This Customs House, in a restrained Renaissance Revival idiom, is one of a number of historic maritime buildings in Williamstown, a port established in 1837 by Governor Bourke. Nearby are the Tide Gauge House, Commonwealth Reserve, Nelson Place (1858–60) and, at Gellibrand Point, Henry Ginn's 1848 Lighthouse (8).

73 Synagogue (Mickva Yisrael)

488 Albert Street, Eastern Hill
1877 Crouch and Wilson
1883 TJ Crouch (completion of facade)
GC, V, A

The Mickva Yisrael Synagogue is Victoria's largest and oldest existing 19th-century synagogue. While the Renaissance Revival facade (1883) and its pair of eight-sided mansard dome roofs are later additions, it is the interior of this building (1877) which is of greatest interest. Containing a bema and tabernacle, the temple volume is encircled on three sides by a gallery supported on cast-iron columns. The East Melbourne Hebrew Congregation, formed after splitting in 1857 from the Bourke Street Synagogue, comprised largely German Jews, who felt somewhat isolated from the predominantly Anglo-Jews of the Melbourne Congregation in Bourke Street.

74

74 Supreme Court

Former Law Courts
192-228 William Street, Melbourne
1874-84 Smith & Johnson and the Public Works
Department (construction supervision: JJ Clark
and Peter Kerr)
GC, V, A

The distinguished classical complex that comprises the Law Courts is planned with a shallow-domed library in a central quadrangle, surrounded by two storeys of courts, chambers and sheriffs' offices. Built of Tasmanian freestone above a bluestone base, the Law Courts are located on a site previously occupied by the 'Old Government House', the Colonial Secretary's office, the first Telegraph Office and the Government Printing Office.

The design arose through a competition, the result of which was scandalous as the winner Smith was partnered by Johnson of the Public Works Department, one of the competition's assessors! Johnson, designer of the General Post Office **(38)** resigned from the PWD and joined Smith in what was to be a long and prosperous partnership.

The plan of the so-called 'modern Italian' complex was a giant square with sides of 95 metres. Eight courts were to be provided, with a centrally placed library which could be used daily by the legal profession. The layout was thus logically: four courts at each corner of the square, four courts in the lateral wings (north and south) and judges' rooms and offices in the east and west wings, with the library as an independent structure in the centre of the quadrangle formed by the building which followed all four sides of the site.

The Supreme Court Library, whose shallow dome supported off 24 Ionic columns, is believed to have been based on James Gandon's Four Courts, Dublin. Once a landmark on the city's western skyline before its dwarfing by postwar skyscrapers, the library houses one of Melbourne's most elegant institutional interiors, an open cylindrical and domed volume with booklined reading alcoves on the ground and gallery floors.

The courts themselves were lavishly appointed in classical style, especially the Banco Court. At the rear of the building, a cobbled right of way stretches from Little Bourke Street through to Lonsdale Street. In the centre of it, leading west, is a covered and cobbled carriageway that passes the Sheriffs' offices and into the central court to give a fine view of the library cylinder. On the principal facade to William Street, the treatment of the central recessed bay is a double open arcade of Ionic and Composite columns.

Remarkably, the seated figure of Justice above the main entrance (a 1967 bronze replica of the original) is not blindfolded as tradition would have it, an idea thought to have emanated from Justice Redmond Barry—an anomaly that the cynical might say was not surprising at all! When the building opened in February 1884, there was no such comment after all the complaints of expense and time overruns. Instead, the *Illustrated Australian News* announced of the Law Courts that they were 'a pile of buildings that is a credit to the city, and equal to any Temple of Justice in the world'.

75

76

75 Scots' Church

140–54 Collins Street, Melbourne
1873 Reed & Barnes
1914–15 Henry Kemp (Assembly Hall)
1981 Peter Staughton (Collins Street fountain)
GC, V, A

Scots' Church is another example of Joseph
Reed's ability to move convincingly amongst the
styles of architecture in search of appropriate-
ness. It contrasts sharply with his Lombardic
Romanesque design for the Independent Church
(58) across the street. For the Presbyterians
who had built an earlier church there (1841–42)
to the designs of Samuel Jackson with additions
by Charles Webb (1859), Reed provided a
disciplined example of Decorated Gothic
(although, according to historians Miles Lewis et
al., this was an unusual choice of style for the
Presbyterians). Built of sandstone and limestone,
it is a fine example of 19th-century Gothic
Revival architects reviving the ideals of Christian
English medieval architecture. Inside, the
spacious nave has a sloping floor, basalt aisle
columns, rich timber fittings and an arcaded
gallery in the main gable. The original spire,
destroyed by lightning, was replaced in the
1930s and the entire stone exterior was recently
restored by Peter Staughton. David Mitchell was
builder of Scots' Church and his daughter (later
to be better known as Dame Nellie Melba) sang
in the choir. Next door at 156–160 Collins
Street, the Presbyterians constructed a four-
storey late Gothic Revival Assembly Hall
(1914–1915) to the designs of Henry Kemp.

76 St George's Presbyterian Church

4 Chapel Street, St Kilda
1877–80 Albert Purchas
GC, V, A

With its extraordinarily tall and banded bell
tower, its double-gabled entrance porch, its rose
window within a bulging triangular opening and
gable-roofed polygonal-shaped buttress-like
corner turret, St George's Presbyterian Church is
a formally striking polychromatic brick Gothic
Revival church in the tradition of English
polychrome specialists such as William
Butterfield and John Loughborough Pearson.
Inside, however, the nave has no aisles, there is
a sloping floor and broad transepts, and the
walls are treated in red and cream brick. It is a
hall-like church with a T-shaped plan which
does not conform to any medieval prototype,
but which instead is a thoroughly modern
adaptation to contemporary religious needs.

77 Kathleen Syme Education Centre
Former Primary School No. 112

Faraday Street, Carlton
1876–77 Reed and Barnes
AC, V, A

An austere version of a polychrome brick Gothic
Revival school building, the two-storey school is
distinguised by its symmetrical end-pavilions,
each with a bell-cast slate roof and a central,
asymmetrically composed bay that comprises a
gable end and four-storey bell tower. Although
some of the windows were enlarged in later
decades to increase daylighting, the overall form
indicates a rational plan and sober language
reflective of the seriousness of intent behind
both the educational mission and the
architecture of the school building program
initiated by the Education Act in 1873.

78

2G A2

78 Tasma Terrace
2-12 Parliament Place, Melbourne
1878-87 Charles Webb
GC, V, A

Tasma Terrace, which comprises six 3-storey, grey-stuccoed townhouses, was designed by notable architect Charles Webb, designer of prominent Melbourne public buildings and residences such as the Windsor Hotel **(90)**, South Melbourne Town Hall **(82)** and Mandeville Hall **(88)**. The restrained cast-iron decoration used as delicate arcading with quatrefoil brackets to verandas over two levels is especially fine and the terrace gains much from its setting amidst trees and a small park. Inside, on the ground floor, each house has two major reception spaces which can be joined to make one large space when a timber-panelled door slides upwards into the wall cavity. Tasma Terrace is owned and has been restored by the National Trust of Australia (Victoria) and is the location of its state headquarters, bookshop and restaurant/café.

2B J3

79 Primary School No. 1252
Lee Street, North Carlton
1878 WH Ellerker (PWD)
1992 Lindsay Holland Pty Ltd
GC, V, NA

Located on the site of a former penal stockade and then the Carlton Lunatic Asylum, the Lee Street state school (No. 1252) was the result of community agitation to have the site, which had been reserved for public institutions since 1853, designated for school use. It also satisfied local demands for a school given the residential boom in 1870s Carlton. The school's form, planning and Gothic Revival styling derives from WH Ellerker's 1873 second-prize competition entry for 'A school for five hundred scholars'. The standard design, with its symmetrical plan, tiered classroom floors, steep gable slate roofs with carved barge boards and inclusion of ventilator funnels, was first built at Buninyong; it became the basis for at least 16 other schools in Victoria, including Carlton.

2B G7

80 Police Station and Lock-up
330 Drummond Street, Carlton
1878 Public Works Department (police station)
1890 Public Works Department (lock-up)
AC, V, A

With its construction drawings signed by PWD Chief Architect, WW Wardell, the Carlton Police Station is a standard design that would influence police stations at Geelong and Kyneton. The two-storey polychrome brick Italianate-styled building is symmetrically planned about a central corridor. Two sergeants and a married constable occupied the ground floor, while upstairs there were two dormitory rooms and more constables' quarters. Behind, the watch-house has a single storey bluestone lock-up and an attached two-storey brick quarters for the watch-house keeper. The lock-up contains six generously proportioned cells (13 feet by 11 feet), the two furthest from Drummond Street reserved for drunkards. A feature of each cell was the special provision for ventilation: perforated iron ceilings and 'Tobin tubes', special flues that exhausted undesirable fumes to the louvred roof monitor which ran the length of the cell block. Across the street, completing this mini-law enforcement precinct is the former Carlton Court House (1887-88) designed by JH Marsden (PWD).

81

81 St Paul's Cathedral

2 Swanston Street, Melbourne
1880–91 William Butterfield, Reed and Barnes
1912 Walter Butler (choir)
1926–31 James Barr (spires)
GC, V, A

Built to replace Charles Webb's St Paul's Church and located on the site of the first official church service in Melbourne in 1836, St Paul's Cathedral has continued the site's history as the centre of the Church of England in Victoria. Designed in 1878 by eminent English Gothic Revival architect William Butterfield (who never visited Australia and who also designed Adelaide's Anglican cathedral), St Paul's is one of his larger commissions, although it was not completed to his original design—the existing spires are not those of Butterfield.

He had envisaged an octagonal crossing tower and two saddle-backed west towers, which would have given an altogether different feeling—a more rugged, robust and some might say even primitive Gothic evocation. Instead, Sydney architect James Barr provided the conventional Gothic spires and in a different stone to Butterfield's bold contrasting textures of Waurns Pond and Barrabool sandstones (described as 'polytexture') which feature on the chequered western facade (in fact, south facade due to having to conform to Melbourne's street grid). Despite this, the interior is almost entirely Butterfield and is a triumph of Gothic Revival architecture inspired by the vibrant striped polychromy of Italian Gothic cathedral interiors.

Butterfield's philosophy of an increasing decorative hierarchy is realised at St Paul's. Encaustic tiled floors and wainscoting give way to marble and glass mosaics as one moves closer to the altar. The kauri pine ceiling, while fine in workmanship and execution, was not part of the Butterfield design. He resigned from the commission in 1888 after a disagreement with the Cathedral Erection Board Committee, but his work was continued in 1888 in an honorary capacity by Joseph Reed of Reed Henderson & Smart (later Reed, Smart & Tappin).

The adjacent four-storey Chapter House and Diocesan Offices were also designed by Butterfield and complement the cathedral design. While St Paul's Cathedral has a mixed architectural pedigree, its skyline of spires is a much-loved Melbourne landmark.

With the 1997 removal of the Gas and Fuel Buildings which had sat over the railyards, the adjacent Flinders Street streetscape was revealed to recapture a view of Melbourne as it had appeared from 1931 until the mid-1960s. Now controversy rages as to whether the proposed structures of Federation Square, set for completion in 2001, will partially obscure the spires and upper half of St Paul's west facade. Whatever the outcome, many people have forgotten that the cathedral had no spires at all for more than 30 years. The cathedral, like Melbourne at the end of the 1870s, was constantly evolving.

Marvellous Melbourne
1880–1890

1880–1890

Marvellous Melbourne … the Boom style, a term which combines wonderment and opulence with decadence and abuse.

'Marvellous Melbourne' is the sobriquet *par excellence* for the image Melbourne likes to have of the decade of the 1880s to early 1890s. The expression of optimism was coined by George Augustus Sala, a visiting London lecturer and journalist, and taken by those who believed in the city to be as much a fulfilment of its destiny as it was praise for the exuberant metropolis.

An image of the wealth, energy and individualism of the city and its suburbs is found in the architecture of the decade. Among its many wonders was one of the tallest buildings in the world at that time, the APA or Australia Building (1888), designed by the architects Oakden, Addison and Kemp. This 12-storey building, which brought together advanced design, engineering and technology, stood on the corner of Elizabeth Street and Flinders Lane until it was demolished in the 1990s – as were many other extraordinary buildings from the 1880s, to the shame of all Melbourne. Many buildings epitomised individualism, each making a claim for itself through striking architectural effects. The architecture of Marvellous Melbourne has long been given its own defining label, the Boom style, a term which combines wonderment and opulence with decadence and abuse.

Events were to prove that the rise of Marvellous Melbourne was to be followed by a dramatic fall. The hubris of Marvellous Melbourne collapsed in a great depression which began in 1891 and reached its nadir in 1893. Later generations found irony in Sala's image: the 'marvellous' overlooked poverty of the 1880s found in the back streets of the city and inner suburbs. Hard times and insecurity followed and the opulent architectural achievements of the previous decade took on a hollow ring of false pretensions and deceit. The Boom style is still spoken of in these terms today, as a warning to architects and clients against decoration and architectural complexity, as if these characteristics presage moral and economic collapse.

The suggestion of a unified approach and of vulgar decorative exaggeration implicit in the term 'Boom style' deflects attention away from the variety of approaches to decorative design during the 1880s and the continuity of practices from previous decades going back to the 1850s. Until the depression, many of the older architects who came to Melbourne in the aftermath of the gold ushes, and who designed in restrained Renaissance Revival and Gothic styles, were still in practice and continued their commitment to the sober aesthetic of those earlier decades. Such was the approach of the architects Charles Webb, Joseph Reed, Lloyd Tayler and William Wardell.

Other somewhat younger architects (in their late forties and early fifties when the depression hit), such as George Johnson, Percy Oakden, John Marsden and GBH Austin (the latter two worked in the Public Works Department), turned to other design sources, Mannerism and to a palette of styles that had been created by English architects in the 1850s and 1860s.

An even younger group (in their twenties and thirties by the early 1890s) were, in some cases, 'off the planet', producing designs that must have shocked their older architectural colleagues as much as they have later generations. It is perhaps these who most deserve to be called Boom Style architects.

A comparison of two Gothic examples—one the former **ES&A Bank** (1883–84) by William Wardell, now the ANZ Bank at 388 Collins Street, and the other, its next-door neighbour, the former **Melbourne Stock Exchange** (1888–91), also incorporated into the ANZ Bank at 376–380 Collins Street) by William Pitt — reveals in the strongest way possible the aesthetic chasm between almost contemporaneous buildings and their designers. Among Classical style examples, differences between approaches can be appreciated if the **South Melbourne Town Hall** (1879–80) by Charles Webb is contrasted to the **Collingwood Town Hall** (1885–90) by George Johnson. The Webb design is impressive because of its calm, if somewhat cramped regularity, while restless Mannerist exaggeration, derived from Michelangelo, and Second Empire picturesque composition are seen in Johnson's work. Webb and Johnson developed their different approaches to design from different sources, although not so different as those of Wardell and Pitt.

Of the partnerships formed in the 1880s, the most interesting were those with the pragmatic realist Joseph Reed. When the practice of Reed & Barnes ended in 1883, two younger architects joined Joseph Reed and the practice became known as Reed, Henderson & Smart. The younger partners shared Reed's aesthetic approach and, although the practice drew on wider sources, including Arts and Crafts ideals of plain brickwork (such as the professorial houses at the University of Melbourne, c. 1886) and Gothic ruggedness in the treatment of stone (**Old Zoology Building**, University of Melbourne, 1887–90), the designs eschew Boom style elaboration and decoration, and have a stern strength far removed from some of their contemporaries.

Even among architects who were most prone to elaborate decorativeness in their designs there can be distinguished personal and idiosyncratic approaches that amount to individual styles. While it seems appropriate to call their work Boom style, the stylistic label—like all such labels which group works together by general characteristics—tends to deflect attention away from individual styles and approaches. Among the masters of cement-rendered decorative works, each had distinctive personal touches which distinguish their work from others such as JAB Koch (**Labassa** (1889–91), formerly Ontario, 2 Manor Grove, North Caulfield), Charles D'Ebro (**Stonington** (1891), 336 Glenferrie Road, Malvern), Walter S Law (Medley Hall (1892), formerly **Benvenuta**, 48 Drummond Street, Carlton), William Wolf (**Lalor House** (1888), 293 Church Street, Richmond), Norman Hitchcock (former Jewish News building (1886), now Brunetti Cakes, 200 Faraday Street, Carlton) and George de Lacy Evans (Lygon Buildings (1888), 98–126 Lygon Street, and **Sum Kum Lee Building**, 1887–88, 112 Little Bourke Street).

Another approach to decorative architecture which came to the fore in the 1880s and 1890s, and almost the opposite of the monochrome decorative stucco architecture, was the use of different-coloured materials on building facades to create contrasting and sometimes quite vibrant effects. Different-coloured stones, tiles, bricks and iron were all brought together in some designs and matched by carved decorative pattern work so that a building would take on a jewel-like character. Two close neighbours by the young architect William Pitt are perhaps the most cherished examples, the **Olderfleet Building** (1889, 477 Collins Street) and the former **Rialto Building** (1889, 497–503 Collins Street). The importance of different-coloured materials and contrasting textures and patterns is also evident on the **Princes Bridge** over the Yarra (1886–88), by Jenkins, D'Ebro and Grainger.

William Pitt and others among his contemporaries designed in many different styles and mixed styles within one building, an approach which later fell into such disrepute that it remains dogmatically condemned to the present day. They also explored picturesque effects of composition, fenestration and the arrangement of materials in their buildings, sometimes with every floor being differently expressed. Eclecticism in the work of some architects also led to extremes of style between one building and another, a feature much derided by later generations. A comparison of two works by George de Lacy Evans—the ponderously elaborate stuccoed **Sum Kum Lee General Store** (1888, 112–114 Little Bourke Street) and a group of his hard-nosed brick warehouses (1887, 23–31 Niagara Lane)—suggests the reason later critics thought these architects were somewhat schizophrenic. William Pitt had such an extraordinary talent for eclectic invention that it seems hardly credible that the same architect designed the **Melbourne Stock Exchange** (1888–91), now part of the ANZ Bank at 376–380 Collins Street; the **Rialto Building** (1889), now Le Meridien at Rialto at 497–503 Collins Street); and the **Princess Theatre** (1886–87) at 163–181 Spring Street.

By a strange irony, the architectural discourse of the 1880s also contained the seeds of destruction for decorative stucco architecture and for eclecticism. The central but difficult feature of the 1880s is that the decade represents both a culmination of architectural endeavour going back to at least the 1850s and, at the same time, the introduction of critical ideas which undermined the glories of the decorative and eclectic approach to the historical styles, especially of the Classical style. The new ideas had their origins in the writings of John Ruskin, leading to the Arts and Crafts Movement, and of AW Pugin and the stern side of the Gothic Revival. These ideas blossomed in the Federation decades and lurk behind Modernist revulsion to decoration and condemnations of the historical styles, especially of the Boom style.

Another legacy of the new ideas was a much expanded interest from previous decades in creating an Australian architecture. The search for an Australian style involved strange ideas—at least to us 100 years later. One line of exploration urged architects to go back to the foundation style, the trunk of the tree of European architecture, Romanesque, and develop an Australian branch from that. Other lines of exploration sought to develop an Australian architecture through climatic correlations — that is, by taking styles from areas with a similar (Mediterranean) climate and developing those styles into a distinctive Australian response. Another was to seek an Australian distinctiveness through the materials used in buildings. Another sought to represent Australian flora and fauna in the decoration of buildings.

Some of the stylistic eclecticism of the 1880s and early 1890s, much derided and even feared by later architects, was perhaps a response to the challenge of creating an Australian architecture, a response which today we cannot read in the buildings, whereas we can still appreciate the representation of Australian flora and fauna as an attempt, though perhaps quaint, to create an Australian architecture.

This search, a legacy of the 1880s, has persisted to the present day, but in such different guises that what may have been built as 'Australian architecture' in the 1880s is now without meaning, wrongly appreciated as a debased architecture of irresponsible decoration and senseless stylism.

GEORGE TIBBITS

82

2K C3

82 South Melbourne Town Hall
Former Emerald Hill Town Hall
208-220 Bank Street, South Melbourne
1879-80 Charles Webb
1940 Oakley and Parkes (interior refurbishment)
1996 97 Daryl Jackson Pty Ltd (interior refurbishment)
GC, V, A

On the suburb's most prominent site, Charles Webb (1821-98) produced one of the period's most accomplished urban designs, as well as an assured complex of giant order Corinthian pilastered and columned pavilion bays flanking a portico topped by a dramatically telescoping pile of classical forms. The exaggerated height of this tower, accentuated by the building's site, results from the missing mansarded towers that once flanked it and the urns that once lined the parapet. The building originally contained offices, a public hall, Mechanics' Institute, fire station, post office, police station and court-house. Some of these were later relocated directly opposite, creating a precinct of distinguished municipal structures.

2B A9

83 Meat Market Craft Centre
Former Metropolitan Meat Market
36 Courtney Street, North Melbourne
1879-80 GR Johnson
1889 GR Johnson (cooling bay)
1906-09, 1918-22 Gibbs and Finlay (additions and alterations)
GC, V, A

Built privately as a convenient place for the sale of wholesale meat, the site was chosen to complement the municipally owned Hay and Corn, Horse and Pig Markets in Sydney Road, and to avoid the cramped conditions of the Queen Victoria Market and the Victorian Meat

Market in Elizabeth Street. George R Johnson (1840-1898), designer of the Collingwood Town Hall **(98)**, included the Metropolitan Hotel in his High Renaissance style design. The main feature (as it still is today) was the market hall, which had a cobbled floor and was flanked by open perimeter stalls with their hanging frames for meat. The ceiling is lined with timber boards and there is foliated cast-iron decoration to the spandrels and soffits of the flanking arched trusses and centrally placed circular vents. Stallholders' names can still be seen above timber columns, and metal and stucco heads of edible beasts decorate the walls and stalls.

2C G5

84 Shot Tower
94 Alexandra Parade, Clifton Hill
1882 Richard Hodgson (builder/engineer)
GC, V, NA

A rare surviving piece of industrial history, the Shot Tower in Clifton Hill, at 160 metres high, is possibly the tallest shot tower in Australia. The shot was made by dropping molten lead through sieves at the top into water at the tower's base. Shaped like a giant tapering chimney and with the colour and texture of a minaret, the brick tower is pierced at regular intervals by arched windows and decorative polychromatic brick bands. Isolated on its skyline, the Shot Tower is a local landmark and a counterpoint in scale to the broad expanse of car-crammed Alexandra Parade.

85

85 Melbourne Exhibition Buildings
Nicholson Street, Carlton Gardens, Carlton
1879–80 Reed and Barnes
1994–95 Allom Lovell & Associates (restoration)
GC, V, A

Completed for the International Exhibition of 1880, the Exhibition Building's magnificent dome was modelled on that of Brunelleschi's Florence Cathedral. Designed by Joseph Reed (1823–90) and his largest work, the main building which remains today was a small but central part of a vast complex of temporary structures that at one time stretched almost all the way to Carlton Street. The Exhibition Building was the scene for numerous trade exhibitions, as well as events such as the opening in 1901 by the Duke of York of the first Federal Parliament of Australia. To celebrate the event, the building and its dome were adorned with 10 000 electric light globes. Afterwards, Federal Parliament sat in Parliament House **(36)** in Spring Street, while the western annexe was used by the Parliament of Victoria until 1927. Soon to gain a new life as part of the Museum of Victoria **(448)**, the Melbourne Exhibition Buildings are rightly regarded as being among Australia's most important 19th-century classical structures.

1A F7

86 Australian Club
100–110 William Street, Melbourne
1879 Lloyd Tayler (Stage I); 1884–85 Lloyd Tayler (Stage II, Chancery Lane extension); 1893 Wilson and Charlesworth (Stage III and completion)
GC, V, NA

Known in its day as 'the domain of the wealthy squatters', the Australian Club is stylistically the king of Melbourne's 19th-century clubs, far more opulent than Leonard Terry's Renaissance Revival Melbourne Club **(40)**. Inside there is lavish interior decoration, ornamented timber panelling and a grand five-metre-wide stair with wrought-iron lamp standards. The ground floor dining room is vast and along its walls are Baroque fireplaces with Corinthian columns and marble bases. The richness in detail and spatial variation continues upstairs with further private dining rooms, a smoking room and a massive billiard room. The second and third floors house bedrooms, each with fireplaces. The significant interior spaces were designed by Wilson and Charlesworth and not by Tayler, who was asked to leave the club after falling out with the club's hierarchy.

2B D10

87 Queensberry Child Care Centre
Former State School No. 2365
225 Queensberry Street, Carlton
1881 Henry Bastow (PWD)
GC, V, NA

From the late 1870s, Education Department policy had been to build compact, two-storey buildings rather than linear, single-storey buildings, and this Gothic Revival school is an excellent example of this shift. Despite the removal of the stepped floors and galleries internally and the insertion of play areas and observation mezzanines, the spatial integrity of the former school is remarkably intact. Externally, the polychromatic brickwork, robust decorative detail and Venetian Gothic windows are all part of the highly adaptable Gothic Revival style, then widely regarded as the modern style of the 19th century. The building now functions as a child care centre.

88

88 Mandeville Hall
Former St George's, later Athelstane
10 Mandeville Crescent, Toorak
1867
1876–78 Charles Webb
GC, V, NA

Commissioned by millionaire businessman
Joseph Clarke to extend St George's, Charles
Webb converted the 1860s house into one of
Melbourne's grandest Italianate mansions and
created one of the landmarks of Melbourne's
so-called Boom style. The house ballooned from
12 to 30 rooms, a conservatory was added and a
lavish new interior was decorated by artist Mr
East of Gillow and Co. of London. The front of
the house was given colonnaded balconies
worthy of Baroque Rome. A central pedimented
entrance portico and a balustraded terrace
leading to gracious lawns increased the sense of
palatial splendour. This was no longer the polite
picturesque Italian villa architecture of the
1860s, but a style attuned to the wealth and
pretensions of its owner. Since 1924, Mandeville
Hall has been home to an exclusive Catholic
girls school.

89 Ormond College, University of Melbourne
College Crescent, Parkville
1879-81 Reed & Barnes (northwest wing); 1885-
87, 1888-89 Reed Henderson and Smart
(southwest wing, Wyselaskie Hall and residences;
northeast wing); 1892-93 Reed Smart and
Tappin (dining hall; Allen House); 1922 HH Kemp
(southeast wing); 1929 Haddon and Henderson
(MacLean House); 1958 Grounds Romberg and
Boyd (Master's House); 1963 Romberg and Boyd
(Picken Court); 1967 Romberg and Boyd
(MacFarland Library); 1969 Romberg and Boyd
(McCaughey Court)
GC, V, A

Constructed of rough-hewn Barrabool
sandstone on a bluestone plinth, with cream
brick dressings around windows and doors
openings, Ormond College is a Gothic Revival
masterpiece and a campus landmark. It was
designed by Reed and Barnes, who had designed
early major buildings on the campus and who
had been retained by the University Council
until the first decade of the 20th century as its
architects. The main building is planned around
a cloistered quadrangle and at the centre of its
three-storey pavilion bay plan is a bell and clock
tower with a belfry and encircling balcony.
Various additions such as the dining hall
(1892-93), with its baronial fireplace, complement the ever-so Englishness of the entire
collection, which owes much to the rigorous
design principles followed by English Gothic
Revivalist William Butterfield. A major
benefactor for the men's residential college
which was built by the Presbyterian Church was
Francis Ormond, member of parliament and
pastoralist. He also donated large sums of
money to the Working Men's College **(95)**, St
Paul's Cathedral **(81)** and to the endowment of
a Chair of Music at the University of Melbourne.
During the 1960s, architects Romberg and Boyd
added to the college with sympathetic and at
times confronting interpretations of Gothic
form. Women were admitted as residents to
Ormond College in 1973.

90

| 1B V6 | 1B P7 |

90 Windsor Hotel
Former Grand Hotel, Grand Coffee Palace
137 Spring Street, Melbourne
1883–84 Charles Webb; 1887–88; 1961 Norris &
Partners (corner extension to Bourke Street)
1983 Allom Lovell Associates (restoration)
GC, V, A

One of Australia's largest and grandest hotels
surviving from the 1880s, the Windsor Hotel
was designed by notable Melbourne architect
Charles Webb and commissioned by George
Nipper of the shipping firm Nipper and See. First
known as the Grand Hotel, the building
contained 200 rooms and, in 1887, it was
extended for the Centenary Exhibition of 1888
to accommodate 360 rooms. It became the
Grand Coffee Palace and one of the city's
symbols of simultaneous lavish speculation and
the intensely fashionable and financially
rewarding habit of morally upright temperance.
Indeed, the hotel did not regain its license until
the 1920s when it was renamed The Windsor
and more than £100 000 was spent on
renovations, especially on the main lounge and
dining room. The original Renaissance Revival
hotel, with its internal Romanesque arcading,
gained its twin cupola, capped French Second
Empire towers in 1888 when the building was
extended north along Spring Street. With its
opulent interiors and vibrant 19th-century
interior colour scheme immaculately restored by
Allom Lovell Associates, The Windsor today
remains one of Melbourne's most prized
reminders of the Marvellous Melbourne of the
1880s and continues to function as one of city's
premier hotels.

91 Georges
162-168 Collins Street, Melbourne
1883 Grainger and D'Ebro
1888 Albert Purchas (alterations and additions)
1997-98 Daryl Jackson Pty Ltd and Sir Terence
Conran (refurbishment)
GC, V, A

This Renaissance Revival building has had a
mixed architectural life, but its name has been
with it since 1890. The first building on the site
was a series of offices and stores erected by
contractor David Mitchell, Dame Nellie Melba's
father, but new tenants, drapers George and
George, required refurbishment. Developer
BJ Fink bought and moved Georges Federal
Emporium from the Block in Collins Street to its
current site and added nearly 2 acres of floor
space. Since 1890, the building has operated as
'George and George Ltd', general drapers, and
later as 'Georges' when it became a Melbourne
institution, the city's most exclusive department
store. In its most recent incarnation, architects
Daryl Jackson Pty Ltd and English good-design
guru Sir Terence Conran have transformed the
interior into a sleek and stylish emporium. The
Collins Street facade has been restored; discrete
parts of the original structure, finishes and
details have been revealed; high-tech steel and
glass stairs and roof lights have been inserted;
and, at last count, four ultra-cool new café/
brasseries as well.

●●●

*The originators of the firm 'Georges' were the
brothers WH and AH George, the latter having
been trained in leading London and Paris fashion
houses. They commenced business in the mid-
1860s as drapers in Collingwood, before moving
to central Melbourne in the early 1870s.*

92

92 ANZ Bank
Former ES&A Bank
390 Collins Street, Melbourne
1883–84 William Wardell
1990 Allom Lovell and Associates (restoration)
GC, V, A

Designed five years after his controversial dismissal in 1878 from his position as Inspector-General within the Victorian Public Works Department, the former English, Scottish and Australian Bank in Collins Street is William Wardell's finest secular work in the Gothic Revival style. English-born Wardell (1823–1899), then practising from Sydney, designed the Venetian Gothic bank office and residential quarter (now immaculately restored, complete with embossed leather wallpapers) for the bank's then general manager Sir George Verdon, a connoisseur of art and architecture. Constructed of Pyrmont sandstone, the bank's restrained facade is graced on the Queen Street elevation by a rendition of a segment of loggia from the Doge's Palace in Venice. The banking chamber is a thoroughly 19th-century concoction—cast-iron columns with scalloped brackets have capitals of wrought copper flowers, foliage and vegetables, and provide an airy space grounded by the Tasmanian black-wood wall panelling. A riot of colours indicate the richness sought by Wardell in a space which evokes the material wealth of English Gothic Revival works by William Butterfield or William Burges—in complete contrast to his church designs, where the rigorous principles of Gothic Revival 'demagogue' Augustus Welby Northmore Pugin are conscientiously followed.

93 Raheen
Formerly Knowsley
94 Studley Park Road, Kew
1884-85 William Salway
1889 extended
1993 Glenn Murcutt in association with Bates Smart & McCutcheon
GC, V, NA

Sitting high above Studley Park with extensive grounds, sweeping drive, four-storey tower and deep shadows cast by its double-storeyed loggia, Raheen evokes the wealth and style of a bygone age. Unusually, red brick was used instead of the typical cement stucco associated with Italianate mansions such as Merridale (originally Pomeroy) at 43 Sackville Street, Kew (c. 1884–85), and Ravenswood at Ravenswood Avenue, Ivanhoe (c. 1890). Raheen was purchased in 1917 by the Roman Catholic Church and its occupant was the charismatic Archbishop Mannix. In recent years, the severe-looking mansion has passed into private hands and been carefully restored by architects Bates Smart & McCutcheon. A highly wrought glass and steel pavilion house designed by Glenn Murcutt has been added to its northwest side.

94

95

2D F11

2F F1

94 Villa Alba
Formerly Studley Villa
44 Walmer Street, Kew
1863 Studley Villa, architect unknown
1882–83 Villa Alba, possibly William Greenlaw
(owner designer)
GC, V, A

Built for William Greenlaw, general manager of
Sir William Clarke's Colonial Bank of Australasia,
the stucco Italianate exterior of Villa Alba
conceals one of the country's most complete
decorative schemes of the 1880s. Executed by
leading Melbourne decorators Paterson Brothers,
the interiors include exquisite hand-painted
ceilings, tiled and decorated fireplaces and
mantles and painted friezes. Charles Stewart
and Hugh Paterson were siblings of fine artist
John Ford Paterson, and they had already earnt
praise for their handiwork in the library of
Parliament House **(36)**. The main rooms of Villa
Alba were painted using the illusionistic
techniques of *trompe l'oeil*. Vases of flowers,
soft blue skies and even cupids engaged in
photography featured amidst elaborately
stencilled ceilings. In the 'Scotch' Room, there is
a panelled frieze with scenes inspired by Sir
Walter Scott's *Rob Roy*. In the vestibule, used as
a ballroom, Greenlaw's vision of the 'Old' and
'New' worlds was depicted. The side walls were
painted to give the illusion of standing on a
terrace. On one side is a panorama of Sydney
Harbour and, on the other, a view of Edinburgh.
Together with Mrs Greenlaw's passion for
Aesthetic Movement furniture, Greenlaw's lavish
additions and 'profligate spending' contributed,
according to historian Jessie Serle, to his
'insolvency, demotion and death in 1895'.

95 Francis Ormond Building
(RMIT Building 1)
Former Working Men's College
124 La Trobe Street, Melbourne
1885–87 Terry & Oakden and Nahum Barnet
(Bowen Street wing)
1890–92 Oakden Addison and Kemp
(La Trobe Street wing & tower block)
c. 1935, 1955, 1997 additions, alterations,
refurbishment
GC, V, A

The first building of the Working Men's College,
and now the administrative headquarters of
RMIT University, the Francis Ormond Building
was constructed in two stages. The Bowen
Street wing (1885–87) housed the main lecture
hall (now the council chamber), workshops,
classrooms and caretaker's quarters. Designed in
rigorous Gothic Revival style, this first stage was
funded one-third by the founder of the Working
Men's College, the Hon. Francis Ormond MLC,
and two-thirds from public donations and levies
raised from members of the Trades Hall Council.
The La Trobe Street wing and its distinctive
donjon tower block, which suggests the
influence of High Victorian architect William
Burges, comprised the second stage (1890–92).
Ormond was again the major sponsor, but this
time through his bequest. Added were offices,
college council and instructors' rooms,
classrooms and laboratories. The final building
was thus completed to the original masterplan
of its architect and instructor at the Working
Men's College, Percy Oakden. The three-storey,
building paralleled in style contemporary
buildings being constructed by Reed Henderson
and Smart at the University of Melbourne, the
major difference being the distinctly urban
setting for what was later to be renamed the
Royal Melbourne Institute of Technology (RMIT).

96

98

2K A6

96 The Biltmore
Former Albert Park Coffee Palace,
Biltmore Private Hotel
152-158 Bridport Street, Albert Park; 1887-89
Walter Scott Law; 1889 Frederick de Garis and
Son; c. 1928 Arthur and Hugh Peck (alterations
and additions); 1992 Conversion to apartments
GC, V, NA

Numerous coffee palaces were built in
Melbourne during the 1880s as part of a
growing temperance movement. Coffee palaces
were rather like residential hotels. The initial
godly aim was to further the cause of
temperance by offering non-alcoholic drinks
and accommodation for the working classes, but
the idea prospered and these establishments
gained respectability. They contained public and
private dining rooms, drawing and sitting
rooms, billiard rooms and a 'family' atmosphere.
The city coffee palaces such as the grandiose
Federal Coffee Palace (1888, now demolished)
on the corner of Collins and King Streets were
enormous places. The Albert Park Coffee Palace
with its gracious arcaded loggias is one of the
few survivors. In the 1930s, it became a private
hotel while in recent years the building has been
converted into residential apartments.

29 E12

97 The Carousel
The Royal Melbourne Zoo, Royal Park, Parkville
1886
GC, V, A

One of a series of architecturally and historically
interesting structures that can be found at one
of Melbourne's most popular tourist attractions,
the Carousel (1886) has exquisitely carved and
painted horses. Other enclosures date from
1861, and continue through to more recently,
when exciting new habitats for butterflies, birds
and lions were constructed.

2C H10

98 Collingwood Town Hall
140 Hoddle Street, Collingwood
1885-90 George R Johnson; 1937-38 AC Leith
and Bartlett (hall and lobby remodelling);
1982 Allom Lovell and Associates with John and
Phyllis Murphy (restoration)
GC, V, A

Built at a time when town councils believed in
municipal magnificence, Collingwood Town Hall
is one the grandest 19th-century Boom style
town halls in Melbourne. When complete, the
complex included a town hall, library, municipal
offices, courthouse and post office. Pavilion bays
and a central three-staged clock tower topped
by a mansard roof and cast-iron 'widow's walk'
balustrade add to the building's opulence and
grandeur—in complete contrast to the predominantly working-class scale of the suburb it
continues to serve. Inside, the hall and foyer
were refurbished in Moderne style in 1937–38
by architects AC Leith and Bartlett. Collingwood
Town Hall's architect George R Johnson (1840–
1898) used a similar lavish style when he extended
the City of Fitzroy's existing premises **(109)**.

1A K3

99 Warehouses
23–31 Niagara Lane, Melbourne
1887 George De Lacy Evans
GC, V, A

A group of four, intact three-storey warehouses,
these handsome, red-brick structures, with their
high Dutch gable facades, were designed by
architect George De Lacy Evans. Their setting
evokes the scale and texture of Melbourne's
19th-century lane architecture. Each store has
an American barrel hoist, and separate entries
for goods and general business. Inside, the
upper floors are lined with Tasmanian ironbark
boards and, on the top floor, raked timber
boarded ceilings rise to a height of 7 metres.

100

100 Princes Bridge

Yarra River at St Kilda Road, Melbourne
1886–88 Jenkins, D'Ebro & Grainger
GC, V, A

Princes Bridge, the southern gateway to
Melbourne, is one of a series of three extant
bridges built across the Yarra River in the
central city between 1886 and 1890. Built to
a competition-winning design (1879), Princes
Bridge (28.5 metres wide and 112.3 metres long),
with its segmental iron girder arches, is the
third such construction at this point in the river,
replacing the single span, arched stone bridge
designed by David Lennox (1850), which itself
had replaced a timber bridge (1845). The current
bridge was built to accommodate the widening
of the Yarra from 130 feet to 316 feet along this
particular length of the river, undertaken to
lessen the possibility of flooding. Another
reason for the new bridge was the increased
traffic to and from the rapidly developing
southern suburbs. The construction was jointly
funded: two-thirds by the Victorian government
and the Melbourne Corporation, and one-third
by the municipalities of South Melbourne,
Prahran, St Kilda, Brighton, Caulfield, Malvern
and Moorabbin. The respective coat of arms of
each contributor was then included in the
ornamentation of the bridge spandrels. The
builder of Princes Bridge, which had inherited its
name from its 1850 predecessor (Prince of
Wales, later Edward VII), was the firm of David
Munro & Co. who were also responsible for the
Sandridge Railway Bridge (1886–88) and Queens
Bridge (1887–90).

101 Baldwin Spencer Building
Formerly Biology Building,
Old Zoology Building

Union Lawn, University of Melbourne, Parkville
1887–88 Reed Henderson and Smart
1889–90 Reed Henderson and Smart
1905–06 Smart Tappin and Peebles
1963 Mockridge Stahle and Mitchell (west wing)
GC, V, A

A handsome Gothic Revival structure with rough-
hewn freestone coursed walls that compare
with the same architects' design for Ormond
College **(89)** and the earlier Medical Building
(now Old Pathology) of 1884–1908, the Baldwin
Spencer Building is also significant for its links
to the foundation professor of biology, who
initiated the various subsequent additions early
into the next century that at one time included
a greenhouse and aquaria. Surprisingly, the
building contains many intact interiors. Original
stairs (including the one in the conical roofed
turret), the library ceiling with its cast-iron
columns and crocket capitals, original laboratory
spaces and equipment, and especially the
steeply tiered lecture theatre (complete with
wooden seats and desks) give a fascinating
indication of what it must have been like to be a
university student in the 1890s. Both the
Biology and the Medical buildings, stylistically
linked, were orientated (together with the
National Museum, now demolished) towards the
large ornamental lake which is now the paved
and grassed Union Lawn.

10

1B V4

102 Princess Theatre

163-181 Spring Street, Melbourne
1886–87 William Pitt
1922 Henry White (interior)
1990 Allom Lovell and Associates in association
with Axia Pty Ltd (restoration)
GC, V, A

The Princess Theatre is architect William Pitt's
most outstanding building in the luscious
French Second Empire style. Built on the site
of two previous theatres, the Royal Princess
Theatre (1864) and Astley's Ampitheatre (1857),
the New Princess Theatre, as it was touted
at the time, featured electric lighting and a roll-
back roof. This roof design solved the critical
issue of the ventilation of a packed theatre.
A circular opening in the ceiling, 8 metres in
diameter, slid open and a cylinder reached up
through the roof space to the top where two
sliding sections of the gabled roof moved apart.
The Princess Theatre opened on 18 December
1886 with *The Mikado*. The theatre's ingenious
mechanical devices were demonstrated to the
audience, who applauded the architect and
scenic artist at the end of the first act. Outside,
mansard domes topped by cast-iron tiaras, a
trumpeting winged female and couchant lions,
and a fabulous stained glassed-in first-floor
foyer completed this theatrical celebration of
architecture. In 1989, the Princess Theatre was
restored—the 1922 auditorium interior by Henry
White was retained—and upgraded, with new
flytower and upgraded air conditioning.

Boom Style

During Melbourne's economic boom of the
1880s, the Italianate and Renaissance Revival
styles were elaborated to Baroque dimensions.
In the hands of architects such as William Pitt,
JAB Koch and Twentyman & Askew, the facades
of buildings were given ever richer and more
sophisticated overlays of trabeated and arcuated
classical schemes: giant classical orders (often
coupled columns) overlaid onto Renaissance
symmetry; balustraded parapets, cement-
rendered swags and festoons of fruit; Mannerist
manipulations of keystones and segmental
pediments; and entire compositions expanding
through decorative repetition and the addition of
encrusted forms and clock towers. With the
influence of Louis Napoleon's grandiose Second
Empire style of domed mansard roofs and
pavilion planning, this effusive manner, which
came to be termed later 'Boom Style', was widely
adopted for public and commercial buildings,
especially town halls and large hotels such as
Pitt's The Windsor and the Federal Coffee Palace,
which once stood at the corner of Collins and
King streets.

103

1A H8

103 Bank of New Zealand (formerly AC Goode House and originally National Mutual Life Building)

389-399 Collins Street, Melbourne
1887-91 Wright, Reed & Beaver
1903 extensions
GC, V, A

Located diagonally opposite William Wardell's ES&A Bank (92), William Pitt's Melbourne Stock Exchange (107) and Melbourne Safe Deposit Building, Goode House completes this precinct's homage to the mercantile associations that became attached to multi-storey Gothic Revival structures of the late 19th century. Taking their cue from high French Gothic sources, Adelaide architects Wright Reed & Beaver then reapplied these ideas to a high-rise office building. Goode House is an exceptional example of robust modelling coupled with flamboyant Gothic detail. It has interiors to match, with exotic dados of grey marble, red marble pilasters and columns, and white marble stairs. Built for the National

Mutual Life Association, Goode House was extended 24 metres along Queen Street in 1903.

104 Wardlow

114 Park Drive, Parkville
1888
GC, V, NA

With its Italianate tower set immediately above the front door, its cast-iron verandas and asymmetrical form with polygonal bays over two storeys, Wardlow is typical of numerous grand mansions built during the boom years of the 1880s by Melbourne's upper middle class. Its most unusual external feature is the balustraded parapet concealing the humble hipped roofs behind. Wardlow was built in 1888 by local merchant John Boyes, who had made money as an ironmonger and then as a speculative house builder in Parkville. Its interior displays a wealth of 19th-century wallpaper designs, wood graining and painted stencilling.

1891 The name 'Commonwealth' rather than Federal Dominion' adopted in Constitution Bill

105

107

1B S4

1A J7

105 Sum Kum Lee General Store
112–114 Little Bourke Street, Melbourne
1888 George De Lacy Evans
GC, V, A

One of the most thoroughgoing examples of bold Baroque massing and Mannerist detail applied to commercial premises of a relatively modest scale, the Sum Kum Lee General Store was erected by Lowe Kong Meng, wealthy merchant and prominent member of Melbourne's Chinese community. The three-storey structure housed business premises, warehouse and a 'first class residence'. On the roof was a flat terrace to enjoy the city skyline. Though briefly owned (c. 1900–1903) by Polish journalist Maurice Brodsky, whose weekly journal *Table Talk* had documented the debts accrued by significant citizens during the 1890s recession, the Sum Kum Lee General Store has primarily had Chinese food and grocery vendors as its owners and tenants since its construction.

1B L6

106 Former City of Melbourne Building
112–118 Elizabeth Street, Melbourne
1888 Ellerker & Kilburn
GC, V, NA

Commissioned by the City of Melbourne Building Society during the heyday of land and building speculation in the 1880s and constructed just before the era's great bust and the society's collapse in 1893, this building is a lavish and free interpretation of classical architecture. Enriched by a skyline of mansard roofs, chimneys and neo-Baroque gable ends, Ellerker & Kilburn's four-storey office design predates Kilburn's trip to the United States, yet its character and densely fanciful decoration suggests the exuberance of that country's late 19th-century American architecture.

107 Former Melbourne Stock Exchange
376–380 Collins Street, Melbourne
1888-91 William Pitt
1990 Allom Lovell and Associates (restoration)
GC, V, A

The former Melbourne Stock Exchange and the Melbourne Safe Deposit Building (1890) at 88–92 Queen Street form two Venetian Gothic bookends to William Wardell's ES&A Bank **(92)** on the corner of Collins and Queen streets. Both designed by William Pitt, one of Melbourne's most successful Boom style architects and responsible for the Windsor Hotel **(90)**, these 'multi-storey' Gothic Revival office buildings possess a style relating to the banking and trade associations of Venice's encrusted Gothic palazzi so admired by English art critic and Gothic propagandist John Ruskin. With the recent annexation of all three buildings for Peddle Thorp Learmonth's ANZ Tower, various Gothic vaulted spaces of the Stock Exchange have been restored, including its gabled roof, clocktower and elaborate cast-iron finials, which had been missing for decades.

2H A7

108 Lalor House
293 Church Street, Richmond
1888 William George Wolf
GC, V, NA

Boom style in its heavy massing, grim grey stucco and exaggerated classical detail, this arcaded, two-storey residence and surgery was built for Dr Joseph Lalor, son of the famous Eureka Stockade leader and politician Peter Lalor (who died at the house in 1889). Its architect, American-born William George Wolf (1855-1898), after arriving in Australia in 1878, lived and worked in Richmond designing numerous hotels, including Swan Street's Council Club Hotel, before shooting himself in 1898.

108

109

2C B9

09 Fitzroy Town Hall

201 Napier Street, Fitzroy
1873 WJ Ellis (hall wing and first tower)
1887-90 George Johnson (hall, offices, library,
courthouse, police station & new tower)
GC, V, A

The complex of Roman Revival buildings that comprise Fitzroy Town Hall, with their monumental flights of steps, Roman Corinthian porticoes and classical-styled clocktower, is the result of two major building programs. The first stage comprised the main hall on the north side of the site and the tower. The second stage involved extensions incorporating new functions, the substantial remodelling of the hall and the addition of a public library. The designer of this stage was George Johnson, perhaps Victoria's most prolific municipal architect, who had been responsible for town halls in Collingwood **(98)** and North Melbourne. The double-height library at Fitzroy is one of Melbourne's most delightful and well-used 19th-century interiors.

●●●

George Raymond Johnson (1840–1898) was born in Edmonton, near London. He completed his articles under George Hall, Chief Architect of the Midland Railway Company, and, after practising briefly in London, emigrated to Australia in 1862. He moved to Melbourne in 1867 and practised there until 1895, designing numerous municipal buildings, theatres and other major works such as the Metropolitan Meat Market (83), the Hosptital for Incurables in Heidelberg (the original Austin Hospital, 1881) and annexes for the Exhibition Buildings for the 1888 Exhibition. Johnson became an expert in town hall design, specialising in grand classical compositions. These include Hotham (North Melbourne, 1875), Albury (1882, not built), Daylesford (1884), Collingwood (1885–87), Fitzroy (1887–89,

extensions), Maryborough (1888), Northcote (1890) and Kilmore (1895). Johnson left Melbourne in 1895 and died three years later in straitened financial circumstances.

2B E8

110 School of Graduate Studies,
1888 Building
Formerly Melbourne Teachers' College

Grattan Street, University of Melbourne, Parkville
1888-91 Henry Bastow and John Marsden
(Public Works Department)
1890-91 west wing
1933 Percy Everett (PWD) (west wing)
1996 Allom Lovell Associates (restoration and additions)
GC, V, A

The Melbourne Teachers' College was planned primarily on the basis of separating the residential quarters of the male (west wing) and female (east wing) students. Following a similar plan which existed at the co-educational Homerton College in London, the red-brick Melbourne college was designed in a novel late-Elizabethan style, complete with mansarded towers and exuberant Dutch gables. The central block, which contained the major teaching spaces, was also organised around the segregation of male and female students, with separate lecture rooms for each sex. Its north wing had a gymnasium at ground level and, upstairs, an examination hall which became the principal lecture hall and which has continued as the building's main auditorium space. Outside, griffins adorn the parapet and, according to the college's first principal, signify swiftness and strength, as well as wisdom and illumination— all appropriate qualities for the teachers of the future.

111

112

1B L7

111 Block Arcade

*280-286 Collins Street; 96-102 Elizabeth Street,
Melbourne*
1891 Twentyman and Askew
1983
GC, V, A

Shopping arcades were the 19th-century answer
to making full use of a deep ground floor plan.
They brought the street inside. The Block Arcade
was the grandest and most fashionable
amongst what would become an extensive
network of retail arcades that provided an
alternative pedestrian route to Melbourne's
major streets. Doing 'The Block' was an 1890s
social institution. It was the place to be seen
and those who frequented the popular
thoroughfare, its shops and teahouses were
often recorded by caricaturists in the city's
social pages. Developed by Benjamin Fink, the
first section of 'The Block' comprised two corner
shops on Collins Street and fourteen arcade
shops all with mezzanine levels above for
showrooms and offices. The arcade formed a
bent L-shape with a polygonal planned space
with a glazed roof at the corner of the L. The
kink in the plan was due to the shape of the
original block subdivison and the location of
Block Place, the lane behind. Fortuitously, it lent
a picturesque quality to the rhythmic classical
composition of the arcade. In 1892-93, 'The
Block' was extended to join Elizabeth Street with
a further two corner and twelve arcade shops.
Linking the two spaces was an elaborately
patterned mosaic floor of tiles imported from
Italy. In 1907, scenic artist Philip Goatcher for
the Singer Sewing Machine Company decorated
the ceiling of their premises on the east corner
of the Collins Street entry to the arcade. It can
still be seen today. On the street, both facades,
especially the Collins Street frontage,
demonstrate extraordinary compositional

virtuosity—it is as if two classically composed
screens have been overlaid onto each other. This
is Boom style facade design at its opulent best.
For devotees of the shopping arcade, next door
at 288–292 Collins Street can be seen a 1920s
version, Harry Norris's Art Deco-styled Block
Court (1929).

2B K11

112 Fitzroy Cable Tram Engine House

Cnr Gertrude and Nicholson Streets, Fitzroy
1886-87 Attributed to Twentyman and Askew
GC, V, NA

The privately owned Melbourne Tramway and
Omnibus Company constructed 11 engine
houses in Melbourne for their cable tram system,
which at the time was one of the largest in the
world. Importantly, the cable trams encouraged
access to the city's premier suburban shopping
streets of the time: Smith, Brunswick, Swan and
Chapel streets, and Bridge and Sydney roads.
Substantial engine houses were built in Richmond
(1885), Fitzroy (1887), Brunswick (1887),
Collingwood (1887), North Carlton (1888), North
Melbourne (1890) and South Melbourne (1890).
The Fitzroy Engine House was the third to be
built in the series and one of the biggest. Three
cables were driven from here, the longest cable
length being 23880 feet. The architects are
likely to have been Twentyman and Askew, who
designed the company's head office and most of
the other engine houses in the system. The
distinctive corner oriel tower, a later addition,
had a practical use as a signal box and sat
above the original corner entrance. The building
itself is a rich composition of two-toned red
brick with cement and bluestone dressings, the
most remarkable being the precast cement
mouldings above the windows that represent
the cables driving this transport system, which
ran in Melbourne until 1940.

113

114

13 Olderfleet Building

477 Collins Street, Melbourne
1889 William Pitt; 1985 Robert Peck Von Hartel
Trethowan in association with Denton Corker
Marshall (renovation and tower behind
at 471–485 Collins Street)
GC, V, A

The stretch of Collins Street that begins with William Pitt's Olderfleet Building and ends with his design for The Rialto (114) at 497–503 Collins Street must be considered Melbourne's most highly prized 19th-century mercantile streetscape. The Olderfleet Building, once stretching all the way to Flinders Lane, is comprised of a four-storey Venetian Gothic screen, an appropriately Ruskinian encrusted facade. Its spandrels are rich in colour, with tile inlays, and the emphasised central bay is crowned by a pinnacled Gothic Revival clocktower. Next door, at 479–481 Collins Street, Record Chambers (1887), designed by JAB Koch, is carried out in Mannerist Classical style with banded pilasters and engaged columns overlaid onto a pier and arch system. The next year, the New Zealand Insurance Company constructed offices at 483–485 Collins Street (1888). Designed by Oakden Addison and Kemp, it was another Gothic Revival office building, rich in polychromatic brick and tile decoration. At 487–495 Collins Street, the exposed red brick and cement-dressed Winfield Building (1891)— built as the first Melbourne Wool Exchange (1892–94) and designed by architects Charles D'Ebro and Richard Speight—reveals the next stylistic phase of the 1890s. Once housing an auction hall where wool sales were held, it incorporates eclectic architectural elements such as the picturesque Franco-Flemish Renaissance gable end and turreted corner tower, and the pier and arches of the brick Romanesque style.

114 Le Meridien at Rialto
Former Rialto Building and Winfield Buildings

497-503 Collins Street, Melbourne
1889 William Pitt
1980 restoration and connection to hotel
GC, V, A

The climax to a distinguished stretch of 19th-century commercial buildings, the Rialto Building gains its style from its famed Venetian namesake. A complex of offices and warehouses that retains its balconies, a cobbled laneway and even its cast-iron privies after being remade as a high-class hotel, the Rialto is William Pitt's second master work for Patrick McCaughlan (the first being the Olderfleet (113) nearby. The Gothic palazzo idiom is followed. Coloured tiles, polychromatic banding, pointed arches and columnettes create yet another fabulous commercial screen, the late 19th century's answer to the late 20th-century curtain wall skyscraper.

•••

Gothic Revival
Influenced by the moralism of English Gothic Revivalists, AWN Pugin and John Ruskin, the revival of medieval Gothic design principles was regarded by many architects as the answer to the problem of a modern style for the 19th century. An 'honest' idiom of direct expression with links to religious virtue, the Gothic Revival was favoured by designers of churches, schools and university buildings. Varying according to religious persuasion, the Catholic and Anglican churches were the most vocal champions of the Gothic, reflected in the commissioning of extreme High Anglican English architect William Butterfield to design St Paul's Cathedral. A different form of Gothic Revival was used in commercial buildings such as the Olderfleet and the Rialto, their rich, repetitive facades evocative of Venetian mercantile exchange.

115

2B G11

115 Medley Hall
Former Benvenuta
48 Drummond Street, Carlton
1892 Walter S Law
GC, V, A

Benvenuta's arcaded loggia, skyline of balustraded parapet, tower and statues, substantial fence and gate, and wealth of decorative stucco work and mouldings smack of Victorian exuberance and excess. The client for this lavishly decorated Boom style townhouse was Mrs Leah Abrahams, the widow of a small arms manufacturer. Now a University of Melbourne hall of residence, its function may have changed, but its sheer ostentation remains unsurpassed in inner Melbourne.

1A A9

116 Grand Central Apartments
and Grand Hotel (Former Victorian Railways Administration Offices)
Spencer Street, Melbourne
1893, 1912, 1922 Victorian
Railways Engineering Office
GC, V, A

Now a hotel and residential apartments, the once very sooty Victorian Railways Administration Offices was the largest office building to be built in Melbourne in the 19th century. A massive Italianate pile with exaggerated horizontal rustication and quoining to its three major pavilion bays, its additional floor and domical towers, added in 1912, and the 1922 attic are clearly discernible. Initially intended to be faced in bluestone, the scale of the building was such that brick, stone and cement stucco were employed instead.

117

117 Illawarra

1 Illawarra Crescent, Toorak
1888–89 James Birtwhistle
AC, V, NA

Designed by the relatively unknown James Birtwhistle, Illawarra was commissioned by infamous landboomer and politician Charles Henry James. Its unusually free mix of full-blown mannerist classical detail, vernacular roof lines and picturesque composition foreshadowed the inventiveness of the Queen Anne Revival that would be experienced for the next 25 years. The house's campanile-like tower is unique in Melbourne for its monumental massing and stacked temple forms, a composition more likely to crown a town hall tower. Now a boarding house under the guardianship of the National Trust, Illawarra is a vast sleeping duchess awaiting an appropriately grand awakening.

118 Lowther Hall, Church of England Girls Grammar School
Former Earlsbrae

17–29 Leslie Road, Essendon
1890 Lawson and Grey
GC, V, NA

Built for wealthy brewer Collier McCracken, Earlsbrae is the grandest Boom period mansion to survive in Melbourne's western suburbs. The house's main feature is the double-height and giant order Corinthian colonnade which stretches across its main facade and halfway down each side of the house's massive block form. Earlsbrae was purchased by the Anglican Church after 1919 and became a girls' school, its new name honouring Archbishop Lowther Clarke.

119

59 C6   **29 E8**

119 Stonington
Formerly Stonnington
336 Glenferrie Road, Malvern
1891 Charles D'Ebro
GC, V, A

Designed by London-born architect Charles D'Ebro (1850–1920), whose firm was responsible for Princes Bridge **(100)**, Stonington was built for John Wagner, owner and founding partner of the Victorian branch of transport company Cobb & Co. Named after Stonington in Connecticut, USA, the birthplace of Wagner's wife, Mary, this huge Boom style, two-storey mansion shares possible design connections to the elaborate German 19th-century Villa Knoop, Bremen (1873–76), designed by JG Poppe. However, D'Ebro's repertoire of buildings in mannerist compositional style paralleled rather than mimicked German contemporary achitecture. At Stonington, the French Second Empire roofscape of steep pitches and areas of concentrated Baroque detail and massing indeed suggest the exaggerated intensity of 19th-century Continental classicism. On the ground floor were vast entertaining rooms giving onto an arcaded loggia/veranda. Upstairs were bed-rooms. A double-storey servants and service wing added further volume to the imposing bulk of the stuccoed mansion. Between 1901 and 1931, when the federal parliament was located in Melbourne and the Governor-General resided at Government House **(66)**, Stonington was, from 1901 to 1932, used as Victoria's vice-regal residence and its name changed to 'Stonnington'. Subsequent uses have been as St Margaret's Girls School (1931–38), hospitals and administrative centre (1938–57), Toorak Teachers College (1957–73) and the State College of Victoria (1973–92). Since 1992, it has been Deakin University's Melbourne adminis-trative headquarters.

120 Former Hoffman's Brick
and Pottery Works
72–106 Dawson Street, Brunswick
c. 1884 (north kiln); 1906 (south kiln)
BC, V, NA

The highlights of this virtually derelict site are the three Hoffman kilns, dramatic pieces of industrial architecture. Features of the massive structures include the seemingly endless tunnel for brick burning, flues, central chimney stack and the external ramped brick walls. A corrugated iron hipped roof covers each kiln. The Hoffman kiln was first patented in Australia in 1865. The Brunswick site was the No. 2 Works of the Hoffman Patent Brick and Tile Company, which had been formed in Melbourne in 1870. No. 1 Works (1870) operated from Albert Street, Brunswick. Clay had been central to the history of Brunswick since the 1840s. From this site, buoyed by the boom of the 1880s, came not just thousands of bricks, but also pottery in the form of sewer pipes, sanitary ware, tesselated tiles and, by 1917, roof tiles.

Below: Plan of Stonington (1891)

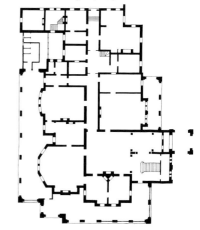

121

121 Labassa
Former Ontario
2 Manor Grove, North Caulfield
1889–91 JAB Koch
GC, V, A

Despite Labassa's site being carved up for subdivision and the house subsequently being hemmed in by 1960s flats (since demolished), the house still induces awe for the sheer density of its rich, overblown exterior and interior decoration. Designed by German architect JAB Koch, this German Renaissance pile was commissioned by Alexander W Robertson, who instructed Koch to design 'the most magnificent house in Melbourne'. Robertson, a Canadian, named the house Ontario, but he died in 1896 and new owner JB Watson, one of Victoria's richest men, changed its name to Labassa. Compared like Stonington to JG Poppe's Villa Knoop, Bremen (1873–76), Labassa is also Italian in flavour, with its double-storey arcading that recalls another earlier Koch design, the single storey Friesia (formerly Oxford) at 21 Isabella Grove, Hawthorn (1888). The overlay of decoration onto the semicircular bay, the heavily modelled cornice and the balustraded parapet, however, give a decidedly Baroque flavour to the asymmetrical Italianate villa form. Inside the entrance hall, every surface is richly veneered: heavily gilded and embossed wallpapers, gilded and stencilled ceilings, gorgeous stained glass and parquet floors. This voluptuous recipe for interior decor continues through the major entertaining spaces of the house on a scale of ostentation never to be seen again after the crash of 1892. For decades, Labassa was a boarding house (albeit luxurious in scale), before being purchased in 1980 by the National Trust. In time, it may become the home of Victoria's first museum of decorative arts.

122 Former Warrington, then Kawarau
405 Tooronga Road, Hawthorn
1891 Beswicke and Coote
1903–1904 Ussher and Kemp (rear extension including billiard room)
GC, V, NA

Kawarau once stood in 22 acres of gardens. Merchant Robert Robinson commissioned his son-in-law's architectural firm to design a substantial 12-room residence and the result was a colonnaded, late Italianate mansion. Of particular note with regard to Beswicke and Coote is their trademark arcaded veranda and balcony that employs stilted segmental arches at the upper level and semi-circular arches on the lower level. The second owner was Frederick J Cato (1858–1935), co-partner of the grocery store empire Moran and Cato. The house was then unfinished and Cato made substantial alterations and additions. Inside, there is a wealth of decorative plasterwork (much of which is in fibrous plaster, a relatively new material for 1904), with noteworthy Edwardian and Art Nouveau designs. The billiard room interior is finished in five different timbers and includes an inglenook. In recent years, Kawarau was home to one of the city's most acclaimed restaurants, Stephanie's, where owner/chef Stephanie Alexander complemented the mansion's rich interiors with equally fine food.

Above: Plan of Labassa (1889–91)

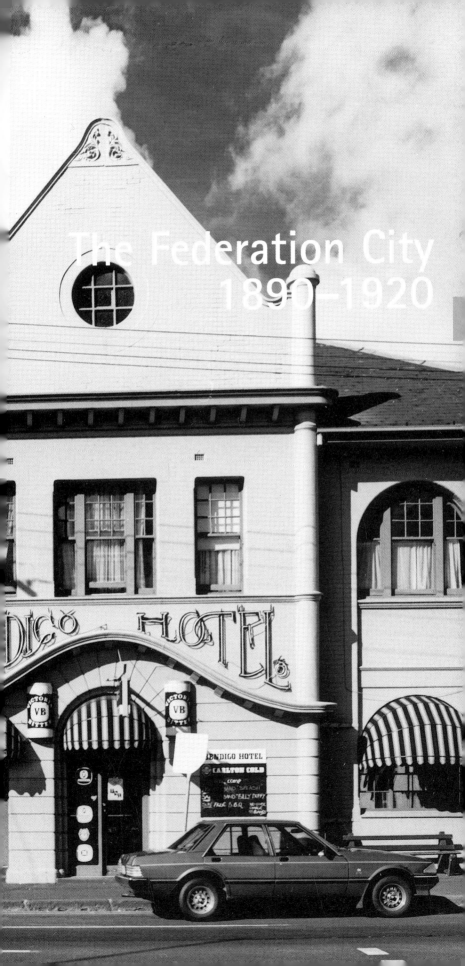

The Federation City
1890–1920

1890–1920

The new outlook combined a series of architectural approaches, fusing them into a virtual 'Federation Agreement'.

The Melbourne of the Federation era (1890–1920) was disliked for decades: from the novelist–architect Martin Boyd's stated desire to 'hold the type up to as much hatred, ridicule and contempt as is possible', to the condemnations of Robin Boyd's *Australia's Home* (1952) or Max Freeland's *Architecture in Australia* (1968). Melbourne after 1890 is often seen as a Sabbatarian shadow of Marvellous Melbourne, racked by economic depression and declining in population (at least until 1900).

Hardly had the 1890s depression set in than Melbourne was swept towards Federation. Still (only just) Australia's largest city, it became the temporary Australian capital from 1901 to 1926. The struggle with Australia's constitution, the rise of industrial arbitration, Australia's early prime ministers and governments, the opera capital, the first Australian motion pictures—all had the Melbourne of 1890–1920 as their public setting. Melbourne was, in many senses, Australia's Federation city.

Architecturally, Federation Melbourne, seen from within the colonial grid, shows its dynamics clearly: its new **State Library** dome (1909–11), **Flinders Street Railway Station** (1901–1911), and **Melbourne Hospital** later the **Queen Victoria Hospital** (1904–10). The spread of the tram and train network changed the city's scale, reshaping the pattern of street and house frontages, and creating a flexibility in building expression across a wider social spectrum. Increasingly, architects looked to a more generalised goal: to an imaging of Australia in architecture, whether a recast composite of European or British inheritances; an affirmation of the rural identity hammered out in contemporary writing and painting; or the synthesis of new, often conspicuously non-British approaches to architectural form. This new outlook combined a series of architectural tendencies, outlooks and movements, fusing them, widely, into a virtual 'Federation Agreement'.

Among architects this lasted from 1890 to about 1905, and in general building culture to about 1914. Gothic Revival attitudes continued from the earlier 19th-century (about ten mid–nineteenth-century churches were still being built or extended), and Italianate massing and veranda shaping continued. Most other things assumed in the 1880s, however, were attacked. Plaster and stucco on walls became falsity. Cast-iron columns and lacework were now cheap and nasty products rom factories, with no genuine embodiment of craft or valid work. Symmetrical composition and planning were artificial, pretentious and false. In the pages of the new building journals, a few such as Lloyd Tayler argued for the classical and the Renaissance—but they were a small minority.

With the new sources came American Romanesque, a free treatment of buildings using the round arches of pre-Gothic churches as a central theme. This came from Henry Hobson Richardson and his contemporaries in the United States, and had reached an ascendancy there in the 1880s. It read as a strong assertion of American identity: beyond the broad form of its arches and towers, its overall shaping was unmistakably geared to American cities and settings, and it explored newer forms, such as open plans and an organic expression of surrounding land. Absorbing newer American techniques of fireproofed iron and steel frame construction, it also reflected America's new skyscrapers, and began to do so in Melbourne. Applied to residential-scale architecture, it powered the first clearly modern forms of American architecture: of Frank Lloyd Wright, Louis Sullivan, Walter Burley Griffin and Marion Mahony.

Cover of Real Property Annual, 1913

In both Melbourne and Sydney, free Romanesque was quickly fused to a new, asymmetrical architecture in plain, unplastered brick, as in the 1880s and early 1890s post offices and courthouses of AJ McDonald for the Colonial Architects' office. McDonald was close to E Wilson Dobbs, a Melbourne associate, *American Architect* correspondent and author of *The Rise and Growth of Australasian Architecture* (1891). As with Melbourne contemporaries such as EG Kilburn's **Cestria** (1891) or Alfred Dunn's remarkable Brunswick and Hawthorn churches (1889–1890), Dobbs and McDonald's designs were linked to the whole, free approach then dominating British architecture and referred to as the 'great Pre-Raphaelite movement' (Dobbs) or, more generally, 'Queen Anne'. The term 'Queen Anne' created problems. The newly forming architecture had several details — unplastered brick exteriors, white or pale-coloured windows, elegant and rather stylised wood treatments, under Japanese influence. Beverley Ussher, author of the signature **Cupples House** of 1900, bemoaned 'the so-called, and wrongly called, Queen Anne'. The term 'Federation', coined by Bernard Smith and others much later, is far more useful in understanding the variety of the mode and its nationalist intention.

Federation architecture gained energy in dynamics and assimilations because of its extraordinary synthesis. From 1887, this shows in a wave of new work by Ussher, Henry Kemp, Alfred Dunn, AB Rieusset, Arthur Fisher, Christopher Cowper and many others. Its large, hipped roofs and flaring, integral verandas resembled parts of the new free styles in the United States. They also resembled the colonial homestead. The round arches of

Federation verandas echoed the heroism and movement against the street seen in the American architecture of Richardson and Louis Sullivan. The valances often used the overlapping line patterns of Japanese decoration – an early but very popular and pronounced Asian reference.

Robert Haddon actually developed the Federation mode, giving it a new simplification and tension between wall surface – which he saw as reflecting Australian light – and the mobility of sinewy line, unfurling each building's meaning in lettering (Swinburne College, 1917), lyrebird tails (**Eastbourne**

Engraving of cable machinery for Glenferrie/Malvern trams.

Terrace, 1901, with Sydney Smith and Ogg), now-vanished lions (Fourth Victoria Building, 1912) or magic swirling ships (Wharf Labourers' Building, 1916, demolished). McCrae and Toole's Catholic Church of St John, East Melbourne (1900), was related in its taut combination of Celtic cross, round arches and bell tower, and Harold Desbrowe-Annear extended a whole range of Federation themes into his Eaglemont houses. All disprove notions that Australian Art Nouveau was somehow blighted by being too heavy. In Melbourne, its robustness stemmed from having to carry the scales and structural loads of wooden valances and newels, unlike the less structural bronze or wrought-iron usage in European Art Nouveau. Nahum Barnet had a similar Nouveau vitality in his city buildings' imagery at this time, either with the **Paton Building** (1905) or the much later Display Block (1923).

Given Art Nouveau's celebration of the natural, American ideas of an organic architecture were the logical sequel. The early precursors of Melbourne's Californian bungalow housing of the 1920s appeared in the Federation years, as in Oakden and Ballantyne's seminal Martin bungalow of 1909 in Malvern. Desbrowe-Annear and other Melbourne architects knew Frank Lloyd Wright's designs and writing, and Louis Sullivan's ideas of linking the organic expression of nature in large city buildings. This work infuses Nahum Barnet's **Auditorium Building** (1913), Butler & Bradshaw's **Queensland Building** (1912–13) and the Tompkins brothers' Tomasetti Building (1905). Less directly, it gave confidence to a spectacular line in engineering, as in HR Crawford's use of the American Turner Mushroom System in his **Sniders and Abrahams warehouse** (1908–09), or the **Public Library**'s Great Dome (1911–13).

Walter Burley Griffin and Marion Mahony arrived in Melbourne in 1913 and their early town design focused on Melbourne suburbs—Eaglemont, East Keilor, Ranelagh and Park Orchards. As with Sullivan and Wright, floral ornament embodied their longed-for harmony with nature. All their Melbourne buildings explore this theme: from Collins House (1913-15; demolished) to their Mary Williams flats in Toorak (1927; built as a house). In their **Capitol Theatre** (1921-24), cave-like foyers (disastrously gutted in 1965) and luminous ceilinged lounges led into an auditorium of changing lights and an intricate, triumphal ceiling in plaster. **Newman College** (1915-18) combined parts of all major Christian styles with an architecture of topography, where piers rose from banks of slanted stone and, turned at a diagonal, became at once both emergent trees and Gothic ribs.

By 1920, the Federation Agreement infusing Melbourne design had come apart. The bungalow, which dominated Melbourne suburbs after 1918, was as much a tightened, rationalised form of Federation as a 'Californian' import. In public buildings, the change was equally fascinating, marked after 1900 by a strong move towards a revived 'English Renaissance', or a synthesis of conspicuously British forms from the period 1661-1740, now seen as English Baroque. Also, the renewed Renaissance offered weight, discipline and systematic grandeur that appealed to architects differently.

Melbourne's new railway works show this, beginning with Fawcett and Ashworth's extraordinary hybrid in **Flinders Street Station** (1901-1911), extending to a whole series of superb stations on the Caulfield, Box Hill, Williamstown and Heidelberg lines (1898-1916). In city buildings came competitions for now-vanished buildings: the AMP Insurance headquarters (1903), the State Savings Bank of Victoria (1912) and some notable survivors: JJ and EJ Clark's **Melbourne City Baths** (1903-04); the Tompkins' more French **Commercial Travellers' Association Building** (1912-13); Oakden and Ballantyne's New Zealand Loan and Mercantile Agency Building (1911), now the Dalgety building; JS Murdoch's brilliant set of **Commonwealth Offices** in Treasury Place (1910-12), with their stepped outline; and the present vestiges of JJ and EJ Clark's vast Melbourne Hospital, later the **Queen Victoria Hospital** (1904-10). There, in a synthesis of the new Renaissance and the movement in red-brick massing that epitomised the earlier free Federation mode, came a building that literally advanced on the city with serried force in four great wings, looming. Today, it is a singular, almost destroyed summary of Melbourne's recovered sense of identity: once, however, it was a complete, composite image, in itself—of the Federation City.

CONRAD HAMANN

12

123 Phillis Spurling House

38 Black Street, Brighton
1888 John Horbury Hunt
GC, V, NA

Phillis Spurling House is the only known house in Victoria designed by the Sydney-based John Horbury Hunt (1838–1904). It is important as it introduced the Shingle style, the Arts and Crafts-inspired North American domestic architecture, to the local scene. Simplified and open plans, the extensive use of shingles creosoted black, bold craftsman timber bracketing and strongly modelled brick chimneys characterise Hunt's residential designs. It is also known that he was an admirer of 19th-century French theorist Emmanuel Viollet Le-Duc, whose belief in an architecture developed rationally independent from conventional stylistic rules informed much of Hunt's distinctive design philosophy. Viollet Le-Duc's *Entretiens sur l'architecture* (1863–72) and *Dictionnaire Raisonné* (1854–68) were to be found in Hunt's architectural library, which was the largest in 1890s Australia. The Spurling House is a notable example within Hunt's collection of 22 house designs built during his lifetime.

45 C6

124 Kew Police Station, Court House and Post Office

190 High Street, Kew
1886, 1888 John Henry Harvey (PWD)
GC, V, A

New architectural influences came to be felt in the 1880s and none more important to the development of the so-called Federation style than the English vernacular free style. The Kew complex of police station, courthouse and post office is a very early example of this inventive new idiom, which was characterised by red bricks and cement-render banding and

detail ornamentation. Also arriving with this style is the increased use of terracotta seen here on the ridge capping and finials, and the use of brick corbelling and strapwork to the chimneys. Rather than domestic architecture leading the way in innovative design as it did in the 20th century, government-sponsored architecture also determined architectural tastes during the last decades of the 19th century.

1B R8

125 Austral Buildings

115-119 Collins Street, Melbourne
1890-91 Nahum Barnet
GC, V, A

Designed as shops and professional rooms, this building housed tenants who enriched the social diversity of this end of Collins Street. Mr William Terry, 'prominent member of the modern spiritualistic movement'; Herr Grundt, 'masseur and medical electrician', and photographer JW Lindt. Another notable tenant was the Austral Salon, a pioneer women's club dedicated to the advancement of women. Nahum Barnet's design is one of the earliest examples in Melbourne of the English Queen Anne Revival office building. The modelling of the brackets, aedicules and bay window consoles is particularly vigorous, foreshadowing the later Edwardian Baroque of the Melbourne City Baths **(142)**.

Below: Plan of Phillis Spurling House (1888)

126

2H K9

126 Tay Creggan
30 Yarra Street, Hawthorn
1891-92 Guyon Purchas
GC, V, NA

This Medieval Revival styled mansion, with its steeply pitched roof from which sprout gables, dormers and decorative chimney stacks, has been described as Elizabethan; however, the generous use of timber and the fine carving of its barge boards suggest possible patternbook influence from early 19th-century American Carpenter Gothic sources. This picturesque, rambling idyll, now owned by Strathcona Baptist Girls School, was home to its architect Guyon Purchas and located in extensive grounds in George Coppin's St James Park subdivision of 1871.

28 J1

127 Former North Park
(St Columban's Mission)
69 Woodlands Street, North Essendon
1889 Oakden Addison and Kemp
1906 Billing, Son and Peck
(ballroom and interior alterations)
GC, V, NA

Commissioned by Essendon brewer Alexander McCracken, North Park is one of the most important early examples in Australia of the English-inspired Medieval Revival style that was to be transformed and popularised as the so-called Queen Anne and Federation style house. North Park is also of technical interest as it was claimed at the time that the house's roofing tiles from Marseilles, France, entailed the first large commission to employ these tiles in Australia. All the features of the future Federation style are here in this free interpretation of a grand English country house. Half-timbered gable ends, crested terracotta ridge-capping, clustered tall chimneys, red brick and Waurn Ponds sandstone dressings and a composition of complex asymmetry laid upon a formally designed garden facade of two gabled wings and an imposing French influenced tower are the house's design elements. The designer of North Park is believed to be Henry Kemp, who later authored distinctive designs in this double-storey gable idiom. The plan of the six-bedroom house is simple, but of grand proportions. An entrance hall with massive flanking arches meets a transverse passage which runs the entire length of the house. The interior decoration in the reception spaces offers fine examples of Art Nouveau foliated ornament on pressed metal ceilings and wall mouldings all still in their original paintwork. A special feature is the series of coloured transfers applied to windows and fanlights throughout the house. A novel alternative to stained glass, some of these transfers indicate landscape scenes and even family members. Galleries, balconies and a tower lookout add to the house's spatial interest and picturesque outline. North Park was eventually acquired by the Roman Catholic Church in the 1920s, which renamed the property St Columban's and has conscientiously maintained much of the original interior. The stables and remnants of the extensive gardens, including a fountain, still exist. The ballroom now serves as a chapel.

128

13

45 D12

128 Cestria

521 Glenferrie Road, Hawthorn
1891 EG Kilburn
AC, V, NA

Fresh from his American and English tour,
EG Kilburn designed this large house for
TB Guest. In May 1891, the *Journal* described
Cestria as being '... designed in the American
Romanesque style, which lends itself readily to
picturesque effects, and at the same time is well
suited to the requirements of the Australians
and their climate'. The next month, Cestria's hall
was described as '... thoroughly American in
feeling ... in mahogany and American walnut'.

The Romanesque overlay is most evident in
the tower, which is modelled like a campanile
with its increasing arched openings towards its
top, but with a steep, pitched roof. The
semicircular arches used on the main mass of
the house and latticed balustrading confirm its
1891 description. American historian Myra
Dickman Orth declared that Cestria's design was
a '... mere Richardsonian shell fitted over a
Melbourne Queen Anne body', overlooking the
subtleties of a third intercontinental translation
of a style that had originally been practised
almost a thousand years ago!

58 C9

129 The Priory (formerly additions to the Priory Ladies' School)

61 Alma Road, St Kilda
1890 Ellerker and Kilburn
GC, V, NA

Together with the influences of the Queen Anne
Revival from England in the late 1880s, there
was also a new influence from North America.
Architecture and building journals discussed
Henry Hobson Richardson, the Beaux-
Arts–trained architect who had developed a
distinctive new style based on French

Romanesque models adapted to American
traditions. The result was a strongly modelled
architecture made distinctive by rock-faced
stone, massive semicircular arches and bunched
Romanesque columnettes. Architect EG Kilburn
visited the United States in 1889 and his design
for Miss Hatchell Brown's Priory Ladies' School
is thought to be the first suburban residence in
Victoria in the new American Romanesque style.

Designed to house more than 20 boarders,
the building was converted to flats, but is now a
single family home. The appearance of the
simulated rock-faced rustication to the ground-
floor Richardsonian arch and veranda pillars and
the almost exaggerated expression of load and
support were strident features in Melbourne's
otherwise prim Victorian suburbs. Apart from
terrace houses in this style in Park Street, South
Yarra (c. 1905), and Clarendon Street, East
Melbourne (c. 1905), and Ellerker and Kilburn's
design for Cestria **(128)** of one year later, the
Priory is an undeniable rarity.

56 E10

130 Royal Hotel

Nelson Place, Williamstown
1890 T. Anthoness
AC, V, NA

Like the Austral Buildings **(125)**, the Royal Hotel
is an early example in Melbourne of the English
Queen Anne Revival. The mixture of red brick
and vertically emphasised facade of Mannerist
compositions of classical detail surmounted by
an oddly English domestic roofline expresses
this hybrid style. The building's appearance is
unusual in Nelson Place, the streetscape of
which dates largely from the 1860s and 1870s.
For a contrast in architectural tastes, compare
the Royal Hotel with the Italianate repose of
Peter Kerr's nearby Customs House **(72)** of
nearly 20 years before.

903 High Court of Australia
tablished

1903 First flight in heavier-than-air
machine by Wright brothers

1904 Australian Public Service
instituted

131

2L H5

131 Former South Yarra Post Office
162 Toorak Road, South Yarra
1892 AJ McDonald (PWD)
GC, V, NA

This unique blend of American Romanesque and Scottish Baronial forms and details is combined with a decorative scheme that features Australian flora and fauna. Stepped gables, soaring chimney elements, a fanciful bulbous turret and a conical roofed tower create a vibrant composition redolent of a Scottish hunting lodge or castle. From Toorak Road, a Richardsonian arch window is surrounded by an ornamental panel of gum leaves, gum nuts, flowers, birds and marsupials—a new symbolic language for a public building. These formal and decorative ideas are explored in McDonald's other major buildings, most notably the Bairnsdale Court House (1892), whereas in the Omeo Court House (1892) and Omeo Post Office (1890), McDonald pursues more overtly Richardsonian themes.

2B H9

132 Sacred Heart Roman Catholic Church
199 Rathdowne Street, Carlton
1897 Reed Smart & Tappin
GC, V, A

The Sacred Heart Roman Catholic Church, with its two tall domed flanking towers, is an impressive, if austere, red-brick interpretation of the Baroque churches of Rome. Highlights of the nave interior are the elliptical barrel-vaulted ceiling, wall frescoes and elliptical painted ceiling and, in the vestibule, an elliptical geometric staircase. Miles Lewis et al. have described this building as 'the first and finest full-blown red brick Baroque church design in Victoria' and a 'radical departure from the usually favoured Gothic'. An earlier church in Melbourne which prefigures this turn towards Renaissance in

Baroque designs by the Roman Catholics in Melbourne is Reed Henderson and Smart's Sacred Heart Church (1884, completed 1922) in Grey Street, St Kilda.

2G A1

133 Victorian Artists' Society Building
430 Albert Street, East Melbourne
1893 Richard Speight and HW Tompkins
GC, V, A

A blend of symmetrical Queen Anne massing and Richardsonian Romanesque detail and fenestration was the recipe for this competition-winning design. Claims have been made that it may have been inspired by Henry Hobson Richardson's rectory for Trinity Church, Boston (1879), but it actually appears to be a reinterpretation of his use of grouped squat Romanesque columns to create clerestorey lighting for library spaces. Here in Melbourne, the same technique is used and, outside, great panels (originally meant to be carved) indicate the gallery walls within. The central entry Richardsonian arch and first-floor loggia are completely different from the Boston rectory and, while the Melbourne designers were knowledgeable about contemporary American developments, there are traces of Queen Anne style in the flattened overlay of cement rendered ornamental detail.

134

137

1B M9

134 Royston House
247-251 Flinders Lane, Melbourne
1898-89 Sulman and Power
GC, V, A

Sydney architects Sulman and Power designed a massive Romanesque-inspired warehouse that extended from Flinders Street to Flinders Lane, but only the latter section remains. The red-brick, giant order Romanesque arches stretching over three floors enabled large areas of glazing to light the warehouse floor. The bay windows were recessed from the brick face and this detail matches, as Miles Lewis notes, Queen Anne Revival designs such as Richard Norman Shaw's New Zealand Chambers, London (1871). Like the Victorian Artists Society Building **(133)**, Royston House is a transitional work blending both American and English ideas in commercial building design.

•••

London-born architect John Sulman (1849–1934) arrived in Sydney in 1888. He had extensive experience, having worked for Sir Gilbert Scott amongst others. He published papers on structural and aesthetic aspects of architecture, taught town planning at the University of Sydney and was heavily involved in Canberra's development. John Sulman was knighted in 1924 for his services to architecture and town planning.

2G E11

135 Morell Bridge
Yarra River at Anderson Street, South Yarra
1898–99 WJ Balzer, Carter Gummow and Company (design engineers)
Monash and Anderson (supervision)
GC, V, A

Generally regarded as the first significant reinforced concrete structure erected in Victoria, the Morell Bridge was designed by WJ Balzer for the engineers Carter Gummow and Company, agents in New South Wales for the Monier system of reinforced concrete. The Yarra River was diverted underneath the bridge once the 'Monier arch' spans and their concrete abutments had been completed. The footpaths were also concrete, while the roadway was macadamised over earth fill, which lay between concrete spandrel walls. Supervising construction were John (later Sir John) Monash (1865-1931) and JTN Anderson, who were to be responsible for other early reinforced concrete structures: their designs for 2–3 Olivers Lane in central Melbourne (1903) are claimed by architectural historian Miles Lewis to be the first conventional buildings in Australia constructed wholly of reinforced concrete.

•••

John Monash (1865-1931) was to achieve fame as an innovative reinforced concrete engineer, an outstanding army officer during World War I, and as the first general manager of the State Electricity Commission of Victoria. The naming of Victoria's Monash University is a testament to his substantial contribution to Victoria.

136 Springthorpe Memorial
Booroondara Cemetery, Park Hill Road, Kew
1897 Harold Desbrowe-Annear
GC, V, A

This elegantly severe Greek Doric temple form was commissioned by John Springthorpe as a memorial to his wife, Annie. It is a moving personal tribute. It appears as a square-planned temple, its roof supported by 12 black, Labrador granite, Ionian order columns. The grey granite entablature is scholarly Doric, but with open metopes housing wrought-iron sculpture by Webb Gilbert. Each side of the temple has its own pediment, suggesting that the roof is a complex meeting of gables, but there Annear has a surprise in store. An angel of mercy tends the figure of Annie Springthorpe lying atop her tomb—a serene white marble carving executed by Bertram McKennal. Above is Annear's climax to what has appeared to be a most sombre composition. A fabulously coloured leadlight domed ceiling is a heavenly sky: an extraordinary contrast of rich reds and oranges to the deathly blacks and greys of the elemental tectonics without.

137 Eastern Hill Fire Station
108–122 Victoria Parade, East Melbourne
1892–93 Smith and Johnson, Lloyd Tayler and Fitts; 1922 Oakden Ballantyne and Hare (alterations); 1994 Meredith Gould (watch tower restoration)
GC, V, A

A headquarters for the Metropolitan Fire Brigade Board was to be designed from competition, and the result is a convincing hybrid of two winning entries. The *Illustrated Australian News* of 1 July 1892 observed that, 'the combination will prove very effective for the purposes required, and be decidedly picturesque. The Queen Anne style of architecture is adopted, and the elevation reveals a substantial and ornamental structure'. Indeed it was. With its red-brick watch tower reminiscent of an Italian Romanesque campanile and its steep pitched roofline studded with tall chimneys, the new fire station was an impressive landmark. The arches on Victoria Parade were the openings for the hose cart and fire engines. Today, the building houses the Metropolitan Fire Brigade's Museum.

138 The Records Office
287–295 Queen Street, Melbourne
1900–04 SE Bindley (PWD)
GC, V, A

A late example of the flamboyant French Second Empire style, complete with a grand internal staircase hall, the Records Offices is one of the last government buildings for which the design relied on a grand classical style. Like Bindley's earlier Crown Law Offices (now the Supreme Court Annexe), 459 Lonsdale Street (1892–93), this building indicates the variety of design styles produced by the Victorian PWD following the austerity of the years under Chief Architect William Wardell. Bindley's recipe for the public building was to create a massive rusticated base at street level, a piano nobile divided into three pavilion bays, an attic storey above a balustraded parapet, topped by the French-derived mansard roofs. It was a vision of Melbourne as a grand Parisian-style capital. The Records Office is freestanding and is joined to the strongroom building at the rear by a courtyard.

139

139 Flinders Street Station
Flinders Street, Melbourne
1901–11 JW Fawcett and HPC Ashworth
(Railways Department)
GC, V, A

Melbourne's Edwardian Baroque masterpiece is Flinders Street Station. A building which responds directly to its urban setting with its angled siting, this Melbourne institution has symbolised the city's rail system for nearly a century. Meeting 'under the clocks' at Flinders Street has long been a favoured location, and this grand dowager has withstood plans to turn it into a podium for high-rise in the 1960s and more recently a festival marketplace. Trains had been arriving at Flinders Street since 1854 and the current building is one of a number that have stood on the site. Like the colonial railway stations of Bombay and Calcutta, Flinders Street was to be a major urban landmark worthy of the Empire. Its wall along Flinders Street is more than a city block in length, it has a giant ballroom and its blend of Baroque and 'blood and bandage' (red brick and cement) styling is enhanced by the grand arch entry to the ticket offices. The platform access ramps and the area beneath the iron trussed sheds have been subject to numerous refurbishments.

140 Eight Hour Day Memorial
cnr. Russell and Victoria Streets, Melbourne
1903 Percival Bell (artist)
GC, V, A

Melbourne was the first place in the world to achieve the eight-hour working day. In 1856, a meeting of employees and employers was persuaded by James Galloway to implement the philosophy of eight hours work, eight hours sleep and eight hours recreation.This monument has a triple eight inscribed in a rectangle beneath a gold leaf orb, atop what looks like a granite pencil. Further celebration was permanently assured (until a future government thought otherwise) with the proclamation of Labour Day as a public holiday for all Victorians.

141 Cupples House
608 Riversdale Road, Camberwell
1900 Ussher and Kemp
GC, V, NA

The Melbourne firm of Ussher and Kemp perfected a domestic style which has been labelled Queen Anne, Edwardian, Federation and now the so-called Melbourne Domestic Queen Anne. The Cupples House is the epitome of this style. Red brick, turned timber veranda posts, half timbering and rough-cast render, terracotta tiles, finials and gargoyles, casement windows and a romantic turret roof are the ingredients which complement a new plan where rooms spin off a central hall space. The use of major gabled wings forming an L-shape and then an all-embracing hip roof, which forms a return veranda between the arms of the L, is the dominant formal pattern of these houses. The so-called Melbourne Domestic Queen Anne style is characterised by a rotation and the lack of frontal symmetry. This perhaps is the first truly Australian style for a suburban house. Beverley Ussher is believed responsible for these spreading hipped roof villas, as seen in the Norman House (151), while Henry Kemp's designs were less roof-orientated in their massing and composition and exemplified by his North Park (127) and Campion College (147).

908 Australia granted its own
bat of arms

1908 First Model T Ford motor
cars introduced into Australia

1909 Canberra selected as site
for new capital of Australia

142

2B E12

142 Melbourne City Baths

Swanston Street, Melbourne
1903–04 JJ and EJ Clark
1980 Kevin Greenhatch & Associates in
association with Gunn Williams Fender
(renovations, alterations and additions)
GC, V, A

The Melbourne City Baths is another grand
Edwardian Baroque pile that balances its
stylistic larger cousin Flinders Street Station
(139) at the other end of Swanston Street.
Architects EJ and JJ Clark (designer of
Melbourne's Treasury **(31)**) skilfully inserted
separate men's and women's swimming pools
and private baths into a difficult triangular site.
The symmetry of the Swanston Street facade
reflects a division into men's and women's
changing rooms on either side of the central
Baroque entry bay. Outside, cupolas atop
belvederes atop highly mannered classical
compositions make this one of the most
exuberant 'blood and bandage' buildings of its
day. Later award-winning additions, including
squash courts and gymnasia, are exemplary
contextual additions to an important landmark.

•••

Edwardian Baroque
This is a grand classical non-domestic style
characterised by turn-of-the-century interests in
Beaux Arts Classicism (filtered through America)
combined with a revival of English Baroque
sources such as the architecture of Sir
Christopher Wren, Sir John Vanbrugh and
Nicholas Hawksmoor. The Edwardian Baroque
found favour in Melbourne in the new
department stores of Sidney Myer and Buckley &
Nunn, and along the booming commercial strip
of Chapel Street, Prahran. Mannered classical
facades were topped by exaggerated deep
cornices often concealing the up-to-date use of
reinforced concrete within.

In Britain, the style's exponents were Sir Aston
Webb and Mewes & Davis in London, and Sir
John Burnet in Glasgow. In Melbourne, the firms
of Bates, Peebles & Smart and the Tompkins
brothers introduced the style to the city's
commercial buildings, while Chief Architect for
the Commonwealth John Smith Murdoch
designed fittingly pompous and occasionally
masterful examples of Edwardian Mannerism for
the imperial outpost.

•••

1B R9

143 Former Metcalfe and Barnard
office–warehouse

145-149 Flinders Lane, Melbourne
1901-02 HW and FB Tompkins
GC, V, A

This office–warehouse was a distinctive early
addition to the emerging pattern of Flinders
Lane as a street of giant order Romanesque-
arched warehouses and offices. With its Art
Nouveau foliated cement ornament adorning
the column capitals and filling the spandrel
panels between the arches, it appears to show
an understanding of the work of Chicago
architect Louis Sullivan. Stylistically, the
warehouse joined Royston House **(134)** and
was followed by Nahum Barnet's Bedggood and
Co. Building, 172 Flinders Lane (1901); the
Tompkins' refacing of the 'Oriental Building'
(now Tomasetti House), 277–279 Flinders Lane
(1905–07); and the Higson Building, 125–127
Flinders Lane (1913).

144

145

1B U9

144 Milton House
21–25 Flinders Lane, Melbourne
1900–02 Sydney Smith and Ogg
GC, V, NA

Milton House is a rare central city example of Art Nouveau detail applied to a red brick, Georgian/Italianate facade. While the building is attributed to Sydney Smith and Ogg, it is believed that 'Design Consultant' Robert Haddon (1866–1929) may have had a hand in the exterior detail design, which exhibits his signature sinuous scenographic compositional technique, curvilinear foliage ornament and a terracotta floral frieze at first-floor level. It is believed that Haddon was also involved in the design of Kilkenny Inn, 248–250 King Street (1914); Napier Hotel, 210 Moor Street, Fitzroy (1916); and the Bendigo Hotel, Collingwood **(159)**. Haddon's only surviving work in the city entirely attributable to him is the former Fourth Victoria Building, 241–245 Collins Street, Melbourne (1912).

•••

Art Nouveau

In Australia, the appearance of Art Nouveau derived not from the work of the Viennese Secessionists such as Joseph Maria Olbrich or Otto Wagner, nor from the seductive liquid-like metal and glass structures of Hector Guimard or Victor Horta, but from the English Free Style and the work of architects such as CFA Voysey, CH Townsend and to a lesser degree, the 'spook style' of Glasgow architect Charles Rennie Mackintosh. Melbourne architects such as Nahum Barnet and Robert Haddon introduced the serpentine whiplash and tulip motifs in decorative panels of render or terracotta. Walter Butler and Bates Peebles & Smart embellished their tapered pylon forms with densely detailed cress. It was, however, Haddon (often through Sydney Smith & Ogg) and AJ McDonald whose compositions

transcended the purely decorative and involved entire facades of fluid free composition, mushroom towers and massing that had dynamic formal balance. Sadly, one of the city's best examples of Art Nouveau with its green majolica lions' heads missing, Haddon's Fourth Victoria Building Society, 241–245 Collins Street while still standing, awaits loving restoration.

•••

2G F5

145 Eastbourne Terrace
62 Wellington Parade, 8–10 Simpson Street, East Melbourne
1901 Sydney Smith and Ogg
C, V, A

One of Melbourne's finest examples of Art Nouveau architecture and a design by Sydney Smith and Ogg where Robert Haddon's presence has been cited, this building was the scene of one of Australia's most intensive murder investigations. The buildings were commissioned by surgeon Samuel Peacock, who was ignominiously tried three times from 1911–12 for the murder of a patient, Miss Davies. It was alleged that Peacock had performed an illegal and failed operation at Eastbourne House, but a corpse was never found. Police detectives at the time believed that the body of Miss Davies had been dissolved in acid and the bones powdered and disposed of through the sewer. Peacock was, however, acquitted and continued to practise at Eastbourne House until 1919. The Wellington Street facade is a tour-de-force of compositional invention, where windows, door, cement ribbon dressings, parapet tiling and curlicued consoles all seem to flow from one to another with scenographic ease. The wrought-iron balustrades to the terrace houses have a three-dimensional fan shape which bulges forward like peacock tails—perhaps a thinly veiled reference to the building's client!

146

31 K7

46 Chadwick House

32–34 The Eyrie, Eaglemont

1903 Harold Desbrowe Annear

1999 Peter Crone (restoration)

GC, V, NA

One of the most important houses in the history of 20th-century Australian architecture, the Chadwick House has only recently regained its original colour scheme. For decades, this Arts and Crafts style house was known as a severe black and white timber house with a radical open plan within—signs of an apparent modernist lineage. The rich ochres and browns derive, through Annear, from William Morris's interest in the pure ideals of Medieval architecture and HH Richardson's notions of rugged simplicity. Contemporary descriptions might have labelled the house as being in a Swiss chalet style, but the timber frame has been found by its current architect-owner to be a balloon frame and the weatherboards have a double bevel—both features of American domestic timber construction. The striking external feature of the house is its fluid collection of gabled and hipped roofs suggestive of a free arrangement of spaces within and the double ox-bow balustrading and veranda bracket detail. Inside, meticulous restoration work has reinstated the dark-stained timber-lined interior, with its raked timber-lined ceilings and handsome built-in timber joinery. Signature Annear details such as the window sashes which slide into the wall cavity and the huge timber door panel which slides away to conceal the front dining room are evidence of his technical ingenuity. Designed for his father-in-law, the Chadwick House is one of three designed by Annear on a single allotment purchased nominally by him and then divided equally into three. He kept the upper corner block at The Panorama and built a corrugated iron-roofed house for himself and his wife Florence at 36–38 The Eyrie, Eaglemont (1903). Annear's initials can be seen in the leadlight of the front door. The middle block (32–34 The Eyrie) and the lowest block (28–30 The Eyrie, now 55 Outlook Drive) were both owned by Chadwick. The three houses on the sloping site are located in the same area that artists such as Arthur Streeton and Frederick McCubbin had come to to paint their famous *plein air* images. Other contemporaneous Annear designs in the Ivanhoe/Heidelberg area can be found at 14 Martin Street, Heidelberg (1903); 234 Rosanna Road, Rosanna (1910); and the MacGeorge House, 25 Riverside Road, Ivanhoe **(170)**. In all the living areas of these houses, Annear followed a theme of open planning that would sustain generations of architects thereafter for decades. It was a simple idea and in Annear's own words, the open plan idea was embodied as: 'The free and constant enjoyment of the whole of the living rooms of the house by all in it is a much healthier ideal ...'

147

147 Dalswraith (now Campion College)
99 Studley Park Road, Kew
1906 Ussher and Kemp
GC, V, NA

One of Henry Kemp's most accomplished residential designs and comparable only with his earlier North Park **(127)**, Dalswraith is one of the most impressive examples of the Old English influence on the so-called Melbourne Domestic Queen Anne or Federation house style. Instead of a dominant picturesque hip roof and return veranda, the main features are the walls—with their bay windows, timber brackets, terracotta shingles and ornamental frieze—and the freestone entry loggia which dominates the composition. Still retaining its sweeping drive, this house has an approach as grand as its neighbour Raheen **(93)**. The entry hall stair is carved with dragons and a domed ceiling is lit by borrowed light from the dormers in the main gable roof. Some of the ceilings have Jacobean-inspired designs and the fireplaces have elaborate timber mantles and glazed Minton tiles. The interior is a wonderful example of Medieval inspiration combined with 19th-century notions of modernity. Ownership of the house passed to the Jesuit Fathers in 1949, who renamed it Campion College, made rear additions and use the residence in connection with Burke Hall, the Xavier Preparatory School next door.

148 Billilla
26 Halifax Street, Brighton
1878
1905 Walter Butler
GC, V, A

Walter Butler transformed this towered 1878 residence into a magnificent Edwardian villa complete with Art Nouveau foliage and floral details. The main body of the house was stuccoed and a new bow-fronted veranda, Ionic columns and bay windows were added. A deep parapet with scallops cut into it and infilled with gridded balustrading is a typical Edwardian motif. Billilla is one of the few remaining Brighton mansions with its substantial grounds intact (Kamesburgh **(68)** is the other). The fence, drive, stables and even the ladies' mounting steps give an indication of the once gracious living of another time.

149 Paton Building
115-117 Elizabeth Street, Melbourne
1905 Nahum Barnet
AC, V, A

The Paton Building is one of Melbourne's gems of Art Nouveau ornament and the American Romanesque idiom as applied to the warehouse or tall office building. Designed by Nahum Barnet—also responsible for the Bedggood and Co. Building, 172 Flinders Lane (1901)and the Auditorium Building **(177)**—it is distinguished by the exuberant curvilinear detail of the bay windows capped by their half saracenic domes, and the lettering of the name panel above the street canopy. The ribbon-like curves were the same decorative motifs that were all the rage in *fin de siècle* Paris and adorned Aubrey Beardsley-designed book covers. Barnet's other major work is the Baroque Classical Melbourne Synagogue, 2–8 Toorak Road, South Yarra (1928–30).

150

151

59 B11

45 G6

150 Anselm

4 Glenferrie Street, Caulfield
1906 Robert Haddon
GC, V, NA

Anselm was designed by Robert Haddon for his own use. Its picturesque and carefully composed asymmetry epitomises the work of this gifted designer and 'architectural expert', who consulted for other Melbourne architectural firms (especially Sydney Smith and Ogg). Anselm is noted for its open-planned living/dining room, which has a strange bulge at the corner tower and is screened from the front door by a stained timber partition. The ceiling is flat with simple, square-edged, stained beams running across its width. The front door with its bottled glass and flat canopy recalls the work of English Arts and Crafts architect CFA Voysey, while the half-timbered dormer expresses the popular interest in Medieval vernacular architecture. Inside the study is a seascape mural painted by Haddon, while at the front gate can be seen his elegantly simple English Free Style/Art Nouveau wrought-iron strapwork designs. The mushroom-topped corner tower and its terracotta ornament are the final flourish. All these elements are brought together with assured complexity. Haddon was one of Melbourne's most artful architectural synthesisers.

Below: Plan of Anselm (1906)

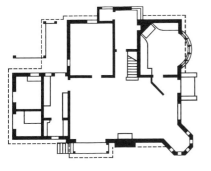

151 Arthur Norman House

7 Adeney Avenue, Kew
1909-10 Ussher and Kemp
GC, V, NA

A classic example of what architectural historian George Tibbits has dubbed the hip-roofed genre of the Federation house, where the second storey is tucked beneath a dominating hip roof, the Arthur Norman House also gives an indication of an authentic Federation colour scheme. The picturesque roofline, with its gables projecting, the terracotta tiles, finials and gable crestings, the corbelled chimney tops with brickwork strapping, the half-timbered gable ends, the shingled walls and balconies, and the idyllic garden setting—all combine to produce the prototype of the immensely popular suburban detached villa of the 1930s, 1940s and 1950s—the forerunner of the triple-front brick veneer. Believed to be primarily the work of Beverley Ussher, for immediate formal comparison with his partner's work, the house next door at 5 Adeney Avenue is Henry Kemp's own home (1912).

●●●

Federation, Edwardian
or Australian 'Domestic Queen Anne'?
What the distinctive Australian domestic style which developed between 1890 and 1920 should be called has bothered architectural historians for years. Characterised by asymmetrical planning, gabled and hipped roofs often with projecting dormers, half timbering and roughcast render infills, red bricks, turned timber columns and timber fretwork, and terracotta for tiles, ridge capping, finials and gargoyles, the Federation house is the unique product of English Domestic Queen Anne Revival of the 1870s and 1880s (as practised by Richard Norman Shaw and others), transformed and adapted to Australian conditions. The return veranda, in particular where its roof is contiguous with the sweeping hip roof of the main house, gives a special quality to these Arts and Crafts-inspired suburban villas.

152

15

152 Professional Chambers

110–114 Collins Street, Melbourne
1908 Ussher and Kemp
GC, V, A

Bringing a decidedly English air to the upper end of Collins Street, the Professional Chambers were built as offices for the much earlier Independent Church **(58)** nearby. Drawing from Elizabethan and Medieval Gothic sources, this fine symmetrical composition with moulded cement-rendered dressings was, like the Austral Buildings **(125)** opposite, a dramatic departure from the stuccoed Italianate residential facades of previous decades. Clustered tall chimneys, a visible terracotta tile roof, bay windows and steep brick gable ends impart picturesque urbanity and a street face of bold projection and recession.

153 Malvern Presbyterian Church

163 Wattletree Road, Malvern
1906 Robert Haddon
C, V, A

This Arts and Crafts–style church has sloping floors to its nave and unusual traceried windows reflecting Robert Haddon's personalised solutions to conventional architectural problems. Like his later St Stephen's Uniting Church, 151 Balaclava Road, North Caulfield (1926), the west window is treated like a giant sign to the street. At Malvern, two central mullions bisect the window and rise through the plain brick gable to form a mini-turret. Another quirky Melbourne church designed by Haddon (in partnership with Henderson) is the former St Andrew's Presbyterian Church, cnr Palmer and Drummond streets, Oakleigh (1928). Each design provides lessons in 'signing' the church, and they forecast innovations that were to occur in the 1970s church designs of Edmond and Corrigan, especially their Chapel of St Joseph **(387)** at Box Hill.

154 Queen Victoria Women's Centre
Former Melbourne Hospital and later Queen Victoria Hospital

172-254 Lonsdale Street, Melbourne
1910 JJ and EJ Clark
GC, V, A

The block bounded by Swanston, Lonsdale, Russell and Little Lonsdale streets once housed the Melbourne Hospital which had been established on the site in 1846. Just one of three pavilions of the innovative hospital complex remains today. The Edwardian Baroque complex was taken over in 1946 by the Queen Victoria Hospital, which was staffed and managed by women for women. The existing structure is the most elaborate bay of the hospital, designed as a series of pavilions with a long central corridor. The palisade fence, bluestone base and entrance gates on Swanston and Lonsdale streets are important reminders of this complex, which once sat back from the street and had its own garden.

155 Brinsmead's Pharmacy

71-73 Glen Eira Road, Ripponlea
1918 Sydney Smith and Ogg
GC, V, A

Brinsmead's Pharmacy contains one of Victoria's best examples of leadlighting to a shopfront and its fittings. Thomas Duff and Bros. designed and fabricated the fanciful elliptical domes over the two recessed front doors and curved glass showcases on the street. Inside, the shop is lined with mirror-backed glass cabinets framed in oak. There is also an elliptical screen framing yet another stunning leadlight dome over the main serving area. Complementing this tour-de-force of shopfitting is the building itself, an asymmetrical Free Style composition with stepped party walls and a roughcast rendered first floor.

156

158

156 The Canterbury
236 Canterbury Road, St Kilda
1914, 1919 HW and FB Tompkins
GC, V, N A

One of Melbourne's earliest blocks of flats, The Canterbury was strategically placed opposite the former St Kilda Railway Station, close to the George Hotel and the shopping strip of Fitzroy Street. It presents a compacted Free Style design, with a red-brick superstructure embracing, at its south-east corner, a mushroom-capped oriel tower bay and a second vertical element which consists of Edwardian curved balconies (now glazed in), supported at each level by Ionic pilastered corner props. The Canterbury is the Tompkins' medium-density response to the picturesque detached Federation house: squeeze it onto a narrow site and extrude it vertically. Each of the first three floors originally contained one flat with a dining room facing the sea and a bedroom at the front. The top floor, added in 1919, had two flats and the balcony was glazed to become a room. The oriel window and its mushroom cupola was extended vertically to maintain the balance of this inventive composition.

29 G11

157 Nocklofty
551 Royal Parade, Parkville
1906–08 Kenneth Munro (engineer)
AC, V, NA

Nocklofty is the example of one's man's retirement obsession: woodcarving. Kenneth Munro designed and constructed this relatively conventional but substantial home for himself. He completed the carving and modelling of the external barge boards, fretwork and terracotta columns and all the internal joinery and furniture. The distinctive aspect of this feat (achieved in Munro's workshops at Nocklofty) was the exploration of Australian themes. The gum leaf and gumnut theme of the barge boards of the projecting gables to the east and north faces of the house are exceptional, and inside Australian flora and fauna appear above doorways, on door panels, on an overmantle and on panel inserts in the hall. Nocklofty must be seen in the light of an emergent sense of national identity after Federation. The other major buildings in Victoria which explore Australiana themes are the designs of AJ MacDonald, in particular his Bairnsdale Court House (1892) and South Yarra Post Office (**131**). Nearby, the Federation villa Auld Reekie at 511 Royal Parade, Parkville (1909–11) gives a sense of the earthy Arts and Crafts tones in which Nocklofty can also be seen.

1A J9

158 Commercial Travellers' Association Building
318–324 Flinders Street, Melbourne
1912–13 HW and FB Tompkins
1997 Buchan Group (renovations)
GC, V, A

With its high-rise facade of glazed brick facing over a concrete-encased steel structure, this building marked the commercial arrival of the Edwardian Baroque in central Melbourne. The choice of style for this competition-winning entry marks a new design phase for HW and FB Tompkins. Designed as a residential hotel for commercial travellers, but also home to gentleman professionals, including Commonwealth Government architect John Smith Murdoch, the interior had grand spaces, including a double-storeyed entrance hall and foyer capped by a domed ceiling. To the street, the facade is a modified palazzo with flanking oriel bays and a massive Baroque cornice. It was a high-rise recipe that would be repeated in the Tompkins' Centreway Building (**163**).

159 Bendigo Hotel

125 Johnston Street, Collingwood
1911 Sydney Smith and Ogg
AC, V, A

One of a number of hotels designed by Sydney Smith and Ogg for the Carlton Brewing Company in Melbourne, this is one of the most flamboyant in a series of English Free Style/Art Nouveau compositions. Unfortunately, the hotel was painted in 1966 and its interiors gutted, and this has dimmed the effect of a design in which Robert Haddon may have played some part. Yet, despite this, the oriel corner towers, the flowing curvilinear cement dressings, the robust massing and the overall symmetry combine to make the Bendigo Hotel a visual highlight of this busy stretch of Johnston Street.

1B M2

160 Former Sniders and Abrahams warehouse

7 Drewery Lane, Melbourne
1908–09 HR Crawford (engineer and designer)
1938 HR Crawford (engineer and designer) –
two extra storeys to original five storey structure
1994–95 Conversion to residential apartments
GC, V, NA

With apartments recently inserted within and on top of its original structure, this former warehouse is of great technical interest. When completed, it contained the first example in Australia of the radical new construction system from the United States known as the Turner Mushroom System: thin concrete floor slabs, reinforced in four directions and supported by columns with mushroom-like column heads. The Turner System's Australian agent, engineer HR Crawford, designed each mushroom capital to be octagonal in shape. It is possibly one of the earliest surviving examples of this structural system anywhere in the world.

161 Wyalla, later Thanes

13a Monaro Road, Kooyong
1907–08 Butler and Bradshaw
1996–97 Boschler and Partners Pty Ltd
(restoration & additions)
GC, V, NA

One of the country's most interesting examples of a Free Style Arts and Crafts house that has distinctive Elizabethan influences, Wyalla was originally graced by extensive grounds with views over the Tooronga Valley. The main living spaces face this view across a projecting garden terrace, while the stair hall and gallery passage face the drive. This was a typical planning technique which English Arts and Crafts architects such as Ernest Gimson and Edward Prior employed when the house could be angled to embrace the sun, the garden and a handsome prospect. The most distinctive aspects of Wyalla are the curving Elizabethan gables, the polygonal bay windows, the scalloped parapet, the entry arch and interior ornament of gum leaves and gumnuts, and the warm, ochre-coloured rough-cast render. Recent additions to Wyalla have not attempted to mimic its formal characteristics, but instead highlight its unique quality as a house that would have earnt the approval of William Morris and his later followers, especially CFA Voysey and Edwin Lutyens.

Below: Plan of Wyalla (1907–08)

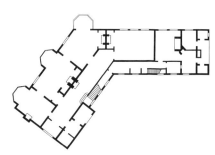

14 ANZAC (Australian and New
aland Army Corps) formed

1914 Australia's first air-mail flight
between Melbourne and Sydney

1915 ANZAC forces land on
Gallipoli

162

2F F1

62 Former Melbourne Magistrates' Court
'nr Russell and La Trobe Streets, Melbourne
911–13 GBH Austin (PWD)
'C, V, A

he former Melbourne Magistrates' Court is part
f a precinct that has been devoted to law and
rder for more than 150 years and that includes
he Old Melbourne Gaol **(42)**, the former Russell
treet Police Headquarters and the City Watch
louse. The Metropolitan Petty Sessions Court, as
: was known at its opening, was designed by
iBH Austin (1860–1921), an architect who,
rom the age of 16, worked in the public service.
lis stylistically diverse works included
nvolvement with the 1888 Building at
Melbourne State College **(110)**, Carlton Court
louse and the Mt Buffalo Chalet. The
Magistrates' Court building followed what the
Age newspaper described in 1911 as the 'Made
n Australia' principle: bluestone, blackwood and
Gippsland marble and Moorabool stone
'Batesford limestone) were used. The style of the
ouilding draws heavily from the Norman
Romanesque aspects of Canterbury and
Peterborough cathedrals in England, rather than
overtly Richardsonian Romanesque sources, and
its overall character respects the French-
influenced Gothic Revival Working Men's
College **(95)** next door. Inside, there were
originally three main court spaces, with carefully
planned circulation routes to separate public,
magistrates and prisoners.

1B M8

163 Centreway Building
259–263 Collins Street, Melbourne
*1911–12 HW and FB Tompkins; 1984–87 Cocks
Carmichael Whitford (arcade refurbishment)*
GC, V, A

Predating the Commercial Travellers' Association
Building **(158)**, the Centreway Building is not
just one of the very early examples of
Edwardian Baroque in Melbourne, but also an
office building which at its base continues
Melbourne's tradition of shopping arcades that
had reached its zenith with the Block Arcade
(111) and Royal Arcade **(57)**. These internalised
shopping streets provide a labyrinthine route
quite different from the wide streets of
Melbourne's grid plan. One of the first all-steel
framed commercial buildings in Australia, the
building facade marks its arcade by a grand
arch, while above decorative panache is denoted
by French style cartouches, oriel bays and
victory wreaths. A new lease of life was given to
the arcade by Cocks Carmichael Whitford,
whose stone resurfacing, overhead bridges and
block letter witticisms inside have added an
upbeat flavour to the already commercially
savvy urban link.

1B N5

164 Leviathan Clothing Store
271–281 Bourke Street, Melbourne
1912–13 Bates Peebles & Smart
GC, V, A

Inspired by designs of clothing emporia in
London, in particular the London Whitely
Building, the Leviathan Clothing Store was the
first major department store constructed in the
central city which began to match the scale and
lavishness of similar stores such as Moore's
(1910–13) and the Colosseum (1915) being
constructed in Chapel Street, Prahran. Striking
aspects of this Edwardian Baroque design were
the enormous consoles, with their wreaths and
dripping foliated detail, and the original white
cement finish to the building's reinforced
concrete (and hence austerely modern) facade.

16

1C D1

165 Mission to Seamen

717 Flinders Street, Melbourne
1916–17 Walter Butler
GC, V, A

One of the earliest examples of Spanish-influenced design in Melbourne, Walter Butler's Mission to Seamen is an intriguing architectural experiment in Arts and Crafts style combined with a somewhat bizarre choice of form, particularly in the stupa-like form of the gymnasium. Built of brick and rendered in rough-cast concrete, the chapel tower and bell turret, courtyard and cloister evoke elements of the Spanish Mission architecture of California. The building houses many elements which are the result of charitable works and donations, such as the marble mosaic compass rose in the entrance hall and the chapel itself, funds for which were raised by the ladies of the Harbour Lights Guild to commemorate British and Australian seamen who lost their lives during World War I. The pulpit in the chapel is a reconstruction of the stern of a sailing ship. It even has a stern-castle and rudder. There are a variety of spaces within the building: a main hall with a vaulted ceiling of reinforced concrete, a lecture hall (now the Celia Little Lounge) and upstairs a self-contained two-storey house for the chaplain and facilities for the officers who were not expected to mix with the seamen.

There was a dance hall, which was turned into a dormitory during World War II, then later converted to a cinema. The domed gymnasium, intended to alleviate the effects of crowded living conditions on ships, was named the Norla Gymnasium (1920) in honour of Sir Simon and Lady Fraser, generous supporters of the mission, and whose home Norla had been used for fetes to raise money. Today, only the staples in the domed roof remain as reminders of the ladders, climbing ropes and trapezes that once hung in this unusual space.

75A G3

166 Conservatorium of Music

Royal Parade, University of Melbourne, Parkville
1909 Bates Peebles and Smart
1913 Public Works Department (Melba Hall)
1926–27, 1934–35 Gawler and Drummond
(Tallis Wing, Marshall Hall wing)
1984–85 Daryl Jackson Pty Ltd (renovations)
GC, V, A

The Conservatorium became the first such institution to be established within a university in the British Empire. Opera diva Nellie Melba laid the foundation stone for this building, which combines an English country house footprint of expressed pavilions, Edwardian domestic-scaled roof forms and wide eaves, a Free Style central entry porch and parapet, and Art Nouveau clover, cress and gum leaf details. Later additions were funded by local luminaries: Nellie Melba, who funded the barrel-vaulted and classically delineated hall; Sir George Tallis, whose contribution was the 1927 wing; and Mr and Mrs Herbert Brookes (daughter of prime minister Alfred Deakin), who funded the 1934–35 Marshall Hall wing.

2G A3

167 Commonwealth Offices

Treasury Place, Melbourne
1910–12 John Smith Murdoch (Commonwealth Department of Works
GC, V, A

Designed by the Chief Architect for the Commonwealth Department of Works, this exuberant classical pile is one of Melbourne's best examples of Edwardian Baroque. The facade facing Lansdowne Street is a Mannerist masterpiece worthy of London's Sir Aston Webb, while,.on Treasury Place, timber eaves strike an ironic domestic note above classical propriety.

168

169

59 A3

31 E11

168 Glyn

24 Kooyong Road, Toorak
1908 Klingender & Alsop
GC, V, NA

Designed by Rodney Alsop, a founding member of the Arts and Crafts Society, Glyn is one of finest surviving Arts and Crafts houses in Australia. It displays the picturesque massing, simplified austere planar walls, references to English vernacular architecture and the exposure of its building materials and textures that typify Arts and Crafts. Alsop, a gifted designer of detail, is believed responsible for the stained glass, built-in timber joinery and especially the wrought metalwork on the gates, lamps and stair newells.

57 K10

169 South African War Memorial

Alfred Square, St Kilda
1905 Arthur Peck
GC, V, A

A fine Art Nouveau design, the South African War Memorial was erected to honour citizens of St Kilda who had fought and died in the Boer War (1899–1902). Significantly, it was the first time Australian troops had fought and died overseas. Funds for the truncated obelisk, which is topped by wrought-iron work, supporting a lamp and clad in olive green faience were raised by public subscription. The overall design is attributed to Arthur Peck, though its free style and inventive decorative scheme suggests the possible involvement of Robert Haddon.

170 MacGeorge House

25 Riverside Road, Ivanhoe
1911 Harold Desbrowe-Annear
GC, V, NA

The pastoral setting of the MacGeorge House gives a unique insight into the artistic ideals of both its client and architect. Norman and May MacGeorge made their home a meeting place for Melbourne's artists, critics and students. (Nearby lived their good friend and fellow artist Napier Waller, at 9 Crown Road, Ivanhoe (1922).) It is believed that the original garden (now in the process of reconstruction) may have been designed by artist William Blamire Young. The house was a single-storey bungalow with a basement studio. Like the Chadwick House (146) and other houses designed by Annear in the Heidelberg/Rosanna area during the first decade of the 20th century, the MacGeorge House is an internally rich spatial amalgam. Each space is finished in dark-stained timbers, with sloping timber ceilings that run counter to the external roof gables—these were originally clad in copper, but later replaced with corrugated iron. There are numerous fine pieces of built-in furniture, handmade hinges and door handles, and a sculpted brass front door knocker. Externally, Annear's adaptation of Medieval and Swiss Chalet forms enclosing open planning typical of American contemporary domestic designs and a skyline of Voysey-esque style chimneys produces a convincing local hybrid.

•••

On May MacGeorge's death in 1970, the house and land, furniture and fittings, paintings and all effects were left to the University of Melbourne. As Bryce Rayworth has noted, '... it was their expressed wish for the house to continue as a centre for arts education in Melbourne, as it had for the previous half century.'

Left: Plan of
the MacGeorge
House (1910)

99

● 1917 Commonwealth Police Force established

● 1917 Revolution in Russia. Bolsheviks seize power and establish communist state

● 1918 Publication of *The Magic Pudding* by Norman Lindsay

171

32 B7

171 Lippincott House

21 Glenard Drive, Eaglemont
1917 Roy Lippincott and Walter Burley Griffin
GC, V, NA

Designed by American architects Walter Burley Griffin and his brother-in-law, Roy Lippincott, for Lippincott and his wife Genevieve, and located on the Griffin-designed Glenard Estate (1916), the Lippincott House is distinguished by its dominating flared gable roof; bold, textured clinker-brick pylons; and battered brick base. Lippincott, a Cornell University trained architect, followed the Griffins to Australia before winning a New Zealand commission and emigrating once again. There he was to introduce Prairie Style architecture and become president of the New Zealand Institute of Architects. Internally and externally, his house in Eaglemont is one of the most intact examples of a Prairie style which celebrated Arts and Crafts ideals in exposing materials, and having exotic sources for the unusual roof profile (scholars debate Japanese or Southeast Asian influence). Surrounding eucalpyts and the lack of fences enhance the Griffins' ideal of an uninterrupted natural and shared suburban landscape.

32 B7

172 Pholiota

Rear of 23 Glenard Drive, Eaglemont
1919–20 Walter Burley Griffin
and Marion Mahony
AC, NV, NA

Next door to the Lippincott House, Walter Burley Griffin and his wife Marion Mahony designed and built a tiny 'doll house' for themselves. Constructed of 'Knitlock', Griffin's patented system of interlocking concrete block construction (1917), the house had a 21-foot square plan (6.4 m x 6.4 m) and a low-pitched pyramid roof with wide eaves, the overall form of which suggests the house's name, 'Pholiota' (mushroom). There were no passages inside. All rooms opened off a central living space. The bedrooms were alcoves with sliding curtains separating them from the living space, while two corners of the square plan were occupied by a kitchen and bathroom. With a major addition and alterations made to it internally, Pholiota is now completely hidden from the street.

1B M5

173 David Jones Department Store
Former Buckley and Nunn Department Store

298–304, 306–312 Bourke Street, Melbourne
1910-12 Bates Peebles & Smart
(298–304 Bourke Street)
1925 Bates Peebles & Smart
(306–312 Bourke Street)
GC, V, A

Located in Bourke Street since the 1850s, this department store expanded in the booming retail years of the early teens of the 20th century. Bates Peebles & Smart gave Buckley and Nunn a new image with this exuberant Edwardian Baroque masterpiece of bold, block, rusticated giant order columns, ox-bow arches and mosaic panels which paralleled the new American Beaux Arts look pursued in London at Selfridges and in emporia across the United States. By 1933, Buckley and Nunn sought further updating for their snappy Jazz Moderne men's store next door **(238)**.

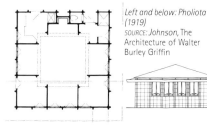

Left and below: Pholiota (1919)
SOURCE: *Johnson,* The Architecture of Walter Burley Griffin

174

2B E5

174 Newman College

Swanston Street, University of Melbourne, Parkville
1915–18 Walter Burley Griffin and Marion Mahony in association with AA Fritsch
1942 Connelly, Dale and Payne (chapel)
1958, 1961 TG Payne (Kenny Wing, Donovan Wing) 1986–1993 Falkinger Andronas P/L (stonework, dome and flèche restoration)
GC, V, A

The second largest building designed in Australia by the husband and wife partnership of Walter Burley Griffin (1876–1937) and Marion Mahony (1871–1961), Newman College was a direct challenge to the adoption of the stylistic models of Oxford and Cambridge colleges which had previously dominated Parkville's College Crescent. The Griffins produced a distinctive response to the idea of education, faith and the monastic cloister.

Named after John Henry Newman (1801–1890), one of the most eminent English writers and theologians of the 19th century, and administered by the Jesuit Fathers, the college was designed to relate geometrically to the centre of the university campus. Two embracing L-shaped arms of student rooms over two storeys defined two quadrangles. At the centre of the composition was intended to be a chapel. At each corner of the L-shapes was a rotunda: one a dining room, the other a library. The dramatically long cloister, the walls faced in Barrabool sandstone, and the dining room

rotunda with its central structure forming a cross combine medieval romanticism, innovative reinforced concrete construction, and a symbology that transcends Christian imagery to provide a universally applicable language of knowledge and faith. While the chapel was not designed by the Griffins, and while only one Griffin-designed wing was constructed, the spatial compression of the cloister, the austere gloom of the dining room and the ingenious fixed ventilation detail of the leadlight windows make Newman College one of the charismatic American couple's most profound contributions to defining a new Australian architectural idiom in the decades following Federation.

Although both Griffin and Mahony had worked for Chicago architect Frank Lloyd Wright (1868–1959), their design for Newman College reveals personal interests that were uniquely different from both the Prairie School architecture of the mid-west and the prevailing Melbourne tastes for the English Arts and Crafts and an emergent Baroque Classicism.

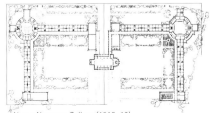

Above: Newman College (1915–18)
SOURCE: *Johnson,* The Architecture of Walter Burley Griffin

1919 Brothers Ross and Keith Smith flew from England to Australia in 28 days, winning a £10,000 prize from the Commonwealth government

1920 QANTAS (Queensland and Northern Territory Aerial Services) formed

171

59 B8

58 A11

175 Malvern/Glenferrie Tram Depot
Coldblo Road, Armadale
1910
GC, V, NA

The Prahran and Malvern Tramways Trust, one of the first suburban tramways trusts in Melbourne, opened its electric tram line along Glenferrie Road, High Street and Wattletree Road in 1910 with extensions to St Kilda and Kew made in 1911 and 1913. The depot in Coldblo Road is a working reminder of this early electric tram line which, among others since 1906, had begun to challenge the supremacy of Melbourne's extensive cable tram network. The Free Style red-brick depot building with its oriel control tower, arched windows and decorative castellated parapet is the formal yet picturesque face to a large saw-tooth roof tram shed behind. The depot's formal qualities are enhanced by its unusual setting off Glenferrie Road.

●●●

Melbourne's much loved trams, tramlines and depots are an intrinsic part, both visually and functionally, of the city's urban environment. The Melbourne and Metropolitan Tramways Board (MMTB) was established in 1919 and, with the expiration of the cable tramways lease pending, began to acquire not just cable tram lines and depots, but also privately operated electric tram lines. The Prahran and Malvern line, for example, was acquired in 1920. From 1925 until 1940, the MMTB gradually replaced all cable trams with electrified lines. Today, Melbourne's tram network continues to expand. Ironically, however, after 80 years of public ownership, a return to privately run tram companies appears imminent.

176 Luna Park
Cavell Street and The Esplanade, St Kilda
1912
GC, V, A

Luna Park, Australia's earliest amusement park, was the brainchild of the Greater JD Williams Company and the Phillips brothers of the United States. Construction began in 1912 and, after 1913, the Phillips brothers ran this unique complex for the next forty years. The giant mouth between two Moorish towers is like the entry to a walled Islamic temple complex; however, with the Big Dipper (1923) and the Scenic Railway creating a dramatic undulating wall above, this is clearly no place for solemnity. From the first year of opening, new attractions were added and removed as their popularity rose and fell. The Whip (1923) and the Giggle Palace have gone, but original rides such as the Carousel and the Dodgems Building remain. The Carousel was built by the Philadelphia Toboggan Company, shipped to Brussels a few years later then ended up in White City, NSW, before being purchased by Luna Park in 1924. Luna Park is returning gradually to its former glory after a few faded decades. A new owner, with the assistance of conservation architects Nigel Lewis and Richard Aitken, is now restoring and rebuilding many of the exotic facades that concealed rides and amusement halls, as well as adding new attractions.

● 1921 Royal Australian Air Force
established

177

179

77 Former Auditorium Building

67–173 Collins Street, Melbourne
1913 Nahum Barnet
GC, V, A

Announcing its stylistic origins as hailing from Adler and Sullivan's Auditorium Building in Chicago, Barnet's building of the same name follows Louis Sullivan's recipe for the high rise, stretching the tripartite division of the early Renaissance palazzo vertically using the Romanesque arch for the shaft of the tower. Designed as offices and a live theatre, this is Barnet's central city masterwork, though altered over the years from a cinema in the 1930s to a failed boutique department store, competitor to Georges, in the mid-1980s. Despite these internal changes, the wrought-iron filigree work, Romanesque arched entry and oriel bay windows bear comparison with the Centreway Building **(163)** as heralding a new standard for city commercial buildings after 1910.

2B C5

178 Trinity College Chapel

Royal Parade, Parkville
1915 North and Williams
GC, V, A

An Arts and Crafts interpretation of the Decorated Gothic style, the Trinity College Chapel is emphatically vertical, with a central lantern spire that is thoroughly original in its reinvention of the conventional tower and spire. Inside, the mood for invention continues with sheer red brick walls and, in the choir stalls, there are wood carvings featuring possums and platypuses. Alexander North and his partner Louis Williams also designed the Arts and Crafts chapel for Merton Hall, Melbourne Church of England Girls' Grammar School, Anderson Street, South Yarra, and modified Philip Hudson and Gerard Wight's 1915 design for All Saints

Chapel at Geelong Grammar School. While the distinctive Arts and Crafts principles that guide these church designs can be attributed primarily to North, Williams was to go on to become Melbourne's most prolific church architect of the 20th century.

1A B5

179 General Post Office, Parcels Building, Mail Exchange

164–200 Spencer Street, Melbourne
1917 John Smith Murdoch (Commonwealth Department of Works)
AC, V, NA

A grand example of Beaux Arts-inspired modern French Renaissance style, the former Mail Exchange was designed by John Smith Murdoch (1862–1945), Australia's first Commonwealth Government Architect and designer of the Provisional Parliament House, Canberra (1921–27), a building which also followed strict symmetry, formality and restrained neo-Grec detailing. Predating the Greek Revival designs and the commercial palazzi of the 1920s, the massive block with its red brick rusticated corners and giant order columns had, for a short while, few stylistic counterparts in Edwardian Melbourne save for Moore's Store in Chapel Street, Prahran and Purchas and Teague's Wool Exchange, 120–138 King Street, Melbourne (1913–14). Murdoch scholar David Rowe notes that an overseas tour in 1912–13 caused Murdoch to shift from a restlessly picturesque Edwardian Baroque to a simplified but nonetheless imperial manner, in effect to pursue a modern and national style for Australian government buildings through the perceived universality of classicism.

181

59 C8

180 St Joseph's Roman Catholic Church
47 Stanhope Street, Malvern
1908 AA Fritsch
GC, V, A

Designed by Augustus Andrew Fritsch, collaborator with Walter Burley Griffin and Marion Mahony on Newman College **(174)**, St Joseph's is part Romanesque, part Baroque. The design is defiantly non-Gothic, paralleling works such as AJ MacDonald's South Yarra Post Office **(131)** in its search for authenticity through new stylistic combinations. The shift from Gothic to this hybrid style was perhaps affected by the construction of JF Bentley's Byzantine-influenced Westminster (Roman Catholic) Cathedral, London (1895–1903). Some of Fritsch's other notable Roman Catholic churchs include Our Lady of Victories, 548 Burke Road, Camberwell (1913–18) and St Mary's Main Street, Bairnsdale (1913, 1937).

1A F7

181 Queensland Building
84 William Street, Melbourne
1912-13 Butler and Bradshaw
GC, V, A

With the same facade division of giant entry arch, flanking oriel bays which stretch vertically through numerous floors and an elaborated attic storey/cornice (in this case, an Italianate-inspired loggia), the Queensland Building joins Barnet's Auditorium Building **(177)**, the Tompkins brothers' Centreway Building **(163)** and the Commercial Travellers' Association Building **(158)**. What makes it different from

these Edwardian Baroque buildings is its stone facade, in particular the rich floral and fruit carved stone decoration around the entry arch reflecting Walter Butler's loyalty to English Arts and Crafts interests rather than American Romanesque or Sullivan-inspired ornamental detail, or even the rule-based language of classical architecture.

23 F9

182 The Robins
Kangaroo Ground–Warrandyte Road, North Warrandyte
1913 Penleigh Boyd (designer and builder)
GC, V, NA

The Robins is remarkable for being a Tudor-styled attic residence with single-skin walls that appear to be constructed of earth mixed with concrete, a primitive form of in-situ concrete construction. The homespun construction techniques and Arts and Crafts interest in vernacular Medieval forms was to be later embraced with enthusiasm by other Warrandyte and Eltham artist residents, most notably at Montsalvat **(244)**. Penleigh Boyd is also credited with the layout of the now overgrown garden. Well known for his paintings of the Australian landscape, Boyd used the attic at The Robins as his studio. Historian Carlotta Kellaway has noted that there also once existed a garden studio of wattle and daub (now demolished) that Martin Boyd, Penleigh's brother, described in his novel *Outbreak of Love*. Penleigh Boyd was killed tragically in a car accident in 1923.

923 Work commences on
ydney Harbour Bridge

1923 A savoury yeast spread
called 'Vegemite' is created

1925 Commercial radio broadcasting begins in Australia

183

1B N7

183 Capitol Theatre

109–117 Swanston Street, Melbourne
1921–24 Walter Burley Griffin and Marion
Mahony in association with Peck and Kemter
AC, V, NA

When this cinema opened in 1924, the public flocked to hear the Wurlitzer organ and see the movies and the spectacular light show afforded by the Griffins' plaster ceiling design. Like a crystal-hung cave, thousands of concealed coloured lights were gradually illuminated to provide a fantastic atmospheric experience. It was a space that evoked spiritual transcendence, but the interior of 'living rock' was not the direct romantic evocation of a Tuscan garden as seen in the later Forum (**218**). It was certainly otherworldly, but the image was distinctly architectural, suggesting a stepped pyramid form, the mystical essence of an original and arguably natural monument.

The Capitol was also of technical interest. To achieve such a dramatic ceiling, massive reinforced concrete portals allowed the interior structure to be hung uninterrupted by any internal columns. Outside, the Capitol is also distinctive. Two deep cornices cap two pylon motifs each of three vertical piers extending over the entire height of the facade. It is, as historian Jeffrey Turnbull has suggested, like a giant gateway. Cinema historian Ross Thorne has described it as, '... not a mere breath of fresh air wafting through the design offices of Melbourne, it was a howling gale of modernity sweeping out every vestige of revivalist decorative stylism'.

Tragically, in the 1960s, the owners decided to insert a shopping arcade right through the middle of the auditorium. A campaign to save the theatre was waged and a compromise was reached: the cave-like foyers were destroyed and a new floor was inserted. Many of the original lobby and vestibule spaces were either destroyed or boarded up, but the ceiling was saved. In recent years, great efforts have been made to restore surviving elements of the theatre. The dramatic cantilevering street canopy with its light globes and skylights is the most significant recent restoration. In 1965, Robin Boyd wrote eloquently in *The Australian* about the Capitol:

> *When you reach the last flight of stairs, you approach one of the architectural sights of Australia. At the top of the stairs it bursts upon you. It is only a picture theatre. It is only plaster. Yet in its own way it is sheer magic.*

Magic, it still is. The Capitol was Melbourne's crowning architectural achievement in the twenty years after Federation.

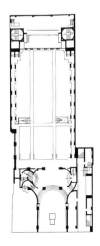

Left: Plan of Capitol Theatre (1921–24), 1963 condition
SOURCE: *Thorne*, Cinemas of Australia via USA

Between the Wars
1920–1930

1920–1930

The ideal of a small house and garden caused a dramatic increase to the metropolitan area

The 1920s can be seen as a time in which architectural innovation was shaped and constrained by the continuing strength of 19th-century architectural conventions.

The decade saw a continuation of the popularity of the bungalow and of various picturesque cottage styles, but also an interest in imported idioms such as the American Spanish Mission and a revival of Georgian and Colonial expressions. These styles shared a common foundation, with their Arts-and-Crafts-based contemporaries, as vernacular expressions from older worlds readily adapted to Antipodean conditions. The familiar Arts and Crafts palette of drab browns and reds, cream and grassy green continued to hold sway. Interiors retained their dark, compartmentalised plans, with an emphasis on small windows and a southern orientation. Society seemed far from embracing the sunlight and bright colours of the suddenly modern spirit of post-Depression Australia.

Dominant amongst the aspirations of the period was the ideal of an individual detached home. The popular ideal of the small house in a garden setting caused a dramatic expansion of the greater metropolitan area and extension of train and tram services. Car ownership also became common amongst the middle class, and the necessary garage increased the width of the standard suburban block. Early in the century, the suburbs had been criticised as monotonous, and it was almost inevitable that domestic architecture after the Great War would be marked by stylistic diversity rather than consensus.

The styling of houses captured the outlook of the period. The bungalow represented the home as suburban-cum-rural retreat close to nature within a garden environment. The California type was commonly held to be the basis of an evolving Australian expression, while Spanish Mission represented an appreciation of things modern, strong light and the contrast of boldly decorated elements against simple wall surfaces. Tudor and Georgian revivalism, on the other hand, represented solid Empire values, although the Georgian Revival also intimated nationalism through its associations with Australia's colonial heritage.

By the 1920s, bungalow architecture had become the builders' preferred choice, exerting an influence in materials and detailing. Two superior examples of the mode include Schreiber & Jörgensen's **Pebbles**, 57A Droop Street, Footscray (1920), and **Parkview**, 512 Racecourse Road, Kensington (1924).

More important to architects, however, were the historicist modes: the Georgian, Tudor and Spanish Mission (or Spanish Colonial) revivals. The architecture of Harold Desbrowe-Annear is perhaps the most innovative expression of the Georgian Revival idiom. The outstanding example of his work was the **Baillieu House** (1929), but other important examples can be seen at Cloyne, 669 Toorak Road, Toorak (1929), at 104 Kooyong Road, Toorak (1922), and in his last building, the Wesley Ince House, 372 Glenferrie Road, Malvern (1931–32). A more relaxed expression displaying specifically American east coast influences was the timber house **Mulberry Hill**, Baxter (1925).

Other important work of the time is that of Walter Butler, including the Old English veneering of a two storey house Marathon, at Mt Eliza, for the Grimwade family (1924), or **Eulinya**, the Sir William McBeath House (1925). Possibly the finest remaining example of the style is **Little Milton** (1925), designed by Muriel Stott in association with Stephenson & Meldrum, with a garden designed by Edna Walling. Walling was one of the vigorous exponents of the mode, particularly through the publicising of her cottages at **Bickleigh Vale** in the 1920s and 1930s.

The rise of the Mediterranean styles in the wake of the war was fed by several stimuli—the experience of soldiers in France and other parts of Europe, and the flood of publications, mainly from the United States. Marcus Martin's own house **Broome** (1925) was one of the more decorated examples, with ochre trowelled render, an arched loggia to the front featuring barley sugar columns, louvred shutters and a cordova tiled roof. While a great many houses were built in the mode, the better known and publicised examples included Ilyuka, Point King Road, Portsea (1929), Belvedere Flats, Upper Esplanade, St Kilda (1928), and Blackett & Forster's very fine house at 9 Gordon Grove, South Yarra (1929).

Bird's-eye view of the Shrine of Remembrance (SOURCE: Art in Australia, March 1924)

The domestic work of Walter Burley Griffin and his Melbourne office continued to exert an influence in this decade. Former students such as Edward F Billson and JFW (Frederick) Ballantyne began to achieve a degree of prominence, and Eric Nicholls had become a more than competent manager of the Melbourne office. The Griffin creative force is particularly evident in Knitlock structures such as **Pholiota**, Griffin's own house, and closely related cottages such as Gumnuts, 619 Nepean Highway, Olivers Hill, Frankston (1922), the **Salter House** and **Stokesay**, the Ballantyne-designed house at Seaford. A broader Prairie influence can be seen in examples such as Ballantyne's **Mrs Craig Dixson house** and Billson's **Revell**.

Griffin attracted other large commissions in the central city, and inner suburbs, the most spectacular of which was Leonard House (1923-24), an innovative curtain wall office building with an ornate, geometric facade, lamentably demolished in the 1970s. A few years earlier he had completed the Melbourne club offices of the Kuomintang, the Chinese Nationalist Party, at 109 Little Bourke Street (1921), since defaced, and the striking interiors of Australia House, also demolished. The remaining jewel from his work in this period is **Capitol House** (1924), of which the facade and the majestic encrusted ceiling survive. In the inner suburbs, Griffin's office also produced industrial buildings for enlightened clients, making architectural quality a priority alongside utility. The two outstanding works to survive are the **Lyddy Polish Factory** and the **Essendon Municipal Incinerator**.

Interior of the Shrine of Remembrance (SOURCE: Art in Australia, March 1924)

Melbourne's city centre developed strongly in the 1920s and 1930s, and a number of key streetscapes retain their original character today. The awareness of a need to cultivate an attractive urban environment, rather than merely hope for its development, was a key feature of the time, manifested through the formation of the Metropolitan Town Planning Commission in 1922, and culminating in the completion of the Plan of General Development, Melbourne, published in 1929.

The introduction in 1916 of new planning regulations enforcing a maximum height of 132 feet (40.3 m) for buildings of steel and concrete and 110 feet (33.6 m) for others was an important modifying factor in the development of this period. From 1922 to 1933, some 17 buildings were constructed to the 132-foot limit, amongst them **Capitol House, Temple Court, Nicholas Building**, Myer, the Hotel Alexander (now the Savoy Plaza), the **T&G Building** and **Coles**, Bourke Street.

Beyond this, the major evidence of the 'City Beautiful' movement is to be found in the contemporary notion of polite, well-mannered architecture. This found expression in the Royal Victorian Institute of Architects Street Architecture Award from 1929, the first nine awards of which were made to buildings located in the central city.

The continuity of classicism within commercial architecture is illustrated by a large number of buildings, many found in Collins Street, including **Francis House** (1928), the first winner of the RVIA Street Architecture award, **Temple Court**, by Grainger Barlow & Hawkins (1923-24), the heavily modelled Renaissance Revival AMP House (1930-31) and the **Port Authority Building** (1929-31). The more severe Greek Revival reflected the sobriety and traditionalism of the period immediately after the Great War.

he **Emily McPherson College of Domestic Economy** (1926) nd the **Shrine of Remembrance** (1927–34), by Hudson & Wardrop, are the two best-known exemplars of this mode, but it was also readily adaptable to the commercial palazzo, as seen at he **Nicholas Building**, by Harry Norris (1925–26). Norris was perhaps the greatest exponent of faience in Melbourne in this period, using it not only for the **Nicholas Building**, but also for he racy Spanish Colonial Revival **Majorca House** (1928–29), and he ground-breaking Jazz facades of the **former GJ Coles store** now David Jones).

Aside from the large emporia of Coles and Myers, the emblematic buildings of the period were cinemas. Like most western world cities, Melbourne experienced a rash of cinema construction in the 1920s and into the 1930s as the industry underwent a meteoric rise. These enormous venues captured the thirst of the times for entertainment on a grand scale, and drew on American precedents in terms of lavish interiors and exotic exteriors, designed to seduce the visitor on their voyage into fantasy before they even entered the premises. Of the inner city's surviving examples, the **State Theatre** (1928) and the (recently restored) **Regent Theatre** (1929–30) capitalised upon the vogue for Mediterranean themes — Spanish, classical and medieval—while Henry E White's **Palais Cinema** (1927) at St Kilda followed a 'French and Oriental style'.

A similar flamboyance was seen in the rise of buildings featuring corner towers, a mode popularised by the competition for the Chicago Tribune Building, 1922, ultimately won by Raymond Hood. A & K Henderson's **T&G Building** (1926–28) was the first major building in Melbourne to build to the height limit and raise a tower above it as an 'architectural feature', but the concept was further developed by Marcus Barlow with the **Manchester Unity Building** (1929-32), modelled directly on the Chicago Tribune Building. With its streamlined verticality, Gothic Modern styling, prominent site and glistening faience, it signalled the high point of 1920s commercial construction in Melbourne and anticipated the imminent rise and triumph of the anti-historical, recognisably modern modes of the 1930s.

BRYCE RAWORTH

Leonard House, which stood at 44–46 Elizabeth Street before being demolished, was designed by Walter Burley Griffin and Marion Mahony housed his third Melbourne office. (SOURCE:Wilson and Sands, 'Building a City').

184

184 Pebbles, House for FG Whitehill
57A Droop Street, Footscray
1920 Schreiber and Jörgensen
GC, V, NA

One of Victoria's best examples of the bungalow and in almost original condition, Pebbles even has its privet hedge and lattice fence to complement its Japanese-inspired timber lych gate. True to its name, pebbles are used extensively throughout, from the crushed quartz rocks and the porches' battered piers to the water-washed pebbles surrounding the fireplace. Designed by a firm noted for their exotic bungalow designs, the house displays all the features associated with the Californian bungalow, the type that would be the speculative house success of the 1920s. Overlapping gable roofs, bold and chunky timber bracket detailing, rough-cast render, cedar gable shingles, clinker brick and Marseilles tiles all form part of this house commissioned by long-time Footscray resident Frances George Whitehill.

185 Revell
9 Toorak Avenue, Toorak
1920 Edward Fielder Billson
GC, V, NA

Designed by Edward Fielder Billson, the Griffins' first articled pupil and the first graduate in architecture from the University of Melbourne, Revell is one of the most important surviving examples of the Prairie-style house in Melbourne. Characterised by low-pitched hipped roofs, exaggerated eaves, banks of casement windows and massive chimneys which all contribute to an overall sense of horizontality, the Prairie style developed in Chicago in the 1890s and was widely publicised through the 1910 Wasmuth portfolio of drawings of Frank Lloyd Wright's houses. Many of these drawings were in fact by Marion Mahony, who had worked in Wright's office. In Melbourne, the Prairie style was practised by other Griffin employees, JFW Ballantyne and Eric Nicholls.

186 First Church of Christ Scientist
336 St Kilda Road, South Melbourne
1920–22 Bates Peebles & Smart
1933 Bates Smart & McCutcheon
(administration block)
GC, V, A

Designed by Harold Dumsday of Bates Peebles & Smart, this church has an amphitheatre form often used by American practitioners of the faith developed by Mary Baker Eddy in Boston in 1879. Christian Scientists had been practising in Melbourne since 1898 and this is the first purpose-built structure erected by them. The building's style, like the nature of the faith it houses, is a hybrid: a Neo-Grec facade with Greek Revival window, lighting and pediment details combined with a centralised plan and large Diocletian windows located beneath a shallow-domed roof. The arrangement is a curious but effective amalgam of Greek, Roman and Byzantine influence.

•••

Bungalow styles
With a myriad of derivations and hybrid forms, from plantation Indian bungalows, the Craftsman Bungalows of Gustav Stickley and the Californian Bungalow with its Japanese oversailing gables and tori-gate door frames, this house type was immensely popular in Melbourne from the 1900s through until the mid-1930s. Part of the attraction was the open planning between dining and living rooms, as well as the generous porch where one could, on a hot night, roll down a canvas blind and sleep outside.

19 Walter Gropius founds Bauhaus
hool of architecture, craft and design

1919 Einstein's theory that light
rays bend near the sun is verified

1920 Population of Melbourne
reaches 1,000,000

187

2L E3

187 Amesbury House

237-239 Domain Road, South Yarra
1921 Walter Butler
1925 Harold Desbrowe-Annear (porte cochere)
GC, V, NA

A gracious Arts and Crafts-inspired block of large apartments designed by one of Melbourne's favoured architects for the wealthy in the 1910s and 1920s, Amesbury House gives the impression of a stately Georgian front to a large single house that, from the rear, reveals extensive use of brick and modelled tall chimneys in a Lutyens-like English country house manner. The addition of the classically styled porte cochère by another darling of Melbourne society, Harold Desbrowe-Annear, is the final scholarly flourish to this haven of respectability. Amesbury House is important as an early block of self-contained apartments. Walter Butler had already designed, when part of the firm of Inskip & Butler: Melbourne Mansions, 91–101 Collins Street (1906; demolished) and Studley flats at 392–400 Toorak Road, Toorak (1918), two early and innovative apartment complexes in Melbourne.

1B T9

188 Former Herald and Weekly Times Building

44–74 Flinders Street, Melbourne
1921–23, 1928 HW and FB Tompkins
GC, V, NA

Designed by the prolific commercial architectural firm of HW and FB Tompkins, the former Herald and Weekly Times Building, a five-storey steel-framed building with 'Permasite' hollow concrete block floors, is an example of a Beaux Arts styled office building and printing works with its grand facade of giant order Ionic pilasters above a massive base and with its flat pediment on heavy brackets.

Its form and style appears to have been borrowed from American department stores and emporia such as Selfridges in London, where the giant order enabled the use of large areas of glass to light the deep, floorplan within (the Tompkins design for the Myer Lonsdale Street store (1927) also adopted the use of the giant order pilaster). In 1928, the seven-bay facade was extended by five bays to the east, introducing access for newspaper delivery trucks at ground level and expanded office and printing space above. In 1930, the radio station 3DB began broadcasting from the building and a steel-framed radio tower was erected. The Herald and Weekly Times building, with its polished metal glass cases at footpath level showing the daily headlines, became a landmark symbolic of two of Melbourne's most popular newspapers.

•••

Sir Keith Murdoch (1885–1952) had worked in journalism all his life. After working first for David Syme's Age *newspaper, Murdoch went overseas in 1908. During World War I, he became a well-known journalist working for the United Cable Service of the* Sun *and* Herald. *By 1920, Murdoch had achieved chairmanship of the Herald and Weekly Times. In 1921, he was chief editor of Melbourne's* Herald, *reshaping the paper's design and content. In 1926, he was appointed a director and, in 1928, was made managing director. By 1935, Murdoch and the Herald's interests were national, including interests in 11 out of 65 commercial radio stations. Keith Murdoch was knighted in 1933. His son, Rupert Murdoch, has continued to expand his father's empire to achieve unrivalled global status in media ownership.*

189

2C A10

189 Lyddy Polish Manufacturing Co. Building
167–169 Fitzroy Street, Fitzroy
1922–23 EM Nicholls
GC, V, NA

Designed by one of Griffin's Melbourne employees who was to move to Sydney to manage the office there, the Lyddy Polish Manufacturing Co. Building was home to, amongst other products, Dubbin, the polish used to revitalise Australians' leather shoes and boots. The design is one of the few Prairie-style buildings in Melbourne that is not a house. With its emphatic horizontality, bandings of squat windows above a massive red brick base, impressed geometric square ornamentation of the concrete fascia and geometric grille work, Lyddy's is a stylistic anomaly amongst the predominantly 19th-century surroundings of terrace houses, workers' cottages and warehouses.

190 Stanley R Salter House

59 B3

16 Glyndebourne Avenue, Toorak
1923–24 Walter Burley Griffin and Marion Mahony
GC, V, NA

The Salter House is one of the best remaining examples in Australia of Walter Burley Griffin and Marion Mahony's Knitlock houses. Knitlock was the concrete masonry construction system developed and patented by Griffin in 1917. He also patented a tessellated concrete roofing tile system. Each tile resembled a diamond patterned flat shingle. The entire system was an integrated expressive whole: part structure, part ornamental, like the interrelated nature of organic form. The Salter House has both these wall and roof systems, as well as the distinctive Griffin trademark of the raked projecting gables,

glazing bars in chevrons patterns that seem to express forces of compression from the ribs that flank them, and an atrium courtyard at the house's centre which, in this cruciform plan, is open to the sky. The Salter House still gives the clear impression of a house in delicate harmony with its landscape and is itself an organic and interconnected whole with an open plan providing for relaxed and informal living. Other Griffin-designed Knitlock houses in Melbourne can be seen at Pholiota, 23 Glenard Drive, Eaglemont **(172)**; Gumnuts, 619 Nepean Highway (1921–22); Julius S Jefferies House, 7 Warwick Avenue, Surrey Hills (1923–24); and the Vaughan Griffin House, 52 Darebin Street, Heidelberg (1924).

191 Stokesay

99 D9

289 Nepean Highway, Seaford
1922 JFW Ballantyne
GC, V, NA

Described in *Australian Home Beautiful*, December 1925, as 'A Pretty Australian Home', Stokesay is one of the most intact Knitlock houses surviving in Victoria. Even the garage is of Knitlock and all the roofs are clad in Griffin's patented tessellated concrete roofing tile. Designed and constructed while Ballantyne was working in the Griffins' Melbourne office, Stokesay's faithfulness to Griffin's planning, detailing and compositional techniques is testament to his considerable influence.

Below: Section of Stokesay

92 Parkview
12 Racecourse Road, Kensington
924
GC, V, NA

escribed as Swiss Chalet in style, Parkview's
old single gable, rough-cast rendered wall
nish, bizarre ogee arch attic window and
round-floor hooded windows account for this
abel. To complete this house of obscure origins
ittle is known of the residents and nothing of
he designer), a large rampant kangaroo
erminates the gable. As if this wasn't enough,
he fence appears to have been constructed of
ron panels recycled from the Flemington
acecourse members' stand (demolished in the
920s) and set between new brick piers.

93 Hartpury Court
1 Milton Street, Elwood
1923 Arthur W Plaisted
GC, V, NA

One of the earliest examples in Melbourne of
a 20th-century Tudor styling to a residential
building, Hartpury Court was the speculative
neighbour to its developer's much older home,
Hartpury. Dr Frank Goon commissioned Arthur
Plaisted to design the English country house
cum village along the western boundary of his
site, with a croquet lawn between the two
buildings. Of the flats themselves, the mixture of
rendered and exposed brickwork, the terracotta
shingled roof, the half-timbering and roofline of
tall bunched chimneys above a variety of roof
forms, and the individually treated entry
porches all contribute to an evocation of 'Back
Home'. This Tudor style was to become popular
in the 1930s as the Old English style. Plaisted
became an accomplished designer of homes in
this romantic idiom and was to achieve
notoriety as the designer of Castle Towers in

Marne Street, South Yarra (1940), the pseudo-
Tudor block of flats that the student pamphlet
Smudges gave a Blot of the Month, earning
editor Robin Boyd a legal writ.

194 Temple Court
422–428 Collins Street, Melbourne
1923–24 Grainger Little Barlow & Hawkins
GC, V, A

Temple Court is an early Baroque and neo-Grec-
inspired example of the commercial palazzo, the
1920s office building type developed primarily
by Louis Sullivan in the United States as a way
of composing the high rise. The commercial
palazzo was almost always characterised by
rusticated base, free interpretation of a piano
nobile (invariably extended over numerous
floors) and an attic storey. Erected to limit
height (132 feet), Temple Court, designed for
the legal fraternity, was thought in 1924 to
have been the tallest building built in Melbourne
since 1888.

195 Mrs Craig Dixson House
23 Moorhouse Street, Armadale
1924 JFW Ballantyne
GC, V, NA

Another of Walter Burley Griffin's employees,
JFW Ballantyne was an apprentice in the
Melbourne office (1921–23). Like EF Billson's
Revell (185), this is an excellent example of the
Prairie style: low-pitched hip roof, wide boxed
eaves, rough-cast rendered walls and concrete
roof tiles, the low scale of the projecting single
storey wing from the main house mass, the
pronounced vertical piers and overall
horizontality. All contribute to a convincing
essay in this style of Midwest American origin.

19

196 Melbourne Boys High School
Alexandra Avenue, South Yarra
1925–28 E Evan Smith (PWD)
GC, V, A

An example of Edwin Evan Smith's eclectic use of historical styles for public buildings, the Melbourne Boys High School, completed in 1928, is an example of Collegiate Gothic, a castellated style of educational architecture popular in the United States at the time and also used by Smith at the University of Melbourne in the Old Geology (1928) and Botany buildings (1926). Part of the attraction of the style was a practical one—the large areas of glass required for classrooms had a parallel in the multi-panelled windows of Elizabethan mansions. Designed to accommodate about 700 boys, the school—with its formal plan, pavilion ends and central entry feature with its octagonal towers, flagpole and clock—is an imposing landmark. Smith's other notable high schools at this time include the Georgian Revival Box Hill High School, Whitehorse Road, Box Hill (1930), and University High School, Storey Street, Parkville (1929).

197 Courthouse and Police Station
209 and 211–213 Bank Street, South Melbourne
1924–28 E Evan Smith (PWD)
GC, V, A

A rare example of the Spanish Mission style used for public buildings, the Courthouse and Police Station opposite the imposing South Melbourne Town Hall (1880) are an example of then Chief Architect of the Public Works Department Edwin Evan Smith's tendency to apply a wide variety of historical styles to public buildings of different function. The choice of the Mediterranean-influenced style, more commonly seen in California in the 1920s as part of the Spanish Colonial Revival style, is unusual, although this idiom was popular in domestic and commercial architecture in Melbourne. The Police Station with its arcaded loggia at first-floor level, hipped roof of half-round Cordoba terracotta roof tiles, balconettes and wrought-iron detailing may also owe something to the Spanish-inspired designs of Sydney architect Leslie Wilkinson. The Courthouse, although attached to the Police Station, appears as a detached structure, complete with a Spanish Baroque parapet of scrolls and a coat of arms set into the render above the front door. Inside, polished timber joinery is used in the entry lobby and for the courtroom benches, and the ceiling has simple strapped plaster detailing typical of the period.

198 Maisonettes
Caroline Street and Domain Road, South Yarra
1925 Marcus Martin
GC, V, NA

Commissioned by art patron Tristan Buesst, this block is a fine example of Spanish Mission style, an idiom appropriate to a closely packed group of apartments modelled on the Andalusian farmhouse as understood through the courtyard houses of Los Angeles. All the features are here: the hand-trowelled render finish, the open grille work, decorative wrought-iron work and Cordoba roof tiles. Another example nearby is 9 Gordon Grove, South Yarra (1928), designed by Blackett, Forster and Craig, while a more openly commercial expression is given in Howard Lawson's Beverley Hills apartments **(248)**. St Kilda also has many Spanish-style flats such as: Edwin Ruck's Aston Court, Acland Street (1919), and WH Merritt's Belvedere Flats, 22 Upper Esplanade (1929).

28 First Australian Formula One
and Prix held at Phillip Island and
on by ACR Waite in an Austin 7

1928 John Flynn establishes the Australian
Aerial Medical Service, later known as the
Royal Flying Doctor Service

199

59 B3

99 Broome
5 Glyndebourne Avenue, Toorak
1925 Marcus Martin
GC, V, NA

Designed in a restrained Mediterranean Revival
manner, Broome was designed by Marcus
Martin, Melbourne society architect of the
1920s and 1930s, for himself. The Spanish
styling of Cordoba roof tiles, original ochre
trowelled render, louvred shutters, the loggia
with its twist columns beneath the projecting
mass of the simply planned house all evoke a
romantic stylistic ambience. Calmness and
discretion were the keywords of Martin's recipe
for domestic living. Banchory at 8 Glyndebourne
Avenue (1928) is another Martin design, also for
himself. The styling this time is Georgian Revival
and, like Broome, contributes to the specific
character of Toorak as a stronghold of domestic
respectability as reflected in gracious historic
style adapted to modern convenience.

59 B5

200 Little Milton
26 Albany Road, Toorak
1925-27 Muriel Stott in association with
Stephenson & Meldrum
Edna Walling (garden)
GC, V, NA

Published three times in *Australian Home
Beautiful* between 1927 and 1929, Little Milton
is a fine example of the influence of Arts and
Crafts-inspired country house and garden
collaborations of architect Edward Lutyens and
garden designer Gertrude Jekyll. Designer Muriel
Stott was described as one of Victoria's best-
known women architects. The garden was
designed by Australia's best-known garden
designer of the period, Edna Walling. The house,
probably inspired by a Cotswold house, has
terracotta shingles, rendered walls which still
have their ochre wash, and window joinery in
the original black. The original front fence, with
its bold posted gate, contributes to the house's
understated character.

2M K8

201 Eulinya
48–50 Irving Road, Toorak
1925 Walter and Richard Butler
GC, V, NA

Designed for Melbourne businessman Sir
William McBeath and later owned by (Sir)
Arthur Coles (of GJ Coles & Co. fame), Eulinya is
a very large house on a corner site. Both the
house and its Italianate-inspired garden are the
work of Walter Butler and his nephew Richard
and reflect their interests in Old English and
Arts and Crafts styles. It was described in 1927
by *Australian Home Beautiful* as "a noble
twentieth century interpretation of sixteenth
and early eighteenth century ideals". The
picturesquely massed house with its vast roof of
terracotta shingles and massive chimneys recalls
the mannered country houses of Sir Edwin
Lutyens. A highlight of the interior is the grand
elliptical stairhall graced by an Ionic colonnade.

•••

Mediterranean and Spanish Mission Styles
*Of the plethora of eclectic historic styles which
found favour in the 1920s and 1930s from
Modern Georgian, Tudor, Old English to French
Provincial, it was the Mediterranean and Spanish
Mission styles that were to provide maximum
flexibility. From the evocation of an Andalusian
farmhouse (which could house a block of
apartments) to a Spanish Moorish palace (which
could be a cinema), this style had two major
sources of inspiration: first, that it was a
climatically appropriate style and secondly, that
it evoked the spirit of Hollywood and the Spanish
Colonial Revival homes of the stars.*

202

202 Langi Flats

579 Toorak Road, Toorak
1925 Walter Burley Griffin and Marion Mahony
(north wing); 1926 Walter Burley Griffin and
Marion Mahony (south wing)
GC, V, NA

With its lemon scented gums in front, signature trees of Griffin and Mahony's landscape designs, Langi is an accomplished essay in the Prairie style as applied to a series of walk-up apartments. The south wing of Langi presents a composition of symmetry and horizontality achieved by capped window bays, low central entry and flanking con-centration of geometric cement render details. The details of geometrically stylised plant forms owe much to Chicago architect Louis Sullivan's notion of organically derived ornament and also possibly to the 'modern' detailing of Viennese architect Otto Wagner. Langi was commissioned by Mrs Mary Williams, who had previously had the Griffins design Clendon Lodge, 74 Clendon Road (1923). Like Langi, Clendon Lodge is substantially intact. Its Eastern-inspired roof forms hint at the Griffins' broader interest in the exotic architectures of Japan and Southeast Asia.

203 Former Temperance and General Mutual Life Assurance Society Building

141 Collins Street, Melbourne
1926–28 Anketell & Kingsley Henderson; 1938
A & K Henderson; 1959 A & K Henderson; 1991
Metier III (internal refurbishment & additions)
GC, V, A

A & K Henderson designed all T & G's major buildings in the so-called 'free Modern Renaissance' style. The 1938 additions extended the building further down Collins Street and replaced the original tower with an even higher central one. As Graeme Butler has observed, you could take a ride to the top in Australia's first tube-shaped lift and enjoy views from Melbourne's highest occupiable structure (220 feet). From the late 1950s, the building was nicknamed the Tooth and Gum Building due to its many tenants being dentists and, in recent years, the T & G has been added to and entirely refurbished, including the insertion of new floors within the original shell. It became the largest facade-propping exercise in Australia as everything except for the tower and the foyer was removed. A landmark to the commercial Moderne and skyline competitor with Melbourne's spires, the T & G was, prior to 1950, one of the city's biggest projects and in architectural and economic battle with another life assurance company head-quarters, the Manchester Unity Building **(231)**.

204 Former Emily McPherson College of Domestic Economy

Russell and Franklin Streets, Melbourne
1926 E Evan Smith (PWD)
GC, V, A

Financed by a bequest from the former Victorian Treasurer Sir William McPherson, and named after his wife, this building was designed in the Greek Revival, a sanitary mode of classicism for the teaching of the virtues of home manage-ment to young women. The RVIA awarded this building its second Street Architecture Medal in 1930. The jury commended its 'austerity and controlled simplicity, real individuality and appeal', and further stated that 'the suppression and omission of superfluous detail displays scholarly judgement of a high order'. Like the first recipient of the RVIA Street Architecture Medal, Francis House **(215)**, designed by RVIA President W Blackett, this building reflects a profession deeply concerned with architectural manners and conservative notions of what constituted a 'proper' architectural language.

205

207

205 St Stephen's Anglican Church
22-24 Merton Street, Ivanhoe
1926–27, 1929 Louis Williams
GC, V, A

A designer of churches for more than 40 years, Louis Williams was one of Melbourne's most prolific producers of religious architecture. St Stephen's is almost domestic in scale and finish. Determinedly Arts and Crafts in spirit, walls internally and externally are in brick, there are simplified hammerbeams and battered walls, and a gabled hood to the bellcote. From Williams's massive oeuvre, this Old English flavoured church is one of his most original contributions. Inside there are three windows by artist Napier Waller.

206 Houses and gardens at Bickleigh Vale
Area bounded by Cardigan, Pembroke and Pine Roads, Bickleigh Vale, Mooroolbark
1921–40 Edna Walling
GC, V, NA

The village of Bickleigh Vale (named after a Devonshire village) began in 1921 when landscape designer Edna Walling (1896-1973) bought a 3-acre lot and determined to design a house and garden in harmony with the landscape. She then bought almost 30 acres of adjoining land, subdivided it and sold allotments with the condition of sale being that she would design and supervise construction of both house and garden. Between 1921 and 1940, 16 such Arts & Crafts inspired house and garden schemes were initiated. In the gardens and along the roadsides, Walling integrated exotic and native plants and trees to achieve a remarkable ecological balance. Working at various times with Walling on the project were future landscape designers Eric Hammond, Glen Wilson and Ellis Stones. Walling lived at Bickleigh Vale for nearly

50 years in three different cottages. In her first house, Sonning, Walling used locally quarried stone, packing cases for lining boards, and saplings for pergolas. After being destroyed by fire in 1936, Sonning was rebuilt by Walling soon after. A dominant figure in Australian landscape design between 1920 and 1973, Edna Walling became a household name, publishing widely on garden design. Her book *The Australian Roadside* (1952) was a pivotal text, redirecting attention to the use of Australian native shrubs and trees alongside highways.

•••

Notable Walling house designs include Sonning, 23 Pine Road; The Cabin (now Sarn), 26 Bickleigh Vale Road; Glencairn, 9 Bickleigh Vale Road; Lynton Lee, 9 Pine Road; Mistover, 92 Pembroke Road; Badger's Wood, 17 Bickleigh Vale Road; Downderry, 10 Bickleigh Vale Road; Winty, 126 Cardigan Road; Hurst, 100 Pembroke Road; Wimbourne, 19 Bickleigh Vale Road; and The Barn (formerly Good-a-Meavy), Edna Walling Lane.

207 Palais Cinema
Lower Esplanade, St Kilda
1927 Henry E White
GC, V, A

Built on the site of another theatre the design of which was widely attributed to Walter Burley Griffin, the new Palais was described by the *Argus* in 1927 as the largest and most beautiful theatre in the country. Seating 2968 people, the 'French and Oriental style' interior was indeed vast. Features of the interior were the open wells in the upper foyer, a rectangular one over the lower foyer and an elliptical one over the back stalls. In recent years, the Palais has been the venue for a wide variety of events, scout gang shows, rock concerts, architects' award nights and even the odd film festival.

208

2L K3

208 Church Street Bridge

Yarra River at Church Street, Richmond
1920–24 Harold Desbrowe-Annear and
TR Ashworth
AC, V, A

Designed by society architect Harold Desbrowe-Annear in association with TR Ashworth and engineered by JA Laing, the Church Street Bridge is composed of three reinforced concrete arches with arcaded infills above to transfer the loads more efficiently. Annear's architectural theme for the bridge piers and four pairs of pylons at street level was a flamboyant Edwardian Baroque style which coincided with his developing ideas on urban design. The processional quality and celebratory decorative scheme of the Church Street Bridge matches Annear's City Beautiful proposals for other areas of Melbourne, most notably his designs for a replanned South Melbourne. Competing under the name 'Ferroconcretor', Annear and Ashworth's bridge design was awarded first prize in a 1920 competition. The bridge was constructed by John Monash's firm, the Reinforced Concrete and Monier Pipe Construction Company, and opened by the then Governor, the Earl of Stradbroke, on 8 July 1924, who described the bridge as 'a thing of beauty for all time'.

2J A3

209 Garden City

Area bounded by Graham Street, Williamstown
Road, Howe Parade, Poolman Street and Walter
Street, Port Melbourne
1926–48 Architects Department, State Savings
Bank of Victoria
AC, V, A

Previously slated as a shipping channel (1851), plantation (1879) and stormwater drain (1883), the extensive area of land adjacent to Port Melbourne at Fishermen's Bend began to attract attention in the 1920s as a possible site to relieve the perceived problems of slum housing. After much publicity citing Britain's Letchworth and Welwyn garden cities, as well as Adelaide's Colonel Light Gardens, the State Savings Bank took up the challenge of providing low-income housing on the site. Between 1926 and 1928, the bank purchased 44 acres and, over the next 22 years, roads were constructed, trees were planted and 322 dwellings were erected. Included also were three recreation reserves and a commercial zone on Graham Street which was developed privately. The six alternative designs of the double-storey semi-detached houses built of cindcrete blocks and rendered in cement were heavily influenced by the *Manual on the Preparation of State-Aided Housing Schemes* (1919) distributed by the British Local Government Board. It is these semi-detached houses with their grey stucco, hipped tiled roofs and Voysey-esque entry porches that earnt for this subdivision the title of 'Garden City'. The curving streets of different widths according to traffic usage, the provision of a shopping precinct, nature strips, street tree planting and public parks made Garden City a model for such welfare housing as the neighbouring Housing Commission estate at Fishermen's Bend begun in 1938. In an extraordinary turn of aesthetic and social events, the cosy English domestic imagery of Garden City's subsidised housing appears to have been borrowed in the design of the adjacent 1990s middle-class speculative subdivision of Beacon Cove.

210

211

1B L5

10 Public Benefit Bootery

23–325 Bourke Street, Melbourne
923-24 Grainger Little Barlow & Hawkins
GC, V, A

esigned as a boot store and offices for Spry
ros., the Public Benefit Bootery is a narrow-
ronted, 1920s commercial palazzo designed to
maximum allowable height for its time. Like its
eighbour Deva House at 327–329 Bourke Street
1926), by Harry Norris, and the nearby London
tores at 349–357 Bourke Street (1924–25), by
W & FB Tompkins, the Public Benefit Bootery
xemplifies the dominant commercial building
tyle of the day, a pragmatic recipe for maximis-
ng floor space and providing inexpensive and
cceptable architectural manners to the street.

•••

*One of Melbourne's most prolific commercial
architects of the 1920s and 1930s, Harry Norris
was a devotee of all things American, including
the Spanish Colonial Revival style and the
various incarnations of the Moderne (both Zig-
Zag and Streamlined), Norris was also blessed
with rich clients. Chief among them were Alfred
Nicholas, the man behind the 'Aspro' fortunes
and developer of the Nicholas Building* **(211)**
and client for Burnham Beeches **(237)**, *and
GJ and AJ Coles, whose department stores Norris
designed across Victoria and interstate. Nicholas
was also a major benefactor in the 1933
rebuilding of Wesley College and funding new
buildings for the Methodist Mission in Lonsdale
Street. Other of Norris's works include: Deva
House, 327–329 Bourke Street, Melbourne
(1926); Majorca House* **(223)**; *Kellow Motors,
St Kilda Road, South Yarra (1928); GJ Coles Store,
Melbourne* **(227)**.; *Ilyuka, Point King Road,
Portsea (1929); Wesley College, St Kilda Road
(1933–39); Melford Motors, Queensberry Street,
Melbourne (1937); Mitchell House* **(257)**.

1B N9

211 Nicholas Building

27–41 Swanston Street, Melbourne
1925-26 Harry Norris
GC, V, A

The Nicholas Building is the grandest 1920s
commercial palazzo in Melbourne. At limit
height and maximum site coverage, it is a Greek
Revival mass with a temple podium, office
floors between giant order columns and
pilasters, implied attic storey and weighty
cornice. American in influence, the building is
also distinguished by its use of Wunderlich's
'Granitex' terracotta faience for its facade. Harry
Norris explained in the *Argus* in March 1926
that the material was used because, '... we
wanted the building to always look new. Now in
the case of public buildings, age tends to give it
a certain dignity which is desirable. But that is
not so in this case of a business building ... We
wanted a surface that would wash down and
which after washing would look as new as the
day that it was erected. For this purpose
nothing equals the new terracotta'. At ground
level, extra retail space was gained with the use
of a glazed leadlight barrel vaulted arcade. The
Nicholas Building, together with other limit
height buildings such as the Port Authority
Building **(230)**, AMP House and Temple Court
(194), gives an impression of a gracious,
classical but solidly commercial city of
consistent skyline, broken only by the spires of
churches, the Supreme Court dome and the
clock towers of the town hall and post office.

212 Bathing Boxes

*Foreshore, between Dendy Street, Brighton and
the Brighton Beach Gardens*
c. 1920s
GC, V, NA

A rare sight now, but one that was common
to many of Melbourne's bayside beaches for
most of this century, the picturesque profile of
a row of nearly 80 timber bathing boxes at the
beach opposite Dendy Street, Brighton, is a
memory of the suburb's role as a Victorian
seaside resort. As early as 1844 in Brighton,
wheeled bathing machines were available and,
from the mid-1870s, permanent timber framed
and weatherboard clad bathing boxes began to
be erected along this stretch of beach. Many of
the 'boxes' have been rebuilt over the years
and it is reasonable to assume that this set at
Brighton dates from the 1920s. Other stretches
of bathing boxes could once be seen at
Mentone, Aspendale, Mordialloc, Mornington,
Mt Martha, Sorrento and Portsea.

107 C2

213 Mulberry Hill

Golf Links Road, Baxter
1925 Harold Desbrowe-Annear
and Daryl Lindsay
GC, V, A

The elegant transformation of a small four-
roomed weatherboard cottage into a large,
American-influenced Georgian style house,
and the result of a close client–architect
collaboration, Mulberry Hill was home to Sir
Daryl and Lady Lindsay from 1926 until Lady
Lindsay's death in December 1984. One of
Annear's early designs was an elaborate Spanish
country house scheme, but Desbrowe-Annear
eventually introduced a distinctively American
Colonial flavour, perhaps through a knowledge
of cottage designs popularised through Sears

Roebuck catalogues of the early 1920s.
Desbrowe-Annear's design coincided with
renewed national interest in colonial architecture generally. Nearby, Desbrowe-Annear was to
transform another existing house and employing
specifically American elements such as an ante-
bellum portico at Cruden Farm (1929) for (Sir)
Keith and (Dame) Elizabeth Murdoch. The
striking feature of Mulberry Hill is not just its
south-facing polygonal porch supported off
white-painted timber Tuscan Doric columns, but
also the inclusion of recycled windows, the
balcony porch balustrade and a cedar staircase
bought from Whelan the Wrecker. Elegantly
furnished with only a few pieces that date from
later than 1830, the Lindsays' interior decor
reflected the conservatism of establishment
Melbourne society and the rule of Georgian
simplicity and good taste that dominated the
city from the 1920s to the 1950s. Director of
the National Gallery of Victoria (1941–56) and
one of the founders of the National Trust in
Victoria, Sir Daryl Lindsay was the brother of the
famous artists Norman and Sir Lionel Lindsay.
His wife, Joan Lindsay, wrote her popular novel
Picnic at Hanging Rock at Mulberry Hill, and it
later became one of Australia's most successful
and widely distributed films. Mulberry Hill, much
loved by the Lindsays, was frequented by their
friends, some of Australia's best known artists,
writers, architects, musicians, politicians and
businessmen, including Nellie Melba, Banjo
Paterson, Sir Robert Menzies, Blamire Young,
Rupert Bunny, and Lord and Lady Casey, as well
as their neighbours, the Murdochs.

Open to the public since 1985, Mulberry Hill
and its entire contents, including the fabulous
collection of Australian paintings, was left to
the National Trust for the people of Victoria.

Street Architecture Medal

215

| 46 B9 | 2M J8 |

214 Colinton

92 Mont Albert Road, Canterbury
1926 Barlow and Hawkins
GC, V, NA

No longer Federation nor a historically correct revival of anything Medieval, Colinton is an early indicator of a new appearance of Tudor styling known as neo-Tudor or Stockbroker Tudor. Like Hartpury Court **(193)** of a few years before, Colinton exhibits the Old English style. It is likely that Barlow and Hawkins would have drawn inspiration from the United States for this light evocation of Olde England; the Tudor Style was being popularised there, even being seen in Hollywood. Built for Walter Gillespie whose money was made in flour, Colinton is also distinguished by its angled siting within landscaped grounds. The prominent corner position confirmed this leafy precinct as home to the city's new suburban gentry.

1B S8

215 Francis House

107 Collins Street, Melbourne
1927–28 Blackett & Forster
GC, V, A

Winner of the first RVIA Street Architecture Medal in 1929, Francis House epitomises the urbanity of 1920s Modern Georgian and the architecture profession's idea that good manners and refined taste were crucial to the postwar metropolis. Its copper shopfront bay is a particularly handsome ornament at street level. Designed by RVIA President WAM Blackett, this commercial office block is a background building, its muted style taking secondary position to monuments of civic and religious importance. The belief was that a city skyline should not possess competing towers, particularly those of grubby commerce.

216 Cranlana

62–62a Clendon Road, Toorak
1929–30 Harold Desbrowe-Annear
(gates and garden)
1933– Yuncken Freeman Bros., Griffiths &
Simpson (house alterations and additions)
GC, NV, NA

The home of retailing giant and philanthropist Sidney Myer and his wife Dame Merlyn has an Italianate garden designed by Harold Desbrowe-Annear. One of his few gardens and one of the few surviving grand Toorak gardens of the interwar period, it contains fountains, urns and statues. The enormous wrought-iron gates, hand wrought by Caslakes, and the flanking stone piers were also designed by Desbrowe-Annear. The house is an amalgam of addition and refurbishment in Georgian and Regency styles, handled by brothers John and Tom Freeman of Yuncken Freeman Brothers Griffiths and Simpson.

•••

Street Architecture

In 1929, the Royal Victorian Institute of Architects established an annual street architecture award to promote an urbane street hugging architecture of manners and subdued architectural good taste. Winners initially were located in the central city but, by the late 1930s, free-standing buildings on suburban sites and even a bush location became winners. Award winners included: 1929 – Francis House (215); 1930 – Emily McPherson College of Domestic Economy (204); 1931 – Lyric House (221); 1932 – AMP House; Collins Street Melbourne; 1933 – Port Authority Building (230); 1934 – Buckley & Nunn's Men's Store (238); – Royal Australasian College of Surgeons (255); 1938 – Second Church of Christ Scientist (247); 1939 – Heidelberg Town Hall (262); 1940 – Sanitarium Health Foods Factory, Warburton (261) .

217

217 Shrine of Remembrance

St Kilda Road, Birdwood Avenue, Melbourne
1927–34 Hudson and Wardrop; 1950–54 Ernest
E Milston (World War II Memorial forecourt)
GC, V, A

The Shrine of Remembrance is arguably
Melbourne's most important public monument;
a focus of cultural identity balancing the
monumental scale of Melbourne's colonial grid
plan across the northern side of the Yarra. When
the hostilities of the Great War ceased officially
at 11 a.m. on the 11 November 1918, discussion
began as to the appropriate form for a
memorial to those who had given their lives.
Early proposals centred on an arch of victory
linked by axial avenues to the rest of the city,
but opinion shifted to a notion of
commemoration rather than celebration.

The existing site was chosen in 1922, the
memorial to be visible from the city, the bay and
surrounding suburbs. It was axially located on
three major streets and its elevated site would
preserve a sense of quiet for its solemn
function. A worldwide competition for a
National War Memorial was held, with a single
winner announced by December 1923. Philip
Burgoyne Hudson and James Hastie Wardrop
were both Melbourne architects who had
studied under Charles D'Ebro. They were also
returned soldiers. Their design was a brilliant
amalgam of classical Greek forms and details.

The overall cubic form with its columned
portico and stepped pyramid roof was derived
from the Mausoleum of Harlicarnassos (353 BC)
and the Parthenon (447–432 BC) provided the
model for the Doric porticos. The crowning
element of the pyramid was based on a detail
taken from the Choragic Monument of
Lysicrates, a prize and symbol of glory in ancient
Greek times, the one concession to victory. There
are two special features of the shrine's interior:

an eye of light at the top of the pyramid which
shed diffuse light; and a ray of light which
moves across the Stone of Remembrance, which
is located at the very centre of the perfectly
symmetrical composition. This ray of light, on
the 11th day of the 11th month (Remembrance
Day), moves across the Stone of Remembrance
and, at exactly 11 a.m., illuminates the word
LOVE on the inscription GREATER LOVE HATH NO
MAN. Architect Hudson claimed that this idea of
the ray had been inspired by the Church of
Santa Maria degli Angeli in Rome. The stepped
pyramid is actually a double skin with a massive
steel frame between.

Outside, the four buttress sculptural groups
represent Justice, Sacrifice, Patriotism, Peace
and Goodwill. In the tympana of the porticoes,
the north-facing one depicts the call to arms
and the south-facing one, the homecoming.
These were all designed and sculpted by English
sculptor Paul Raphael Mountford. Public
response to the final design was mixed. Second
place-getter William Lucas accused Hudson and
Wardrop of plagiarism, Arthur Streeton thought
it should be higher and Norman Lindsay
declared that:

> It takes a long time to get used to a
> monument like this. But if it is erected I
> hope that Melbourne will live up to it, and
> become, as I have always thought it will,
> the Athens of Australia.

The Shrine of Remembrance was dedicated on
11 November 1934. It was, for many, the
crowning ceremony of Victoria's centenary
celebrations. But wars had not ended and the
need for further commemorative memorials at
the shrine continued. In 1950, Czech emigré
architect Ernest E Milston was declared the
winner of a competition for a memorial to World
War II. His design comprised a large forecourt

1929 The New York stock market
crashes, starting a worldwide
economic depression

218

to the shrine in the shape of a giant cross of sacrifice, three flagpoles, the perpetual flame and the elevated sculptural tableau all as they exist today. Later inscriptions recording combat in Korea, Borneo, Malaya and Vietnam were added to the various piers of the approach landscaping and a Garden of Remembrance specifically commemorating the four post-World War II conflicts was officially dedicated in 1985.

●●●

Near the Shrine can be seen the 'Lone Pine', grown from one of the five seeds of a cone taken from the single pine tree at Gallipoli by a soldier serving with the 24th Battalion. In its shade is sculptor Wallace Anderson's rendition of Simpson and his donkey.

1B Q9

218 The Forum
Former State Theatre, Rapallo Cinema
150 Flinders Street, Melbourne
1928 Bohringer Taylor and Johnson
GC, V, A

One of the greatest 'atmospheric' cinemas in Australia, the State Theatre was built with extraordinary decorative effects. The Flinders Street facade is topped by a minaret, while at the Russell Street corner is the 'jewelled' clock tower with its flanking minarets—a marvellous Moorish fantasy. Inside, the romance continues. The *Argus* in January 1929 described the new interior: 'By a clever illusion an imitation Mediterranean sky, with twinkling stars and a gibbous moon, takes the place of the ordinary canopied roof, so that patrons can, if they like, imagine themselves seated out-of-doors ... On one side will be a balcony, said to have been copied from that in the Doge's Palace, Venice; while opposite is a Florentine garden, with its peacock walk. The proscenium represents the facade of a Venetian palace.' The dress circle

even had a pergola running across the entire width of the auditorium's blue sky, complete with artificial vines, and the projection box was designed to look like a rustic 'outhouse'. The building with its Greek and Roman statues ironically changed its function in the 1980s to a Christian revival centre, and only recently has the theatre been refurbished to return as a venue for popular entertainment.

31 K7

219 Mervyn Skipper House
45 Outlook Drive, Eaglemont
1927–28 Walter Burley Griffin
and Marion Mahony
GC, V, NA

This is the only Griffin-designed house to be built on the Griffins' Mount Eagle subdivision. The house's most distinctive features are the flared gable roof profiles of each wing enclosing the sun-trapping court and the massive block chimneys. Conservation architect Graeme Butler has suggested that Mervyn Skipper, who commissioned the house with his wife Lena, sold it to help finance Montsalvat **(244)**. Skipper's son Matcham, who grew up in this house, was a silversmith at Montsalvat.

45 C7

220 Xavier College Chapel
Barkers Road, Kew
1927–34 Schreiber & Jörgensen
GC, V, A

The crowning landmark of one of Melbourne's largest Roman Catholic boys schools, the chapel, designed by architects better known for their bungalow designs, signals its links to Rome with a formal High Renaissance (almost Baroque) design. The Renaissance pulpit was carved by Robert Prenzel, noted for his carvings of Australian flora and fauna in domestic furniture.

221

223

1B M7

221 Former Lyric House
250 Collins Street, Melbourne
1929–30 A & K Henderson
GC, V, A

Built as a music showroom for Hugo Wertheim Pty Ltd, hence its name and the use of musical motifs in the facade ornamentation, Lyric House is a fanciful departure in style for the Modern Renaissance stylists A & K Henderson. Faced in golden faience and with a tiled roof and eyelid window, the compacted vertical windows suggest a Germanic Modern Gothic style different from the firm's later Modern Gothic Shell Corner (1933; now demolished), but reminiscent of something one might see in the Berlin or Hamburg of the early 1920s. Oddly enough, the building's quirky style mustn't have appeared strange at the time. Lyric House was awarded the RVIA Street Architecture Medal for 1931.

2M H8

222 Mullion, Smith House
6 Stonehaven Court, Toorak
1927-28 EM Nicholls
GC, V, NA

Designed by Nicholls while he was working in the Melbourne office of Walter Burley Griffin and Marion Mahony, the stone and stucco house of Mullion is located at the end of Stonehaven Court, then a newly created cul-de-sac off Orrong Road. With enormous conifers on its north side, the darkly shaded site provides a mysterious setting for this fairytale house of steeply pitched gable, muscular chimney elevation, heavy barge boards, random stonework, and leadlight windows. Yet Mullion is not like the gingerbread Tudor houses of northern California, but owes much instead to the Griffins' Prairie style, particularly their Lippincott House **(171)** in Eaglemont and earlier houses in the United States' Mid-West.

1B M8

223 Majorca House
258–260 Flinders Lane, Melbourne
1928–29 Harry A Norris
GC, V, A

Majorca House is an exercise in the exotica of Spanish Colonial Revival architecture, seen by Harry Norris on his tour of California in the 1920s. Perfectly framed at the end of Degraves Street, the distinctive feature of its Spanish/Moorish-inspired facade is its facing in blue terracotta faience and gold foliated and rope moulding ornamental details. The shallow barrel vaulted elevator/stair foyer is especially rich in its use of terrazzo and inlaid stone. Norris's other Spanish-inspired works included Kellow Motors, St Kilda Road, South Yarra (1928), designed in the effusive Spanish Churrigeresque style, while at Ilyuka, Point King Road, Portsea (1929), he designed a lavish Andalusian mansion (now partly demolished) for an American oil baron.

1B P8

224 Regent Theatre
191–197 Collins Street, Melbourne
1929–30 Cedric H Ballantyne; 1945 Cowper Murphy & Appleford (restoration); 1994 Allom Lovell & Associates (restoration)
GC, V, A

Arguably surpassing the State Theatre (Forum) in lavishness, the Regent is one of the sumptuous Regents built by the Hoyts Group across Australia when the 'talkies' arrived. Its fabulous golden interior decor amalgam of High Medieval, French Second Empire, Spanish Baroque styled lobby and lounge interior, and massive auditorium in a semi-classical style can only be described as 'Hollywood'. Disaster struck in 1945 when it was destroyed by fire. Rebuilt by Cowper Murphy & Appleford, the Regent has seen cyclical success, desertion and threats of destruction. It is now used mainly for blockbuster stage shows.

225

2G B3

25 Conservatory

Fitzroy Gardens, East Melbourne
1929 MCC City Engineer's Department
GC, V, A

Constructed in the Fitzroy Gardens as a
horticultural showpiece, the Conservatory was
the brainchild of the Nurserymen and
Seedsmen's Association and supported by
T Smith, Curator of Parks and Gardens for the
City of Melbourne. This Spanish Mission–styled
building was seen at the time as a possible
threat to the 'restful and quiet sylvan beauty'
of the gardens. The building was later graced by
sculptures outside either entrance, *Meditation*
(1933) to the north and *Diana and the Hounds*
(1940) to the south, both of which were efforts
at beautification. Despite the building's frothy
decoration and subdued surrounding landscaping, the Conservatory and its five annual
displays continue to be an immensely popular
tourist attraction.

2M H6

226 Baillieu House

729 Orrong Road, Toorak
1929 Harold Desbrowe-Annear
GC, V, NA

Designed by society architect Harold Desbrowe-
Annear, this grand house is one of the most
accomplished of the mannered classical compositions that he developed in the 1920s for his
Toorak and South Yarra clientele. Commissioned
by Maurice Howard Baillieu, youngest son of the
immensely rich estate agent and entrepreneur
WL Baillieu, No. 729 is faced in brick rather than
Annear's favoured stucco. What distinguishes
the Annear designs from other Georgian-
inspired houses in the same area are the
inventive combinations of classical window and
door details combined with Annear's collection

of construction details such as angled sills,
cantilevered entry porch canopies and wide
exposed eaves. The brick wall with its circular
motifs completes this particularly idiosyncratic
departure from Georgian conformity. Other
Annear designs in the Toorak/ Malvern area can
be seen at 1 Heyington Place, Toorak (1925);
4 Heyington Place, Toorak (1922); 104 Kooyong
Road, Armadale (1922); Cloyne, 669 Toorak
Road, Toorak (1929); and Katanga, Wesley Ince
House, 372 Glenferrie Road, Malvern (1931–32).

1B M5

227 Former GJ Coles Stores
(now David Jones)

299–307 Bourke Street, Melbourne
1928 Harry Norris; 1938–40 Harry Norris; 1984
Bates Smart McCutcheon (conversion to David
Jones)
GC, V, A

Built on the site of EW Cole's book arcade, the
new Coles Store was one of a series of
department stores and warehouses across
Victoria which architect Harry Norris designed
for the retail giant. The arched facade was clad
in a striking pinkish-red faience and the
decorative Hispanic/Indian/Jazz details of
chevrons and sunbursts in yellow, orange, green
and black suggested influence from Mexico or
Southern California. In 1938, an extension was
added continuing these themes. One of the
interior highlights was the first-floor Coles
Cafeteria, a Streamlined and Jazz Moderne
destination for lunch on the run. Today, the
workaday shopping aisles have been replaced by
the black glass and marble, and upmarket swish
of the David Jones department store. Vestiges of
the building's more humble commercial origins
can still be seen in wall and column tiling and
plaster column capitals.

127

228

22

28 D6

228 Essendon Municipal Incinerator
Holmes Road, Moonee Ponds
1929–30 Walter Burley Griffin and Eric Nicholls
GC, V, A

Between 1929 and 1937, the office of Walter
Burley Griffin enjoyed a productive association
with the Reverberatory Incinerator and
Engineering Company (RIECo). The incinerator
designs were handled by Griffin and his
assistant Nicholls, and it is the latter whose
name appears on drawings for the Essendon
building which, with the incinerator designed
for Ku-ring-gai, New South Wales, was the first
designed and constructed by the Griffin office.

The process of rubbish incineration was
relatively simple: refuse travelled in a diagonal
flow path downwards through three levels, so
the building required a three-level structure and
location on a slope or artificial embankment. At
Essendon, this diagonal path was indicated by a
single continuous enveloping roof, a giant gable
with chimneys and grilled vents. A local
newspaper enthused over this 'beautiful asset of
the council':

> *Essendon should be proud of its new
> destructor ... Not only does this destructor
> mark a new era in sanitation and the handling
> of household refuse, but the actual plan is
> housed in an imposing Spanish Mission type
> building ...*

While Griffin and Nicholls may have disagreed
about the stylistic label, Griffin would surely have
been pleased with such municipal enthusiasm as
he later remarked:

> *It has been intended that these buildings
> awaken an aversion to the fundamentally
> uneconomic conditions of industrial ugliness.*

Only one other RIECo incinerator was constructed
in Melbourne—in Brunswick in 1936 (now

demolished). Others proposed for St Kilda (1936)
and Caulfield (1937) were never built. The
Essendon incinerator has recently been sympathetically restored and refurbished by architect
Keith Streames to become a performing arts space

1B V7

229 Alcaston House
2 Collins Street, Melbourne
1930 A & K Henderson
GC, V, A

Alacaston House is one of A & K Henderson's
typically free interpretations of a Modern
Renaissance style and its massing recalls
American high-rise buildings of the 1920s. The
composition of the massing was functionally, as
well as aesthetically, determined. The podium
contained a series of medical consulting rooms,
while the recessed bays between the three
upper blocks maximise the provision of natural
light for the apartments within. This urbane
design, which respected the Italianate sense of
mannered propriety in Collins Street, had other
contemporary neighbours in Blackett, Forster
and Craig's Francis House, 107 Collins Street
(1927–28) **(215)**, winner of the first RVIA Street
Architecture Medal in 1929; and the later Anzac
House, 4–6 Collins Street (1937–38), designed
by Oakley & Parkes. Another Modern Renaissance
design can be found at Meldrum and Noad's
National Bank of Australasia Ltd, 77–89 William
Street (1939).

Below: Plan of Alcaston House (1920–1930)

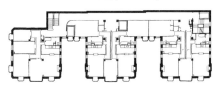

231

230 Port Authority Building
29-31 Market Street, Melbourne
1929-31 Sydney Smith, Ogg and Serpell
GC, V, NA

A sober Greek Revival style applied to the 1920s commercial palazzo form, this stone-faced building continues the conservative trend of mannered street architecture. Awarded the 1933 RVIA Street Architecture Medal, the Port Authority Building respects the Grecian restraint of the neighbouring Customs House **(35)** with its Ionic columns, but in scale the nine-storey office building was reflective of the Beaux Arts techniques of expanding classical models into modern programs. Nearby, the previous winner of the Street Architecture Medal, Bates Smart & McCutcheon's former Australian Mutual Provident (AMP) House, 419–429 Collins Street (1930–31), also adopts the commercial palazzo form, but in a free interpretation of Modern Renaissance. Together with Temple Court **(194)** and Leslie M Perrott's Savoy Plaza, former Alexander Hotel, 122–132 Spencer Street (1929), these four buildings combine to give an excellent impression of government, hotel and speculative office building design in the late 1920s.

231 Manchester Unity
91 Swanston Street, Melbourne
1929-32 Marcus Barlow
GC, V, A

The pinnacles of the Manchester Unity Building made it the tallest building in Melbourne when it was finished in 1932. Built during the Depression using round-the-clock eight-hour shifts, the termination of Manchester Unity's corner tower in Commercial Gothic Modern style had its inspiration in Raymond Hood's competition-winning design for the Chicago Tribune Tower (1922). The building is faced in a gold-brown glazed faience and elaborated by figures of benevolence and charity. As if in commercial challenge to the municipal clock tower of the Melbourne Town Hall **(55)** and the spires of St Paul's **(81)**, the size of the limit-height building proclaimed that the new force in the urban skyline was commerce. The ceiling and upper walls of the ground floor arcade reveal the mores of the day, with sculptural tableaus of industrious Victorians. Outside, the street canopy is a fine example of the sophis-ticated move from posted verandas to decorated cantilevered canopies. Perhaps Marcus Barlow's crowning achievement as an architect, it was joined by Barlow's Century Building (1938–40) **(272)**, thus creating one of Melbourne's most distinctive limit-height streetscapes between Swanston and Little Collins streets.

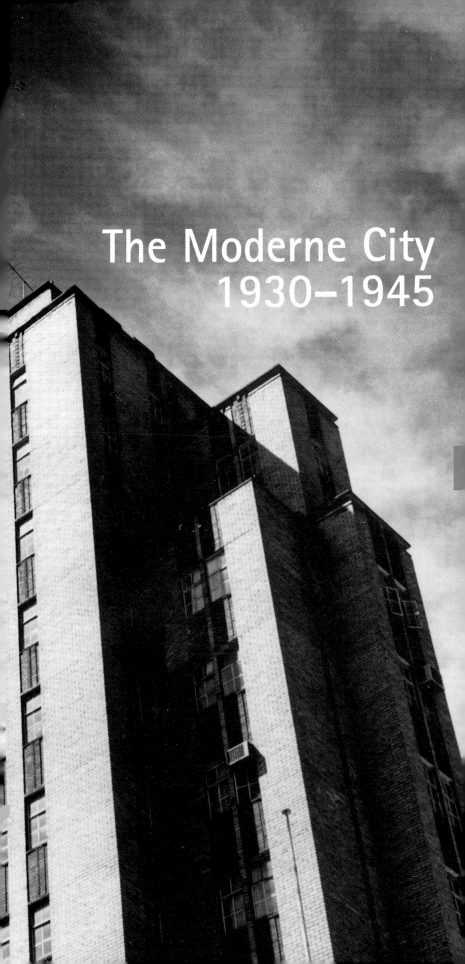

The Moderne City
1930–1945

1930–1945

As Melbourne emerged from the Great Depression, its skyline reflected new aspirations.

The pinnacles of the commercial moderne city now began to compete with the city's church spires. After three years of chronic unemployment and the occasional mass protest in Melbourne's streets, the completion of the splendid Modern Gothic **Manchester Unity Building** in continuous eight-hour shifts masked the economic malaise that had cast a blanket of gloom over the city. Some inner suburban areas never fully recovered and were labelled as 'slums'. F Oswald Barnet's newspaper articles in the *Herald* highlighted this dire urban crisis and were a catalyst for the eventual formation of the Housing Commission of Victoria (HCV), an impetus which led to the **Fishermens Bend Housing Estate** in Port Melbourne.

The year of 1934 was a signal one. By that date, building in the central city had resumed in earnest. It was also the year chosen to celebrate Melbourne's centenary of foundation (even though the exact date was 1835). In terms of building and changes to the physical face of Melbourne, the celebrations were significant.

The Shrine of Remembrance (1927–34) was dedicated on 11 November 1934 as part of the visit of the Duke of Gloucester. There was a Centenary Bridge built at Port Melbourne as a new gateway from Station Pier, so that the trains could still go out to the piers. Melbourne businessman Russell Grimwade funded the relocation of Captain Cook's Cottage to the Fitzroy Gardens, despite the fact that it was his parents' house and Cook had in fact never visited Melbourne. There was a Centenary Homes Competition to determine a modern Melbourne house and there was also a competition sponsored by chocolate manufacturer MacPherson Robertson for the design of a new girls high school. With its cream brick walls, glazed blue brick trims, steel window frames in vermilion and abstract cubic composition, **MacRobertson Girls High School** (1933–34) appeared to confirm that 1934 marked, as Robin Boyd wishfully observed, the 'Revolution' of modern architecture in Victoria.

But while there had been young architects such as Oscar Bayne, E Keith Mackay, Roy Grounds and Geoffrey Mewton who had spent the greater part of the Depression travelling or working in Europe and the United States and looking at the latest avant-garde architecture, there was no real aesthetic revolution in Melbourne. What occurred was simply an expansion of a reper-toire of accepted architectural styles—only now that repertoire included the new functionalist style from Europe.

Indeed, it was in hospital design, most notably Stephenson & Meldrum's (later Stephenson & Turner) **Mercy Hospital**, that was to be found the most convincing stylistic and functional grounds for adoption of the new abstract and appropriately hygienic idiom. The architecture profession's idea of appropriate contemporary architecture continued to be modernised versions of historic styles such as the Scandinavian-inspired classicism of the **Royal Australasian College of Surgeons**.

By the late 1930s, however, taste had modified. In 1939, the RVIA Street Architecture Medal was awarded to the cubic forms of **Heidelberg Town Hall** and, in 1940, to the functionalist **Sanitarium Health Foods Factory** at Warburton. Design inspiration came not from French Modernist Le Corbusier or the German Mies van der Rohe, but from the textured cream brick de-Stijl compositions of Dutchman Willem Dudok. Even Edgar Gurney, architect for Albert Victor Jennings at the **Beaumont Estate**, Melcombe Road, Ivanhoe, put forward new cubic forms in cream and red brick as just one of a number of style alternatives to Old English, Spanish Mission and Contemporary Bungalow.

The Jennings houses were typical speculative houses of the 1930s: the front of the house was graced by a modest brick porch; walls were solid brick; and roofs had clipped eaves and terracotta tile roofs. Inside, the colours of walls, kitchen and bathroom fittings were cream and green—deadly dull shades that were to become the bane of the postwar architect. Melbourne grew in the 1930s to be truly suburban, its houses and its new churches, confirming conservative middle-class tastes and aspirations.

In progressive house design, young architects such as Mewton & Grounds tended to favour adaptations of the low-key gable-roofed forms of Californian architect William Wilson Wurster or the interlocking forms of Dudok. Yet in the Georgian strongholds of Toorak and Malvern, the proliferation of 18th-century manners continued in the hands of Marcus Martin, Geoffrey Sommers and the emerging firm of Yuncken Freeman Bros., Griffiths and Simpson, this latter partnership to become one of Melbourne's major architectural forces in the 1960s.

By contrast, the Streamlined Moderne in faience or cement-rendered reinforced concrete became the fashionably racy commercial style in the city — for office blocks and car show-rooms — and, in the suburbs, for cinemas such as the Rivoli, Camberwell (1940), and the **Astor Theatre**, St Kilda. Similar to the new train which ran between Sydney and Melbourne, the 'Spirit of Progress', whose interiors had been designed by architects Stephenson & Turner, the Streamlined Moderne expressed movement and symbolised speed. In the architecture of retail, Streamlined Moderne came into its own. The **Myer Emporium** was expanded in Bourke Street with a vast new vertically streamlined store, while Arthur Coles employed architect Harry Norris to designs scores of new Coles stores across the state in the new smartly horizontal format. Norris's Moderne *pièce de resistance* was **Mitchell House**, Elizabeth Street, a convincing amalgam of asbtracted vertical classicism overlaid onto horizontal layers of concrete spandrel panels and broad expanses of steel-framed glass. JH Wardrop's **Alkira House** in black and green faience was perhaps the best of these radiogram fronts which accompanied the launch of commercial radio broadcasting in Melbourne and the construction late in the decade of the ABC Radio Studios at Lonsdale and William streets (now demolished). Of the few commercial office blocks to depart from the recipe of faience-clad streamlining, Seabrook & Fildes **Barnett's Building**, 164-166 Bourke Street (1938), had a curtain wall complete with blue fluted metal spandrels and originally a sculptural tableau on its top face concealing a rooftop squash court.

The Myer Emporium
(SOURCE: *RVIAJ, January 1933*)

Stylistic diversity within the Moderne also informed the output of the Public Works Department. When Percy Everett became Chief Architect, the design style shifted to reflect modernistic themes of every persuasion. For RMIT, he designed horizontal Streamlined Moderne **Buildings Nos 7 and 9**; for the University of Melbourne, however, it was cream brick Collegiate Gothic for its **Chemistry Building**. In the city, Melbourne gained its first Gotham City silhouette with the construction of Everett's **Russell Street Police Headquarters**. Even the Commonwealth Department of Works began tapping its feet with stylish classical Moderne designs for drill halls in Victoria and William streets.

By the late 1930s, central Melbourne still had plenty of 19th-century houses and pubs, and early 20th-century apartment buildings. Little Lonsdale Street was the haunt of harlots. In Collins Street and nearby in the minor streets, artists rented attics and backrooms as studios. Outside the city, certain areas were becoming thoroughly urbanised with increased densities arising from the proliferation of apartment buildings. A new demographic mix of bachelors and single women encouraged acceptance of new housing types. Some flats such as **Denby Dale** were designed to appear as if a very large single Tudor-style country house. Others (a very few) such as the **Cairo Flats** demonstrated the latest ideas in *existenzminimum* living, brought back to Australia by architect Best Overend after working in London for arch-Modernist and Canadian expatriate Wells Coates. Swiss emigre architect Frederick Romberg teamed up with local architect Molly Turner Shaw and constructed three modernist apartment blocks: **Newburn**, 30 Queens Road, Melbourne; **Glenunga**, 2 Horsburgh Grove, Armadale; and arrabee, Walsh Street, South Yarra; and produced designs for another, **Stanhill**, before the onset of World War II. Meanwhile, in the bushy outskirts of Melbourne at Warrandyte and Eltham, artists and intellectuals returned to the earth and savoured the bush, building from recycled materials such as at the artists' colony at **Montsalvat**. At Mooroolbark, Edna Walling continued to design and build her Arts and Crafts – inspired cottages, complete with gardens also to her design, at **Bickleigh Vale**.

With the onset of World War II in September 1939, Melbourne's cosy suburban shell was broken. Melbourne became the administrative headquarters for the Allied Forces in the Southwest Pacific theatre. US General Douglas MacArthur lived in Sir Keith Murdoch's Toorak mansion. His headquarters were in the Leslie M Perrott – designed Australia Hotel in Collins Street. Schools were turned over to military use and parks and gardens were dug up for trenches and air-raid shelters. Large architectural firms continued to operate, designing large hospitals and barracks. Leighton Irwin & Co. designed the massive Heidelberg Repatriation Hospital (1943), while Stephenson & Turner's recently completed **Royal Melbourne Hospital** became a US military hospital. Builders such as Jennings sought commissions from the government for the construction of huts, camps and low-rise hospitals. The smaller architectural firms and builders simply closed shop and ceased working. Many architects worked for the government, joined the armed forces or worked for the US armed or support services in an architectural or engineering capacity. Local artists such as Albert Tucker viewed the American presence in wartime Melbourne with bitterness.

Building in the central city and the suburbs came to a virtual standstill. Everyone dreamed of release from rationing and waited for friends and relatives to come home. Others thought about the future. The editors of *SALT*, the Australian Army's education journal, prophetically remarked in a 1942 article, 'After the bombs' that: '... our whole postwar plan is linked with building. Thus the perspective drawing of a five roomed cottage is linked with a perspective drawing of Australia.'

PHILIP GOAD

232

233

2K J4

1B L6

232 MacPherson Robertson Girls High School
Albert Road and Kings Way, South Melbourne
1933–34 Seabrook and Fildes
GC, V, NA

Built to a cost of £40 000 and financed from an overall donation of £100 000 by Sir MacPherson Robertson to the state government to mark Melbourne's centenary, this is one of the first and most convincing introductions to Australia of the cream brick de-Stijl architecture of Dutch modernist Willem Marinus Dudok. Robin Boyd described 'MacRob' as the building that announced 'the revolution of modern architecture' in Victoria. The flat-roofed, cream brick design, with its steel-framed windows painted vermilion and its glazed blue sill bricks and composition that relied on sophisticated arrangements of interlocking form, was almost certainly inspired by Dudok's Hilversum Town Hall (1927–31). MacRob is testament to Melbourne architects' search for a modern architecture whose forms and design could be reapplied in an Antipodean context of an Arts and Crafts tradition of craft, texture and buildability, and a modified Beaux Arts design education that practised emulation and propriety.

233 Yule House
309–311 Little Collins Street, Melbourne
1932 Oakley & Parkes
GC, V, A

Arguably Victoria's and possibly even Australia's first example of a Moderne-style commercial building, Yule House is a diminutive office building of emphatic horizontality achieved by deep and protruding horizontal spandrel panels separated by horizontal strips of uninterrupted steel-framed glazing. The narrowness of the building enables this streamlined appearance, as a single span means no internal columns are required. Glazed terracotta cladding (faience), vertical fins, elegant flat plate-metal lettering, incised lines infilled with different colours to highlight the lines crossing the surface, tiered linear ornament and curving glass shopfronts and showcases complete this stylish vocabulary of what has now become known as the Streamlined Moderne.

Right: Drawing of MacPherson Robertson Girls High School (SOURCE: RVIAJ, March 1934)

31 The caterpillar tractor is
veloped in the USA for farming

1932 Bodyline bowling by the
English cricket team causes major
sporting controversy

1933 First edition of the
Australian Women's Weekly

234

1B M8

34 Newspaper House

47–249 Collins Street, Melbourne
932–33 Stephenson and Meldrum
Japier Waller (mural)
GC, V, A

his 1884 Renaissance Revival warehouse had a
andstone horizontal Moderne facade with a
oloured mural directly above shopfront level
pplied to it. Angular balconettes are the
orizontal strips across a giant window opening
hat rises vertically through the facade—a direct
hallenge to the original building, with its
ndividually punched, rectangular window
penings. The rather solemn mosaic mural by
Napier Waller, 'I'll put a girdle round about the
earth', was an unusual introduction of colour
nd street art to sedate Collins Street, but it was
lso a clear and entirely appropriate indication
of the aspirations of media baron Keith
Murdoch, whose son Rupert in later years was
o literally do just that.

101 K5

235 Portland Lodge
First Henty House
GC, V, NA
1 Plummer Avenue, Frankston
1933–34 Roy Grounds (Mewton & Grounds)
C, V, A

Part of a series of house designs from 1933–37
that display Roy Grounds's interest in the
progressively planned houses of San Francisco
architect William Wilson Wurster. Portland
Lodge reflects the practical planning of houses
as single-room width linear blocks strung
informally together to create protected
courtyards and terraces to shelter from a fickle
climate of wind, rain and sun during any one
day. While the resulting plan was often open
and casual with generous gallery passages, the
exterior of Portland Lodge was treated in a low-
key American ranch style evocative of Wurster's
portfolio: gabled roofs, multi-paned windows,
block chimneys and white-painted eaves. In
1936, Portland Lodge was awarded First Prize in
the Ideal Home and Building Exhibition for a
house of more than eight rooms.

●●●

Other Grounds designs in this idiom include:
Lyncroft, Tucks Road, Shoreham (1934); Fairbairn
House, 236 Kooyong Road, Toorak (1936);
Ramsay House, 29 Rendlesham Avenue, Mt Eliza
(1937) and, outside Melbourne, Chateau Tahbilk,
Nagambie (1935).

101 E11

236 Ranelagh, Grounds House
35 Rannoch Avenue, Mt. Eliza
1934–35 Roy Grounds, (Mewton and Grounds)
GC, V, NA

Ranelagh was designed in 1933 to be built of
prefabricated wall panels of steel and composition sheeting with open-web steel joists for
ceiling and floors. As observed in *Australian
Home Beautiful* in June 1934, this was so it
'could be dissembled, sold and re-erected
elsewhere virtually without waste, or the use of
skilled labour'. What eventuated, however, was a
house with walls of standard timber frame
construction clad with asbestos cement sheets
with horizontal cover strips, banks of timber
French doors instead of steel ones and thick
draped rope balustrading instead of a ship's
railing. There were other inclusions of influence:
a Dudok-like entrance door of receding brick
panels and a yellow and white striped front
door which opened in half like a stable door.
Pragmatic construction techniques had created
a local interpretation of the International Style.
Grounds was to build another house nearby at
29 Rendelsham Avenue (1937) which was to
become his own house when he married Betty
Ramsay, his client.

137

237

238

237 Burnham Beeches
Sherbrooke Road, Sassafras
1930–33 Harry A Norris
GC, V, A

Burnham Beeches is the vast three-storey house built in the Dandenongs for Alfred N Nicholas, the 'Aspro' King, the man who had made his millions by the shrewd purchase from the Germans of the patent for the little white headache pill. Designed by prolific commercial architect Harry Norris, Burnham Beeches is one of the finest examples of the Moderne in Australia. Its design sits uniquely at the midpoint between the decorative Zig-Zag Moderne style of the 1920s (commonly called the Jazz style in Australia) and the Streamlined Moderne of the 1930s. Described alternately as 'Xanadu in Jazz' and a 'battleship', Burnham Beeches was built in reinforced concrete and massed as if it was a huge ship with curving bays and long stretches of cantilevering decks. In describing his design, Norris said: 'Our man wants fresh air, sunshine and outlook at command and under control. These then shall be the keynotes of the building'. The building's ornament is uncompromisingly Jazz: bold zig-zagging chevrons to the iron balustrading and diamond motifs containing representations of Australian animals. Despite 1980s additions which palely mimic the original house, Burnham Beeches and its gardens (which can be visited separately as the Alfred Nicholas Gardens) are still the most impressive Moderne answer to a summer domicile in the cool of the hills.

238 Former Buckley and Nunn's Men's Store
294–296 Bourke Street
1933 Bates Smart & McCutcheon
GC, V, A

With its cement-rendered men in knickerbockers and suits, suavely smoking or leaning on their golf clubs, this building's tall facade was the raciest addition to Bourke Street's retail heart in the early 1930s. Buckley and Nunn's Zig-Zag or Jazz Moderne facade reflected the popularity of the new stylised geometries that had come out of Paris at the 1925 *Exposition des Arts Decoratifs*, the place where the term 'Art Deco' was born. Sunburst motifs, chevron zig-zags and abstract classical forms frame a steel and glass window that passes over several storeys. In 1934, the Royal Victorian Institute of Architects awarded it its annual Street Architecture Medal.

239 St Monica's Roman Catholic Church
Mount Alexander Road, Moonee Ponds
1934–41 Thomas G Payne
GC, V, A

One of the largest churches built in Melbourne during the 1930s, St Monica's demonstrates the persistence of interpretive historical styles in church design adopted by the Catholic Church before World War II—in this case, Arts and Crafts Gothic suggestive of some craggy hilltop site in windswept Scotland or Ireland. A tall, deep west window, octagonal turrets and tall, massive piers—all in freestone—contribute to this rugged abbey image. The church's narrow and lofty interior is complemented by exceptional stained glass.

240

240 Former McPherson's Pty Ltd Building
546-566 Collins Street, Melbourne
1934-37 Reid and Pearson in association with
Stuart P Calder
GC, V, NA

Melbourne's most convincing homage to horizontality in architecture is a fine example of the Streamlined Moderne. While historians have adopted this building as a leading example of the International style, its use of terracotta faience, vertical punctuation by stair tower, black vitrolite glass and the deliberately incised lines on the three boldly horizontal spandrels mark its commercial origins and similarity to the diminutive Yule House **(233)** in Little Collins Street. Designed as a warehouse, office and showroom for the hardware empire run by Sir William McPherson, later Premier of Victoria, McPherson's has attracted praise also from those who would prefer to relate its design to German Expressionist architect Erich Mendelsohn's Schocken department stores and avant-garde works of other European architects. Its huge areas of glass still today appear as a stark and visually dramatic contrast to the sedate streetscape at the top end of Collins Street.

1B M7

241 Kodak House
252 Collins Street, Melbourne
1934–35 Oakley and Parkes
GC, V, A

Kodak House's polished and shaped stainless steel spandrels gleam like a seven-storey camera and its 'K' medallions still decorate the tops of the facade's abstract fluted faience pilasters. The narrow exterior's 'picture frame' composition houses a vertical Moderne curtain wall. According to Graeme Butler, Kodak House has the first city facade to use stainless steel and is the first to use a combined spandrel and framing system set within vertical mullions. The original interior was, by contrast, all horizontal with walnut panelling and chrome strips, its curving glazed shopfronts sweeping in the prospective film buyer.

1B M5

242 Myer Emporium
314-336 Bourke Street, Melbourne
1933 HW and FB Tompkins
Napier Waller (Mural Hall)
GC, V, A

The Myer Emporium is the vertical Streamlined Moderne member of the series of Myer buildings that lie between Bourke and Lonsdale streets. Sidney Myer replaced his 1913 store with this one in 1931, during the Depression, a brave move achieved only through 24-hour shifts that enabled the store to open for Christmas in 1933. The building is externally relatively undistinguished, apart from its clock, repetitive facade and parapet of fins. Its most striking feature is inside. The Myer Mural Hall features the work of artist Napier Waller, who had lost his right arm during World War I, then learnt to paint with his left arm and went on to become Melbourne's major mural artist. His Myer murals depict women in all manner of fields; womens' fashion throughout history; and sea and land transport vehicles throughout history.

•••

Sidney Myer, born Simcha Baevski Myer in Moghilev, Russia, in 1878, emigrated to Melbourne in 1898 and opened a drapery store in Bendigo in 1907. Four years later, he expanded his business to Melbourne and employed architects HW and FB Tompkins (as Myers would continue to do for the next 60 years) to design his new Bourke Street store (1913) based on the San Francisco Emporium.

1933 The town of Stuart in the Northern Territory renamed Alice Springs after Lady Alice Todd

1934 The pavlova, a dessert made with meringue and passionfruit, was created in Perth by Bert Sachse, in honour of the eponymous Russian ballerina

243

47 G10

243 Sidney Myer Tomb, Box Hill Cemetery

Middleborough Road, Box Hill
1934–38 Sir Edwin Lutyens in association with
Yuncken Freeman Bros. Griffiths and Simpson
GC, V, A

Designed by British architect Sir Edwin Lutyens, planner of New Delhi, great proponent of the English country house and arguably England's finest 20th-century classical architect, this stately pergola tomb is a fitting memorial to one of Victoria's most important figures of commerce, Sidney Myer (1878–1934), and his wife, Dame Merlyn Myer. The plot is designed as a contemplative garden setting. Two garden beds flank a path leading to a pergola which shades the simple altar stone. A surrounding screen of Tuscan Doric columns is backed by a plain stone seat and wall. Above, triangular slats of bleached teak carry wisteria vines. The entire memorial is executed in Stawell stone.

•••

Edwin Lutyens, one of a group of architects appointed to the Imperial War Graves Commission and architect of the famous Cenotaph in Whitehall, designed one other structure in Melbourne in 1933—the tomb of Australia's greatest opera singer Dame Nellie Melba (1861–1931) in the Lilydale General Cemetery. A simple composition, the pedestal-like stone bears the words from her favourite role, as Mimi in La Boheme*: 'Addio senza rancor'.*

22 A8

244 Montsalvat

Hillcrest Avenue, Eltham
1934–72 Justus Jorgensen and others (all main buildings); 1937 student quarters and studio 1938-58 Great Hall and gallery; 1942 store, stable; 1943 Skipper's wood turning studio, enamelling studio and residence; 1946 craft shop; 1954 studios, foundry, greenhouse;
1957 jewellery shop, joinery shop; 1960 painting studio, lead lighting studio; 1961 metal spinning studio; 1970s chapel
GC, V, A

An extraordinary and unique collection of 'medieval' and vernacular styled buildings built of mud brick, stone and secondhand building materials comprises Montsalvat, the artists' colony founded in 1934 by Justus Jorgensen (1894–1975). Carlotta Kellaway has noted that 'Montsalvat was the temple or home of the Grail, the most precious chalice which only the most perfect Knight could hope to find in his ultimate quest'. With such high aspirations, Montsalvat became a living and working environment devoted to art. The ad-hoc collection of structures erected by Jorgensen, his students and fellow artists over 38 years encouraged a sense of community through building and came to influence the social and physical life of the Eltham district. The Great Hall, a large baronial space, is the most notable building. Built with Gothic bay windows supplied by Whelan the Wrecker, stone blocks and lintels scavenged from Melbourne, New Zealand and Ireland, and roofing slates from Wales, the Great Hall also contains tables, stools and carved chairs made by Welsh joiner Phil Taffe.

•••

Notable people who have been associated with Montsalvat include Mervyn Skipper (novelist and journalist), Clifton Pugh (artist), Matcham Skipper (gold and silversmith and sculptor), Myra Skipper (painter, enameller and silversmith), Sonia Skipper (painter and sculptor), Leonard French and Albert Tucker (painters), and Arthur Mundy (builder). Twenty artists still have studios at Montsalvat, now managed by Sigmund Jorgensen (designer and entrepreneur, and the founder's son).

34 The parking meter is
vented in the USA by CC Magee

● 1934 RM Williams establishes
company in Adelaide catering
to the needs of bush people

● 1935 Cane toads imported
from Brazil to counter grey-
backed beetle

245

247

59 C2

45 Littlejohn Memorial Chapel

cotch College, 491 Glenferrie Road, Hawthorn
934–36 Scarborough Robertson and Love
GC, V, A

vocatively sited above the playing fields of
cotch College and against a backdrop of
orthern European trees, this chapel, built in
onour of a former headmaster, is one of the
most convincing late works of Arts and Crafts–
nspired Gothic architecture in Melbourne. With
ts asymmetrical octagonal turret tower, triangular buttressing and protruding minor chapel,
t recalls the work of US architects Cram
Goodhue and Ferguson. Elsewhere on the
cotch College campus are red-brick and half-
imbered buildings designed by Henry Kemp
ating from the early years of the 20th century
the Gate Lodge at the northeast corner on
Glenferrie Road is the most notable of these).
hese are further complemented by a series of
notable Scottish Baronial Moderne buildings
uilt in the 1930s by Scarborough Robertson
and Love.

59 A4

246 Redheath, CD Finch House

202 Kooyong Road, Toorak
1934 Yuncken Freeman and Freeman
GC, V, NA

Here is urbane, Georgian Revival, formality with
convenience. Its low front fence reveals the
house in all its symmetrical finery with an entry
centrepiece of classical rectitude— the elements
that characterise the soberly respectable
architecture that dominates Melbourne's
wealthiest suburb. Brothers Tom and John
Freeman were masters of this ever-so-polite
idiom. Another of their houses is the Lempriere
House, Illawarra Crescent, Toorak (1939). Other
exponents of the style included Marcus Martin,
Geoffrey Sommers and Osborn McCutcheon.

45 J11

247 Second Church of Christ Scientist

41 Cookson Street, Camberwell
1934–36 Bates Smart & McCutcheon
GC, V, A

Christian Science was introduced to Australia in
the 1890s. The First Church of Christ Scientist
was built in St Kilda Road **(186)**. This is the
second and there is a third church in Elsternwick.
The monumental design is at once daring in its
departure from Gothic, Byzantine or Classical
revival models and, at the same time, grimly
sombre. With a stripped Classical Moderne front,
exquisite Art Deco style wrought-iron gates and
grill work in black and gold, it could have been
derived from contemporary American Beaux
Arts Moderne examples of the temple. The
overall massing of overlapping cubes is austere
and abstract—this is neoclassical Modern—a
theme which also makes its way into the
decoration of the interior. Possibly the first
convincing Moderne-styled church in Victoria,
this building was awarded the RVIA Street
Architecture Medal for 1938, the first such
award given outside the city of Melbourne.

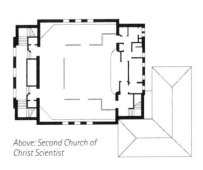

*Above: Second Church of
Christ Scientist*

141

248

2L H2

248 Beverley Hills flats

61–65 Darling Street, South Yarra
1935–36 Howard Lawson
GC, V, NA

An ode to Hollywood with its frosting of
Spanish Mission styling and swimming pool
with viewing window below water level,
Beverley Hills flats is architect/developer
Howard Lawson's largest and most flamboyant
work. Part of a precinct of apartments built and
designed by Lawson from the 1920s until 1942,
Beverley Hills is the dominant complex and
features two tower blocks. Each block has the
same vocabulary of barley sugar columns, bay
windows, decorated cement-rendered panels
above each window, and cast concrete
balustrading detail of circles crossed
by diagonals that makes a Lawson flat easily
recognisable.

2B K9

249 Cairo flats

98 Nicholson Street, Fitzroy
1935–36 Taylor Soilleux and Overend
GC, V, NA

Best Overend had worked in London with arch-
Modernist Wells Coates. On his return to
Melbourne, Overend began writing on the
minimum flat concept—an entirely functional
living unit with built-in or fold-down furniture
and complete with labour-saving technological
devices. Cairo is a series of serviced bachelor
flats arranged in a two-storeyed U-shape
around a courtyard. The busy bachelor or single
woman slept on a divan, had built-in storage
cupboards, ate in a dining nook, could have
food delivered to the flat which could be left in
a cupboard, or could eat in the communal
dining room which is now a milk bar. The
interiors were finished with coved ceiling to
eliminate cornices, simple Bauhaus style light-

fittings and portholes to each front door. A
dramatic cantilevering concrete stair leads to
the roof where residents were intended to dry
laundry and sunbake with uninterrupted views
to the Exhibition Gardens. The most rigorously
functional building in 1930s Melbourne, Cairo's
only concession to history was the old brick
garden wall on its north side, a remnant of the
original site of 19th century Uxbridge House.

31 G5

250 Beaumont Estate

Melcombe Road and culs-de sac off Melcombe
Road, Ivanhoe (Hampton Court, Tudor Court,
Surrey Court and Lincoln Court)
1935–36 Edgar Gurney, architect for AV Jenning
GC, V, NA

In 1935, Albert Victor Jennings embarked on
another speculative housing venture after his
earlier and first success as a builder/developer ir
Murrumbeena in 1932. Here, in Ivanhoe, the
Beaumont Estate was aimed at a solidly middle-
class market. Built around a series of four culs-
de-sac off a single street and including a set of
tennis courts and playground, the Beaumont
Estate of 70 houses was to be, according to its
promoters, 'the most up-to-date and
picturesque estate in the Commonwealth'. The
estate displays the variety of styles available in
the mid-1930s: Tudor, Old English, Spanish
Mission, Modern, Modern Bungalow—all
designed by in-house designer, Edgar Gurney.

251

253

251 Woy Woy flats
7 Marine Parade, Elwood
1935-36 Mewton and Grounds
GC, V, NA

Woy Woy Flats are the stuccoed version of Geoffrey Mewton's nearby Bellaire Flats at 3 Cowderoy Street, St Kilda (1936). Those flats point to Mewton's interest in the work of Dutch architect Willem Dudok. By contrast, austerely functional with all ornament stripped away, the Woy Woy flats still evince a daring minimalism. The name of this pacesetting block of international style flats is its only flight of fancy.

252 Grainger Museum
University of Melbourne, Royal Parade, Parkville
1935-36 Gawler & Drummond
1938 Gawler & Drummond
GC, V, A

Designed for Percy Grainger (1882-1961), Australia's most notable composer and pianist, the Grainger Museum is a peculiar product of its idiosyncratic client. In 1933, Grainger proposed to the University of Melbourne that he fund the building of a museum to contain items about himself and that it would also chronicle Australia's musical achievements. The result is a curious building (often mistaken for a public convenience) constructed in glazed brick. The plan is like a half-spoked wheel with a central courtyard. One semi-circumambulates through the interior of bookcases, paintings and glass cases of memorabilia of a truly unique man devoted to conflicting extremes of experimental 'free music' and a Wagnerian spirit of Nordic purity.

253 Mercy Hospital
Grey Street, East Melbourne
1934-36 Stephenson & Meldrum
AC, V, A

The Mercy Hospital was designed shortly after the return of Arthur Stephenson (1890-1967) from his tour of American and European hospitals, during which he had been especially inspired by Alvar Aalto's Paimio Tuberculosis Sanatorium, Finland (1928-32). Stephenson's firm had already designed several hospitals in Melbourne, including St Vincent's Hospital, Victoria Parade (1933) and Jesse McPherson Maternity Hospital, William Street (1928)(demolished), but neither of these approached the sheer modernity of the Mercy. With its reinforced concrete structure, expressed escape stairs, broad sweeps of balconies and sparklingly clinical interiors, the Mercy was followed by a succession of hospitals (the Freemasons' Hospital, East Melbourne (1936), Bethesda Hospital, Richmond (1936), the Royal Melbourne Hospital **(273)** (1936-41) all designed in the uncompromising forms of the new functionalism.

254 Evan Price House
2 Riverview Road, Essendon
1935-36 Roy Grounds (Mewton & Grounds)
GC, V, NA

Built in cream brick, Melbourne's answer to the International Style's white stucco, the Evan Price House, is a convincing Modernist composition of interconnected cubic forms complete with the requisite metal corner and strip windows, flat concrete porch roof and roof terrace. The Price House joins the Watt House, Grosvenor Court, Toorak (1935; much altered) and the Ingpen House, Aphrasia Street, Newtown, Geelong (1936), as the last remaining houses by Grounds in this uncompromising style.

257

1B V2

255 Royal Australasian College of Surgeons

Spring Street, Melbourne
1935 Irwin & Stevenson
GC, V, A

Winner of the RVIA Street Architecture Medal
for 1937, the Royal Australasian College of
Surgeons is Melbourne's most convincing
example of Nordic Classicism, the restrained
idiom where abstracted classical forms are
combined with regional building materials such
as local bricks and roof forms determined by
local climate. The building's temple front, with
its square sectioned columns, its impossibly tall
entry doors and its stripped-back interior lobby
all contribute to a cool Teutonic elegance.

1A H6

256 Australasian Catholic Assurance Co Ltd Building

118–126 Queen Street, Melbourne
1935–36 Hennessy, Hennessy & Co in association
with R Morton Taylor
GC, V, A

Presenting one of Melbourne's most distinctive,
intact and late Jazz or Zig-Zag Moderne facades
to Queen Street, this rose pink building also
rewards visitors with its rear view of
accomplished cement-rendered styling in
horizontal Streamlined Moderne. Its facade
material was a challenge to the prevailing
popularity of faience for cladding commercial
buildings. In a remarkable commercial venture,
the Roman Catholic Diocese of Brisbane had
acquired, in the early 1930s, the rights to
manufacture the appropriately named 'Benedict
Stone', a concrete cladding block originally
developed in the United States in the 1920s
which could be produced in a variety of colours.

1A K3

257 Mitchell House

352-362 Lonsdale Street, Melbourne
1936 Harry Norris
GC, V, A

The commercial equivalent of Burnham Beeches
Mitchell House is Harry Norris's finest central
city design in the Streamlined Moderne style.
With its prominent corner siting and off-centre
vertical frame to emphasise its curved corner,
and its curlicued Art Deco wrought-iron gates,
Mitchell House is an exemplar for devotees of
the Moderne. Norris was a prolific designer of
1920s and 1930s commercial buildings such as
the Nicholas Building (1926–27) **(211)**, Majorca
House (1928–29) **(223)**, Kellow-Falkiner Car
Showroom, South Yarra (1928) and Melford
Motors, Queensberry and Elizabeth Streets.

●●●

Mitchell House is different from Harry Norris's
other near intact Moderne work in central
Melbourne; the almost cubist and faience-clad
Carlow House, 34–36 Elizabeth Street (1938),
with its emphasised horizontality to the north
contrasting with the vertical strip glazing to
Elizabeth Street.

59 C4

258 Former Dr Boyd Graham House

68 Hopetoun Road, Toorak
1936 A Mortimer McMillan
1994 *Synman Justin and Bialek (restoration)*
GC, V, NA

A rare example of the stripped forms of 1920s
European Modernism, widely known as the
International style, this house was described in
Australian Home Beautiful in March 1936 as:
'Conspicuously placed, ultra modern in style,
and with the cement rendering tinted to a
decided pink, the building has been angled to
take as great advantage as possible of sunlight
and air'.

260

58 D8

59 The Astor Theatre
Chapel Street, St Kilda
1936 R. Morton Taylor
GC, V, A

complete with its original illuminated sign and
substantially intact, the Astor is one of
Melbourne's most loved movie house interiors,
sometime location of the Melbourne Film
Festival and also one its best (if restrained)
examples of a Moderne styled cinema. Designed
by R Morton Taylor, formerly of the firm of
cinema architects Bohringer Taylor and Johnson,
designers of the State Theatre (1928) **(218)**, the
Astor is part of the boom in the cinema building
across Australia during the 1920s and 1930s.
Externally the bulky brick volume of the building
is divided into two parts, the smaller section
indicating the main entrance foyer which has a
marvellous elliptical cutout to the lounge above.
The larger mass contains the auditorium with
shops externally at ground level (which are
period pieces in themselves in terms of glazing,
tiles and shopfront finishes). Tiered ceilings with
concealed indirect lighting appear throughout.
Light fittings and furniture also date from the
period. Another cinema of similar pedigree is H
Vivian Taylor and Soilleux's Rivoli Cinema, 196-
200 Riversdale Road, Camberwell (1940).

67 B2

260 Windermere Flats
49 The Broadway, Elwood
1936 architect unknown
GC, V, NA

One of the best examples of Streamlined
Moderne flats in Melbourne, Windermere's front
elevation is a tour-de-force of aerodynamic
composition inspired by the likes of American
industrial designers Raymond Loewy and
Norman Bel Geddes. With its Buck Rogers
balconette, curved cantilevering corners,

projecting planter box, and incised linear
decoration, the block of flats suggests that it is
about to move. St. Kilda/Elwood/Brighton are
rich in Moderne style apartments including WH
Merritt's Valma, Victoria Street, St. Kilda (1936);
SJ Hall's Del Marie, St. Leonard's Avenue, St.
Kilda (1936) and IG Anderson's Ostende,
Seacombe Grove, Brighton (1937) which has
boatsheds opening directly onto the sand.

290 D4

261 Former Sanitarium Health Foods Factory
Warburton Highway, Warburton
1936-39 Edward Fielder Billson
GC, V, NA

Yet another major modern building in
Melbourne that owed a visual debt to Dutch
Modernism and a recipient of an RVIA Street
Architecture Medal (1940), this is an exemplar
of the combined horizontal and vertical
composition of interlocking cream brick
geometric forms. Its aspirations towards pure
functionalism are made ever more clear with
the unbroken expanses of steel-framed glazing
and portholes windows — this is a ship designed
for industry. It was to provide a model for much
postwar industrial and commercial architecture.
Next door to Sanitarium, the Signs Publishing
Co. Building (1936-37) also by Billson, is
another accomplished tribute to Dudok.

262

262 Heidelberg Municipal Offices and Town Hall

253-277 Upper Heidelberg Road, Ivanhoe
1936-37 Peck and Kemter in association with
AC Leith & Associates
GC, V, A

A monumental structure owing much to Dutch architect Willem Dudok's Hilversum Town Hall (1927-31), the Heidelberg building was much more massive and more formally designed. The entry feature, like the Second Church of Christ Scientist in Camberwell **(247)**, was an abstracted temple front with flanking brick pavilions, and the corners of each of the cubic volumes of brickwork had incised brick quoin rustication—an allusion to classically composed form. While the tower design was an assured Dudokian composition, the rest of the building is a hybrid Modern/Moderne design—a free and overall picturesque disposition of symmetrically composed volumes. There have been extensive internal alterations, but most have been sympathetic. The architectural profession approved of this massive pile and awarded it the RVIA Street Architecture Medal for 1939.

263 Denby Dale

424 Glenferrie Road, Kooyong
1937 Robert Bell Hamilton and Marcus Norris
GC, V, NA

Denby Dale is the apotheosis of Old English/ Tudor style garden court apartment design in the 1930s. Designed to appear like a single, spreading English country house with a sweeping drive and rustic pergolas, the complex in fact contains 12 flats in three blocks. Hamilton, a devotee of the Arts and Crafts who was to become a Liberal member of the Victorian Parliament and effectively quashed the prefabricated Beaufort House scheme **(290)**, was a noted designer of Tudor style houses and apartments in the leafy Melbourne suburbs most likely to evoke memories of 'back home'. While Arthur Plaisted's Hartpury Court (1923) **(193)** is one of the earliest designs in this idiom, Denby Dale is the most generous in terms of site, appearance and accommodation. Trademark features of this style include the clinker bricks, massive tall chimneys, steep roofs of terracotta shingles, half-timbering to gables, leaded glazing and wrought-iron lamps and weathercocks.

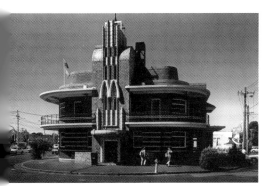

264

265

2C H1

264 Former United Kingdom Hotel
Queens Parade and Dummett Crescent,
Clifton Hill
1937-38
GC, V, A

This former hotel, at its prominent corner site, is a Moderne landmark. The sculptural building up of cubic forms and fins in glazed terracotta tile is the building's most dominant feature. It is a dynamic sign. By contrast, the hipped roofs, terracotta tiles, domestic-scaled windows and frosted glass temper the building's smartness. This 1930s watering hole (now a fast food outlet), with its hose-down external walls, was a new building rather than, as was usual in 1930s Melbourne, the Moderne makeover of a 19th-century pub.

1A J9

265 Alkira House
18 Queen Street, Melbourne
1936-37 JH Wardrop
GC, V, NA

The tall, narrow facade of Alkira House presents the materials, colours and composition of the Moderne. Green faience tiles in the spandrels, black faience tiles elsewhere that appear shiny and streamlined, steel-framed windows and glass blocks are composed into a vertically emphasised abstract design. The central element of the facade culminates in a crystalline grouping of fins, as if the building were an enlarged Bakelite radiogram or ebony and jade brooch. If there is a case for describing buildings as urban jewellery, then Alkira House fits such a description. The designer, JH Wardrop, was a principal of the architectural firm responsible for Melbourne's most convincing example of 1920s Greek Revival, the Shrine of Remembrance **(217)**.

2B D11

266 Royal Melbourne Regiment, 6th Battalion Drill Hall
49-53 Victoria Street, Melbourne
1937 George H Hallendal, designer
Horace J McKennal, Chief Architect
Commonwealth Department of Works
AC, V, NA

The Royal Melbourne Regiment's 6th Battalion Drill Hall has a severe Moderne-styled temple front. With columns that are streamlined, weapon-like vertical fins, this building attempts to bring the armed forces architecturally up to date, but remains strictly within conventional limits with allusions to a classical past—a common theme of the 1930s not just in Melbourne, but also in Europe and the United States. Relief is given by continuous bands of cream brick running around the whole building, and fine Deco-styled metal curlicues to grilles, doors and vents. Another drill hall (1938) by the same designer, can be seen at the corner of William and A'Beckett Streets.

45 C10

267 Glenferrie Sports Ground Grandstand
Linda Crescent, Hawthorn
1938 Stuart P Calder in association
with Marsh & Michaelson
GC, V, A

A practical sculpture of curved Moderne forms, this grandstand makes great use of its required curved plan to arrive at a dynamic three-dimensional composition. A daring cantilevering canopy sweeps horizontally away from the obligatory vertical termination of flagpole and tower. The impressive composition recalls Angiolo Mazzoni's similarly styled service buildings in Italy at Florence Railway Station. The Glenferrie Grandstand is, together with the McPherson's Building, Stuart Calder's other highly notable contribution to the Moderne.

147

268

27

1B L8

268 Former Royal Banking Chambers
287–301 Collins Street, Melbourne
1939–41 Stephenson & Turner
GC, V, A

A blend of stripped Classicism and the Streamlined Moderne, the former Royal Banking Chambers is a perfect example of 1930s architects attempting to insert new architectural forms discreetly into an existing streetscape. Even the all-glass cornice-level restaurant attributed to Frederick Romberg, who was working within the Stephenson and Turner office at the time, is an elegant termination of the parapet of this stylish modernised palazzo. The polished stone podium, entry portals and stairwell interior to Collins Street are particularly fine examples of Moderne detailing. Inside, the banking chamber tellers were not housed behind bars, but stood for the first time giving customers counter-type service.

2B E12

269 Buildings 5, 6, 7 & 9
RMIT, Bowen Street, Melbourne
1937–38 Building 5 & 9 Percy Everett (PWD)
1948 Building 7 Percy Everett (PWD)
1955 Building 6
GC, V, A

Constructed over more than15 years, these buildings are unified by their consistent architectural style: the horizontal Streamlined Moderne. Continuous bands of brown manganese brick spandrel panels separated by bands of uninterrupted glazing (except at vertically marked entry points) emphasise horizontality. Buildings 5, 7 and 9 in fact form a continuous facade. They epitomise Percy Everett's favoured idiom for technical schools. The basements of Buildings 5 and 9 were enlarged during World War II and used for defence training.

1A G7

270 FAI Insurance Building
412 Collins Street, Melbourne
1941 Percy Everett (PWD)
GC, V, A

A late Moderne piece designed by Percy Everett for the State Accident Insurance Office, this building is distinguished by its green and white faience cladding, its bay windows which curve in a reverse bow out from the facade, and its interpretive copper shop window and glazed entry joinery added in the 1980s. The building's flagpole completes this Moderne intrusion into Collins Street's financial heart—one of the last city buildings completed before World War II effectively halted commercial office building for nearly seven years.

56 H3

271 Housing Commission Estate
Garden City, the area bounded by Williamstown Road, Todd Road, The Boulevard, Barak Road and Howe Parade
1938- Architects' Panel, Housing Commission of Victoria
AC, V, NA

In 1938, the first major scheme of the new Housing Commission of Victoria (HCV) was at Fishermens Bend in Port Melbourne. An estate of detached and semi-detached houses was laid out according to the garden suburb principles of Ebenezer Howard. Included in the estate were parks, shopping centre, community centre and preschool facilities. The urban impact of these humbly formed houses and the humanistic garden layout has been underestimated— overshadowed by the vilified high-rise housing schemes of later decades. Pre-war Melbourne estates included Ashburton, Coburg, Oakleigh and North Williamstown. Today, the houses at Fishermens Bend are mostly privately owned.

272

274

1B N7

72 Century Building

25-133 Swanston Street, Melbourne
938-40 Marcus R Barlow
C, V, A

ne Century Building is Marcus Barlow's vertical
treamlined Moderne updating of his Modern
othic Manchester Unity Building **(231)** on the
ext corner, completed six years earlier. With its
ostracted corner tower, uninterrupted vertical
ns and boldly horizontal and stepping stream-
ned canopy (the soffit is particularly notable),
ne limit-height Century Building is smartly
Moderne. Common to both buildings, however,
as the external cladding material: faience-
lazed terracotta tiles, which Barlow used
equently as they provided a permanent and
mpervious finish. Wunderlich Limited,
roducers of faience, used the Century Building
n their advertisements, saying of it: '[it] gives
permanent freshness and sparkle to this fine
uilding. Window spandrels are in hand
moulded terracotta glazed neutral grey to
chieve an arresting architectural contrast'.

2B B7

273 Royal Melbourne Hospital

132 Grattan Street, Parkville
1936-41 Stephenson and Meldrum (later
Stephenson and Turner) in association
with WAM Blackett
1990- Daryl Jackson Pty Ltd
refurbishment & additions)
GC, V, A

Designed principally under the direction of
Arthur George Stephenson, who went on to
receive an RIBA Gold Medal in 1954 for his
contribution to hospital design, the Royal
Melbourne Hospital is Melbourne's largest
monument to interwar International Modernism.
Almost as soon as the building was completed,
t was occupied by the US government and

equipped and used as a military hospital during
World War II. The original northern facade, with
its broad cantilevering balconies at each floor
painted white and contrasting with the orange
brick behind, was the building's most striking
visual note. Additions all around the original
building have lessened its landmark siting. While
compromised by this plethora of (albeit
sympathetically designed) additions, one can
still discover 1930s elements, both internal and
external, and read the health and hygiene
message in the stripped back surfaces of this
functionalist design.

2B F12

274 Russell Street Police Headquarters

354 Russell Street, Melbourne
1940-43 Percy Everett (PWD)
AC, V, NA

Located next door to the 1888 Italianate Police
Barracks, the Russell Street Police Headquarters
is the central city's most obvious landmark to
Percy Everett's career as Chief Architect within
the Public Works Department. A Beaux Arts–
influenced skyscraper of emphasised vertical
orange brick panels and a stepped tower form,
this ode to Gotham City was further linked to its
New York counterparts with a steel-framed
communications tower. Associated for decades
with TV police dramas such as 'Homicide' and
the symbolic home of Victoria's police force, as
well as the site of the infamous Russell Street
bombing of 1986, this monument to the
Moderne is now vacant.

1940 A human skull, estimated to
be 13,000 years old, is found near
Melbourne

1940 Prime Minister Robert
Menzies places a ban on the
Communist Party

275

27

275 Brunswick Fire Station & Flats
24 Blyth Street, Brunswick
1937–38 Seabrook and Fildes
GC, V, NA

The Brunswick Fire Station and flats is one
of 12 metropolitan fire stations designed by
Seabrook and Fildes. With a father who
happened to be Chairman of the Metropolitan
Fire Brigade (MFB), Norman Seabrook took
advantage of this good connection to transform
the MFB's architectural profile completely—from
polite domestic Georgian Revival to
uncompromising European Modernism,
specifically the de-Stijl Modernism of Dutch
architect Willem Dudok. The bold, horizontal
glazing counterpointed by vertical elements
such as the flagpole and vertical slit stair
windows and the simply modelled prismatic
forms became part of the new vocabulary for
the MFB. Brunswick was special because of the
layout of separate station and offices with
(originally) two detached blocks of flats for
firemen and families behind. This allowed
garden courtyard spaces between and northern
orientation for all the flats. In overall massing
and precinct planning, the complex refers to the
most advanced urban planning ideas then being
employed in Europe.

•••

The use of large areas of cream brick, a typical
feature of modern buildings in the 1930s also
has a special meaning in Brunswick, as the
cream brick was first developed by Brunswick
brickmaker John Glew some 80 years earlier
and was used as a design feature of several
notable buildings in the locality from as early
as the 1860s.

Trust News, February 1995

276 Moonbria Flats
Mathoura Road, Toorak
1941 Roy Grounds
GC, V, A

One of the important series of apartment
buildings completed by Roy Grounds (1905–81)
between 1939 and 1942, Moonbria is
distinguished from the others by its possession
of an elevator (which is circular, hence the
glazed tower) and its neat disposal of car
parking beneath its cream brick mass. From the
street, one doesn't realise that the plan of
Moonbria is in fact a U-shape with a courtyard
to the north. At the upper levels, the north-
facing access balconies (with balustrades topped
with Swedish blue tiles) are extremely wide—big
enough to serve as outdoor living rooms.
Balancing the cylindrical tower on Mathoura
Road is a corkscrew reinforced concrete stair at
the east end of the block.

•••

In addition to Moonbria, Grounds's other
important apartments from this period include:
Clendon (1939–40) and Clendon Corner
(1940–41), 13–15 Clendon Road, Armadale; and
Quamby, 3 Glover Court Toorak (1941–42). Each
block is slightly different and comprises a simple
set of geometric forms and a common set of
architectural elements. They reflects Grounds's
new interest in contemporary Scandinavian
housing design and the work of Australian
expatriate architect Raymond McGrath.
Clendon's eight flats are planned in a U-shape
around a court; Clendon Corner's six flats are
arranged along an external breezeway; while
Quamby's six flats and one maisonette are
arranged in a fan shape set out from the centre
of a cul-de-sac.

277

279

59 A7	2L A8

277 Glenunga Flats

Horsburgh Grove, Armadale
1940-41 Romberg and Shaw
GC, V, NA

The design of Glenunga does not conform to commonly held notions of the stripped white abstract forms of the so-called International Style. Instead, it is a complex hybrid of folk-inspired *heimatstil* elements such as the rubble rock chimneys, obvious domestic elements such as window blinds and timber-framed roofs with projecting rafters combined with conventional brick construction and elements of the new functionalist architecture from Europe: cantilevered balconies, pipe steel handrails, porthole windows and generous areas of glass. Of special note at Glenunga are the angled glass bays which echo Romberg's admiration of Alvar Aalto's Villa Mairea, Finland (1937–38).

75A G9

278 Chemistry Building

Masson Road, University of Melbourne, Parkville
1938 Percy Everett (PWD)
1963 Stephenson and Turner (east addition)
1970-71 JFD Scarborough & Partners (penthouse laboratory)
GC, V, A

One of Percy Everett's most accomplished designs in Collegiate Gothic style, the Chemistry Building demonstrates Everett's skill in asymmetrical block composition, brickwork detailing and precinct planning. It has been given a massing evocative of Dudok's Dutch modern work, detailing that echoes the Griffins' innovative rotating of the square pier to explore diamond forms at Newman College, and a layering of stone dressings and foliated decoration that pays tribute to the Gothic pedigree of the university's original quadrangle buildings. It is an effective hybrid.

279 Newburn Flats

30 Queens Road, Melbourne
1939-42 Romberg and Shaw
GC, V, NA

Designed by Frederick Romberg (1913-1992) and Mary Turner Shaw (1906-1990), Newburn is one of the finest contributions to the emergence of European Modernism in Australian architecture. Built in off-form reinforced concrete (the impression of the square steel forms are visible beneath the paintwork), the north face of this linear block of apartments has a serrated edge to give each apartment a view and a degree of privacy. Each flat has a balcony whose outside edge has been formed using corrugated iron as formwork. At the front of the block, larger apartments are separated from the linear block by a stairwell and a full height steel-framed glazed wall. A former highlight of this wall flanking the stairwell and visible from Queens Road was a giant painted sundial executed by emigre artist Gerhart Selheim. Selheim had also painted aboriginal motifs outside the front doors of each apartment. These have all since been painted over. This north face was further enlivened by gold canvas blinds, balcony soffits painted light blue and vermilion painted steel glazing. A rooftop pergola at the front of Newburn was glazed in by Romberg to become a penthouse apartment and office. On the south face, open cantilevered balconies recall Cairo flats (where Romberg lived while designing Newburn) and at the very rear of the block there is a tiny caretakers' flat, shop (which still operates) and garages for residents. Newburn is one of a series of important prewar buildings designed by Frederick Romberg in association with Mary Turner Shaw, both former employees within the Stephenson and Turner office.

1945–1955

For just £5, prospective home-owners could purchase working drawings for an architect-designed house.

Between 1945 and 1950, there was a dire shortage of houses in Melbourne. Returning to normal life after six uncertain years of war, Australians were encouraged to repopulate and thus rehouse the nation. In Melbourne's outer eastern suburbs of Balwyn, Box Hill, Blackburn and Ringwood, and along Port Phillip Bay from Beaumaris southwards, new austere brick and timber versions of pre-war bungalows appeared. Some were jerry built. Some were part of developer AV Jennings's re-emergence as the nation's biggest homebuilder. There was also a sprinkling of flat-roofed architect-designed houses. All of these houses were subject to size restrictions (generally 12–14 squares) and had been since 1940. The standard postwar house was an unlovely thing. In numbers, they became the bleak setting for George Johnston's *My Brother Jack* (1964) and the target of ambivalent satire for Melbourne's most celebrated dame, Edna Everage.

One government strategy to increase housing numbers was to encourage prefabricated housing programs such as the steel-framed and sheeted **Beaufort House** scheme (1948), which made use of redundant wartime industries, new technologies and industrial production. The schemes were branded socialistic in intent by their detractors and the enthusiasm for prefabrication was shortlived but more significant in planned townships outside Melbourne such as Eildon for the State Rivers and Water Supply Commission and Mt Beauty for the State Electricity Commission's Kiewa Hydro-Electric Power Scheme.

The Royal Victorian Institute of Architects (RVIA) focused their efforts on improving the design quality of postwar houses. The RVIA Small Homes Service began in July 1947, as a joint initiative with the *Age* newspaper. Its first director was architect Robin Boyd (1919–71), who had just completed his first house, the **Pettigrew House**, Kew (1946) and was about to publish *Victorian Modern* (1947), the first history of modern architecture in Victoria. For just £5, prospective home-owners could purchase sketch plans, working drawings and specifications for a new architect-designed house. Publicising the service and the cause of modern architecture with a weekly newspaper column, Boyd soon became a household name. In 1953, directorship was handed onto Neil Clerehan and the promotion of modestly progressive planned houses continued to make minor inroads into

Melbourne's sprawl.

Shortages of conventional building materials such as bricks and terracotta roofing tiles meant that some designers turned to alternative construction methods. In the hills of Eltham and Warrandyte, mud cost nothing. Builder–designer Alistair Knox perfected mud-brick construction in the **Busst House**, Eltham 1948–49), continuing a regional building tradition pioneered at Montsalvat (1935) and by local residents such as John Harcourt. Amongst the artistic and literary community in the bush, the participatory hands-on nature of mud-brick construction evoked the noble ideals of the Arts and Crafts movement. By contrast, recently graduated architects such as Kevin Borland experimented with sprayed concrete and hessian in the **Rice House**, Eltham (1951), while husband and wife team's **Peter and Dione McIntyre House** (1955) employed steel angles and Stramit (compressed straw) board infill panels. The result was a dramatic elevated and cantilevered house on the Yarra River at Kew. It was these latter so-called structural–functional experiments of engineering that drew national attention.

Other Melbourne architects were also turning to alternative design methods. Chief among them was Roy Grounds, who from 1950 designed a series of houses with pure geometric plan shapes. The plan of the **Henty House**, Frankston (1950), was a perfect circle, while the plan of his own **Grounds House**, Toorak (1953), was a perfect square with a circular courtyard. Other architects looked to overseas heroes for inspiration. On the Mornington Peninsula, the spreading plans and low-pitched gable roofs of Chancellor and Patrick were assured local interpretations of Frank Lloyd Wright, the Griffins and Richard Neutra. Harry Seidler's arrival in Sydney had immediate effect. As learnt from his Harvard mentors Marcel Breuer and Walter Gropius, Seidler's white, cubic East Coast International style forms as built at Turramurra were transferred to Melbourne in the **Keith Mann House**, Balwyn (1954) and in numerous other houses by architects such as Ray Berg, Douglas Alexandra, Kevin Borland and Robin Boyd.

While there had been a few notable blocks of postwar high-rise flats built such as the reinforced concrete **Stanhill**, South Melbourne (1945–50), and **Caringal**, Toorak (1948–51), by 1952 the theme of the single family house in Melbourne's architectural culture held pre-eminent sway. Robin Boyd, in his seminal text *Australia's Home* (1952), was to say 'Australia is the small house' and, in doing so, he seemed to cast progress in the next four decades of Australian architecture solely within the realm of domestic design.

But there were other equally significant architectural activities under way. While building in the central city was certainly slow to recover and Melbourne's streets indeed appeared as grim as John Brack's *Collins Street, 5 p.m.* (1955), the announcement in 1948 that Melbourne had won the right to stage the 1956 Olympic Games began a minor flurry of building activity. The Olympic Village

(1953–56) built at Heidelberg West became a controversial site amidst Housing Commission houses not yet completed. In the city, the Graham Hotel, Swanston Street (1954), and **Hosies Hotel,** Flinders Street (1954), were direct outcomes of the need for new tourist accommodation for overseas visitors. A small number of limit-height (40 metres) office buildings were built. **Gilbert Court**, Collins Street (1954) was the first high-rise glass box in the city – and one of the earliest in Australia. The Melbourne City Council enthusiastically continued with 1920s delusions that to modernise Melbourne meant the removal of 19th-century cast-iron posted verandas

R160 armchair, c. 1951, designed by Grant Featherston (SOURCE: Featherston Chairs)

and their replacement with cantilevered awnings. There were competitions for new sporting stadia, chief among them being one for the main Olympic stadium at Princes Park, which was subsequently shelved in favour of upgrading the existing Melbourne Cricket Ground. The most important design competition (1952) was for the **Olympic Swimming Stadium** (1953–56), a building which came to symbolise Melbourne's coming of age in architectural engineering.

There was also great activity in Victoria's long-range development plans for postwar industry and education. In Dandenong, new factories for Heinz Foods, International Harvester and most important of all, the vast **General Motors Holden** plant (1955–56) signalled enthusiasm for the United States not just in terms of consumable products, but also in architectural ideas. At the University of Melbourne, **Wilson Hall** (1952–56) and the **Beaurepaire Centre** (1953–56) signalled institutional moves away from Percy Everett's Collegiate Gothic and towards external architectural consultants and crafted International Modernism which included commissioned artworks by artists Leonard French, Tom Bass and Douglas Annand. Everett and the PWD, meanwhile, were preoccupied with **Upwey Primary** (1945) and Red Hill Consolidated schools (1951) and the perfection of the LTC prototype that would be used statewide throughout the 1950s and 1960s as the standard school type.

Massive postwar immigration from Europe to Australia enabled the first espresso bars to be seen at the top end of Bourke Street. A new continental flavour in the social mix was a tonic to the essentially drab Anglo-centric culture that was Melbourne in the late 1940s. Melbourne experienced a dramatic influx of migrants from Greece and Italy, displaced persons from the Baltic States and Jewish refugees such as Prague architect Ernest Milston, who contributed one of the very few significant pieces of postwar urban design, the cross-shaped **Memorial Forecourt** (1950–54) in front of the Shrine of Remembrance, and Viennese architect and urbanist Dr Ernest Fooks, who wrote *X-Ray the City* (1946), urging a thorough survey of Melbourne's metropolitan area as the basis from which to plan seriously for a postwar future.

Large-scale plans were indeed being made for Melbourne. In 1954, the Melbourne Metropolitan Board of Works (MMBW) released its masterplan for Melbourne, which had been in the making since 1948. A landmark planning scheme which planted the seeds for future sites such as the **National Gallery of Victoria**, a ring road for Melbourne and future roofing of the Jolimont railyards, its breadth of scope from an institution that was for the most part responsible for the removal of Melbourne's sewage was remarkable. It included plans to turn the space in front of Parliament House into a massive city square and hinted at transport links such as freeway underpasses and the idea of a city as a multi-level functioning organism. The **Degraves Street pedestrian underpass** (1955–56) was a diminutive indicator of a future Melbourne rationalised by circulation. In construction terms, a change in building regulations showed a hint of Melbourne's future. In July 1955, permission was granted for **ICI House**, East Melbourne (1955–58), which exceeded the 132-foot height limit, with the provision of an open garden plaza at ground level to compensate for its increase in height. Melbourne had been an urbane metropolitan street city from the 1860s to the mid-1950s, structured largely throughout that time by its legacy of 19th-century public buildings, grid plan and the distant axially connected Shrine of Remembrance. In the 1960s, as Melbourne become a skyscraper city, all that would change.

PHILIP GOAD

Sketch: Olympic Swimming Stadium (1953 - 56)

280 Stanhill

34 Queens Road, Melbourne
1945–50 Frederick Romberg
GC, V, A

Stanhill is the largest of the distinguished series of apartment buildings designed by Romberg before entering into partnership with Roy Grounds and Robin Boyd in 1953. Generally regarded as the masterpiece of Romberg's career, Stanhill is a compositional tour-de-force in reinforced concrete. As one moves around this building which has been massed like an oceanliner, each facade reveals a different and accomplished amalgamation of International Modern motifs. Designed in the early 1940s, Stanhill's construction dragged over five years due to postwar labour, material and financial shortages. Its critical reception, once complete, was mixed. The student broadsheet *Smudges* gave it a 'Blot of the Month', suspecting its busy, sculptural appearance. Historians have since hailed Stanhill as a landmark of postwar International Modernism in Australia which recalls the work of German Expressionist architect Erich Mendelsohn, but the building's formal pedigree is far more complex. One must admit influence from the humanistic modernisms of Finnish architect Alvar Aalto and Austrian Josef Frank, and the fenestration of Le Corbusier's Porte-Molitor apartments, Paris, and Romberg's early training under Otto Salvisberg (an expert in reinforced concrete design), and also Romberg's experience, albeit brief, within the office of Stephenson and Turner, whose hospitals included generous cantilevered balconies and the extensive use of reinforced concrete. A streamlined Moderne front with cantilevered balconies to the north and a fully glazed facade to the south suggest a blend of 1930s functionalist architecture with the commercial Moderne. When viewed from the south, given the domestic-scaled railings and the different scales and textures of window treatment, the building is at its most sculptural, revealing Romberg's *heimatstil* (folkloric) interests which combine with his use of that most modern of building materials, reinforced concrete.

•••

Stanhill's formal opposite, at a completely different scale (though commissoned by the same developer, Stanley Korman), was Hilstan, Nepean Highway, Brighton (1950). A series of cube-like two-storey blocks from the road appeared as free-standing modern townhouses, but all were in fact connected at the rear by a linear slab with garages below grade. This innovative Romberg design was demolished in the 1970s.

280

281 Pettigrew House

71 Redmond Street, Kew
1946 Robin Boyd, Boyd Pethebridge & Bell
1951 Pethebridge & Bell (first-floor additions)
GC, V, NA

From a partnership between 1945 and 1947 only three Pethebridge and Bell designs out of twenty-three commissions were constructed: the Pettigrew House; Boyd's own home, 666 Riversdale Road, Camberwell (1946–47; 1951 additions); and the Dainty Shoe Co. Factory, Church Street, Hawthorn (1947). The Pettigrew House had an L-shaped plan with zoned living and sleeping wings, with banks of French doors to the north and east opening up to the garden. The two zoned blocks interlocked, the roof of one continuing on to become the carport. While Conrad Hamann suggests that this first completed residential commission by Boyd refers to 'Roy Grounds's pre-war work in its elevations', the house owes more to Frank Lloyd Wright's ideas for an ideal house in the suburbs, his 1930s Usonian houses. Wide oversailing eaves, blank wall and carport to the street, flat roof hovering above a horizontal strip window, block chimney, repetitive vertical window break-up and an overall emphasis on horizontality confirm this. Pethebridge and Bell's first-floor additions (1951) accentuated the two-wing composition and retained the original 1946 fence design of spaced white painted horizontal timber boards. In 1947, Robin Boyd wrote *Victorian Modern*, the first history of modern architecture in Victoria. The Pettigrew House was featured in it.

282 Upwey Primary School

15 Darling Avenue, Upwey
1945 Percy Everett (PWD)
GC, V, A

Upwey Primary School, with its layered flat roofs, bold projecting eave pergolas and random rock base, demonstrates the influence of the Griffins' Prairie style buildings combined with Everett's own skill in cubic massing. This school together with the polygonal classroom plan at Red Hill Consolidated School (1951) and reinforced concrete Windsor Girls High School (1948) are part of an underestimated contribution by Everett to educational architecture in Victoria.

283 Ascot Estate, Housing Commission of Victoria

Epsom and Union Roads, Ascot Vale
1948 Architects' Panel, Housing Commission of Victoria (Best Overend)
GC, V, A

A complex of low-rise walk-up flats, the Ascot Estate represents the social realist design approach of the Housing Commission of Victoria's Architects Panel before their embrace of precast concrete construction for houses and apartment towers in the late 1950s. Small-scale communal and green spaces and a mix of gable and flat-roofed blocks were part of a humble and pragmatic approach to subsidised housing, demonstrating Overend's interest in finding a humanistic basis to the provision of *existenz-minimum* living.

284

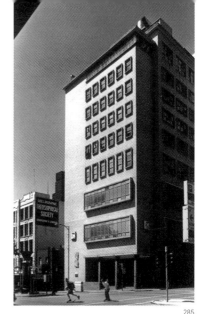

285

284 Caringal Flats

3 Tahara Road, Toorak
1948–51 JW Rivett
GC, V, NA

A strangely luxurious composition in terms of site coverage, Caringal exhibits a rigorously stripped aesthetic that 1950s architects associated with the most progressive work of the 1930s. Built in two stages, the first was the gently curved three-level block with full-height glazed walls on the upper two floors. The second stage was the six-storey point tower. A folding wall between bedroom, living room and sunroom opened up to provide one rectangular living space. JW Rivett, Caringal's designer, had a fetish for technology, which is evident in the construction and servicing of the buildings. Steel forms were used for the walls and, in an experiment which terrified engineer John Connell, who worked on its structural design, 1-inch diameter drawn steel tubes in the floor slabs acted as both structural steel reinforcing and heating and cooling coils!

Below: Plan of Caringal Flats (1948–51)

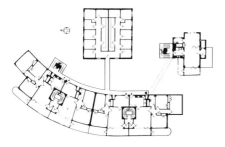

285 Russell Street Telephone Exchange and Post Office

114–120 Russell Street, Melbourne
1948–54 Commonwealth Dept. of Works
Hammond and Allan (bas-relief sculpture)
AC, V, NA

The first postwar government building of any size completed after 1945, the Russell Street Telephone Exchange and Post Office marks a crucial stylistic shift between pre- and postwar attitudes to the metropolitan public building. Construction took five years, with the result that its interlocking cubic design, projecting glazed panels and cream brick appeared dated when it was finally completed in 1954. Another exchange at 378 Flinders Lane (1952–54) follows a similar compositional palette. Unusually, the Russell Street building combined a postal hall (since closed) at ground level, the interior design of which echoed 1930s Italian Modernism. A dashing striped floor and outside smart metal grill work, stainless steel telephone booths (since removed), three massive pink granite stylised Doric columns and a bas-relief sculpture mounted on the cream brick wall above the footpath were mannered ornamental inclusions beneath large first- and second-floor glazed panels that, in functionalist fashion, revealed the machinery of the exchange within. As the exchange is located on Russell Hill, in 1956 the building gained special status by briefly serving as a relay station for newly arrived television.

286

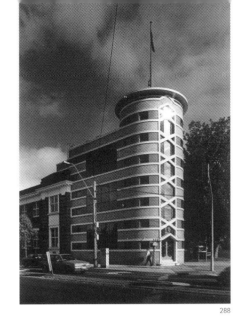

288

| 75A F5 | 68 G1 |

286 Babel Building

Professors Walk, University of Melbourne, Parkville
1948, 1957 Godfrey Spowers Hughes Mewton
and Lobb
GC, V, A

With an entirely appropriate name for a structure devoted to the teaching of languages, the Babel Building is a masterful composition of interlocking cream brick forms. After returning from Europe in 1932 and during his partnership with Roy Grounds (1933–37), architect Geoffrey Mewton consistently put building forms together inspired by Russian Constructivist Iakov Chernikov and Dutch architect Willem Dudok. The Babel Building is the largest of these designs and one of the University of Melbourne's most convincing examples of the functionalist idiom. It met with early controversy, however, with a sculptural tableau on its north side being removed after being considered by university authorities as unsuitable for general viewing.

2L B7

287 Sheridan Close

485–489 St Kilda Road, Melbourne
1950 Bernard Evans
GC, V, NA

With its generously glazed and serrated side elevations (to give each flat a view, however narrowly focused, of St Kilda Road), its faux Regency porch of white, rendered cement columns and its concave brick facade with Georgian-proportioned windows, Sheridan Close is a stylistic hybrid. Its architect Bernard Evans, an avid developer, became Melbourne's Lord Mayor. The apartments at Sheridan Close, the formal impurities of which were at the time a clear flaunting of contemporary architectural tastes, are rare survivors from the single family house period.

288 Former Caulfield Institute of Technology

Dandenong Road and Sir John Monash Drive,
Caulfield East
1950 Percy Everett (PWD)
GC, V, A

Owing much to Dutch Modernist JJP Oud's Shell Building, The Hague (1938–42), Percy Everett's design falls within his 'buildings for trades' idiom, a functionalist style of banks of industrial steel glazing separated by horizontal brick strips for the main mass of the building with articulated and vertical emphasis at each entry point. Like his Essendon (1938–39) and Oakleigh Technical Schools (1938) and Buildings 5, 6, 7 and 9 at RMIT (1938–55) **(269)** this building, at the risk of appearing dated even in 1950, blends its homage to Dutch Modernism with an earlier model of industrial architecture, Walter Gropius and Adolf Meyer's Fagus Shoe Last Factory at Alfeld-an-der-Leine, Germany (1910–11).

75 B6

289 Berneray (formerly Ventura), Miller–Short House

55 Mast Gully Road, Upwey
1948–49 Frederick Romberg
AC, NV, NA

Romberg's Miller-Short House is an extension of his prewar interests in texture and dynamic form-making. Sited on a steep hillside, the house is built off a huge retaining wall which forms the backbone of the house. A massive fireplace in local natural stone is the functional divider between the living and sleeping zones of the house, which are expressed on either side of the mass with simple skillion roofs which have generous overhangs and cutouts which form pergolas to a first-floor balcony. Another Romberg house design, 'St Quentin' (1940), can be seen nearby at 8 Sayers Road, Upwey.

290

29

29 B1

101 K5

290 Beaufort Prefabricated Steel House

19 Gallipoli Parade, Pascoe Vale South
1948 Arthur Baldwinson (Beaufort Division of the Department of Aircraft Production)
AC, V, NA

Conceived as a solution to postwar housing shortages, the Beaufort House was one of a series of prefabricated metal house designs developed after 1945. In 1946, the Beaufort Division of the Department of Aircraft Production conceived the Beaufort House, which was further developed through the Victorian Housing Commission. This house is one of a series built in Coburg/Pascoe Vale during the late 1940s, each designed with standard units that were faced in spot-welded sheet steel and bolted together using a frame of steel sections. The external wall panel sheeting was designed as a stressed skin which braced the entire structure, a construction technique derived from aircraft building.

•••

A Beaufort House prototype for public demonstration was erected in early June 1946 in the Treasury Gardens, Melbourne, and later removed. Other Beaufort Houses in Pascoe Vale can be seen at 17 Fontaine Street; 31 & 35 Gallipoli Parade; 16 Heliopolis Street; 17 & 27 Reynolds Parade; 15 & 21 Somali Street; 5, 11, 15, 19 Vaux Street; and 3, 9, 13 & 15 Moascar Street. A steel-framed but asbestos concrete-clad Myer House (1946) can be seen at the corner of Moreland Road and Johnson Street, Pascoe Vale South.

Below: First floor plan of Busst House (1948–49)

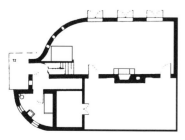

291 Henty House

581 Nepean Highway, Frankston
1950-53 Roy Grounds
BC, V, NA

Built below the first Henty House, Portland Lodge (235) also by Grounds), the second Henty House was a double-storey cylinder built on a sloping site overlooking Port Phillip Bay. At the centre of the circular plan (actually a 48-sided polygon), a brick cylinder housed the fireplace, an internal gutter for the inward sloping roof, a central core for services and the support for a slate-paved concrete spiral stair. Originally, the external vertical lining boards were treated and left to weather to a natural grey. Colours elsewhere were black with accents of white to the steel columns, window frames and balustrade. Bricks were local grey sand-lime. The house is a subtle blend of Grounds's interest at the time in Frank Lloyd Wright's obsession with primary geometries, William Wurster's restrained palette of colour and materials and, oddly enough, in spirit, Buckminster Fuller's Dymaxion House. Original sketch drawings show that the central chimney was to act like a mast with steel cables supporting the roof beams cantilevering from the centre. Now painted and partly obscured by a house in front, the Henty House awaits overdue and deserved restoration.

21 H4

292 Busst House

Cnr Diamond Street and 71 Silver Street, Eltham
1948-49 Alistair Knox (building designer)
AC, V, NA

Phyllis Busst, who had been a member of the Montsalvat colony, commissioned Knox to design a mud-brick house with a studio for a steeply sloping site. One enters the three-level house at mid-level, ascending to the bedroom and studio, or descending to the open living/dining/kitchen. From above, the house seems to be embedded into the slope, while the roof eaves slide gracefully around the corner. On the ground floor, a concrete slab was used, a rare use of such construction at a time of no ready-made concrete mixers. The heart of the house was a vast fireplace and ingle.

293

Alistair Knox built mud-brick houses in the Eltham–Warrandyte area for the next 40 years and became one of the leading figures of an environmental design tradition in Victoria. His house at 2 King Street, Eltham (1962–63), is a wonderful example. Knox was often aided by landscape designer Gordon Ford, whose own house at 141 Pitt Street, Eltham (1950–1980s), epitomises the bush house and garden design idiom that was to become popular in the 1960s and 1970s.

21 G4

293 Rice House
59 Ryans Road, Eltham
1951 Kevin Borland
AC, V, NA

Together with Robin Boyd's Wood House and Supermarket, cnr High Street Road and Cleveland Road, Jordanville (1952; much altered), the Rice House is thought to be one of the only two surviving examples in Victoria of Ctesiphon concrete construction. A novel means of experimenting with roof shape, the Ctesiphon Arch had been patented by local builders McDougall and Ireland. Constructed by forming timber arches at 1200-mm centres, with hessian suspended between and 75 mm of concrete sprayed over the top, the arches provided structural stability across the surface of the roof. The beauty of the technique was that a single structural element acted as both roof and walls. Inspired by a British journal article explaining the system, Kevin Borland told Boyd about it and experimented with it himself. Borland created a complex of spaces beneath four arches, a suspended catenary, arched, covered entryway and another separate, double-arched structure. This was radical new domestic architecture when it was thought that modern engineering could provide formal answers for a new postwar lifestyle.

294 Gillison House
Yarrbat Avenue and Kireep Road, Balwyn
1951 Robin Boyd
AC, V, NA

One of Robin Boyd's experiments in structural-functional design, the Gillison House demonstrates his attempts at finding alternatives to the typical timber stud structural frame and conventional sheeting materials. A facade of diagonally set windows sits between timber posts, thus providing bracing to the simple post-and-beam structure. The whole north face of the house is an emphatic open diagram of structure welcoming the sun. The plan is split into two functional zones by an open entrance court—living to the east and sleeping to the west. A circulation spine of stair, passage and storage space to each bedroom further splits the house into north–south zones—living and bedrooms to the north; garage, kitchen and utility to the south. Where the window wall was not expressed as a diagonal grille, walls were sheeted externally with painted asbestos cement panels (originally a deep navy blue) and internally with masonite, hardwood lining boards and a natural caneite ceiling—all part of Boyd's determinedly different palette for the everyday home.

Below: Plan of the Gillison House (1951)
SOURCE: Architecture and Arts, August 1954

295

295 Wilson Hall

Wilson Avenue, University of Melbourne, Parkville
1952-56 Bates Smart & McCutcheon; Douglas
Annand (mural); Tom Bass (bas-relief sculptures)
GC, V, A

Described by Robin Boyd as 'the crowning jewel of Australian Featurism', Wilson Hall is one of the most crafted and well-decorated box-buildings of the 1950s. The university community, devastated by the burning in 1952 of Joseph Reed's Gothic Revival Wilson Hall (1879), decided on modern architecture for their major space for orations, examinations and graduations. What arose through the designs of Osborn McCutcheon was a finely veneered interior with four different external facades.

Inside the foyer, a curved ceiling sweeps low overhead before one passes through a glass wall enhanced by an intricate mosaic by Douglas Annand. One then enters what Boyd described as 'the beautifully fitted jewel-box' of the hall's main volume. The ceiling is panelled with Swedish birch in an off-centred brickwork pattern which folds down the wall and floats above the floor where glazing to the west reveals the South Lawn. Ahead is a massive mural by Annand, a giant male nude reaching upward with his feet in intellectual clay ('elegant lobster salad' according to Annand!), arms aloft to an eye-like sun of knowledge.

The major pieces of furniture on the dais, such as the Chancellor's throne, were designed by Grant Featherston. Outside there is a massive glazed wall to the east and a series of elms planted at the time of construction. To the north, a textured brick wall is relieved by a bronze bas-relief sculpture by Tom Bass, located directly above the main glazed entry doors. To the west, a translucent vertical egg-crate west window diffuses western light onto the dais within. To the south, there are textured bricks sprinkled with Gothic bosses and decorative details retrieved from the Reed building, and a protruding copper-clad bulge which houses the university organ. The entire building feels crafted; there is no overbearing expression of structure. The attention to colour, materials and introduced artworks owes much to the beautifully detailed university buildings by Arne Jacobsen in Denmark, which McCutcheon visited as part of his research for the new Wilson Hall design.

•••

Wilson Hall puzzled hardline Modernists such as Robin Boyd. Not only the building's decorativeness, but also its craftsmanship and artworks of such high quality, raised questions about the austere forms of modern architecture. Boyd summarised his feelings in The Australian Ugliness *(1960), the book which launched the term 'Featurism': the 'subordination of the essential whole and the accentuation of separate selected features.' He went on:*

'The new building was a success, but not as modern architecture.... this building frankly elevates features to the major emotional role. All its ornament—including the giant mural.... is truly contemporary to the 1950s. It is ornament applied with imagination ... and in many cases with such sophistication that few people viewing it recognise it as ornament.'

50 Australian troops take part
Korean War

1951 ANZUS security alliance is formed
(Australia, New Zealand, United States)

1953 Britain explodes atomic
device at Woomera, SA

296

2G B9

46 B1

96 Former Olympic Swimming Stadium

Swan Street and Batman Avenue, Flinders Park
1952–56 Kevin Borland, Peter McIntyre,
John and Phyllis Murphy; Bill Irwin (engineer)
1980-1982 Borland Brown (alterations)
AC, V, A

The former Olympic Swimming Stadium realised Robin Boyd's statement that Melbourne was the 'cradle of modernity' in 1950s Australian architecture. Public outcry over the sacrifice of South Yarra parkland for a building prompted a change of site to the present location. With engineer Bill Irwin's assistance, the team of young architects took on the challenge of supporting a roof over sloping seating on either side of a swimming and a diving pool. The solution was brilliantly simple: tie the building together via the roof and let the forces balance. The seating provides the lateral bracing to the expressively angled girders. The top chords of the trusses take most of the outward thrust of the girders so that the span-depth ratio of the truss is extremely economical. Pin joints at ground level form a determinate structure and vertical ties stabilise the building and effectively hold down the building. Major alterations in the 1980s attempted, with their overlay of expressed service ducts and industrial glazing, to complement the original. The infilling of the end walls and removal of the pool all but doused the flame of Olympian bravado that made this one of Melbourne's most prized contributions to modern architecture.

297 'Stargazer' (Castle) House

Aquila and Taurus Streets), North Balwyn
1953 Peter McIntyre
BC, V, NA

Nicknamed the 'Stargazer' House, the Castle House was one of Peter McIntyre's first completed house designs. He proposed that his clients, instead of looking at terracotta roofs, should look to the stars. The resulting two-storey house is an unusual one. It was built on a concrete slab with a ground floor of concrete bricks and an upper floor framed in timber. Bedrooms and bathrooms were contained on this floor on a mezzanine balcony supported on the south wall and held with tie rods to the north wall. The section through this bizarre house was a scalene triangle, with its apex centred over the cantilevered section. It appears to recall Oscar Niemeyer's staff housing, Sao Paolo (1947), but McIntyre's design is structurally far more adventurous than the Brazilian example. On the north side, it was roofed with corrugated aluminium sheet. The south side was the skylight wall, almost entirely glazed. This was cavalier technique and romantic engineering. Now looking slightly worse for wear, the spirit of invention is still there, even if its present condition suggests otherwise.

*Below: Section of former Olympic Swimming Stadium
(1952–56)*

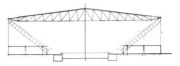

298 Snelleman House

40 Keam Street, Ivanhoe
1953–54 Peter McIntyre
GC, V, NA

The Snelleman House has a geometry which is
site-induced rather than an abstract placement
of a geometric shape upon an untouched site.
This 'coil' curves down a steep slope and around
two very large eucalypts; McIntyre scraped a
line down and around the trees with the heel
of his shoe. The house presents to the street
a curved sold brick external wall with small
punched openings. To the courtyard, there faces
a lightweight timber and glass wall which internally was originally a carousel of red, yellow and
white Mondrian-fenestrated window walls. Each
of the interior spaces steps down the slope as
an individual platform. The carport has since
been filled in and is now a master bedroom. At
the entry, a diamond timber screen is like a
symbolic structural claw holding the house from
sliding downhill. Next door at No. 42 is Peter
and Dione McIntyre's Stephenson House (1955)
in a completely different idiom—a diagonally
braced steel-framed house with masonry veneer
infills and triangular timber pergolas which are
revealed internally and externally.

299 Richardson House

10 Blackfriars Close, Toorak
1953–54 Robin Boyd
1980–81 Peter Crone (additions)
1997 major alterations
AC, V, NA

Instead of a tiny hill which had determined the
arch form of the Foy House **(301)**, here it was a
tight triangular site cut through by a creek bed
which was also a drainage easement. Building
was not permitted on the easement, but
permission was granted to build across it if the
ground was kept free. The solution was a
wedge-shaped house suspended between two
steel open girder arches, spanning between
concrete buttresses set on either side. A steel
frame was hung from the arches and the long
sides of the wedge were glazed in timber frames
set between steel members, with (originally)
deep blue spandrels for privacy. Inside, the
curtains were bold, black-and-white vertical
stripes. An open living/dining/study space
occupied most of the wedge, with bedrooms,
kitchen and bathroom squeezed into the broad
end of the wedge. This is a fine example of a
structural–functional idea 'solving' the design
using the latest marvels of engineering.

Below: Plan of the Richardson House (1953)
SOURCE: *Architecture and Arts, December 1955*

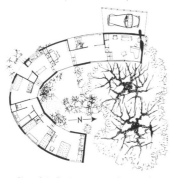

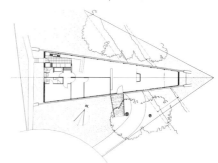

Above: Plan of the Snelleman House (1953–54)
SOURCE: *Australian Home Beautiful, January 1956*

954 Queen Elizabeth II and
ince Philip tour Australia

1955 Structure of DNA discovered
by Francis Crick and James Watson

1955 European Coal and Steel
Community develops into EEC

300

| 2M G3 | 86 G7 |

300 Grounds House and Flats

24 Hill Street, Toorak
1953-54 Roy Grounds
GC, V, NA

One of a series of Roy Grounds designs that involved pure geometric shapes in plan, this house is the most well known. Designed by Grounds (1905–81) for himself and his wife, Betty, and winner of the 1954 Victorian Architecture Medal, this little house is a gem. The plan is a square with a circular courtyard at its centre. Maximising a narrow site to fit flats at the rear, the house was built close to the street and is thus similar to the 1930s Georgian houses of South Yarra. By concealing the circular court and providing windows only at eaves level, Grounds created an inward-looking house, almost Japanese in its retreat from the outside world. The signature doorknocker on the oversized front door, the hovering roof and the perfect symmetry conjure images of Frank Lloyd Wright's Winslow House, Chinese courtyard houses or the geometric plans of High Renaissance architect Andrea Palladio. This is an ideal villa for the Antipodes. Contributing to its exotic ambience was the landscaping, also designed by Grounds, which originally comprised a persimmon and black bamboo, two plants featuring in Grounds's National Gallery of Victoria (1959–68). Indeed, the overall form of the National Gallery owes much to this little experiment in blending East and West.

301 Foy House

2 Deauville Street, Beaumaris
1953 Robin Boyd
GC, V, NA

Originally intended to be roofed by one all-encompassing arch formed by two steel lattice girders which swept up and over a small sandy hill, the Foy House was finally constructed beneath a gently curved arch, but one which was supported off timber posts. The resulting house is a graceful example of Boyd's penchant for creating shelter with a single idea roof—a parasol, a giant arch or a draped curtain. Amidst ti-tree and an informal garden, the spaces of the house step backwards and forwards under its curved canopy, blurring the distinctions between inside and out.

•••

Nearby the Foy House at the corner of Sparkes Street and Beach Road, Beaumaris, a house designed by Mockridge Stahle and Mitchell in 1954, employs a quite different roof solution. The butterfly roof, a shortlived fashion for a reverse gable (that tended to leak) was a daring signature of difference. Inspired by the butterfly roofs of Marcel Breuer and Harry Seidler, Mockridge Stahle and Mitchell added their own signature, the distinctive Swedish Red paint that appeared on many of their houses at the time.

Below: Plan of Grounds House and Flats (1953–54)

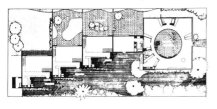

Below: Plan of Foy House (1953)

302

302 Beaurepaire Centre
Tin Alley, University of Melbourne, Parkville
1953–56 Eggleston MacDonald and Secomb
Leonard French (internal mural, external glazed mosaics)
AC, V, A

Financed through generous donations by Frank Beaurepaire, former Olympic swimming champion and car tyre tycoon, the Beaurepaire Centre was designed to serve Melbourne University as its major sporting complex and also as a training pool for the 1956 Olympics. The building is composed as three major volumes, each housed within a portal-framed structure of a different size, but same shape. These portal frames are externally the centre's most dominant feature. Perhaps more than any other Melbourne building, the Beaurepaire Centre exhibits the combination of modern art and engineering, each element visually separate, but brought together to suggest a new form of monumental public architecture.

303 Classrooms, Melbourne Church of England Boys Grammar School
Bromby Street, South Yarra
1954 Mockridge Stahle and Mitchell
GC, V, A

These classroom blocks, with their contextually appropriate use of bluestone, perforated metal balustrades and concrete grid frames, are the first of many postwar buildings on the South Yarra campus. They herald an association between the architects and the school that resulted in a range of progressive buildings which fitted seamlessly into the school's 19th-century Gothic Revival core. These rectilinear blocks frame the space of the oval and, despite minor alterations over time, their scale, colour and texture remain of the moment. Nearby, the Myer Music School, Domain Street (1960), with its butterfly roof, is of particular note.

304 Boiler House, Australian Paper Mills
South of 626 Heidelberg Road, Fairfield
1954 Mussen McKay and Potter
AC, V, NA

Visible today from the Chandler Highway, the Boiler House was an icon of rigorous functionalist design to young 1950s architects. Not only did the building demonstrate sheer glazed curtain walls which veiled its mass of machinery within, but also its industrial function was signalled by chimneys belching forth the emissions of industry. With precedents such as Brinkmann and Van der Vlugt's Van Nelle Tobacco Factory, Rotterdam (1929) and Mies van der Rohe's Boiler House at Illinois Institute of Technology, Chicago (1940), here was a local example of absolute utility of envelope coupled with the desire for transparency and visible structure.

•••

305

305 Hosies Hotel

186 Flinders Street, Melbourne
1955 Mussen McKay and Potter
GC, V, A

One of two new hotels constructed in central
Melbourne in anticipation of tourist trade from
the 1956 Olympic Games, Hosies Hotel is the
most dramatic in its visual departure from the
more common model of the 19th-century
corner hotel. Unlike Best Overend's Town Hall
Hotel (more commonly known as The Graham)
at 67–73 Swanston Street (1955), Hosies boldly
expressed its functions in Constructivist style. A
low block of four floors topped by a roof garden
interlocked into a rear high-rise slab of hotel
rooms. On the Elizabeth Street facade is a four-
storey abstract ceramic mural by Richard Beck,
perhaps best known for his Wynns wine bottle
labels, which also date from the 1950s.

306 Degraves Street Underpass

Flinders Street/Degraves Street, Melbourne
1955–56
GC, V, A

Hidden from view and little known even by
Melburnians, with the exception of shrewd
commuters looking for a shortcut from Flinders
Street Station directly into the central city, the
Degraves Street Underpass is a time capsule of
early 1950s attempts to modernise Melbourne's
pedestrian circulation infrastructure. Pale yellow
tiles, stainless steel trim, moderne curved styling
and dim lighting appear unremarkable, but the
intention, inspired by the MMBW 1954 Master
plan, was to envisage a new Melbourne that
was multi-level in access. It was an early
attempt to separate people and cars, hence
relieving commuter crowd crushes at the two
major station entry points at Swanston and
Elizabeth streets.

307 Gilbert Court

100–104 Collins Street, Melbourne
1954–55 John A La Gerche
GC, V, A

One of the first multi-storey 'glass box'
buildings in Australia, this is also one of the
earliest buildings in Melbourne to use the glazed
curtain wall aesthetic of American high-rise
buildings. The impression of a glass box is given
by the sheer aluminium and glass curtain wall
wrapping around the corner into Alfred Place.
Here, where the glass wall meets the second
escape stair the facade steps back over the top
floors, accentuating the glass prism appearance.
At 18–22 Collins Street, architect JA Le Gerche
continued his curtain wall experiments with the
limit-height Coates Building (1957–59). Both
buildings were the only intrusions at the east
end of Collins Street until 1960, and only
minimally affected the street's Italianate charm.

Melbourne and Structural-Functionalism
Robin Boyd referred to 1950s Melbourne as the
'cradle of modernity'. In 1967, in Architecture
Australia, he was to write: '... The Melbourne
School was forward looking, daring all and
damning all aesthetic rules.. The two climactic
buildings of the period (in parkland) were on
opposite sides of the Yarra River: the Olympic
Pools Buildings (1952–56) and the Sidney Myer
Music Bowl (1956–59) – palaces of sport and
culture respectively. These buildings had in
common two elements: tensile construction and
Bill Irwin, an engineer with the courage of his
architects' convictions. As well, they had the
ingredients of the Melbourne School: a great
structural–functional idea carried out with an
enforced austerity and a cavalier technique.'

308

308 Peter and Dione McIntyre House
2 Hodgson Street, Kew
1955 Peter & Dione McIntyre
GC, NV, NA

The first building on a glorious riverfront site which has now become a compound of later buildings designed by Peter, Dione and son Robert McIntyre, the McIntyre House has a giant triangle as its structural and spatial delineator. Built on a steeply sloping bank of the Yarra, the McIntyre House is suspended above a concrete base between two steel frames and has two floor levels within. Originally, the steel frame was exposed with infill panels painted in the bright new colours of the Tip-Top paints range. In 1956, *Vogue* magazine likened it to a Paul Klee butterfly. One entered through a front door that slid upwards, then ascended a central spiral staircase to each of the hovering platforms of space with open balconies high above the trees. The house was altered during the ensuing decades and is now one of the McIntyre Partnership architectural drawing offices on site. The kitchen, however, retains its Mondrian colours and remains a true 1950s period piece.

309 Keith Mann House
39 Inverness Way, North Balwyn
1955 Montgomery King and Trengove
GC, V, NA

One of the best examples in Melbourne of the influence of Harry Seidler's Rose Seidler House, Turramurra, New South Wales (1948–50), the Keith Mann House is also notable for its first-floor concrete slabs laid on pre-stressed concrete beams and finished with a thin concrete screed. The house displays the design language taught to Seidler by teachers Walter Gropius and Marcel Breuer at the Harvard Graduate School of Design. Transferred faithfully by Neil

Montgomery to a different situation, this house cut from a cube—with its window break-ups inspired by Mondrian, internal garden court and interiors flooded with daylight—epitomises a stylish departure from the postwar vernacular of brick veneer walls and terracotta tile roofs.

310 Brett House
3 Buddle Drive, Toorak
1955 Grounds Romberg and Boyd
GC, V, NA

In contrast to Robin Boyd's obsession with the experimental, the Brett House is his venture into the 'classical modern' house. His client wanted a Georgian house in this conservatively styled suburb, and Boyd offered a sympathetic alternative. The formal front of columns and French doors contribute a classical order to what is essentially a description of brickwork panels with windows between. Boyd had abstracted the Georgian house into a modern and rational equivalent. What visitors do not see are Boyd's decorative touches which were later removed: jaunty drooping chain balustrades and shallow planter dishes which framed the offset front door.

•••

Boyd continued to experiment with a subdued mode of brick and glazed infill panels for the next 15 years. Houses in this style include: McNicol House, 19 Gordon Grove, South Yarra (1959); Burgess House, cnr MacKennel and Longstaff Streets, Ivanhoe (1964); and Lawrence House and Flats, 13 Studley Street, Kew (1967).

Left: First floor plan of Brett House

310

311

311 St Leonard's Uniting Church

nr New Street and Wolseley Grove, Brighton
1956 Bruce Kemp
GC, V, A

All building types appeared to undergo a personality crisis in the immediate postwar decade. The church was not exempt from the mood of experiment and St Leonard's is an expressionistic answer to the 1950s new church form. The segmented curving walls have panels of translucent coloured glass at each change of angle of the nave wall. The roof is a flat plate the fascia edge of which is unbroken, hence accentuating the faceted fish 'scales' of the walls below. Designed by the favoured church architect for the Presbyterian church in the 1950s and also architect for Hailebury College's Memorial Hall on its Brighton campus (1952), this is one of Melbourne's largest and intact postwar suburban churches.

2D G12

312 Former Milston House

5 Reeves Court, Kew
1955–56 Ernest Milston
GC, V, NA

With its butterfly roof and lightweight walls, this house designed by its architect owner and recently sympathetically renovated by another architect owner typifies the possibilities of post-war living—a close relationship with the outdoors, simple construction and a modesty that bespeaks humility in terms of site and landscape. Ernest Milston was one of numerous sophisticated central European emigres who arrived after the late 1930s and enriched the city's Anglo-centric focus, bringing cosmopolitanism and diversity. Arriving in Adelaide in 1940 and after serving under the Engineer-in-Chief during World War II, Milston became naturalised and set up private practice based on his winning the 1950 competition for the 1939–45 War Memorial Forecourt to the Shrine of Remembrance. This house gives an indication of Milston's skills in functional domestic construction, which were given full expression in his later partnership with Don Henry Fulton when they designed all the buildings for the Mary Kathleen Township, near Mt Isa in Queensland (1955–57).

91 A12

313 GMH Factory

Princes Highway, Dandenong
1955–56 Stephenson & Turner
AC, V, NA

Home to the Holden, the all-Australian car of the 1950s, the design of this massive factory complex owes much to its bigger American brother in Warren, Michigan, the General Motors Technical Centre (1948–56), where US architect Eero Saarinen designed a virtual 'industrial Versailles'. The Dandenong aspirations were similar, but more pragmatic in finish and scale. The new corporate language of Modernism, the curtain wall, made its way out to the suburbs to signal the industrial campus which included office, plant and high-grade facilities. The vast GMH plant, indicative of vigorous expansion in industry nationwide and a decisive shift to American models of production and consumption, was joined by other factory complexes of similar pedigree such as Hassell and McConnell's impressive Heinz Factory, Princes Highway, Dandenong (1954–56).

The Contemporary City
1955–1970

1955–1970

By 1955, a whole decade after
a war from which Australia had
emerged victorious, the long-
awaited building boom had
only just got under way.

Housing had flourished since 1945 and, at that time, it had meant
individual villas with the proscribed maximum of 135 square
metres (14 squares) located on Melbourne's unserviced fringe
Building and rental controls imposed in 1940-41 were lifted in
1952. The inner suburbs abandoned since the Great War and the
home of the postwar generation's grandparents continued to be
ignored; the larger houses provided cheap accommodation for
the indigent, while workers' cottages housed an increasing
number of European migrants.

The XIV Olympiad in 1956 had provided a stimulus and a
deadline for many projects, but its architectural legacy was scant:
namely the former **Olympic Swimming Pool**; the **Beaurepaire
Centre** and the athletes' village in West Heidelberg. The former
two were eventually to receive heritage listing, while the Olympic
village houses were ultimately systematically demolished.

Most postwar houses were scaled-down versions of their
1940s prototypes, but soon the new architecture began to appear.
The 'Contemporary style' became a popular topic and newspapers
and magazines carried regular articles on domestic architecture
and its architects. The advanced houses of the late 1950s, such as
Chancellor & Patrick's **McCraith House** and Grounds Romberg &
Boyd's **Haughton James House**, presented an immediately
recognisable contrast to the all-pervasive hip-roofed, asymmetrically fronted 1950s suburban villa. Such houses took the forms of
ells and aitches; they were slewed, cater-cornered or even reversed
on their blocks to seek sun or notoriety. In the **Delbridge House**,
entire walls were given over to glass. Compartmentalisation, under
threat since the 1930s, was now reduced almost to the point where
the only walls remaining shielded beds or plumbing fixtures.

The new houses introduced fragmented forms and contrasts in
texture and colour, capped with skillion (asbestos cement or
galvanised iron) or flat roofs (with bituminous felt). For most
architects, tiles were unacceptable; slates were unthinkable. The
arrival of steel decking in 1958 meant that the new roofs could
at least be relied on to keep out rain—a quality the old hipped and
gabled roofs had always possessed. The inventive architects
constantly introduced new and untried materials. They sought
lightness of structure and sparseness of detail. The shift away

om the traditional quest for solidity also reflected the wartime ulture of austerity. Forty years later in the mid-1990s, that earch for lightness proved to be the undoing of these over-fined and frail buildings. As their sites increased dramatically in alue, the buildings (especially 1950s houses) came to be egarded as expendable, no matter what their significance.

By the late 1950s, apartments (then still called flats) had ecome a significant building type. Entire streets in suburbs such s Armadale and East St Kilda were lined with solid blocks. Many vere built in yellow, then brown, bricks with little or no nvolvement with professional designers and were rarely more han three storeys high. A few private 'elevator blocks', such as **dgewater Towers** and Yuncken Freeman's Fairlie, Anderson treet, South Yarra (1963), appeared understandably in the east nd south, but for more than a decade the Housing Commission, nder the direction of Chief Architect Roy Prentice, erected a score f tower blocks mainly in the north and west.

Commercial development took second place o housing. It had been slow to recommence, ut, after 1955, standardised aluminium curtain valling began to appear. Released in 1954 and nveiled at the National Gallery no less, the MMBW Plan for Melbourne resulted in, amongst thers, two far-reaching changes: the eventual bolition of the 132-foot (40-metre) height limit nd the introduction of plot ratios.

The most significant building to emerge from he decade was **ICI** (now Orica) **House** 1955–59). It occupied a fraction of its site and ose to 24 storeys. Its open ground floor, curtain valling, sunshading devices, isolated service ower and inevitable courtyard sculpture ncapsulated the aspirations of the period. But he press gloatingly reported minor failures of its glass panels. One reviewer described the building as 'deciduous'.

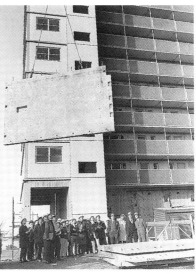

A concrete slab is lifted into position during construction of the Housing Commission of Victoria's Park Towers, South Melbourne.

In the late 1950s, churches, schools and universities, tradition-ally enlightened patrons of architecture, began, after an absence of nearly 20 years, to commission buildings. Some of the period's most important free-standing public buildings are found on the old and new campuses, and along the outer highways. While the new architecture, with its emphasis on human scale, rational planning, climate and comfort control, was eminently suitable for educational buildings such as **Preshil School**, the churches of the times, much like religion itself, seemed alien to the new world. Bogle & Banfield's **St James Anglican Church** and Mockridge Stahle & Mitchell's **St Faith's Anglican Church** were two such startling new arrivals.

Despite the dramatic expansion of industry, the new standard. of design and amenity were generally confined to the street fronting curtain walled administrative block backed by basic industrial shed structures. Such was the case for the **ETA Factory** and D Graeme Lumsden's now demolished Nicholas Aspro Factory, Chadstone (1956). The 1960s also witnessed the destruction of many Victorian and Edwardian landmarks such as Inskip & Butler's Melbourne Mansions, 91-101 Collins Street (1901-1906), one of the city's first apartment buildings Innovative 'modern' house designs such as HD Annear's Troon (1919) and Inglesby (1915), both in South Yarra, were lost before their significance had been reassessed. In 1960, after a decade of intense building activity and inflation, credit controls were introduced to slow the racing economy. The results were immediate, dramatic and unexpected. Major buildings were left half built and subdivisions, even in rudimentary were left with only survey pegs to delineate the decade's optimism.

In South Yarra, the **Domain Park** apartments designed to take advantage of new planning and height laws sat for more than a year as a basement garage waiting for the ensuing 20 storeys. At the lowest point of the credit squeeze, designs for the **National Gallery of Victoria** and **Victorian Arts Centre** (1959–84) were unveiled in 1961 and more than a decade of controversy and construction began.

While the CBD still produced spectacular examples of the new architecture, the privately commissioned suburban house remained the design laboratory. When construction recommenced in the early 1960s, there were notable changes. Commercial buildings were sealed and the reliance on artificial climate and comfort control began. The occupants had a much lower standard of comfort at home, but there, for the first time since settlement, the rigours of Melbourne's winter were accepted and rudimentary heating systems became general. City buildings were still framed and clad with the ubiquitous curtain walling, but now glass had been supplanted by precast concrete, with various aggregate finishes and reconstructed stone. The striving for lightness which had distinguished the previous decade was over, replaced by an equally strong preference for massiveness. Chief among these new city buildings in search of mass were **Royal Insurance** and **BP House**. Houses now sought darkness and texture after the ineffable brightness and smoothness of earlier years. Clinker bricks and sawn-finish timber were now acceptable after 40 years of sleek surfaces and dynamic asymmetry. Rising standards of living now assumed central heating and an additional bathroom, double garages and a television-engendered reversion to separated living areas — levels of amenity unimaginable a decade earlier.

The early 1960s also saw a minor Wrightian revival. Although mainly confined to houses such as the **Godsell** and **Freiberg** **houses**, the movement produced Chancellor & Patrick's **ES&A** **Bank** (Elizabeth Street), the **Hoyts Cinema Centre** and most notably the **Brighton Municipal Offices**, an intriguing tribute to the master's Guggenheim Museum in New York. The period also introduced new patrons to the new architecture. Large shopping centres in outer suburbs and motels in all areas became staple items in mid-century life; bowling alleys and drive-in cinemas had uncertain futures.

Builders were responsible for the design of the great majority of houses with architects catering only for the bigger building budget. A more significant influence was the appearance of construction firms which often employed prominent architects to make design a facet of their marketing strategy. Generally they failed to achieve the hoped-for success, but a notable exception was Merchant Builders. A Melbourne firm established in 1965, it borrowed the idea (and part of their name) from Pettit and Sevitt, a Sydney firm which had achieved spectacular success a year earlier by retaining top architects and producing houses of a high level of design.

Chadstone Shopping Centre, 1961 (SOURCE: Architecture Library, University of Melbourne)

Influences from the United States and, to a lesser degree, western Europe affected planning and construction, but the philosophical controversies of the era did not cross the Pacific. Melbourne architects remained loyal to the International style. Redevelopment in the CBD and along St Kilda Road was on a new and enormous scale. The heritage movement was, as yet, private and lacking political and professional acceptance. As the 1960s drew to a close, two new forces emerged. Planning law became a fact of building life and a new age of architectural imperialism began. The city's biggest project, **Collins Place**, was designed in New York (by IM Pei & Associates) just as the earlier **AMP Tower** **and St James complex** had been designed in San Francisco by Skidmore Owings & Merrill. By the end of the decade, that firm had been involved in the design of three building's at the city's highest intersection at Bourke and William streets. The remaining corner was occupied by **Goldsborough Mort**, a 19th-century bluestone warehouse protected by new heritage controls. Indeed, it now appears that it may outlive them all.

NEIL CLEREHAN

314

3

314 ICI House

1 Nicholson Street, East Melbourne
1955-58 Bates Smart & McCutcheon
GC, V, A

ICI House was one of the first free-standing fully glazed curtain wall commercial skyscrapers in Australia. As one of the nation's most stylish skyscrapers, it represented the most refined example of Bates Smart & McCutcheon's efforts in the 1950s to perfect high-rise office design. Raised on pilotes, the blue glazed linear slab of open-plan offices, with its lift core expressed as clearly separate, broke the city's 132-foot height limit and changed Melbourne's previously consistent skyline forever. It was the provision of the open space at ground level as a garden—designed collaboratively by the architects, sculptor Gerald Lewers and landscape architect John Stevens—which enabled the limit height rule to be broken. While the design is often cited as having the glass curtain wall of Skidmore Owings & Merrill's Lever House, New York (1952), as its precedent, the Melbourne tower is an amalgam of Wallace Harrison et al's United Nations Secretariat (1945–52) and Niemeyer & Costa's Ministry of Education & Health, Rio de Janeiro (1936–39). Recent renovations and additions at ground level by the original archi-tects have been sympathetic, although none of the original upper floor office interiors remain.

315 Former R Haughton James House

82 Molesworth Street, Kew
1956 Grounds Romberg & Boyd
GC, V, NA

The house has an unusual eye-shaped plan of living spaces on the ground floor, surmounted by a rectilinear entry and bedroom wing on the first floor. An open tread stair descends through a circular cutout in the ceiling, marking the iris of the eye-shaped plan. The design is one of Boyd's most concerted attempts to resolve the rational versus the organic. Here in Kew, Boyd blended the ground-hugging solar hemicycle houses of Frank Lloyd Wright with the simplified box forms of Philip Johnson's neo-Miesian house designs in New Canaan, Connecticut, of the early 1950s.

Below: Plan of former R Haughton James House (1955)

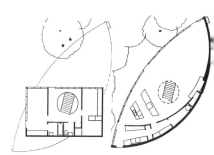

316

67 D9   **2L E1**

16 Lloyd House

Newbay Crescent, Brighton
1958 Grounds Romberg & Boyd
GC, V, NA

Robin Boyd's interest in Frank Lloyd Wright's
semicycle plans was realised in the Lloyd House
as a flat-roofed, crescent-shaped block facing
into a northerly courtyard. It was as if a sensible
rectangular plan had been bent into a curve to
create a private garden. A wide roof overhang,
forming a curving pergola of shade battens, was
later infilled as solid eaves. At the centre of the
circle which had determined the plan there was
intended to be a sculptural 'focal piece'.

17 Clemson House

24 Milfay Avenue, Kew
1957 Grounds Romberg & Boyd
GC, V, NA

Designed by Robin Boyd and originally landscaped by Ellis Stones, the Clemson House is
comprised of a sloping wedge of rooms sitting
beneath an all-embracing parasol roof. The
rooms of the house step down the slope under
an all-protective butterfly roof made up of
crossed roof beams (like a pair of scissors!).

318 Robin Boyd House II

290 Walsh Street, South Yarra
1957 Grounds Romberg & Boyd
GC, V, NA

Robin Boyd's second house for his own family
was planned as a long rectangle roofed by a
sweeping catenary of planks suspended on wire
cables. The draped roof is the guiding idea of
the house, an open plan with rooms as free
floating timber platforms all roofed by one
single gesture. The catenary sweeps the length
of the sloping site, containing within it a central
courtyard, a living and parents' zone at one end
and the children's block at the other. The
horizontal break-up of the window mullions, the
refined built-in furniture and the obscure glass
side walls of the courtyard suggest an interest
in Japanese design, allusions which enrich the
bold structural-functional idea. At the street/
entry side of the house, a band of highlight
windows emphasises the floating roof.

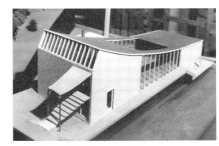

Above: Model of Robin Boyd House II (1957)
Below: Plan of Robin Boyd House II

Below: Section of Boyd House

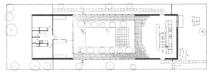

319

Above: Drawing of former ES&A Bank, Elizabeth Street (1959–60) (SOURCE:: *Architecture Library, University of Melbourne*)

2B B8

45 B5

319 Elizabeth Tower Motel
Former Ampol Building
792 Elizabeth Street, Melbourne
1958 Bernard Evans & Associates
AC, V, A

While its massing and detail suggests that it could have been built in the late 1930s, the former Ampol Building is in fact a product of the late 1950s. With its dramatic glazed corner housing a concrete spiral stair and framed by blue tiles, this landmark building is now a motel. The painting of the orange bricks, the introduction of bluestone at ground level and the olde-worlde lettering detract from this design, which emanated from the office of one-time Lord Mayor and real estate speculator, Sir Bernard Evans.

320 Clerehan House
18 Fawkner Street, South Yarra
1955 Neil Clerehan
GC, V, NA

Neil Clerehan's first house for himself and his family in South Yarra was significant for its inner suburban siting. Built on one of its side boundaries, this flat-roofed townhouse had a Stegbar window-wall and, unusually for the time, an upstairs kitchen and living room. The glass wall facing the garden was held off the structure of the first floor, and double-storey curtains could be drawn to shade this side of the house. This was one of the first 1950s houses to acknowledge the spatial potential of the inner city site.

321 Freiberg House
26 Yarravale Road, Kew
1959–60 Chancellor & Patrick
Edna Walling (landscape designer)
GC, V, NA

The plan of this house, which graced the cover of Neil Clerehan's *Best Australian Houses* (1961) is a T with low-pitched gable roofs, horizontal bands of windows and oversailing major internal rafters. The broad eaves recall not only the Melbourne houses of Walter Burley Griffin, but also the Californian houses of Harwell Hamilton Harris, where a similar technique of exposed purlin beams overran the roof to project beyond the line of the house. One enters between two square brick piers and ascends to arrive at the centre of the cruciform/ T plan. Each arm of the T houses a function: sleeping and bathrooms; living room with corner fireplace; or kitchen/dining. In the corridor of the sleeping wing, oregon timber joinery suggests Japanese inspiration for the interior fittings and colour scheme. The garden designed by Edna Walling, with its bluestone walls built by Eric Hammond, is a completely Australian native garden and represents Walling's almost complete shift to indigenous plants after 1952.

Below: Plan of Freiberg House
SOURCE: *Clerehan,* Best Australian Houses

322

22 Former ES&A Bank
nr High Street and Glenferrie Road, Malvern
958-60 Stuart McIntosh (ES&A Architects'
ranch)
C, V, NA

together with Geoffrey Danne within the
Architects' Branch of the ES&A Bank, Stuart
McIntosh designed scores of postwar suburban
and country town bank premises in the 1950s.
Like the dramatically different architectural
image given to the 1950s church, the ES&A
Bank was styled with the latest abstract composition in veneers of stone, sculptural shading
devices and entrance canopies. With tinted glass
and deep horizontal fins (painted mint green on
their underside) which wrap around the corner
and a mixture of massive forms clad in stone,
the bank's sculptural composition owes much to
McIntosh's interest in Surrealist painters' free
experimentation with shape. The ES&A Bank was
an unorthodox modern building, flaunting its
lack of structural truth, and as such was omitted
from purist historical views of the period.

23 McCraith House
tunga Terrace and Caldwell Road, Dromana
956 Chancellor & Patrick
GC, V, NA

The McCraith House is a small elevated weekend
house, of four triangular frames supported on
just four points. The structure is 3-inch diameter
steel tube and 6-inch by 3-inch steel channels
with timber infills. Four triangles are then hung
off either end to extend the available area of the
first floor. The overall profile of the house, with
its inverted butterfly roof, is like a hovering pair
of angular binoculars.

324 Former ETA Factory
Ballarat Road and Annesley Street, Braybrook
1958 Grounds Romberg & Boyd
BC, V, A

Designed by Swiss emigre architect Frederick
Romberg, the long, repetitive facade of the ETA
Factory, together with other factories such as
GMH, Dandenong **(313)** and DG Lumsden's
Aspro Factory, Warrigal Road, Chadstone (1956;
demolished), exemplified the US-inspired move
of the curtain wall into the suburbs as the new
stylish corporate face to the office/factory
complex. Romberg introduced another com-
ponent to his rigorously modulated clear and
black glass wall: diagonal structural bracing
which gives the building added dynamism.
Originally designed by John Stevens, Melbourne's
devotee of Roberto Burle Marx and co-designer
of the garden at ICI House **(314)** the courtyard
garden and the landscaping along Ballarat Road
once included succulents, cacti, rocks and
geometric-shaped sections of river pebbles.

325 Former ES&A Bank
453-457 Elizabeth Street, Melbourne
1959-60 Chancellor & Patrick
GC, V, NA

Originally intended to be an office tower of
12 storeys with floors of alternating balcony
projections and a north-facing decorative sun-
grille rising from the ground floor to pierce a
floating roof, this is Chancellor & Patrick's only
central city building and a tribute to not only
Frank Lloyd Wright, but also Walter Burley
Griffin. The bluestone stone corner piers recall
the Griffins monumental geometries and
penchant for capped piers. Despite its truncation,
the former bank is a convincing example of the
survival in Melbourne of the organic principles
of Frank Lloyd Wright following his death in 1959.

181

● 1958 Qantas starts first round–the–world
service through North America

● 1958 Slim Dusty tops the record
charts with 'The Pub with no Beer'

● 1959 Population of Australia
reaches 10,000,000

326

32

60 G6 **59 H8**

326 St Faith's Anglican Church

8 Charles Street, Burwood
1957–58 Mockridge Stahle & Mitchell
GC, V, A

Inspired by the formal invention of new
churches in postwar Europe such as Basil
Spence's Coventry Cathedral, John Mockridge's
plan for St Faith's was a 'round square', a circle
extended by a shallow triangle to house the
altar. The narthex, chapel, baptistry (all faced in
stone) and vestry were additions to this
centralised plan which was crowned by a spire.
The Anglican Diocese initially rejected
Mockridge's unusual design, but finally accepted
it on the grounds that it was located in a side
street and not on a public thoroughfare! Inside,
the supporting structure of steel portals can be
seen as well as furniture, pews, candlesticks,
lectern and stained glass all designed by MSM.
Esther Harris, a parishioner, designed the panels
depicting apostolic symbols in the narthex doors
in memory of her brother Richard Hall.

•••

*Other significant postwar Melbourne churches
include: Mockridge Stahle & Mitchell's Mother of
God Catholic Church, 63 Wilfred Road, East
Ivanhoe (1955); Ray Berg's Christ Church
Anglican, 485 Whitehorse Road, Mitcham
(1957); Louis Williams's St Andrew's Anglican
Church, 230 New Street, Brighton (1961); and
Romberg & Boyd's St George's Anglican Church,
46 Warncliffe Road, East Ivanhoe (c. 1962).*

*Right: Plan of St Faith's
Anglican Church (1957–58)*

327 St James Anglican Church

1461 High Street, Glen Iris
1959 Bogle Banfield & Associates
GC, V, A

With its box-like form, black portal frames and
cement-rendered screens of cruciform cutouts,
St James Anglican Church is an exemplar of
austere postwar modernism. The combination of
structural clarity and the repetitive use of the
cross as pattern and symbol make this a unique
contribution to religious architecture in postwar
Melbourne.

2B C1

328 International House

231–241 Royal Parade, Parkville
*1956–57 Raymond Berg in association with
Leighton Irwin & Co.*
GC, V, A

The 1950s buildings of International House are
period pieces of postwar thinking on institutional
interior design finishes and fittings. The dining
hall, stairwells, recreation rooms and rear
residential wing convey a sense of smart
postwar cosmopolitanism intended for the
university's overseas guests.

1A G5

329 Former London Assurance Building

468–470 Bourke Street, Melbourne
1959 Bernard Evans & Associates
GC, V, A

Together with Allans, 276–278 Collins Street
(1956–57); the OPSM Building, 82 Collins Street
(1960); and JA La Gerche's Coates Building,
18–22 Collins Street (1959), the London
Assurance Building displays the scale and
modulation that enabled such generously glazed
buildings to fit comfortably within Melbourne's
19th century structure while being clad in the
latest building materials.

59 Fidel Castro becomes
esident of Cuba

1960 First production of Alan Seymour's
play *The One Day of the Year*

1961 Current affairs program
'Four Corners' begins on ABC

330

2F K9

30 Sidney Myer Music Bowl

ings Domain, Melbourne
956–59 Yuncken Freeman Brothers
Griffiths & Simpson
VL Irwin & Associates (structural engineers)
GC, V, A

Designed by Barry Patten and assisted by Angel Dimitroff within the office of Yuncken Freeman Bros. Griffiths & Simpson, the Sidney Myer Music Bowl was the first major purpose-built outdoor venue to be constructed in Melbourne. Named after its benefactor, the Sidney Myer Music Bowl is perhaps the best-known project of the Sidney Myer Charity Trust. Its planning, design and construction were overseen by members of the Myer family, especially the late Kenneth Myer, Sidney's son. The design of the tent-like roof suspended from its two tapering cigar-shaped masts and floating above the grass originated from Patten and Dimitroff's experimentation with various structurally expressive ideas. Patten has recalled their interests then in "the similarity of cable structures like the Brooklyn Bridge and the section through Satchmo's trumpet". A model of 6-inch nails, cotton thread and Japanese rice paper was used to develop the concept and the final draped structure covered a stage, orchestra pit and fixed audience seating with an extensive open sloped lawn area to the south. The intended capacity of the Bowl was for an audience of 20 000. The structure was based on a complex web of prestressed steel cables which support a skin of 'Alumply', aluminium-faced plywood panels developed by Sydney manufacturer and inventor Ralph Symonds. The Bowl was officially opened by Prime Minister Robert Menzies before an estimated crowd of 30 000 at a free concert held on 12 February 1959. Under the baton of American conductor Alfred Wallenstein, the combined orchestras of Melbourne and Sydney performed, as well as the famous pianist Andor Foldes. The scene of thousands of concerts since, as well as the 1959 Billy Graham evangelical crusades, the Sidney Myer Music Bowl continues to play host to free opera, rock concerts and even ice-skating in winter.

58 A11

331 Edgewater Towers

12 Marine Parade, St Kilda,
1959–60 Mordecai Benshemesh
AC, V, NA

A 13-storey slab of 100 single- or two-bedroom apartments, isolated on the skyline, Edgewater Towers is a St Kilda landmark. One of Melbourne's early truly large-scale privately developed apartment blocks, it was described by the *Age* in November 1960 as 'everything you'd find in a Manhattan building ...'; however, this white, generously glazed slab seems more akin to 1950s Miami Beach, Florida, than New York.

Below: Section through Myer Music Bowl (1956–59)

183

● 1961 East Germany builds the
Berlin Wall

● 1961 Cosmonaut Yuri Gagarin
orbits the earth in first manned
space flight

● 1962 Australian Ballet Company
established

332

*Above: Rendering of the proposed National
Gallery of Victoria and Cultural Centre, 1961*

2F G8

332 National Gallery of Victoria
St Kilda Road, Melbourne
1959–68 Roy Grounds
GC, V, A

Currently the subject of controversial major alterations and additions proposed by Italian architect Mario Bellini and local firm Metier III, Roy Grounds's National Gallery of Victoria (NGV) has been a locus for controversy ever since its commissioning. The project caused the 1962 split between Grounds and his erstwhile partners Robin Boyd and Frederick Romberg. At the gallery's opening in August 1968, architectural critics alternately savaged and praised this bluestone treasure house. Much of the controversy has to do with Grounds's quixotic and arguably brilliant design—a giant Oriental palazzo with a geometric plan, a city block in length, and with three square courtyards inside.

On a 1960 trip to Europe and the United States with NGV Director Eric Westbrook, Grounds was inspired by the 18th-century Palazzo di Capodimonte outside Naples and the medieval Castello Sforzesco, Milan. Grounds was also keen to use a local stone and took the NGV Buildings Committee to look at the bluestone walls and great arch of the old Melbourne Gaol (a gesture ironically echoed in Premier Sir Henry Bolte's opening speech, when he praised the gallery as a perfect place for 'hanging').

Grounds's design is like a renovated neo-classical palazzo/castle sitting in a moat, but with Oriental overtones, especially given the floating roof and its upturned eaves, the timber gridded ceilings and the Bamboo Courtyard

(now the Coles Court) with its fountains, black bamboo and bluestone pebbles, which was designed to relate directly to the collection of Oriental art encircling the courtyard. Other original features of the NGV include the state's coat of arms above the Richardsonian entry arch designed by Norma Redpath; the waterwall, long derided as a fishmonger's window, but loved for decades by the Victorian public; the circular lift within its bush-hammered concrete core; the Victorian ash panelling in the galleries and foyer; and the Great Hall where Leonard French's stained-glass ceiling, thought to be the largest in the world, is the baronial climax to this eclectic masterwork of the late Sir Roy Grounds (1905–1981).

59 A3

333 'Naliandrah'
3 Glendye Court, Toorak
1967 Holgar & Holgar
GC, V, NA

A striking modern house with a cement-rendered sun-grille stretched across its first-floor facade, this design by Polish-born husband and wife team of John and Helena Holgar is one of a small number of similarly designed houses nearby that favoured luxuriant curves, terrazzo floors and an imagery of postwar Modernism that might have been found in Tel Aviv, Mexico City or Oscar Niemeyer's Brasilia. Overlooked by orthodox architectural historians and heritage bodies, 1960s houses such as this one and others in East St Kilda, Caulfield and Elsternwick are in danger of disappearing entirely from view.

334

334 Former Brighton Municipal Offices

15 Boxshall Street, Brighton
1959-60 Oakley & Parkes
GC, V, A

The former Brighton Municipal Offices are a red-brick miniature of Frank Lloyd Wright's Guggenheim Museum, New York (1946–59). Designed by architect KF Knight within the office of Oakley & Parkes, the feature of the main circular public lobby is a ceramic mural and a spiral ramp which leads to a semi-circular public lobby at first floor. The tapering red-brick drum houses the council chamber on the floor level above the main lobby space, while the attached flat-roofed ground- and first-floor spaces contain offices and circular planned rooms. Broad, flat concrete eaves have square cutouts to become pergolas and act as horizontal counterpoints to the vertical volumetric composition of intersecting cylinders. Additional to these skilfully rendered Wrightian spaces and forms are the peacock blue interior furnishings and furniture created by industrial designer Grant Featherston.

86 C5

335 Godsell House

491 Balcombe Road, Beaumaris
1960 David Godsell
GC, V, NA

David Godsell was an architect with a strong interest in Frank Lloyd Wright's principles of an organic architecture, Coomaraswamy's *Transformations of Nature in Art* (1956), the module of the tatami mat and the Japanese love of asymmetry. This house for his family is the embodiment of his ideals. Built on a steeply sloping site, it is a skilful interplay of horizontal roof and floor planes over a number of levels. With cantilevered eaves and a linear skylight in the living room glazed with smoked topaz glass, this house planned around a courtyard was designed on a 4-foot module. Fawn coloured bricks, glass and Californian redwood were the sole materials used, all left in their natural finish throughout. The notched bricks at wall corners and the brick returns emphasising mass, the coved lighting and wide horizontal boards give warmth to this Usonian reformulation.

•••

Another convincing interpretation of Wrightian ideals is the former Don Breedon House, 34 Were Street, Brighton (1966), winner of a 1966 RAIA citation for house design and designed by Geoffrey Woodfall.

32 A7

336 Williams House

4 Glenard Drive, Eaglemont
1962–63 Charles Duncan
GC, V, NA

Charles Duncan is one of the most gifted 1960s interpreters of Frank Lloyd Wright in Melbourne. His first new house for the Williams family won him the 1965 Victorian Architecture Medal for single house design. Built in clinker brick, with layered flat roofs and planar walls that encompass and enclose both indoor and outdoor space, this is a house blending the spareness of a Richard Neutra plan with the mass and warm textures of Frank Lloyd Wright.

Below: Plan of Godsell House (1960)
SOURCE: *Beryl Guertner,* Gregory's 200 Home Plan Ideas

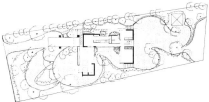

185

● 1962 The United States begins
military build-up in Vietnam

● 1962 Nuclear confrontation over
Cuba between USA and USSR

● 1963 Ord River irrigation scheme
begins in Western Australia

337

338

2L D3

337 Domain Park
193 Domain Road and Park Street, South Yarra
1960-62 Romberg & Boyd
GC, V, NA

Domain Park is Robin Boyd's most visible
Melbourne landmark. Based on his interest in
Walter Gropius and TAC's Interbau housing,
Berlin (1957), Japanese Metabolist notions of
stacked trays of living space served by point
vertical elevator towers and also Paul Rudolph's
similar formal concerns for spatial platforms,
the building contains a variety of plan types and
rooftop penthouses, all served by the rear lift
towers which rise high above the roof. The north
facade is a free and abstract composition of
glazed balconies, recessed bays and the leading
edge of each floor slab. Markedly different from
its neighbours, this vertical tower slab was initially
criticised for its lack of scale and for its visibility
from the adjacent Royal Botanic Gardens. Today,
however, immaculately maintained, its location
and its views are unsurpassed.

2B G6

338 Jimmy Watson's Wine Bar
333 Lygon Street, Carlton
1962 Romberg & Boyd
GC, V, A

Designed by Robin Boyd, this is the amalgamation of three 19th-century shop/residences into
one. The brick party walls of the existing
buildings can still be seen inside the new shell.
The bagged brick cubic facade, which was painted
white, evokes a vernacular Mediterranean image,
a shift for Boyd away from strictly abstract ideas
of truthful structure and the single line solution.
Instead there is an investigation of humble
building forms that might have universal
application. Boyd's design might also have been
inspired by the whitewashed outbuildings of
Australian homesteads. There are mulberry-

painted deep reveals to the doors and windows
on Lygon Street. Inside, the cellar theme of quarry
tiles and whitewashed walls is consistently
applied, while upstairs sliding timber screens
and private dining spaces provide a completely
different atmosphere to the bar below.

1A G7

339 Royal Insurance Group Building
430-444 Collins Street, Melbourne
1962-65 Yuncken Freeman
GC, V, A

One of Melbourne's most elegant and early
precast concrete-clad International Modern
office designs, this 18-storey tower was
awarded the Victorian Architectural Medal in
1967. It was the prelude to a series of black-clad
commercial and institutional buildings designed
by Yuncken Freeman. Set back from the street, a
gesture which gives the simple black form its
significant presence, the tower is clad in precast
panels finished in reconstructed black granite.
Each of the panels was pre-double glazed with
dark thermal tinted glass before erection, and
the glass was fitted so that no frame was visible
externally. Referred to by some as the 'Black
Stump', the broadsheet *Cross Section* concluded
that Royal Insurance was 'realised as an
architecture playing it so cool that it makes
every other city building in Melbourne look like
an overdressed juke box'.

•••

Another distinguished precast concrete panel
design by Yuncken Freeman can be found at the
Scottish Amicable Building, 128-146 Queen
Street, Melbourne (1966).

340

31 K6

340 Delbridge House
55 Carlsberg Road, Eaglemont
1960-61 owner-designed and built
Emery Balint (engineer)
GC, V, NA

Designed by its owner, a builder not an architect, with assistance from RMIT lecturer in structural engineering Emery Balint, Delbridge House is a tour-de-force of glass and reinforced concrete. It is a 1960s period piece: sheer minimalism externally and exuberant 'Featurism' inside. Located deep on its block, each of the floor slabs seems impossibly thin and the sliding glass walls tempt fate for those inside. On entry from the open undercroft of the house into a glazed hall, stair treads cantilever from a Castlemaine stone wall and lead to a first-floor living room. The balustrade is a series of overlapping open brass squares, while the main bathroom is a chromatic delight of Italian glass mosaic tiles. The top floor contains an open terrace and a bedroom/study with views to the Yarra Valley.

Observing the fact that all kids love to climb and be on different levels, I designed a building that would reflect this, by use of levels, and low spaces for example. They like the comfortable feeling of the low scale—it's almost the womb-like syndrome.

•••

Kevin Borland's beliefs in participatory design, his egalitarian methods of design delegation within the office, and his bushman-like experimentation with structural techniques and expressive form were to influence a generation of young Melbourne architects. A crucial text for Borland was Serge Chermayeff and Christopher Alexander's Community and Privacy: Towards a New Architecture of Humanism (1963). These beliefs resulted in a rough-and-ready timber architecture, a baroque, ad hoc celebration of vigorous structural and functional expression which was especially attuned to bush sites and the exploratory lifestyles of the 1970s.

2F K3

342 Victorian State Offices and Premier's Office
1 Macarthur Street and 1 Treasury Place, Melbourne
1962-70 Yuncken Freeman
GC, V, A

The result of a competition where Yuncken Freeman went against requirements that an office tower be placed behind the Treasury Building, the Victorian State Offices is an examplar of 1960s precast concrete facade treatment of high-rise office buildings. Designed by Barry Patten, the offset tower on Macarthur Street and the low-rise Premier's Department on Treasury Place, have their window module designed to respect the proportion of the windows of the neighbouring 19th-century government buildings.

45 H8

341 Preshil, The Margaret Lyttle School
395 Barkers Road, Kew (view from Mount Street)
1962-70 Kevin Borland
GC, V, A

In 1962, Kevin Borland designed a hall at Preshil, one of a series of buildings awarded the RAIA Victorian Chapter Bronze Medal in 1972. The low-cost timber buildings were the result of an intimate process involving user, client and architect. The commission was a turning point for Borland: the consolidation of his design philosophy of an informal, client-based architecture. The task-orientated educational philosophy at Preshil where students and teachers worked together to solve problems was pivotal to Borland's design thinking. In a 1974 interview about these buildings, he was to say:

343

● 1964 The Beatles
tour Australia

Above: Plan of Richardson House (1963)

28 H3

343 Richardson House
14 Brewster Street, Essendon
1963 Graeme Gunn
GC, V, NA

Winner of the 1966 Victoria Architecture Medal in the domestic category, Richardson House was designed for maximum privacy and to provide an intimate relationship between the living areas and adjacent courtyard gardens, which were landscaped by Gordon Ford. The house was constructed in concrete block left exposed with timber ceilings and exposed beams in western red cedar. All floors except the two bedrooms and sunken formal living room were paved in quarry tiles. The design's centre was a rectangular court crossed by a timber pergola and paved in brick. On the house's external wall, the windows are deeply recessed slots which give the house its austere and massive formality. This planning of served and servant space suggests a knowledge of Louis Kahn and an interest in Mediterranean and Japanese courtyard houses, and also Clerehan & Bell's award-winning Simon House, Mt Eliza (1962).

2B A5
344 Saunders House
Cnr Gatehouse and Morrah Streets, Parkville
1962–63 David Saunders
GC, V, NA

Designed by University of Melbourne academic David Saunders for his family, this is one of the first convincing Brutalist house designs in Melbourne. It is an important work in Melbourne and rates beside Sydney houses such as Ken Woolley's own house, Mosman (1962), and Peter Johnson's own house, Chatswood (1963). In 1967, Neville Quarry said of the Saunders House that it was unique as an example of a new house of 'serious modern un-imitative architecture' inserted into a terrace house street. Materials were frankly expressed: reconditioned slate roofs, dark grey concrete bricks, stained timber stairs, internal walls lined throughout with old hand-made Hawthorn bricks and an off-form concrete slab ceiling to the ground floor. The typology of the 19th-century terrace house was respected by the use of double-storey form, balconies and a dominating linear orientation along the length of the block. With its contextual allusions, the Saunders House departs radically from the 1950s. Unfortunately, the severity of the original interiors has been lost with all exposed internal surfaces either plastered or painted.

●●●

Other important 1960s Melbourne houses indicating the shift towards the ascetic aesthetic rigours of New Brutalism are architect Neville Quarry's former house, 23 Duke Street, Kew (1966), and architects Judith and John Brine's (of Brine Wierzbowski) former house at 78 St Vincent's Place, South Melbourne (1967).

1B L4
345 Myer Department Store Aerial Crossover
At 290 Little Bourke Street, Melbourne
1963 Tompkins Shaw & Evans
GC, V, A

Designed by long-time Myer Emporium architects Tompkins Shaw & Evans, the Crossover was Victoria's first multi-level, public pedestrian enclosed bridge to cross a public thoroughfare to be approved by the Melbourne City Council. For this right, Myer's paid a yearly fee to connect, over 4 storeys, its two city stores. The elegantly detailed aluminium and glass curtain wall on both sides of the bridge revealing the ramped walkways within is complemented by illuminated bands of ceiling diffusers. The bridge concept was typical of 1960s urban ideals, where it was thought that bridges and platforms were ideal ways of avoiding the 'traffic jungle' below.

964 Dawn Fraser becomes only woman in
lympic history to win three successive gold
nedals for the 100-m freestyle

1965 Opera singer Joan
Sutherland returns to Australia

Photograph: Kenneth Ross

346

2L E3

346 Fenner House

228 Domain Road, South Yarra
1964 Neil Clerehan
GC, V, NA

The Fenner House exudes an image of privacy,
urbanity and attention to detail. Built in grey
concrete Besser block, the design is typical of
Neil Clerehan's efficient planning to gain as
much from the site as possible. Two internal
courts and a rear garden give northern orientation
to every room. Gracious entry stairs are a simple
but essential addition to the sobriety of this
modern home. Like Martin & Tribe's Van Straten
House, 44 Anderson Street, South Yarra (1937),
the careful composition of the blank front
facade ensures the car slips beneath the ground
floor. The Fenner House won the 1967 Victorian
Architecture Medal in the domestic category.
Next door is Guilford Bell's Bardas House,
222 Domain Road, South Yarra (1958).

•••

At the end of 1961, Neil Clerehan resigned from
directorship of the RVIA Small Homes Service
and went into full-time practice. Between 1962
and 1964, he was in partnership with Guilford
Bell. Clerehan's houses of the 1960s and early
1970s are understated Melbourne homes, high-
lighting efficient entry from car to house and a
minimum of building materials and finishes.

33 B8

347 Reid House

72 Macedon Road, Lower Templestowe
1964 Keith & John Reid
GC, V, NA

The 1960s houses of Keith and John Reid
demonstrate renewed interest in the enclosing
and centring qualities of the individual room. In
1964, *Cross Section* described John Reid's own
house as 'outside a simple and "anonymous
non-featurist" type of architecture that makes it

virtually unique. The interior is given a touch of
theatricality with eight peeled radiata pine logs
which support the exposed rafters of the
cement tiled roof. Internally, the log columns
created three celebratory zones of lofty interior
space within the exposed volume of the roof.
Outside, the house appears as a modest pavilion.
A simple symmetrical front to the street, white
planar walls and a hipped roof are modest
domestic signs concealing a rich interior.

2K J2

348 The Domain
Former BP House

1 Albert Road, South Melbourne
1962-64 Demaine Russell Trundle Armstrong &
Orton; 1993 Synman Justin & Bialek
GC, V, NA

One of the most important office buildings to
be built along St Kilda Road in the 1960s, BP
House became a benchmark for quality
corporate design in the move to decentralise
from the city centre. In charge of design was
director Tony Armstrong and his assistant Don
Webb. These two architects produced distinctive
Wrightian-influenced designs for the Royal
Melbourne Golf Club, Blackrock (1967); Kew Golf
Club (1972); and the Australian Medical
Association offices, Parkville (1969). The final
design, a curved high-rise slab, its plan an
eighth part of a circle, was chosen partly
because its form referred to the shape of BP's
London headquarters; a low-rise, convex and
classically styled Edwardian baroque pile. By
contrast, Australia's BP House was to be tall,
boldly concave and uncompromisingly modern,
with its floating linear balconies with an incised
geometric key pattern. It was a completely
different corporate language to the glazed
curtain wall of the 1950s. In 1993, BP House
was converted into 104 residential apartments.

349

1B R4

349 Total Carpark

170-190 Russell Street, Melbourne
1964-65 Bogle Banfield & Associates
GC, V, A

The Total Carpark is one of Melbourne's best examples of Japanese-inspired Brutalist architecture where off-form concrete is employed in emphatic structural and functional expression. The balustrade treatment and clear expression of load and support is comparable with Kenzo Tange's Kagawa Prefectural Offices, Japan (1958). The mixed-use building, with an office block resembling a giant television set supported on cruciform concrete beams above a series of floating parking decks, is also possibly the first building in Australia to combine a multi-storey carpark, an office building above, shops at ground level and a theatre in the basement. With Bernard Joyce as project architect, the Total Carpark was one of a number of this firm's innovative designs which included the boldly expressive Mid-City Cinemas, 194-200 Bourke Street, Melbourne (1977); St James Church of England, Glen Iris **(327)** and St Vincent's Private Hospital, Victoria Parade, Fitzroy (c. 1972).

31 K9

350 Purcell House

17 Hartlands Road, Ivanhoe
1964 Guilford Bell
GC, V, NA

Like Philip Johnson's Hodgson House, New Canaan, Connecticut (1951), the Purcell House is comprised of slim brick wings which create a private courtyard. The plan is an H-shape, with the two wings of formal living spaces and bedrooms bridged by a kitchen/family room which opens onto the courtyard. On the front, north face of the house, outrigger beams form a pergola. Bell employed a standard dimension for

all wall openings and a formal symmetry dominates each elevation. The floor-to-ceiling window, the width and height of which was also the dimensional module for a door or French window, was to be a continuing theme in his work. Bell detested windows cut out of walls and rarely in his houses after c. 1960 is there a traditional window to be found.

1A F8

351 National Mutual Life Centre

435-455 Collins Street, Melbourne
1965 Godfrey Spowers Hughes Mewton & Lobb
Grace Fraser (landscape architect)
GC, V, A

Built on the site originally occupied by the Western Markets, the National Mutual Life Centre is one of Melbourne's best examples of the postwar urban design concept of a high-rise slab with an open landscaped plaza at ground level. The office tower does not have a conventional glass curtain wall. Instead, it has deep horizontal spandrels and thin vertical brass rod-like elements—glass has disappeared in favour of floating horizontal mass and vertical decorative delicacy. The north-facing plaza with car parking underneath offers welcome spatial relief and also the opportunity to stand back and see surrounding towers and street facades rarely seen in full elevation.

Above: Plan of Purcell House (1964)
SOURCE: *Imrie*, 1952-1980 Architecture of Guilford Bell

1966 Australia changes to decimal
currency, introduces dollar and cents

1966 The film *They're a Weird Mob*
has record run

1966 The satirical magazine *Oz*
moves from Australia to London

352

32 E5

352 Museum of Modern Art at Heide
Former Heide II

7 Templestowe Road, Bulleen
1965 McGlashan & Everist (David McGlashan);
1991 Gregory Burgess Pty Ltd (rose garden pavil-
ion); 1993 Andrew Andersons (gallery extensions)
GC, V, A

Heide II is located on a site rich in association
with Melbourne avant-garde painters of the 1940s
such as Albert Tucker, Joy Hester and Sidney
Nolan, who lived and painted in the adjacent
Victorian weatherboard farmhouse, now known as
Heide I, which also housed its owners, noted art
patrons John and Sunday Reed. They commissioned David McGlashan to design 'a romantic
building, ageless, and with a sense of mystery; a
quality of space and natural light appropriate to
a gallery, and the sense of walls within and
extending into a garden'. Described by Neil
Clerehan as 'International style set down amongst
the melaleucas', Heide II was built in Mt Gambier
limestone, timber and glass, and massed as a
series of L-shaped masonry walls interlocking to
form a sequence of internal and external spaces
—a sophisticated de-Stijl composition in plan
and section. Each space has its own external
court, all of which interconnect to form a maze
of outdoor rooms. In 1968, Heide II was awarded
the RAIA Victorian Chapter Bronze Medal. In
1980, the Reeds donated it to the National
Gallery of Victoria. Heide II was subsequently
converted into an art gallery and various
additions have been made to it and the 15-acre
sculpture garden which fronts the Yarra River.

●●●

*Other residential designs which display
McGlashan and Everist's masterful open planning
and fine detail can be found at: Grimwade House,
Old Melbourne Road, Rye (1960); Reed House,
7 Gladstone Avenue, Aspendale (1961, much
altered); Guss House, 18 Yarra Street, Kew
(1963); and Carnegie House, Kildrummie Court,
Sorrento (1967).*

263 C2

353 Saper House

60 Dunmoochin Road, Cottles Bridge
1965 Morrice Shaw
GC, NV, NA

Due to the excellent building possibilities of the
local soil and a limited budget for this house,
pise construction and secondhand materials were
used. The main fireplace, den, bedroom and bathroom cells were formed in curved mud-brick
enclosures. Collections of beer bottles set into
some of the mud walls give a mellow amber light
to their interiors. The tall volume of the central
living area is roofed by radiating timber beams
which form two mushroom-like roof umbrellas.
The geometry of the roof was that of two intersecting circles with organic extensions on either
side to provide extra functional space. Telegraph
pole columns were located at intervals around
the circumference of the circles and the resulting

*Above left: Plan of Museum
of Modern Art at Heide*

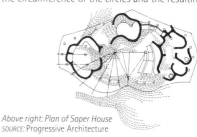

Above right: Plan of Saper House
SOURCE: *Progressive Architecture*

354

1A E6

354 AMP Tower and St James Building
527-555 Bourke Street and
111-141 William Street, Melbourne; 1965-69
Skidmore Owings & Merrill (San Francisco) in
association with Bates Smart & McCutcheon;
Clement Meadmore ('Awakening')
GC, V, A

The AMP Tower and St James Building are important indicators of the shift towards monumental tower and urban plaza design in the mid-1960s. The tower's design is believed to have been partially inspired by Eero Saarinen's CBS Tower, New York (1962-64). The vertical lines of the tower of russet-coloured reconstituted granite panels contrast boldly with the splayed and angled colonnade of the St James Building, which forms an L-shaped arcade of shops on two sides of the tower plaza. A further counter-point is expatriate Australian Clement Meadmore's 'massive bent box of Cor-ten steel', 'Awakening'. The AMP Tower and St James Building remain in almost flawless condition, and are a rare example in Melbourne of a public space enclosed by a tower and perimeter block.

165 D10

355 Former BP Administration Building
Crib Point Refinery, The Esplanade, Crib Point
1966 Don Hendry Fulton
GC, V, NA

With its upturned eaves and dainty formality, this building signifies attempts to find new ways of expressing monumentality. Designed by Don Hendry Fulton, designer of the Weipa mining township (1958-1965), Far North Queensland, and, with Ernest Milston, the uranium mining township of Mary Kathleen (1956) near Mt Isa, the former BP Administration Building is planned with offices at first-floor level and staff dining and meeting rooms at ground level. Meticulously detailed with folding ventilation panels and louvred windows, the overhanging glazed first floor and colonnade detail recalls Walter Gropius and TAC's US Embassy, Athens (1956). Like Romberg & Boyd's Zoology Building, ANU, Canberra (1965) and Bunning & Madden's National Library of Australia, Canberra (1968), Fulton's Modernist temple in the bush sits within a group of institutional and commercial office buildings of the period that sought acceptance through abstract classicism and the rigours of structural and material modulation. In 1966, this building was awarded the RVIA Architecture Medal in the General Buildings Category.

1B R5

356 Hoyts Cinema Centre
134-144 Bourke Street, Melbourne
1966-69 Peter Muller
AC, V, A

The Hoyts Cinema Centre is the largest Frank Lloyd Wright-influenced design in central Melbourne. It is also the largest and most elaborately detailed off-form concrete tower in the central city. Inside, the foyer is split level, walking half-up and half-down into each foyer, with an escalator being provided for the highest level. When complete, the complex contained three cinemas and ten floors of office space. The Centre is Muller's largest commission in Australia. A designer of numerous Wright-inspired houses in Sydney and Adelaide, his other major works are luxury hotels such as the Bali Oberoi and Amandari hotels, Bali. Peter Muller achieved recognition early as a brilliant house designer with a flair for reinterpreting the organic architecture of Frank Lloyd Wright. He was the first Australian architect to win a Fulbright Travelling Scholarship and graduated MArch from the University of Pennsylvania in 1950. Muller set up a highly successful practice in Sydney in 1953.

357

2B C1

57 Whitley College

71 Royal Parade, Parkville
1962–65 Mockridge Stahle & Mitchell
C, V, A

split face, grey Besser brick, Whitley College recalls the geometric forms of Roy Grounds's houses of the early 1950s. A university and theological college, the circular main building is planned like a doughnut. Inside is a central courtyard landscaped by Beryl Mann, with curved concrete seats and Australian native trees, palms and tree ferns, a complete contrast to the avenue of elms in Royal Parade. The slight protrusion from the circular form at the site's corner indicates the college chapel inside.

67 C10

58 House

700 The Esplanade, Brighton
1966 Chancellor & Patrick
GC, V, NA

Chancellor & Patrick, Melbourne's most skilled interpreters of Frank Lloyd Wright's Usonian house principles, produced convincing modern house designs through the 1960s after their residential practice had boomed on the Mornington Peninsula in the 1950s. With its T-shaped plan, vast areas of glass, flat roofs, wide eaves, and grey Besser bricks, this house repeats themes of emphasised horizontality contrasted by vertical brick piers explored in earlier elevated houses such as the Iggulden House, Wells Road, Beaumaris (1956), and another house in White Street, Beaumaris (1959). As with virtually all of the Chancellor & Patrick houses, the carport is completely integrated into the overall composition.

•••

The partnership of David Chancellor and Rex Patrick began in 1953. In addition to their mutual interests in Wright's Usonian and Prairie style house designs, they had an abiding interest in the works of Walter Burley Griffin and Marion Mahony, and also the structural logic and expressive devices employed by Austrian emigre architect resident in Los Angeles, Richard Neutra. In the 1960s, they expanded and major commissions included: Frankston Community Hospital (1963–79); halls of residence at Monash University (Deakin, 1964–65; Farrer, 1967; Howitt, 1967; Robert, 1972; Richardson, 1972); halls of residence at La Trobe University (Chisholm, 1970-74); St Matthew's Presbyterian Church, 8 Park Road, Cheltenham (1964); and St Peter's Church, Mornington (1966).

2L D2

359 Kurneh Flats

Cnr Domain Road and Anderson Street, South Yarra
1966 Bernard Joyce
GC, V, NA

A devotee of Mies van der Rohe, modular planning and the court spaces and structural standardisation of Japanese architecture, Bernard Joyce was also an inventive planner of flats, designing numerous blocks in 1960s Melbourne. Kurneh is an example of Joyce's commitment to the Modernist principle of the plan as generator of form and his belief in making architectural design available to the general public. At Kurneh, the planning principle is remarkably simple—four central double-storey flats with four double-storey flats at each corner. Each of the eight flats has a private courtyard garden. The lower ground floor provides undercover parking and storage space. This formal arrangement of cells about an implied communal centre recalls Louis Kahn's Trenton Bath House in New Jersey, USA (1955), and the 1950s house designs of American John Johansen.

360

360 Menzies College
Menzies Drive, La Trobe University, Bundoora
1965–70 Romberg & Boyd
AC, V, A

One of Robin Boyd's largest built projects, Menzies College exemplifies his attempts to shrug off his reputation as just a designer of houses. The choice of materials—concrete, brick and vertical slot windows—follows the La Trobe University masterplan by Roy Simpson (Yuncken Freeman), which aimed to achieve a unified character for the campus. Boyd's robust use of off-form concrete, pod projections and bold angled struts, however, indicates a more openly Brutalist idiom, which contrasts with the subdued character of neighbouring 1960s buildings. Inspired by contemporary Japanese architecture and the latest British university buildings, Menzies College, while a striking Brutalist landmark, was not without controversy. Its design emasculated by budget cuts, Menzies College was briefly the cause of student unrest at the harshness of its finishes and appearance.

361 Harold Holt Memorial Swimming Centre
High and Edgar Streets, Glen Iris
1967–69 Kevin Borland & Daryl Jackson
GC, V, A

Unfortunately named after the prime minister who drowned in surf off Portsea, this complex is one of Melbourne's significant Brutalist landmarks. It is distinguished by its concrete block and off-form concrete construction, industrially glazed walls and the timber trusses which span the indoor pool. Circulation elements such as the pedestrian ramp and semi-circular stair become sculptural features at the point of entry. Elsewhere, chamfered walls and skillion roofs indicate a shift in Melbourne from a restrained 1960s Modernism to a sculptural, more expressive idiom.

362 Featherston House
22 The Boulevard, Ivanhoe
1967–69 Romberg & Boyd
GC, V, NA

In 1967, Robin Boyd produced the epitome of the 'idea' house. During initial client discussions Grant and Mary Featherston remarked that, 'We wish we could live in a courtyard'. On a steeply sloping site, Boyd provided them with just that. Between two solid brick wing walls lay an exposed garden of moss and ivy. At each end, a wall of glass implied the unimpeded slope of the ground passing down towards Darebin Creek. The living, dining, study and master bedroom spaces inside this shed, which was roofed in translucent fibreglass with dacron fibre underneath, were solid timber platforms supported off massive beams which hung within the wide open glasshouse volume. The only vertical element was a massive, pier-like brick fireplace. The house was a rationalised version of Bruce Goff's Bavinger House (1950), a spiral house with a garden interior and open floating balcony saucers. The extraordinary idea of the Featherston House had its antecedents in Boyd's own house (318) of platforms beneath an all-encompassing roof slung on cables, and in the Wyn (1954) and Date House (1955) projects, the earliest examples of Boyd's free floating platforms or trays of living space within a shed.

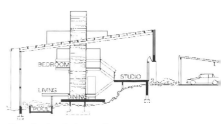

Above: Section, Featherston House
SOURCE: *Architecture in Australia, February 1971*

363

363 BHP Research—Melbourne Laboratories

245–273 Wellington Road, Mulgrave
1969 Eggleston MacDonald & Secomb
1992 additions (Eggleston MacDonald & Secomb)
GC, V, NA

Constructed in Aus-ten 50 (or Core-Ten, as the Americans call it), a steel which rusts to form a protective coating, BHP's research laboratories at Mulgrave are an excellent advertisement for the company's founding product. Eggleston MacDonald & Secomb's Brutalist design is an elegant and minimalist expression of load and support, two steel and concrete platforms, glass and nothing else! At the rear, a sunken court with a centrally placed sculpture opens off the staff dining area. Based on Ludwig Mies van der Rohe's elevated Farnsworth House, Plano, Illinois (1945–50), and Eero Saarinen's rusted Core Ten corporate campus, the Deere Corporation Headquarters, Moline, Illinois (1960–62), these award-winning laboratory buildings epitomise the interests in rational and robust structural expression of the firm's design director Roderick MacDonald. In 1992, the firm added a second wing to this complex, employing a similarly bold structural expression in steel, but painted white and with glass smoky black instead of clear.

•••

Other significant 1960s and later buildings by Eggleston MacDonald & Secomb (EMS) include: offices for Wes Lofts (Aust) Pty Ltd, 135 Abbotsford Street, North Melbourne (c. 1966); EMS's former offices, 215 Grattan Street, Carlton (1967); Educational Resource Centre, University of Melbourne, Parkville (c. 1972); and the former State Bank and Galleria, corner Elizabeth & Bourke streets, Melbourne (1975–80).

364 Clerehan House

90 Walsh Street, South Yarra
1968 Neil Clerehan
GC, V, NA

Extending the townhouse themes of his earlier Fenner House **(346)**, Neil Clerehan in designing his own house emphasised themes of privacy and the exposure of structure and materials. Hidden from the street by a dower house which occupies about one-third of the site, the double-storey Clerehan House has an off-form concrete ceiling and the main structural south wall has cantilevering terrazzo stair treads connecting the two levels. The house is set back from the northern boundary, enabling all the main rooms to face a paved court containing a pool and terrace garden. Honest structural expression throughout the house can be seen in the heavy concrete lintel of the first floor north wall, providing both sill and spandrel panel to the windows of the first-floor bedrooms. The elimination of passage space is achieved by implying circulation routes within the house by changes in floor surface. In the living room, a large, circular opening in the brick wing wall provides visual continuity between the other entertaining spaces on the ground floor. Possessing a rigorously linear plan and minimal palette of materials and colours, this under-stated modern home is characterised by the honest pursuit of, as Clerehan himself puts it, contemporary 'living patterns' rather than 'intriguing forms'.

The City and the Bush
1970–80

1970–1980

During the 1970s, Melbourne's architecture appeared polarised between city and bush.

In Melbourne's CBD, the consolidation of sites continued to produce giant skyscraper and plaza developments. The twin towers of **Collins Place** (1970–80) and its state-of-the-art space-frame broke the contiguous building line of Collins Street, while the black-painted steel of the free-standing **BHP House** (1967–72) was corporate cool at its most elegantly severe. These slick skyscrapers of international pedigree contrasted with efforts to humanise street level with the Bourke Street Mall and, after the 1976 competition, the achievement of a new city square (1979, now demolished) at the corner of Swanston and Collins streets designed by young architects Denton Corker Marshall. More gritty aspects of social feeling were also experienced as Melbourne's streets came alive with a different sense of *civitas* with the Vietnam moratoria of the early 1970s.

Outrage had begun to smoulder over the way in which the physical face of city was being changed. While the Melbourne Underground Rail Loop (1974–82) signalled completion of infrastructure plans that dated from the 1920s, the move to construct new freeways—in particular, the Eastern Freeway—met with stern opposition from local residents. The Melbourne Strategy Plan of 1974 compiled by Interplan, a group led locally by the McIntyre Partnership with American consultants including Donald Wolbrink and Daniel Mandelkar, encouraged intensive development at the east and west ends of the CBD. It was met with lukewarm response and only acted upon a decade later. In the city and inner suburbs, resistance to development became stronger and more vocal.

The most public issue was conservation and community concern over the 19th-century building stock that had been rapidly depleted during the 1960s urban building boom. The Collins Street Defence Movement was formed in September 1976 by members of the architectural and planning profession led by Evan Walker and Professor Charles Robertson. Its aim was to redress the progressive decimation of one of Melbourne's premier streetscapes. This resurgence of interest in local history was matched by the training of architects skilled in conservation practice. Local resident groups such as the Carlton Association formed to combat unsympathetic development and successfully challenged government programs of slum clearance. Controlled development, planning guidelines, ideas about context and historical styles all experienced new appreciation by the end of the decade.

Amidst this urban tension, in Melbourne's outer eastern suburbs, project house developments such as Merchant Builders' Winter Park, Doncaster (1970) and Vermont Park, Vermont (1974), were landscaped with Australian natives, railway sleepers and volcanic rocks. Bagged brick or brick seconds, window frames stained brown or pale eucalypt green, diagonal timber lining boards and purple and orange plastic hemisphere light shades were part of the new 1970s house. Architects were interested in informality, woodsy detailing, mezzanine floors, sliding doors living onto timber decks. The houses and schools of Graeme Gunn, Kevin Borland, Daryl Jackson and Evan Walker had free and inventive compositions and were programmatically innovative. The early 1970s were characterised by a continuation of the traditions of Brutalism. Built in off-form concrete in bold chunky angled shapes with black smoked glass and adorned with appropriately unadorned numbers and letters, the **Plumbers and Gasfitters Union Building**, Carlton (1970) was politically and architecturally de rigeur for a profession intent on being seen to be up to date. For even smarter architects, concrete block and angled industrial glazing gave these chamfered buildings a correspondingly smarter finish.

By the late 1970s, a mood of change and debate influenced Melbourne architecture. Some architects went into politics. *Transition*, Australia's first journal of architectural criticism was founded in 1979. There was a shift in commonly held aesthetic ideals and this was exhibited in houses and small-scale institutional buildings designed by young architects outside the central city. Common to the work of architects like Edmond & Corrigan, Peter Crone, Greg Burgess and Norman Day was an architecture that celebrated not just function but the artifice of design. The polychrome brickwork, ordinariness and openly suburban nature of Edmond and Corrigan's **Chapel of St Joseph**, Box Hill (1976–78) and their **Resurrection Church and School**, Keysborough (1976–81) were locally and nationally, the most confronting works of this late 1970s shift.

Robin Boyd's untimely death in 1971 seemed to close the door on an earlier generation's tasteful extension of modernism and open another door for a younger generation to a new and liberating understanding of function, and the value of the suburbs whose relentless sprawl was an unavoidable part of Melbourne. The change was swift, so that by 1980 most Melbourne architects had gone postmodern.

PHILIP GOAD

367

369

1A F5

367 Former BHP House

140 William Street, Melbourne
1967–72 Yuncken Freeman
GC, V, A

Intended to promote the use of steel in building construction and to set new national standards for the height of a steel-framed building, the former BHP House was also claimed to be the first office building in Australia to use a 'total energy concept'—the generation of its own electricity using BHP natural gas. Yuncken Freeman sought advanced technological advice from structural engineer Fazlur Khan of Skidmore Owings & Merrill (SOM), Chicago. Khan's innovative idea of the high-rise tower was the principle of a giant stiff structural tube where the tower became a pure cantilever. Back in Melbourne, under the direction of Barry Patten, the design of the steel structural sheath was refined to a strikingly simple concept comprising four basic elements: a central steel-framed core; a stiff steel and glass facade; steel trusses to link the core to the facade; and a steel deck flooring system. With no interior columns, all structural loads were carried down by an outer skin of steel and a central services core rising the full height of the building. The facade was a 10-mm thick skin of welded steel over 50 mm of concrete insulation fire protecting and housing the main steel frame. This steel skin was erected before the placement of the concrete and in effect constituted permanent formwork. Yuncken Freeman experimented with the tower's proposed finishes with the construction of their own offices at 411–415 King Street, Melbourne (1970), a black Miesian building that recalled the Bacardi Building, Mexico City (1957-61).

•••

BHP House was the third in a trio of fine commercial office towers designed by Yuncken Freeman in this part of the central city that *included Eagle House, 473 Bourke Street (1971), and the former Estates House, 114–128 William Street (1974–76). It was also complementary in period, scale and expression to Shell House (now demolished), cnr William and Bourke Streets (1958) and AMP Tower (1963–65) opposite, and both designed with SOM assistance. Despite mixed views within the profession, BHP House received an RAIA Award of Merit (1973) and RAIA Bronze Medal in 1975.*

Even with recent changes by Geyer Design, BHP House remains Melbourne's most sophisticated and elegantly severe tower of the postwar decades.

2G B1

368 Catholic Archdiocese of Melbourne

383 Albert Street, East Melbourne
1969–71 Yuncken Freeman
GC, V, A

Designed by Roy Simpson of Yuncken Freeman, the offices for the Catholic Archdiocese are an accomplished urban design which defers to the grandeur and scale of William Wardell's bluestone St Patrick's Cathedral **(37)** next door. On Albert Street, stepped fountain pools act as a foil to the offices behind, while in the centre of the complex is a circular courtyard giving light to the collection of humble low-rise forms. The repetitive formal language and blue-grey colour of the battered piers evoke the qualities of a Gothic monastery. Located on the site of St Patrick's College (demolished 1968), the bluestone tower of which remains, this complex is now admired as a sensitive contextual response to a difficult site by one of Melbourne's unsung architectural figures, RAIA Gold Medallist (1997) the late Roy Simpson, master planner of La Trobe University and designer of the Civic Theatre and Library, Canberra, in the Australian Capital Territory.

368

1B T8

369 Collins Place
45 Collins Street, Melbourne
1970–80 Harry Cobb (IM Pei) in association
with Bates Smart & McCutcheon
GC, V, A

In the 1970s, Collins Place represented the dramatic consequences of the consolidation of numerous sites in the CBD where the final complex could entirely change the quality and scale of an existing urban character and streetscape. The twin tower concept, one housing an international hotel and the other originally housing the headquarters of the ANZ Bank, was joined at ground level by a sunken plaza roofed by the wonder structure of the 1970s, the space frame.

1D U5

370 Victorian Arts Centre
St Kilda Road, Melbourne
1969–84 Roy Grounds; 1981 Roy Grounds
(Concert Hall); 1984 Roy Grounds, later
Suendermann Douglas McFall (State Theatre);
1995–96 McIntyre Partnership (spire extension);
1996–97 Ashton Raggatt McDougall (corporate
lounge & restaurant refurbishments); sculptures
(Inge King; Carl Milles; Clement Meadmore)
GC, V, A

After the National Gallery of Victoria (NGV) opened in August 1968, Roy Grounds set to work on the remaining part of the proposed Victorian Cultural Centre. He died before seeing the final completion of a project which had first begun in 1959. The brief outgrew the site and eventually the Victorian state government was persuaded to annex the land all the way to the Yarra River. The State Theatre grew to accommodate 2000 patrons and the spire was lifted to house the flytower, becoming an enormous latticed space frame (unfairly called a frame for a tutu). The Concert Hall, originally intended to be underground, became a massive cylinder. Grounds was happy to acknowledge its formal similarity to Rome's Castel Sant' Angelo. The Concert Hall became, like the National Gallery of Victoria, another fortified gateway to Melbourne. While Grounds and his partners provided world-class facilities within, Academy Award-winning expatriate set designer John Truscott (*Camelot* and *Paint Your Wagon*) was called in to decorate the interior. He made the underground theme, especially in the Concert Hall foyers, an idea of a rich jewelled cave. Grounds's faceted cave interior to the Concert Hall was retained and, in the State Theatre, the wire mesh chandelier-like ceiling, a Grounds idea, was also kept. Elswhere, Truscott overlaid a Morris Lapidus-like lushness which contrasted dramatically with Grounds's sombre exteriors. He introduced traditional theatrical colours of gold and red. Recently, the Amcor and Commonwealth Bank corporate lounges have been refurbished in daring ways, adding a new level of richness to this popular complex.

45 A4

371 Townhouses
76 Molesworth Street, Kew
1968 Graeme Gunn
Ellis Stones (landscape design)
GC, V, NA

This set of six concrete block townhouses won the 1970 RAIA (Victorian Chapter) Bronze Medal for Graeme Gunn and Merchant Builders. Each house was designed for family living with at least three bedrooms and provided with private courtyards, a double carport and at least one large reinforced concrete balcony at first floor level. Landscaped with bluestone blocks and Australian natives while retaining existing trees where possible, the village-like complex employed honestly expressed materials and construction, realising the 1960s shift towards a more humanised and textured communal living environment.

372

75A I6

33 B10

372 South Lawn Underground Car Park, University of Melbourne

South Lawn, University of Melbourne, Parkville
1970–72 Bryce Mortlock (Master Planner)
Loder and Bayly (Structural Engineers)
Rayment and Stones (Landscape Architects)
GC, V, A

A building with no elevations and the result of Bryce Mortlock's 1970–71 Master Plan for the University of Melbourne, this underground car park for 400 cars in one master stroke solved the problem of too many cars on campus and provided a green heart for the state's oldest university. Hyperbolic paraboloid concrete shells, supported off concrete columns, provided sufficient depth of soil on the surface for substantial trees and a broad expanse of lawn, paving and a reflecting pool which directed foot traffic on axis towards the historic Law Quadrangle **(41)**. Below ground, the resulting space resembles a vast Gothic crypt (for cars not coffins), a wonderfully mysterious space that was used as the setting in a scene from the Australian film *Mad Max*. In addition to the brilliant landscaping by Ron Rayment and Ellis Stones, which combines native and exotic planting, and the now signature unmortared brick paving which is the unifying surface treatment for the remainder of the campus, at the east entrance can be found a door from a house in St Stephen's Green, Dublin (1745), while the west entrance is framed by two atlantes from the demolished Colonial Bank, Elizabeth Street (1880).

373 Winter Park

137-141 High Street, Doncaster
1970–75 Graeme Gunn for Merchant Builders
Ellis Stones (landscape architect)
GC, V, NA

This cluster development of 20 houses (four clusters) has them grouped around common access courts and facing onto a park. Each cluster of five houses was made up of five different house types: the Studio, the Courtyard, the Cellar, the Two Storey and the Terrace House. Each of the houses was simply planned, of brick veneer construction and with a mix of terracotta tile and steel deck roofs, a discreet and low-key vernacular of muted good taste— the recipe of the Merchant Builders project house. The design, planning and ownership structure of Winter Park marked the high point of Merchant Builders' director David Yencken's idealist hopes for an alternative vision of suburbia. The reallocation of what had normally been high-maintenance private garden space to collective parkland maintained by the body corporate was an attempt to provide public amenity. The strata title provided for common ownership of the driveways, courtyard and public parkland by a body corporate formed from the individual homeowners at the same time that the strata subdivision was registered. Winter Park became a demonstration model of the possibilities of the cluster concept and was built prior to the Cluster Titles Act and Interim Cluster Code (1975) established by Yencken on behalf of the Victorian government.

●●●

The influential project house building company
Merchant Builders Pty Ltd was established in
1965 by David Yencken and John Ridge. Inspired
by the success and quality of the Pettit and Sevitt
houses in Sydney, Ridge and Yencken asked Gunn
to design three prototype houses to fill the void

375

n the Melbourne project housing market. andscape designer Ellis Stones, who had worked with Gunn on his Dawson-Grove House, Frankston 1962), supervised the landscaping for all Merchant Builders projects until his death in 1975. The Terrace House, the Studio House and he Courtyard House were built as display homes on the corner of Springvale Road and The Boulevard, Glen Waverley, in 1965 and were an immediate success.

76 F3

374 Former Fletcher House
3 Roslyn Street, Brighton
1972 Morris & Pirotta
GC, V, NA

This collection of angular forms is one of the early so-called chamfer style houses in Melbourne. The parents' bedroom is situated at the front of the house with its own private walled court. Dining and living rooms are separated by a fireplace, while above is a mezzanine study open to the dining room below. Upstairs is a separate children's bedroom block, with its own bathroom and outdoor terrace. The house is organised off a linear spine which bends at 45 degrees to avoid the carport and was conceived as a skylit gallery of angled glazing, rather than as a passage.

Above: Plan of Fletcher house

375 Plumbers and Gasfitters Union Building
52 Victoria Street, Melbourne
1970 Graeme Gunn
GC, V, A

One of Melbourne's toughest examples of Brutalist architecture, the chunky expressionistic forms of this building contrast dramatically with the sober classicism of Reed & Barnes's Trades Hall **(69)** next door. Down the side lane and from the rear, however, Graeme Gunn's office block sits comfortably with its neighbour in scale and modulation. A bold statement of growing trade union power, Gunn's chamfered volumes are a no-nonsense response for a no-nonsense client. The imprint of the vertical, timber-boarded shuttering and the regular set of filled holes indicating rod supports for the formwork is the subtle texture of these 'brut', functionally expressive elements. Smoked black glass increases the sculptural nature of the forms, which echo work by Japanese Brutalist architects Arata Isozaki and Kunio Mayekawa. Gunn also designed the chamfered concrete block Amalgamated Metalworkers Foundry Shipwrights Union (AMFSU) Building, Victoria Parade, East Melbourne (1974; altered).

•••

Brutalism
A critique of the uniformity of pre-war Modernism was New Brutalism, a term coined in 1952 by London architects Peter and Alison Smithson. Expressed structure and materials, especially exposed brick and off-form concrete and graphically functional external expression were the 'honest' design recipe. Inspiration varied and included outright emulation of the off-form concrete (beton brut) postwar architecture of Le Corbusier. In Melbourne ,the Harold Holt (361) Pool and Plumbers and Gasfitters' Union Building (375) are two of the best examples.

376

2K G2

376 City Edge

Park Street, Kingsway, Napier Street,
Eastern Road, South Melbourne
1972-76 Daryl Jackson Evan Walker Architects
AC, V, A

City Edge, a 180-unit development, was designed as an alternative to the suburban house and also the high-rise apartment tower which had, given the dominating presence of the Housing Commission towers, become a vilified housing choice. A variety of townhouse unit types were located around a vehicle-free central garden platform above a concealed ground-level car park. A raised 'footpath/street' also ran through the development between each 'wall' of housing. The form of the new units echoed the 19th-century terrace house with diminutive front gardens, individual front doors and balconies. The vocabulary of tan bricks, off-form concrete and stained timbers combined with Australian natives was, however, a complete contrast to the local context. The bush had entered the city.

86 G4

377 Leonard French House

22 Alfred Street, Beaumaris
1973 John Baird, Cuthbert & Partners
AC, V, NA

The plan of this house is an elaborated dumb-bell with a gallery spine on both levels connecting a very large, double-height living block to a double-storey bedroom and studio block. The materials are exposed concrete blocks, natural galvanised steel deck, concrete slabs and slate paving. On a typical suburban site, with such a palette of materials and the client requirement for large areas of internal wall space, this chamfer style house appears as a giant fortress.

45 D8

378 Methodist Ladies College (MLC) Resource Centre

Glenferrie Road, Hawthorn
1973 Daryl Jackson Evan Walker Architects
GC, V, A

This reinforced concrete library building has a robust sculptural manipulation of ramps and stairs about the building's entry. While arguably overscaled and brutish even for the asceticism of its clients, the Resource Centre nevertheless solves circulation and access problems on a cramped and sloping site. The Jackson/Walker partnership (1965–79) was designing similarly gutsy education buildings for other private schools in Melbourne, including Lauriston Girls School (1967), Presbyterian Ladies College (1971), St Leonard's College (1972), Mt Scopus Memorial College (1974), St Paul's School, Woodleigh, Golf Links Road, Baxter (1974–79) **(382)**, and, in the public system, Princes Hill High School (1973).

76 F4

379 Coakley House

4 The Avenue, Hampton
1975 Peter Crone
GC, V, NA

At the Coakley House, the principal materials are concrete block, natural galvanized steel decking, angled glazing and limed timber. All the materials are hard-wearing and suggest a non-suburban industrial vernacular of steel and concrete. Inside on the floor, black rubber Pirelli sheet is used. The house has a dumb-bell plan with a central kitchen/bathroom/ laundry spine separating the parents' suite and living rooms from the children's playroom and bedrooms. The chamfer in plan reduces floor area and there is a sculptural manipulation of the volumes which have been saddlebagged off the dumb-bell spine. This plan was refined in Crone's Porritt House, Osbourne Drive, Mount Martha (1978).

380

67 D7	166 K1

380 Former Seccull House
2 North Road, Brighton
1972 Guilford Bell
GC, V, NA

he former Seccull House is the epitome of the
rbane walled haven and patrician architect
Guilford Bell's rigorous control of the ritual of
ntry and receiving. The house is entered along
a wide pergola-covered loggia and beside white
walls. The end of this passage is blank. One
urns to the right and enters a square skylit hall
and immediately engages with another axis of
arrangement. This flat-roofed house with an
-shaped plan is Bell's tour-de-force of white
tucco, black steel and travertine. Enclosed
courts off bedrooms and the family area, and
major court spaces adjacent to the living and
dining wing create a dense network of carefully
controlled interiors.

●●●

*Interviewed by Australian House and Garden
(1980), Guilford Bell was quoted as saying:
'Almost every city home I design has its roots in
Middle Eastern architecture—where one enters
the home through a single opening in a
protective wall and comes into the environment
of a garden and inner buildings. People feel safe
in such a place.'*

Below: Plan of former Seccull House (1972)

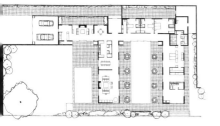

381 Woodley House
Keating Avenue, Sorrento
1974 Cocks & Carmichael
GC, V, NA

The 1970s beach houses of Cocks & Carmichael
are exemplars of fine detail and craftsmanship—
a return to the generous open plan and also the
art of architectural formalism. Interested in the
work of the New York Five, especially the work
of Charles Gwathmey, Robin Cocks designed this
holiday house so that its first floor had a 360-
degree outlook to the bay on one side and the
ocean on the other. The walls of this living area
have large areas of sliding plate glass opening
onto generous living decks, which almost
doubled the living spaces within.

107 E3

382 St Paul's School
Woodleigh, Golf Links Road, Baxter
1974–79 Daryl Jackson, Evan Walker Architects
1998 Sean Godsell (additions)
GC, V, A

St Paul's School at Woodleigh was typical of
Jackson/Walker's inventive approach to progressive curricula and bushland sites that enabled
experimentation in circulation and the creation
of urban groupings of buildings. A school with a
focus on the gaining of practical skills and
community participation, its design process and
the informal timber buildings of standard components paralleled Kevin Borland's participatory
design methods employed at Preshil **(341)**.
Jackson/Walker continued to explore these
themes in the planning of large institutional
facilities such as the State Bank Training Centre,
Baxter (1976–78).

383

67 C9

383 Abrahams House

17 Seacombe Grove, Brighton (view from beach)
1979 Daryl Jackson Architects
GC, V, NA

A rare case of a Melbourne house sitting right on the beach, the Abrahams House has a brick box core with a series of large angled pergolas/ gazebos. The outdoor rooms created by these robust timber structures provide shade and wind protection, as well as the familiar bleached seaside colours and textures. The ground-floor plan of living spaces is airy and open, but the shading and volume is graded and a complex layering of light and zoning occurs. Jackson's conscientious knowledge of contemporary living patterns had informed his own holiday house at Shoreham (1978). Given his experience with Evan Walker in school design in the 1970s, this skill in understanding complex programs and resolving them in workable plans was to make Jackson one of the most sought-after designers in the 1980s not just of houses, but also of large-scale institutional buildings.

2A F6

384 Former Gillies House/Studio

Rear of 22 Shiel Street (view from Kerrs and Norris Lane), North Melbourne
1976 Suzanne Dance
GC, V, NA

A tightly planned collection of corrugated iron-clad forms, this house/studio is hidden within a garden at the back of two terrace houses. Suzanne Dance, noted for her ability to create intimate and whimsical forms, provides an inner suburban reading of corrugated iron, a material mythologised by others for its literal associations with rural buildings. With each space given its own differentiated volume and fenestration— the dining table, for example, sits within a circular room—Dance has created a gritty urban jewel.

89 C8

385 Resurrection Church and Resurrection School

402 Corrigan Road, Keysborough
1976–81 Edmond & Corrigan
AC, V, A

Like their Chapel of St Joseph **(387)**, Edmond & Corrigan's Resurrection Church and Resurrection School provide an alternative to traditional notions of Catholic worship and educational buildings. This complex and the adjacent residential units have a startling array of raw expressionistic forms, and planning that provides personal spaces such as bay windows, balconies and porches around buildings. These are 'communities of buildings' and their forms encourage the making of judgments based on familiarity and taste—the same principle as the catechism. While the architectural sources range from German Expressionists Fritz Hoger and Hans Scharoun to Americans Robert Venturi and Charles Moore, the overall sense is that of a very local palette of materials and forms. This larrikin cry from the suburbs remains a potent reminder of the extraordinary influence that the challenging work of Edmond & Corrigan was to have on the next generation of Australian architects and students.

2M G11

386 Former Prahran High School Library

Orrong Road & Molesworth Street, Prahran (view from rear)
1979 Gregory Burgess
AC, V, NA

This two-level extension (currently vacant) is perhaps the most directly mannerist work in Burgess's spiritually based oeuvre. It is like a polychrome brick Villa Savoye which has its own inner life and has grown with curved corners, curved end bays with circular windows and curved hit-and-miss brickwork screen walls.

387

387 Chapel of St Joseph
Strabane Avenue, Box Hill
1976–78 Edmond & Corrigan
AC, V, A

One of the pivotal buildings of the 1970s and also one of the most hotly debated for the bombshells this building aimed at conventional architectural taste, the award-winning Chapel of St Joseph is a most unusual church. The architects were briefed to provide a space that was filled with light and could be understood not just as a place of worship, but also as a community hall or clubhouse. Architecturally, the church is a tribute to the expressionism of Erich Mendelsohn and Hans Scharoun, a celebration of the banal (hence its vilification by half of the architectural profession) and a rallying cry for the suburbs. The ironic painting of the steel portals in duck-egg blue (a reference to the Virgin's pale blue cloak?), the corner cut-out window up high, and the overall sense of unpretentious and ordinariness suggest that there is hope in the everyday.

Below: Chapel of St Joseph (1976–78)

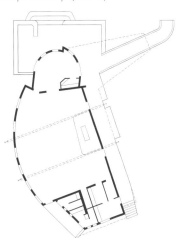

388 Scroggie House
52 Kensington Road, South Yarra
1976–78 Gunn Hayball
GC, V, NA

Within the simple white cubic forms of the Scroggie House, white-walled rooms are planned around a light court that is also a double-height garden room defined by glazed and latticed ceiling and walls. The idea of a translucent centre to a house was not unknown to Graeme Gunn, who would almost certainly have been aware of his former employer Robin Boyd's design for the Featherston House, Ivanhoe **(362)**. The use of a volume defined by a frame also appears in Gunn's Redlich House (1979), where a double-height and angled pergola delineates an outdoor room.

389 Fuzzell House
15 Russell Street, Toorak
1979 Max May
GC, V, NA

This is one of the most fanciful houses ever to be produced by Max May, whose career to date had comprised a series of award-winning, sleekly detailed and relentlessly modern houses. This vast apricot picturesque 'ruin' sits behind high walls, together with a pool, a crumbling wall of cyclopean stone blocks, a decaying brick wall (concealing a tennis court), a date palm and a giant ladder truss hovering in mid-air, forming a cantilevered sunshade to an entire wall of glass. Were these the ironic ruins of modern architecture or had the romantic pleasures of architecture returned?

Modern Metropolis
1980–1998

1980–1998

A framework for future development sees Melbourne 'on the move'.

Informed by themes of urban consolidation, heritage and context, Melbourne came to be understood as an entity that could be enriched by strategic design. As a result, the Modernist rush to raze sites slowed dramatically. While there continued to be casualties—ironically hospitals and most notably **Queen Victoria Hospital** in Lonsdale Street and Leighton Irwin's Prince Henry's Hospital (1939) in St Kilda Road—the management of a minor economic boom in the mid-1980s raised the city skyline considerably and with seemingly little fuss.

The incoming Labor government had introduced the Central Business District Interim Development Order (CBD–IDO) in 1982. It was the first attempt in decades to wrest planning control from the hands of the Melbourne City Council (MCC) and provide a framework for future development. Part of this plan was the idea that the CBD have a low centre and high edges to retain view corridors and maintain urban scale in historically sensitive areas. As the eastern and western ends of Melbourne's CBD rose in height, the valley of Swanston and Elizabeth streets was retained to highlight the spires of **St Paul's Cathedral** and the clocktower of the **Melbourne Town Hall**. New skyscrapers **101 Collins Street** (1986–90), **333 Collins Street** (1990) and **120 Collins Street** (1991) adopted 1920s street architecture at footpath level and, at their peaks, the pinnacles and temple tops of New York. The mirrored **Rialto Towers** (1986) continued Mies van der Rohe's 1920s visions of skyscrapers as soaring glass crystals, while the **Telecom Tower** (1988–92) paid homage at ground level to Melbourne's rich spatial grain of arcades and lanes, and, above, to local high-rise favourites, ICI House and BHP House. In a joint venture with state government, the MCC created Swanston Walk (1992), a semi-pedestrian precinct. The MCC's Urban Design and Architecture Division initiated an inspired program of footpath widening, new street trees, public art and police and newspaper kiosks, complementing their city-wide program of upgrading community spaces.

With the 1987 stockmarket crash, architectural attention was drawn to issues of urban consolidation through re-housing the inner city. Melbourne City Council instituted 'Postcode 3000', a scheme encouraging the refurbishment of existing buildings for housing and the building of new inner-city apartment buildings. Developers also began to convert 1960s skyscrapers such as **BP House** into apartments. New medium-density housing developments sprang up at a rapid rate. Some, such as Nonda Katsalidis's **Melbourne Terrace Apartments** (1994) were exuberant architectural cocktails that included sculpture and serrated fins. Others such as Craig Rossetti's **Townhouses**, Richmond (1995), were inventive reinterpretations of the row house, while the **Yarra Park Housing**, Richmond (1993), and **Tyne Street Housing**, Carlton (1992), were more complex amalgams of different housing forms and scales.

Over this same period and after decades of turning its back on the Yarra, the city began to look at the river as the next axis of potential development. The result was a strategy to replace industrial buildings on the river's south side and make use of the north sun, city views and the potential to link Roy Grounds's **Victorian Arts Centre** (1969–84) with a proposed Museum of Victoria between Spencer Street and the Grimes Bridge. The **Southbank Promenade** (1989) designed by Denton Corker Marshall became the link for a 3-kilometre stretch of mixed-use development, the most prominent early addition being Southgate (1988–91), designed by Buchan Laird & Bawden in association with San Francisco-based Sprankle Lynd & Sprague. Part of the overall strategy was the **Yarra Footbridge** (1987–89), a picturesque 'coathanger' that made a pedestrian connection to Melbourne's grid.

In 1990, during the economically flagging Labor years, the idea of a casino to raise revenue was floated. A Casino Control Act was instituted in 1991 and, when the Liberal government swept to power in 1992, the idea was pursued with vigour. South Bank became the preferred site for the **Crown Casino** (1993–96) and for three years it became one of the largest building projects in Victoria's history. Other changes, meanwhile, had already been made to the South Bank masterplan. The site for the new **Museum of Victoria** (1996–99) was shifted to the Exhibition Gardens, Fitzroy, and another competition held for its design. Back on its former site, the museum's reinforced concrete beginnings were cloaked and extended as the **Melbourne Exhibition Centre** (1995–96).

The new casino, exhibition centre and museum were part of Agenda 21, the Liberal state government's program of major civic projects launched in 1992. Included in one of the most politically charged building programs of the century in Victoria were the redevelopment of the **State Library of Victoria**, the restoration of **Old Customs House** and the **Treasury Building** for public use, redevelopment of the **Regent Theatre** and the City Square, and a tram line that would loop Melbourne's grid. By the end of the 20th century, the city was to be transformed by an 'edifice complex', experiencing an astonishing shift both politically and architecturally from the socially conscious years of the 1970s.

With the rise of Postmodern theory, the idea of architecture as a bearer of meaning had become popular again. Buildings were adorned with symbols and ideas of reference and context were explored. At **Parliament Station** (1982), there were fibreglass Tuscan capitals in the ticket lobbies copied directly from nearby **Parliament House**. Even arch-Modernist Harry Seidler at **Monash Civic Centre** (1982–84) produced a sign of municipal authority with his Pop-scale Veronese battlement which doubled as a gargoyle. Paralleling this interest in signs and symbols was the revision of urban theories which had led to the slum clearance of the 1960s and the erection of numerous high-rise Housing Commission towers. Demonstrating both this revision and an interest in Postmodernism was the Ministry of Housing's **Kay Street Housing**, Carlton (1981–83). Under the direction of John Devenish, progressive architects such as Greg Burgess, Peter Crone and Edmond & Corrigan explored brick polychromy and 19th-century terrace house forms on diminutive infill house sites. At Racecourse Road, Flemington, and Sutton Street, North Melbourne, some of the bases and tops of the commission towers were refurbished; brave attempts to humanise entry spaces and redress problems of alienation and neglect.

Overshadowed in public perception were the activities of Melbourne's less obvious but lively architectural subcultures. In the tradition of compositional experts such as Haddon, Desbrowe-Annear and Griffin, in the Boom style and Federation traditions of layering, veneers, expressive composition and complex ideas of representation, Melbourne architects demonstrated a hearty respect for the local, as well as idiosyncratically assimilating overseas trends. Unlike the impressive sporting structures of the **Great Southern Stand** (1990) and the **National Tennis Centre** (1987–88), which draw on 1920s Russian Constructivism and Melbourne's 1950s structural–fuctional tradition, the specifically Melbourne experiments have generally been confined to three main building types: the institution, the university and the house. Institutional buildings such as Edmond and Corrigan's **Windsor Fire Station** (1997), Peter Elliott's **Carlton Baths** (1989), the **Brunswick Health Care Centre** (1985–90) of Ashton Raggatt McDougall and the community buildings of Gregory Burgess such as his **Box Hill Community Arts Centre** (1990) and **Eltham Library** (1994) are all predicated on breaking down scale, creating communities of buildings rather than one overall image.

In the 1990s, there was a renaissance in university architecture. Enlightened patronage at RMIT University set the pace with Edmond and Corrigan's postmodern tour-de-force **Building 8** (1991–94) and Ashton Raggatt McDougall's **Storey Hall** (1995), two controversial landmarks signalling a new civic sensibility.

While Melbourne's suburbs in the 1980s and 1990s continued their crawl outwards, speculators promoted the neo-Georgian townhouse, threatening to consolidate single house/garden sites in the leafy suburbs of Toorak, Malvern and Canterbury. The days of the grand Melbourne garden may soon be gone in the wake of dual occupancies and the historicist townhouse. Dotted throughout this resurgent suburbanism of mannered anonymity, a new generation of architects such as Robinson Chen, John Wardle, Wood Marsh and Sean Godsell persevered with the traditions of Modernism and their own crusades for difference in the design of the family house.

By 2000, Melbourne's population is expected to reach 3.5 million. New development is focused on water again. The docklands will become the site of sporting stadia and huge residential projects. More recently, the state government began to rationalise the network of freeways, completing projects planned for decades. The $2 billion City Link project due for completion in 1999 will link the Tullamarine, West Gate and South Eastern freeways and includes the Domain Tunnel beneath the Botanic Gardens. On the Western Ring Road, landscape designers and architects beautified cuttings and verges, the **Bell/Banksia Street Freeway Link** (1992) being one of the best. The final scheme of the century will be Melbourne's proposed Federation Square (1997–2001) in front of St Paul's Cathedral. With this, the city will have reached yet another stage of cyclical completion—another episode in its perpetual reinvention of itself as a modern metropolis.

PHILIP GOAD

390

2B J5

390 Kay Street Housing for
the Ministry of Housing
Station Street, Kay Street, Carlton
1981–83 Gregory Burgess; Edmond & Corrigan;
Peter Crone
GC, V, NA

As a direct response to the Housing Commission
of Victoria's slum clearance and 1960s high-rise
estates in inner suburban Melbourne, the
Ministry of Housing under the direction of the
late John Devenish initiated a completely
different response—urban townhouse infill. The
Kay Street precinct in Carlton became the
benchmark for this shift in philosophy, with
progressive architects outside the Ministry being
invited to design specific responses to specific
sites. The idea was to blend in with the local
streetscape and not signal this housing as being
clearly low-income. Each architect's response
was very different. Gregory Burgess (cnr Kay
and Canning streets, and also 78, 80 Station
Street) designed expressionistic, red-brick
townhouses. Edmond & Corrigan (75, 79, 78 Kay
Street) introduced polychrome wire cut brick
and neo-Baroque curves, hinting at Carlton's
rich postwar Mediterranean migrant past. Peter
Crone (51, 53, 56, 62 Station Street) produced
townhouses that fit seamlessly into the
surrounding urban fabric.

Below: Ground floor plan of Kay Street Housing (1981–83)
SOURCE: *Hamann,* Cities of Hope

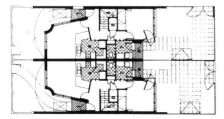

115 B6

391 Mowbray College
Centenary Avenue, Melton
1981– onwards Norman Day & Associates
GC, V, A

A thoroughly inventive and rich complex of
school buildings, Mowbray College is Norman
Day's most notable work. A staged development,
this low-cost school is community sponsored.
Planned like a mini-city with streets and lanes,
and buildings such as the cylindrical library
(1986) and arts centre (1987), with its silhouette
of skylights, the college's teaching spaces are
like houses where, as Day says, 'Each house
[classroom] becomes the home for a particular
student group for the year and is "lived-in"
accordingly'. Multi-coloured patterned brickwork
and lattice screens complement the simultaneous ironic critique and celebration of Australian
building types. This is Melbourne's most joyful
set of Postmodern structures.

1B V3

392 Parliament Station
Spring Street, Melbourne
1982 McIntyre Partnership Pty Ltd
GC, V, A

Part of Melbourne's attempt to rationalise its
commuter train network , Parliament Station is
one of three stops on the city's underground
rail-loop which circles the Hoddle grid. Located
next door to Parliament House, the dimensions
of the stairways and concourses are generous
and the palette of materials is understated:
silver-grey granite panels, blue metal wall panels
at platform level, and charcoal and off-white
floor tiles throughout. As a counterpoint, details
from Knight and Kerr's building reappear in the
public concourse and on the platform. Near the
ticket barriers, giant white fibreglass replicas of
the fluted Roman Doric column capitals provide
an instant point of recognition.

395

104 H7

393 Sea House

Caraar Creek Lane, Mornington
1982 Peter McIntyre
GC, NV, NA

Perched high in the ti-tree on a cliff above the water, Peter McIntyre's own beach house is an intimately scaled timber getaway—a house of window seats and spectacular views; of different levels and decks; of sliding screens to shade or close the house. It owes much to Charles Moore's Sea Ranch, California (1965–), and also McIntyre's own design for the family's ski lodge at Mt Buller (1961–onwards). At the Sea House, in a single, highly resolved composition of simple shed-like forms, McIntyre has achieved a wonderful collection of open and closed spaces which captures perfectly the spirit of the holiday house as haven and prospect.

71 C3

394 Monash Civic Centre

293 Springvale Road, Glen Waverley
1982–84 Harry Seidler
GC, V, A

One of four Melbourne buildings by Sydney architect Harry Seidler, this is a rare case of Seidler using a giant sign in a building. The profile of the council chamber is a Pop-scaled medieval battlement from Verona. Seidler would argue, however, that the shape was determined by the dramatic internal shape of the chamber and the subsequent draining of water from the unusually shaped roof—a gargoyle shoots water into a pool below. Concrete and split-face brick frames detached from the building announce entry points—unlikely semiotic devices from the Sydney rationalist. Seidler's 1980s planning technique of using opposing semi-circles appears, as does his familiar massive brise-soleils (sunshades), which have been a trademark of his enduring late Modern works.

Viennese-born Harry Seidler (1923–) emigrated to Australia in 1949. Educated at the Harvard Graduate School of Design under Professor Walter Gropius, his Australian designs of the 1950s were emulations of the houses of his idols Gropius and former employer Marcel Breuer. His first commission in Sydney, a house (1948–50) for his mother Rose Seidler at Turramurra, earnt him international notoriety. From the 1960s, Seidler skyscrapers began to appear in Sydney, then later in virtually every Australian capital city. In Melbourne, Seidler's built works include: Ringwood Cultural Centre (1980); Monash Civic Centre (1982–84) **(394)**; Shell House, 1 Spring Street (1988) **(403)**; and the Waverley City Gallery, 170 Jells Road, Wheelers Hill (1990).

1B V8

395 No. 1 Collins Street

1 Collins Street, Melbourne
1983 Denton Corker Marshall in association with Robert Peck YFHK
GC, V, A

No. 1 Collins Street was unusual in Melbourne at the time of its construction for restoration of several historic buildings on the same site, as well as the design of a contextually responsible high-rise tower behind. The stepped form of the pre-cast concrete panel-clad tower comfortably creates a new grain of height and scale in comparison to the foreground of small 19th-century houses. The gradation of window reveals across the facades is a subtle means of increasing the modelling and appearance of height of the corner tower. The lift lobby is located deep within the plan behind the required 9-metre depth of historic buildings, with axial entries from Collins Street and Spring Street.

396

398

29 H8

396 Brunswick Community Health Centre
11-13 Glenlyon Road, Brunswick
1985-1990 Ashton Raggatt McDougall
GC, V, A

Drawing on Ian McDougall's innovative Kensington Community Health Centre, 12 Gower Street, Kensington (1981-85), in Brunswick, Ashton Raggatt McDougall mined the architectural imagery of the surroundings as a means of direct identification with the place. Instead of quotation, however, the bay window, the warehouse shed (about to turn into a high-rise building) and the tilt-slab speculative office building were amalgamated into a literally compacted street facade. Inside, a vibrant geometric carpet design creates the next jarring addition to what has become a productive melange of human-scaled spaces, including a sun-trapping courtyard at the rear which evokes the scale of 1970s pre-fab classrooms. This is Melbourne architecture with an intellectual twist: good humoured, functionally responsible and mannerist all in one.

•••

In 1979, architects Ian McDougall and Richard Munday founded Australia's major postwar journal of architectural discourse Transition.

12 C12

397 Harvey–Beavis House
Narida Court, Eltham
1987 Lindsay Holland
GC, V, NA

The work of Lindsay Holland remains staunchly faithful to Modernist precepts and this house exemplifies Holland's meticulous attention to rational planning. This minimalist glass and corrugated iron-clad house of four bedrooms is an attempt to find a viable aesthetic and economic alternative to the typical suburban house.

2K C2

398 Macrae and Way Film Production
3 Francis Street, South Melbourne
1985 Biltmoderne
AC, V, NA

A surviving work of the flamboyant partnership (1983-87) of Biltmoderne—comprising architects Dale Jones-Evans, Roger Wood and Randal Marsh—the Macrae and Way Film Production offices are an exercise in decorative excess and formal fun. Studded with off-the-shelf concrete rosettes, the facade is like a giant brooch with a mirror glass cartouche and pointy ears.

2B G8

399 221 Drummond Street
221 Drummond Street, Carlton
1986 Ashton and Raggatt
GC, V, A

Built as a speculative venture for the Anglican Church of Australia, this is an exercise in making the skin of a building a provocative and formally inventive subject—a collage of tilt-slab concrete, brick veneer, mirrored glass curtain wall, pebble-tex and a series of faux bolt heads. The facade has the formal capacities to deceive, humour and confound the onlooker. The corner where pieces meet and others don't is the highly wrought climax of this theatrical exploration of surface.

Below: Brunswick Community Health Centre (1985-1990)

400

402

88 J9

400 Haileybury College Chapel

Springvale Road, Keysborough
1985–88 Philip Cox Richardson & Taylor;
mural, stained glass — Leonard French
GC, V, A

Built in a soft, orange red-brick to blend with the 1960s modern box buildings of Haileybury College, Philip Cox's design for the school chapel is a calm and clever box, its scale, warm textures and structural simplicity reminiscent of his best work in the 1960s in New South Wales. Cox has referred to the chapel's design as being loosely based on the image of a Norman 'keep'. A pyramid-roofed entry pavilion located on axis with the main school building opens onto a pergola facing onto a sunken courtyard. The chapel itself is planned as a box with four thick, habitable brick 'walls', but pulled apart at each corner to allow entry or light into the rectangular volume within. Each 'wall' then has its own function: altar, ante-chapel with organ above, gallery vestibule and choir, and vestry and side chapel.

1A D8

401 Rialto Towers

525 Collins Street, Melbourne
1986 Gerard de Preu & Partners in association
with Perrott Lyon Mathieson Pty Ltd
1997 podium alterations
GC, V, A

At one time the tallest building in the Southern Hemisphere, Rialto Towers comprises two sheer, uninterrupted irregular prisms, with their only definition a horizontal line of balcony below each crown. A highly controversial development that was prefaced by the demolition of the 19th-century Robb's Building at the corner of King Street, the most striking qualities of this ode to Mies van der Rohe's expressionist glass skyscraper projects of the 1920s are the building's changing colours as the sun sets. The towers have recently obtained an overscaled stripped neoclassical colonnade at ground level.

1B S8

402 101 Collins Street

101 Collins Street, Melbourne
1986–1990 Denton Corker Marshall Pty Ltd
1990 Johnson Burgee (foyer & entry columns on
Collins Street)
GC, V, A

101 Collins Street appears to be based on the New York skyscraper model—a tower that steps inward up its height and terminates in a pinnacle. In fact, the tower is essentially a square-planned stone-clad shaft with projections and recesses. The five-storey podium level on Collins Street is the building's most successful aspect—an abstract composition of modular frame, randomly filled and left empty, and vertical rods and baffles that fits seamlessly into the surface modulation of historic Collins Street. With a change of developer, however, Denton Corker Marshall (DCM) were passed over in favour of the New York firm of Johnson Burgee, who added the granite Tuscan Doric columns at street entry and the extravangant and opulent Tuscanesque foyer within.

•••

As a formal model, 101 Collins Street was predated by the completion of DCM's 222 Exhibition Street, Melbourne (1989), another square-planned tower. DCM's skill in street level urban architecture is also demonstrated in the expressed structural frame and variously infilled and finned facade of the office and carpark for 101 Collins Street which is located at 114–128 Flinders Street (1989).

403

404

1B V9

403 Shell House
1 Spring Street, Melbourne
1988 Harry Seidler & Associates
GC, V, A

Built on a corner of the city's defining grid, Shell House had one major limitation in its planning: the tower core had to avoid railway tunnels under the corner of the site. With extensive views over the Treasury Gardens and towards the Yarra River and Botanic Gardens, Shell's new Australian headquarters are designed as a snaking curve set back into the northwest corner of the site. Blinker-like walls screen out the rest of 19th-century Melbourne in favour of Seidler's late Modern baroque skyscraper with its faceted 'leg', the open plaza and sculpture that is a geometric transformation of the scallop shell.

2C A7

404 Office Building
61 Victoria Street, Fitzroy
1989 Carter Couch
GC, V, NA

Designed by Paul Couch, an employee of Romberg & Boyd in the 1960s, this quietly unassuming building is evidence of other traditions at work in Melbourne in the late 1980s. Its face masked by a louvred timber screen, of the sort favoured by Spanish Modernist Jose Luis Coderch, the structural principle behind this unpretentious infill building is that of tilt-slab concrete walls with propping beams and slabs in between. Inside, missing floors provide unexpected spatial richness, while elsewhere details are simple and industrially inspired. At street level, a veranda echoes nearby 19th-century shop verandas.

2G B8

405 National Tennis Centre
Batman Avenue, Melbourne
1985–87 Philip Cox Richardson & Taylor in association with Peddle Thorp & Learmonth
GC, V, A

Home to the Australian Open tennis championships, the National Tennis Centre includes numerous practice and competition courts, as well as a centre court that seats 15000 spectators. Much of the development is softened and concealed by earth berms. The main architectural features are the two massive, white-painted steel trusses which enable a retractable roof to slide back and forth.

122 G12

406 Athan House
Lot 1 Carcoola Road, Monbulk
1988 Edmond & Corrigan
GC, NV, NA

A madly bristling castle in the bush, Athan House is planned as a big V-shape. One wing houses living spaces; the other a string of bedrooms. At the point of the V is an eyrie reached via a triangular stairwell, a memory not just of Louis Kahn's Yale Art Gallery, but also of Roy Grounds's platonic geometries of the 1950s. This house does not refer to a romantic rural tradition of verandas—the decks on the north seem like drawbridges from the safety of the house into a bush wilderness.

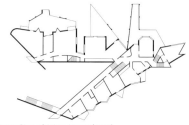

Above: Plan of Athan House (1988)

409

2G H7

07 Wheeler House

1 Rowena Parade, Richmond
988 Robinson Chen Pty Ltd
GC, V, NA

n internally focused house with complex
nterior volumes, Wheeler House also has careful
window placement to ensure privacy and the
apturing of sunlight. Devotees of the volu-
netric manipulations of Le Corbusier, the
mphatic massing of Louis Kahn, the use of
ght on sheer walls by Japanese architect Tadao
Ando and the space-defining walls and saturated
ues of Mexican architect Luis Barragan, Ian
Robinson and Kai Chen have created a
nonumental domestic work. Complementing
he intensity of this carved and sculpted haven
s the landscaping by Kate Cullity.

2B J4

108 Carlton Baths Community Centre

248 Rathdowne Street, Carlton
1989 Peter Elliott Pty Ltd
GC, V, A

Winner of the 1991 RAIA Victorian Architecture
Medal, the Carlton Baths Community Centre
redeveloped the 1890s outdoor Carlton Baths.
Using a palette of galvanised steel, glass block,
concrete pavers and tilt-slab reinforced
concrete, Peter Elliott provided a community of
buildings that indicated a de-institutionalised
notion of what a public building might be—a
picturesque *civitas*. The building's grey tones
and careful tectonic compositon compare with
contemporary Japanese architecture by the likes
of Itsuko Hasegawa and Toyo Ito. Each outdoor
space is composed as a separate urban design
vignette. Steel pergolas become new public
loggias.; circulation routes become public
streets. Peter Elliott's architecture has continued
to pursue a modestly urbane but consistently
humane progression towards contextual fit.

1D S2

409 Yarra Footbridge

Yarra River at Southbank
1989 Cocks Carmichael Whitford Pty Ltd
GC, V, A

The Yarra Footbridge has formed a much-
needed pedestrian link between the southern
edge of the city grid and the new developments
along the river's south bank. From afar, the
simple gesture of the bridge's arch and its
suspended triangle is a bold one; the experience
of crossing is dynamic and picturesque. Cocks
Carmichael Whitford are experienced domestic
designers, and their forays of into matters urban
have met with professional acclaim. Awards
have been received not just for this bridge, but
also for their refurbishment of the Centreway
Arcade **(163)** and the Bell-Banksia Streets
Freeway Link **(426)**.

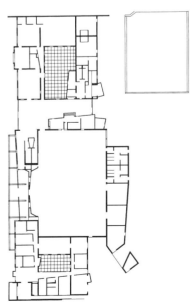

Above: Carlton Baths Community Centre (1989)

219

410

410 Great Southern Stand, Melbourne Cricket Ground

Brunton Avenue, Jolimont
1989–92 Daryl Jackson Pty Ltd in association
with Tompkins Shaw & Evans Pty Ltd
GC, V, A

Built to replace Purnell and Pearce's much-loved and austerely funtional Southern Stand (1937), the Great Southern Stand precinct accommodates a total of 60 000 spectators. Externally, the articulation of spectator movement through inclined ramps with lines of porthole windows and glazed stair bays is crowned by a dramatic half-ring of steel roof stays, masts and cantilever truss supports for the grandstand roof, recalling the kinetic engineering aesthetic of Constructivist stadia designs of the 1920s. The structurally expressive design reflects the involvement of Daryl Jackson (1937–), renowned in Australia for his expertise in sporting structure and stadium design. Each of the elevated seating galleries has uninterrupted, column-free views, with corporate sponsors' boxes stacked neatly between and above the two lower level galleries.

Below: Ground floor plan of Hildebrand House (1990)

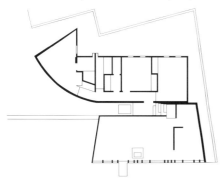

411 Adelphi Hotel

187 Flinders Lane, Melbourne
1990 Denton Corker Marshall Pty Ltd
GC, V, A

A refurbishment of Joseph Plottel's Moderne-styled Yoffa House (1937–38), the Adelphi Hotel is a minimalist boutique hotel and club. The original building becomes the neutral frame for an overlay of de-Stijl-like coloured and metal plates, planes, inlaid lights and random rhythms of vertical rods. On the roof, there is a glass-bottomed lap pool which overhangs the street like some Constructivist gesture. On the floors between, the hotel rooms are sharply detailed, while at lobby level there is a reception and restaurant graced by contemporary Australian artworks.

412 Hildebrand House

Lot 10, 57 Parklands Avenue, Somers
1990 Robinson Chen
GC, V, NA

The last house designed by the partnership of Ian Robinson and Kai Chen, the Hildebrand House is a testament to their skill in formal and spatial manipulation. From the street, the house appears as an introverted black mollusc partially embedded into the site. The street-facing side of the house is dark and mysterious, containing bed-rooms. The sea-facing side of the house contains the open living spaces with a wall of unevenly spaced glass panels and vertical rods which Le Corbusier called *ondulatoires*. The Hildebrand House is about themes of openness and closure, darkness and light, protection and release—a house about the experience and fundamentals of dwelling.

413

415

13 Box Hill Community Arts Centre

70 Station Street, Box Hill
990 Gregory Burgess Py Ltd
C, V, A

Vith its bulging and heaving roofscape, its
urved corners and vaulted ceilings, the Box Hill
ommunity Arts Centre has the feeling of a
uilding bursting with its own inner energy.
reg Burgess brought his collaboration skills to
ear in the building's design, with its adornment
y community artists, ceramicists and landscape
rchitects Kevin Taylor and Kate Cullity. Glazed
ricks and capping tiles; inlaid tiles; warm
hades of pink, orange and blue; and mottled
rickwork to a massive chimney give this
uilding a magical air. Influenced by the
nthropomorphism of Rudolph Steiner,
urgess's design is resolutely Arts and Crafts,
nd a challenge to conventional notions of what
modern architecture might mean and what we
xpect it to look like.

14 333 Collins Street

333 Collins Street, Melbourne
*1990 Nelson Architects International and Robert
Peck von Hartel Trethowan Pty Ltd*
GC, V, A

A late example of American Postmodern
Classicism in Melbourne, the tiered and domed
profile of 333 Collins Street recalls the 1920s
kyscrapers of New York. At ground level, large
bracket light fittings and luscious marble floors
continue the tradition that such buildings were
to be regarded as temples of commerce. The
abstracted tripartite facade sits comfortably in
Collins Street, while inside can be found Lloyd
Tayler and Alfred Dunn's fully restored Baroque
Revival dome of the Commercial Bank of
Australia (1891).

415 Telstra Corporate Centre
Former Telecom Corporate Building

242 Exhibition Street, Melbourne
1989-92 Perrott Lyon Mathieson
GC, V, A

In the tradition of No. 1 Collins Street **(395)**,
the former Telecom Corporate Building
incorporates a number of historic buildings at
ground level, as well as three former laneways.
Skilfully orchestrated by project designer Carey
Lyon, there is a layering of urban traces at
ground level, with the inclusion of striking new
infill buildings which adopt the principle of a
structural armature, the cantilever and anti-
gravity to mark their difference from the 19th-
century buildings between. Entry points to the
building other than the main corner are aligned
with the dimension and position of the former
laneways and become mini-galleria, echoing the
tradition of Melbourne's glazed arcades as well
as being mini-glazed skyscrapers when viewed
at entry. This technique of finding previous
layers of urban form and inventing new ones
reinforms the hybrid morphological structure of
the city. When one reaches the lift lobby after a
Piranesi-like experience of aerial bridges and
massive hanging forms, however, one finds the
pure form of the skyscraper core. The complex
tower form and its sleek black skin makes
another local reference: ICI House **(314)** with its
sun-hoods (more decorative than sensible), and
the sheer skin of the Rialto Towers **(401)**.
Behind all of these local evocations lies the Mies
van der Rohe-inspired skyscrapers of Chicago.

416

41

1B R7

1A K1

416 120 Collins Street

120 Collins Street, Melbourne
1991 Daryl Jackson Pty Ltd in association with
Hassell Architects Pty Ltd
GC, V, A

A slender skyscraper reflecting its origins in the high-rise projects of Chicago architect Louis Sullivan, 120 Collins Street also defers to the skyline of 1920s and 1930s New York. Designed with a recessed central shaft, this means that the corner bays, delineated as more solid elements, give the impression of soaring height. The base is planned with multiple entry points off surrounding streets. A garden plaza with fountain is formed in the space between the new and old, and a Jackson signature diagonal slash in plan indicates a deliberate urban gesture to create an access route to the lift core.

251 J7

417 Beach House

St Andrews Beach, Rye (view from beach)
1991–92 Nonda Katsalidis
GC, V, NA

Like a washed-up cargo crate, Nonda Katsalidis's beach house for his own family is a weathered box built to withstand the elements. A simple linear plan with a raised volume over the living spaces and a lowered section denoting bedrooms, the skeleton of the house is a hefty timber hard-wood frame with horizontal timber slabs stacked between. Above plate glass to the living areas, the raised volume is externally clad in steel which has rusted to its protective finish. At the junction of the two forms, a Luis Barragan-like gargoyle directs water onto cyclopaean boulders.

418 Argus Centre

300 La Trobe Street, Melbourne
1991 Katsalidis Architects with Axia Pty Ltd
GC, V, A

An exuberant collage of elements that recalls Constructivist experiments in dynamic composition, the Argus Centre is typical of Nonda Katsalidis's richly sculptural urban structures. Layers of facades and the implied intersection of three-dimensional forms break down the building's scale. The podium and foyer veneered in all manner of marbles and with an inverted and truncated cone are the theatrical street-level setting for this speculative office building. The absolute virtuosity of the composition transcends empty corporate formalism. Further up the street at 170 La Trobe Street (1991) is another Katsalidis-designed development with a collage of elements and a crown of double-storey apartments.

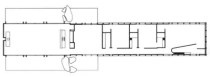

Above: Plan of Beach House (1991–92)

419

2B E12

80 F7

419 RMIT Building 8

Swanston Street, Melbourne
1991–94 Edmond & Corrigan in association with
Demaine Partnership
GC, V, A

Sitting on top of John Andrews's incomplete Union Building, RMIT Building 8 is Edmond & Corrigan's most significant central city building and the university's flagship building on Swanston Street. Built on a tight budget and with the constraints of having to accommodate the buildings below and next door, Building 8 is like the Athan House **(406)**, another magic castle. A new lift and service core were built and account for the medieval passage accessing the upper floors. The deep floor plate was maximised, resulting in rabbit warrens of rooms to the upper floors. Balustrade details, handrails and dadoes are built to last and the entire interior has the chaotic vibrancy of a pre-Renaissance city. From various points along Swanston Street, the expressionistic roofscape reveals more and more formal fantasy from the crystalline cornice and the Darth Vader exhaust hoods over the fire escape stairs, to the corrugated iron Matterhorn of the lift overrun. The coloured stone facade and its knitting needle, steel pipe strut supports continue the bastion theme, while on the Bowen Street side of Building 8, a polychrome and polygonal brick fire stair turret acknowledges Percy Everett's 1930s workshops **(269)** and provides the visual focus of one of RMIT's few outdoor spaces. Building 8 has revitalised RMIT's urban campus and is the first major expression of that institution's enlightened patronage of comtemporary architecture in the 1990s.

420 The Necropolis Crematorium and Chapel Complex

East of North Drive, The Necropolis,
Princes Highway, Springvale
1991 Bates Smart & McCutcheon
GC, V, NA

Like an unearthed monumental urban artefact, this design is indebted to Italian architect Aldo Rossi's seminal urban text *The Architecture of the City* (1966), which argued for the rethinking of the city in terms of building types being open to different uses over time. Bates Smart & McCutcheon's cylinder is the ghost of former building types—from Roman tombs to bases for gas containers. Adding to the building's serious function, skull-like white panels hover above the processional entry points. The centre of a greater urban plan, the crematorium will eventually be surrounded by chapels, thus creating an ideal city of the dead.

2F D10

421 Fire Station No. 28

Moray and Catherine Streets, South Melbourne
1992 Simon Swaney Pty Ltd
GC, V, NA

Located in South Melbourne in a freeway environment of grey concrete and light indus-trial structures, this smart, high-tech, image for the brigade was produced by Simon Swaney Pty Ltd. Tilt-slab concrete panels, natural anodised aluminium, obscure glass panels and clear structural and tectonic expression evince an image of no-nonsense efficiency.

1992 Mabo land title claim is decided in the High Court

1993 International Olympic Committee awards 2000 Olympic Games to Sydney

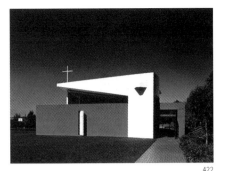

422

42

45 D7

422 Trinity Grammar School Chapel
Charles Street, Kew
1992 Crone Ross Architects
GC, V, A

The Trinity Grammar School Chapel is one of a series of award-winning buildings designed by Crone Ross for this Kew campus. The quadrant plan of the chapel is like a pair of hands opening to receive its congregation. From the forecourt, the resulting curved facade is composed as a series of doors. Peter Crone, one of Melbourne's most proficient detailers, has employed a white baked-enamel steel panel as a cladding material. Inside the chapel, the intersection of planar walls and simple volumes continues, concealing vestry spaces and allowing slots of light to illuminate the altar. White walls and pale timber pews give a feeling of Scandinavian simplicity.

2B F7

423 Tyne Street Housing
Tyne Street, Carlton
1992–1993 Williams & Boag
GC, V, NA

The Tyne Street Housing is a Melbourne City Council-sponsored development aimed at consolidating inner urban density with increased residential development located above a large carpark. Peter Williams and Gary Boag produced a sensitive development based on the urban grain of the 19th-century terrace house. Introducing a range of townhouses, studio apartments and terraces, Williams and Boag also intended that the home/office concept be easily adapted to each of the house types. An understated vocabulary of varying brick colours, ubtle evocations of pediments and diverse balcony treatments has resulted in a seamless urban fit and earnt for Williams & Boag the 1994 Victorian Architecture Medal.

Left: Plan of Trinity Grammar School Chapel (1992)

2L G5

424 Offices
5 Avoca Street, South Yarra
1990 Guilford Bell & Graham Fisher
GC, V, NA

This tilt-slab concrete box has a black steel and glass double-storey front. While the building's appearance is that of polished late Modernism, the reading is more complex. The form of the 19th-century terrace, with its double-storey cast-iron veranda attached to a simple brick box, is reinterpreted as a complete bay of glass and steel attached to a concrete box regularly perforated with openings of graceful Georgian proportion. This is undemonstrative and carefully calculated urban architecture.

2L K5

425 Country Road
Cnr Toorak Road and Chapel Street, South Yarra
1991 Metier III
GC, V, A

An entirely new store commissioned by this retail chain, this is an accomplished exercise in architectonics. On the corner, a huge suspended display case is the store's major sign, the flanking walls of which are made up of rectangular portals infilled with aerodynamically shaped shading baffles. Inside, the palette of finishes is calm and neutral—ivory and pale blond timber tones given an extra edge, with stainless steel cables, rails and balustrade details.

31 J4

426 Bell/Banksia Street Freeway Link
Bell Street, Heidelberg
1992 Cocks Carmichael Whitford Pty Ltd
GC, V, A

Like a scaly reptile skin that changes colour and shape with each change in direction, each wall of this freeway link is treated as a series of modular panels intended to be viewed at speed. The north wall, invariably in shade, has a convex shape and the grey tapered panels lean forward in the direction of travel. By contrast, the southern wall, invariably in sun, is concave, terracotta in colour, with a raised top border of exposed quartz aggregate triangles like the cresting of a chameleon.

427

429

427 Lecture Theatres/Computer Centre/Bookshop & Bistro

Caulfield Campus, Monash University
Sir John Monash Drive and Queens
Avenue, East Caulfield
1993 Denton Corker Marshall Pty Ltd
GC, V, A

Designed to make urban sense out of a campus of unrelated buildings, Denton Corker Marshall's (DCM) series of tilted, aluminium-clad volumes projecting through and above a neutral concrete grid frame relies on the placement of a colonnade of concrete 'sticks' across the building's northern front to link two undistinguished buildings and provide a north-facing entry to this campus. The crucial aspect of the scheme is the new relationship with the ground level, where shops and cafeterias create a sun-trapping street. Inside finishes are typically DCM: sheets of natural galvanised steel, sometimes acid-etched, perforated metal, fibre-cement panels; plasterboard and, occasionally, sheet steel.

428 Altona Meadows/Laverton Uniting Church

Cnr Central Avenue & Whitehead Court, Laverton
1993 Philip Harmer
GC, V, A

This award-winning church is a response to the most striking monumental architectural forms of the area — the aircraft hangars at Point Cook. Planned as a flexible preaching space beneath a curving corrugated iron roof, movable walls can open or close various spaces. Harmer's bold shapes, strong colours and graphic structural expression also hark back to the structural–functional era of the 1950s, when churches such as St Faith's, Burwood **(326)** reflected postwar liturgical advances.

429 Storey Hall, former Hibernian Hall

344–346 Swanston Street, Melbourne
1887 Tappin Gilbert & Dennehy;
1992-95 Ashton Raggatt McDougall with Allom
Lovell Associates; 1997 Grant Amon with ARM
(re: VAULT café)
GC, V, A

Storey Hall is a tour-de-force of cerebral architecture and formal virtuosity. Restoration and refurbishment of Hibernian Hall and replacement of its ghastly 1960s interior was complemented by an entirely new structure to the hall's south. Containing now a 750-seat auditorium, conference centre, lecture theatre, seminar rooms, art gallery and café, Storey Hall is a remarkable architectural advertisement for RMIT University. Green is the dominant colour and refers to the Hibernian Irish Catholic community who built the 1887 hall, and also, when combined with purple and white, the colours of the Women's Political Association (associated with the hall from 1916). There are other references, too—architectural, mathematical and social, religious. The building is devotional— fragments of much-loved Melbourne monuments such as the Griffins' Capitol Theatre **(183)** ceiling and Ron Robertson-Swann's canary yellow Vault (now at Batman Park) appear in the upper level foyer and the auditorium. Mathematician Roger Penrose's deliberations on the pentagon are given expressionistic range in the auditorium ceiling and also recalled is Buckminster Fuller's folded map of the world in triangles. The annexe foyer is like walking around the outside of the inside skin of a cathedral dome before reaching a foyer with a purple padded balustrade. Outside sculpted metal panels embossed with lacy suspender belts and the words 'Resurrection City' hint at the finally most profound layer of embodied meaning.

430

430 Melbourne Terrace Apartments

Cnr Franklin and Queen Streets, Melbourne
1994 Katsalidis Architects
GC, V, NA

The Melbourne Terrace Apartments are the city's answer to the Roman *palazzine* of the 1950s, the speculative apartments which explored exuberant decorative and formal potentials available to an urban facade. Nonda Katsalidis has here enriched his facades with copper oxide–etched balcony slabs, weathered metal, mannered window surrounds, glass blocks, serrated edges to brutish off-form concrete and a skyline that verges on a description such as post-apocalyptic Baroque. At the entry to each lift and stair lobby, copper doors and figurative sculptures by Peter Corlett announce the four buildings: Equus, Mondo, Roma and Fortuna. With this exciting urban hulk, Katsalidis offers the vibrancy of mixed use and a taste of decorative excess.

431 Yarra Park Housing

Punt Road, Webb Lane, Jolimont
1993 Perrott Lyon Mathieson Pty Ltd
GC, V, NA

Incorporating the former Yarra Park State School as part of a large, medium-density speculative housing development, project designer Hamish Lyon combined a series of housing typologies: single-level apartments, terrace houses and double-storey studio apartments. Lyon's interests in Italian urban theorists Giorgio Grassi and Antonio Monestiroli come to the fore in this tautly controlled study in urban morphology. Another project that reflects these ideas is the Lyon Jenkin House, 38 Rathdowne Street, Carlton (1993), designed by Lyon and Astrid Jenkin in association with Charles Salter.

432 St Kilda Town Hall Redevelopment

Cnr Carlisle Street and Brighton Road, St Kilda
1994 Ashton Raggatt McDougall
GC, V, A

The gutting by fire of the 19th-century St Kilda Town Hall was the impetus for a major redevelopment of its interior and existing 1960s additions. Ashton Raggatt McDougall (ARM) resolved a formerly convoluted plan with the addition of a skylit spine running down the back side of the hall. This 'street' is an extraordinary space. For the architectural afficionado, it's a surprise. Finnish architect Alvar Aalto's Finlandia Congress Hall has been simulated in medium-density fibreboard as an internal facade. This is one of ARM's favoured techniques: dismantling architectural icons and rejecting notions of authorship. At their Howard Kronborg Clinic, 16 Eleanor Street, Footscray (1991–92), for example, the side facade is a polychrome brick version of Robert Venturi's mother's house stretched almost beyond recognition by a xerox machine. At St Kilda, the result is a thrilling light-filled almost Baroque space. In the main hall, another icon is given the treatment. The plaster canopies of Philip Johnson's Kneses Tifereth Israel Synagogue, Port Chester, New York (1956), are reintroduced within the previous burnt-out shell as a flat ceiling plane studded with cut-out stars and with scalloped cut-outs at its edges. Outside, facing Carlisle Street, a small plaza is created with yet another simulacrum, this time Richard Serra's torqued curves of steel are painted bright green and conceal disabled ramps to the entry terrace.

●●●

Opposite St Kilda Town Hall is another ARM project, an addition (1994) to Enrico Taglietti's St Kilda Library, 150 Carlisle Street, St Kilda (1969). An open, giant stone book forms the obvious sign for the new additions.

433

21 J5

433 Eltham Library
Panther Place, Eltham
1994 Gregory Burgess Architects
GC, V, A

Gregory Burgess's panoptic plan has, at its centre, an egg-like control desk which sits beneath an elliptical light well. Instead of evoking a feeling of being watched, however, this information heart is like the generating centre of a roofscape and building section that unfolds like the cross-section through a flower. Concentric, curved clerestorey windows reinforce the radial plan and bathe the library in diffuse light. Victorian mountain ash battens line the curved ceilings. The main floor is elevated above the ground to avoid a once-a-century flood, and above this mud bricks rest on a brick base protected by broad eaves and verandas. Burgess's library is a brilliant exposition of organically-driven planning combined with ingenious structural and material invention.

434 Traffic Entry and Security Office, University of Melbourne
Masson Road at Swanston Street, Carlton
1994–95 Peter Elliott Pty Ltd
GC, V, NA

A tiny but distinguished design for the Swanston Street/Masson Road Traffic Entry and Security Office, this sleek, modernist accretion is grafted neatly onto the existing red-brick Richard Berry Building and its ivy-clad wall. Elliott has then punched holes in this otherwise unremarkable wall to give light to office spaces behind. One of numerous award-winning small and finely detailed urban fragments, alterations and additions designed by Peter Elliott Pty Ltd. Across the university campus, the office's deeped eaved roof, with its sloping

soffit, recalls in miniature a much larger building at the other end of Swanston Street, the National Gallery of Victoria **(332)**.

•••

Other Elliott designs on the University of Melbourne campus include: internal alteration and additions to Department of Fine Arts, Classical Studies & Archaeology, Old Pathology Building (1994); International Office (1996); Staircase, western end of Union Building (1988); Principal's Residence, St Mary's College (1994); and Genetics Building (1994-96).

435 Gottlieb House
40 Lumeah Road, North Caulfield
1994 Wood/Marsh Architecture
GC, V, NA

The Gottlieb House is an exercise in the sculptural arrangement of geometric forms. From the street, the house is announced as an elliptical planned volume in reinforced concrete with a silvered glass box protruding at first-floor level. Inside this volume, a huge entrance hall contains a spiral stair. Beyond is a vast living room with narrow slots of double-height space indicating the individual cubic volumes of the bedrooms above. Two solid, pylon-like volumes then mark entry to a family room overlooking the rear garden.

Below: Plan of Gottlieb House (1994)

436

437

2G G11

436 Townhouses

106-112 Cremorne Street, Richmond
1994 Rossetti & Holmes
GC, V, NA

Designed by Craig Rossetti, these six, 4-metre wide, three-storey townhouses built in a semi-industrial precinct are a refreshing alternative to the rash of neo-Georgian townhouses being built all over Melbourne in the 1990s. The hard-edged, no-nonsense architectural imagery and limited choice of materials was inspired by nearby factories and commercial buildings.

70 F11

437 Performing Arts Buildings, Buildings 67 & 68

Monash University, Clayton
1995 Allan Powell Architects in association with Pels Innes Neilson & Kosloff (PINK)
GC, V, A

The 1960s modernist campus planning of Monash University has been revised in the mid-1990s. From that revision has emerged Allan Powell's Performing Arts Buildings adjacent to Roy Grounds's orange brick monolith, the Robert Blackwood Hall (1965). The deep desert red-coloured Performing Arts Building, an L-shape in plan, has been designed to create a north-facing plaza and attempt an enclosure of urban proportions. In the centre of the 'L', a series of folded planes becomes the sculptural foil to the massive building bulk behind. At Monash, the urban character is one of bigness and bold, formally independent objects. Powell's choice of abstract forms and the resulting De Chirico-like spaces between are powerful.

●●●

Another Allan Powell Architects and PINK collaboration is Building 94, RMIT Vocational Educational Training School of Design, 23–27 Cardigan Street, Carlton (1996).

45 D4

438 Kitamura House

123 Pakington Street, Kew
1995 John Wardle
GC, V, NA

A finely crafted family house that responds programmatically and architecturally to its Japanese clients, the Kitamura House exemplifies John Wardle's attention to subtle spatial manipulation and the careful framing of views out to the garden. This house and another Wardle design, the Isaacson-Davis House, 23 Masonsmith Road, Balnarring Beach (1997), both RAIA award-winners, demonstrate the ongoing tradition in Melbourne of the design of the single family house as a major focus of architectural experiment, research and refinement.

1C K4

439 Crown Casino

Queensbridge Street at the Yarra River, Melbourne
1993-97 Bates Smart; Daryl Jackson Pty Ltd; Perrott Lyon Mathieson, architects in association
GC, V, A

One of the largest and most expensive postwar building projects ever to be constructed in Melbourne, Crown Casino, by its very size, demands comment and even a visit. Designed by a consortium of local architects, the choice of architectural imagery is externally understated (and largely picturesque) urbanity, rather than the burlesque hype and glamour of Las Vegas.

Below: Plan of Kitamura House (1995)

440

1C F5

440 Melbourne Exhibition Centre
Clarendon Street, South Melbourne
1996 Denton Corker Marshall
GC, V, A

Built over and around the fragmentary beginnings of the new Museum of Victoria before its move to the Carlton Gardens, the collage-like array of forms, fins and planes of the Clarendon Street end of the Melbourne Exhibition Centre cleverly cloaks its unwanted skeleton. This sculptural (and internally chromatic) excitement is where the major lobby entry, auditorium and administration spaces are located. The rest of the long, linear structure comprises an exhibition building containing a series of all-purpose large-span spaces gained by a clear structural system of giant curved steel girder trusses. With a cross-section that resembles a modern airport, parking underneath and multiple entry points along a linear circulation spine, the centre has Melbourne's Yarra River as its giant urban tarmac. Facing the river is a very long public glazed concourse and a virtual forest of angled steel 'stick' columns. It is Melbourne's biggest urban veranda.

Below: Plan of Atlas House (1996)

58 D8

441 Windsor Fire Station
Albert Street, Windsor
1997 Edmond & Corrigan
GC, V, NA

Replacing a 1938 cream brick fire station by Seabrook & Fildes (1938), the new Windsor Fire Station is one of a series of robust expressionistic fire station designs by Edmond & Corrigan in suburban Melbourne including: Keilor Fire Station, Milleara Road, Keilor (1991); Heidelberg Fire Station, Bell Street, Heidelberg (1993); and Oakleigh Fire Station, 100 Atherton Road, Oakleigh (1995). Each of these fire stations is different and dependent on its immediate locality for urban and formal inspiration.

59 D2

442 Atlas House
80 Kooyongkoot Road, Hawthorn
1996 Kovac Architecture
GC, V, NA

Tom Kovac's architecture is sensuous and organic. Fluid curves and sculptural forms that seem to emerge from nowhere characterise his idiosyncratic house and interior designs. The Atlas House in Hawthorn is no exception. With a plan that would have any rationalist tearing their hair out with frustration, the expressionistic serpentine lines and womb-like spaces, the free forms and kooky shapes recall the emotive drawings and models of German Expressionist Herman Finsterlin. From the street, the undulating white walls and blank street face given no indication of the remarkable spatial complexity within.

444

38 D7

2H H1

443 Student Union Building
Lilydale Campus, Swinburne
University of Technology
Melba Avenue, Lilydale
1996 Glenn Murcutt with Bates Smart
GC, V, A
Eastern Institute of TAFE,
Lilydale Lake Campus
Melba Avenue, Lilydale
1997 Perrott Lyon Mathieson with Carey Lyon
GC, V, A
Located virtually next door to each other, these
two educational facilities demonstrate two
distinctly different approaches to architecture.
Sydney architect, Glenn Murcutt, and Bates
Smart have designed a student union building
that is an exercise in structural and formal
clarity – a big shaded steel box (the main
cafeteria and gathering space) flanked by brick
offices and lecture theatres detailed in brick the
way Murcutt and his confreres in Sydney in the
1960s used to do. By contrast, the Eastern
Institute of TAFE is a giant and folded landscape
sign, a remnant slice of quarried escarpment on
one side and rolling green hills on the other.
These two buildings evidence different traditions
which are keenly pursued. One is the orthodox
notion of tectonics in building and the classical
placement of an object within the landscape.
The other is about allegory and building as a
sign, and about an uncertain reciprocity
between landscape and object.

444 Godsell House
6 Hodgson Street, Kew
1997 Sean Godsell
GC, V, NA
An intentionally rusted tribute to the 20th-
century house, the Godsell House is an heroic
gesture. Its design nods to the cavalier
structural-functionalism of the McIntyre House
(308) nearby, to glass-and-steel houses of the
1940s and 1950s by Philip Johnson, Mies van
der Rohe, Craig Ellwood and Paul Rudolph, and
to the rusted monumentality of Eero Saarinen's
Deere & Co. complex, Moline, Illinois (1960-62),
and, even more recently, works by French
architect Jean Nouvel. Derivations aside, this
house is a reverie in minimalism – in a town
currently noted for the reverse.

34 C6

445 Alessio House
9 Glendarragh Road, Templestowe
1996-97 Ivan Rijavec
GC, V, NA
An extraordinary piece of live-in sculpture, the
Alessio House is planned as the amalgam of
three curved blade shapes and an almost
rectangular bedroom block (all the external
walls bulge out or in). Ivan Rijavec's architecture
is boldly forthright with an external overlay of
super-scaled stripes.

Above: Alessio House (1997)

446

447

61 B5

446 Buildings 1–5, Burwood Campus, Deakin University
Burwood Highway, Burwood
1996-97 Wood Marsh Architecture in association with Pels Innes Neilson & Kosloff (PINK)
GC, V, A

A series of five low-rise tertiary education buildings pinwheeling from a central spiral stair tower, Buildings 1–5 have become the award-winning centrepiece of Deakin University's Burwood Campus. Comprising the Stage One redevelopment of a former teachers college into a university campus, the group of dynamically place and deftly 'skinned' buildings was intended to give identity and architectural distinction to a campus lacking in urban continuity. Following Deakin University's policy of ecologically sustain-able buildings, the buildings ranged from three to eight storeys with openable windows, flexible interior volumes and minimal lift capacities. The exception was the biggest structure, a sleek, double-curved slab of reconstituted stone panels punched with slot windows and visible like a giant sign from Burwood Highway. The other four buildings have interesting and different skins—three have woven metal blade 'chain mail' skins in black painted or galvanized steel, while the fourth, floating above the ground has a folded facade of exposed aggregate. Thoroughly urbane, these buildings and the fortuitous residual spaces between each are compelling evidence that to be sustainable doesn't require or mean an architecture obsessed with sunshade and solar collectors. Another Wood Marsh and PINK award-winning outer suburban campus building can be seen at the Faculty of Education, Language & Community Services, Bundoora West Campus, RMIT (1997).

2H B7

447 Silo Residential Apartments
22 Abinger Street, Richmond
1996 Katsalidis Architects
GC, V, A

Another sculptural tour-de-force from the hand of Nonda Katsalidis, this time in the form of the refurbishment of four existing wheat silos from the Daly's Malthouse, these apartments command stunning views over the nearby eastern suburbs. The tower consists of six three-bedroom apartments (one per floor) and a double-storey penthouse. At each level, three bedrooms occupy three of the silos, while the fourth contains a stair and bathroom. A lift tower, service block and a living room which terminates in an arrowhead-shaped terrace were added to the north face of the silos. The result, especially given the off-form concrete, rusted steel balustrades and crown of thorns eaves details at the building's top, is a brutish totemic tower of inner-city living.

2B J10

448 Museum of Victoria
Rathdowne Street, Carlton
2000 Denton Corker Marshall Pty Ltd (DCM)
GC, V, A

The result of a nationwide design competition, DCM's Museum of Victoria stretches right across the site. Beneath a giant steel frame supporting solar panels and screening devices, the gallery and exhibition spaces are housed in black boxes. Different functions earn different shapes and the ground is carved away beneath the overriding order of the frame. Enter from either side beneath DCM's signature tilted blades, while to the north another massive and controversial blade appears above the trees.

231

GLOSSARY

acanthus

ACANTHUS a herbaceous plant whose leaves were used as a decorative motif in classical architecture.

ARCHITRAVE ornamental moulding around exterior of arch, doorway, or window.

ARRIS the sharp edge formed by angular contact of two planes.

ASHLAR squared hewn stone used as facing for masonry.

ATRIUM an interior space of a building either open to the sky or covered with a skylight.

BALUSTER a slender upright post supporting a rail. Usually in sequence, thus balustrade.

BARGE BOARD a board running along the edge of the gable of a house.

BATTLEMENT an indented parapet.

BOND a method of placing bricks or stone so that the whole is bound together in one mass.

bossaged

BOSSAGED stones (usually in columns) left uncut and projecting, often to be carved later.

BUTTRESS a structure of brick, stone or wood built against a wall to support or strengthen it.

CANTILEVER a structural projection supported from a wall or column, such as a beam or balcony, which is unsupported at its outermost edge.

CAPITAL the uppermost part of a column, usually decorated.

CASEMENT a frame which forms a window that opens outwards on hinges.

CASTELLATED built like a castle with battlements.

CLERESTORY the highest level of the nave or transept of a church containing windows clear of adjacent roofs.

CONSOLE an ornamented bracket or corbel which projects about half its height.

COPING the top course of a brick or stone wall, usually sloping, which throws off the rain.

capital

CORBEL a timber or stone projection from a building which supports a load.

CORNICE a horizontal projection which crowns the top of a building; also the moulding around the wall where it joins the ceiling.

CUPOLA a small dome-shaped structure forming the roof of a building. The word can also be used to describe the ceiling of a dome.

CURTAIN WALL the non load-bearing skin, usually of glass, that encloses the framework of a building.

DADO the finished lower part of the wall of a room.

DENTIL a type of moulding consisting of small (toothlike) rectangular blocks.

castellated

DORMER a projecting vertical window in the sloping roof of a house.

EAVES the lower edges of a roof, that overhang the walls.

ENTABLATURE the horizontal assemblage, in classical architecture, above the column. It comprises architrave, frieze and cornice.

cornice

ENTASIS the almost imperceptible swelling of the shaft of a column.

FANLIGHT the window above a door usually, but not always, in the shape of a fan.

FASCIA a flat horizontal band or moulding of stone or wood.

FINIAL an ornamental piece on top of a gable, spire or other roof projection.

FORMWORK a temporary construction of wood or metal either into or on top of which concrete is poured.

FRIEZE a decorative band at the top of an interior wall. In classical architecture it is the middle division of the entablature.

GABLE the vertical triangular part of an external wall at the end of a ridged roof.

dentil

GALVANIZE to coat one metal with another by means of an electro–chemical action. Most coatings are of zinc.

HEADER a brick or stone laid with its end or head in the face of the wall.

HIP a projecting inclined edge on a roof extending from the ridge or apex to the eaves.

JOIST one of the timbers on to which a floor or ceiling is attached.

KEYSTONE the wedge-shaped central stone which locks an arch in place.

LANTERN a small superstructure on a dome or roof to provide light or ventilation.

keystone

LINTEL a horizontal member of timber, concrete, stone or metal, which supports the weight above a door or window opening.

LOGGIA an arcade or gallery with one or more of its sides open to the air.

LOUVRE an arrangement of overlapping slats of glass, timber, or other thin material in such a way to allow flow of air but exclude rain, or light if opaque.

MANSARD a roof with a double pitch, the lower section being longer and steeper than the upper.

MOULDING an ornamental contoured band either carved or in relief used to add interest to a wall or surface.

MULLION a vertical member that divides the surfaces of a window, door or panel, often used decoratively as well as to add support to a frame.

NICHE a shallow hollow in a wall intended to contain a statue or ornamental object.

console

pediment

pilaster

roundel

NOGGING a non-structural horizontal piece of framing used to provide support to brickwork or internal plastering.

ORDER the design, arrangement and proportion of all parts of a column and its entablature allowing for a method of classification. The Classical Orders include Greek (Doric, Ionic, Corinthian) and Roman (Tuscan, Doric, Ionic, Corinthian, Composite) examples.

ORIEL a projecting bay window often of polygonal plan supported at an upper level by brackets or corbels.

PARAPET the part of a wall that continues past the eaves line of a roof to give protection and conceal roofing surfaces and drainage.

PEDIMENT a triangular low gable found in many classical buildings and similarly used in varying geometrical forms to decorate a window, doorway, archway or other wall opening.

PERGOLA a system of posts supporting a lattice roof intended for climbing plants and vines.

PERISTYLE a row of columns surrounding a building or open court.

PILASTER a flattened, shallow column that protrudes slightly from a wall, acting as a decorative element rather than being structure.

PORTICO a colonnade or roofed entrance open on at least one side.

PRESTRESSED a condition of concrete where high-strength steel cables are used as reinforcement instead of steel rods. The cables are placed in ducts cast in the concrete and then stressed, inducing compression in the concrete before it is loaded.

PURLIN a horizontal roof beam placed parallel with the upper wall plate and the ridge beam at regular intervals along the slope of the roof, in order to support rafters.

QUOINS decorative or reinforcing corner stones of a building.

RAFTER one of the construction members of a roof giving slope and form, as well as support to the external surface material.

REINFORCED CONCRETE concrete strengthened by steel bars or steel mesh placed in formwork before concrete is poured.

REVEAL the side of a window or door opening showing the thickness of the wall.

RISER the vertical part of a step connecting two treads in a stair.

ROUNDEL a circular decorative panel, window or plaque.

RUSTICATE stonework finished with a rough surface and deeply cut bevelled joints . Various types include diamond-pointed, cyclopaean and vermiculated (worm-eaten).

SASH a frame which holds the glass of a window. A sash window is created using two or more vertically sliding sashes, usually counter-weighted.

SKILLION a one-way single pitched roof falling from the highest point of a structure to the lowest at the opposite side.

SPACE-FRAME a triangulated framework which encloses a space. The members of the framework are interconnected and are frequently used to cover large spaces without need for intermediate supports.

SPANDREL the roughly triangular space between adjoining arches or above the curve of a single arch, bound by the rectangular frame enclosing it.

STILE the vertical framing member in joinery, used most frequently in doors and windows.

STRING COURSE a projecting course, moulding or band running horizontally across a facade.

STUD a vertical supporting member of a timber wall frame on to which wall coverings and linings are fixed.

STYLOBATE a continuous stepped base supporting a colonnade.

TENSIONING the process of applying a permanent stress opposite to that expected from the working load, used in structural reinforced concrete work.

TERRACOTTA a fired clay material of red-brown colouring that can be molded or shaped .

TRANSOM the horizontal member that divides the surfaces of a window, door or panel.

TREAD the flat horizontal part of a step connecting two risers in a stair.

TRUSS a structural framework of timber or iron with increasing load bearing capacities used in the construction of bridges and roofing systems.

TUCK POINTING the process of applying a narrow strip of mortar over the face of the joints in brickwork to giving the appearance of precision and regularity.

VALANCE a decorative strip or border edging below a roof, usually running between veranda posts.

VAULT an arched structure of stone or brick, sometimes imitated in stucco, plaster or timber, usually serving as a roof or ceiling.

VOUSSOIRS wedge-shaped stone blocks or bricks, which combine to form an arch or vault.

WATTLE AND DAUB a system of wall construction involving the interlacing of slim pieces of wood (wattles) which are then fixed to framing members and thickly plastered with mud (daub).

WEATHERBOARD one of a series of long thin boards fixed horizontally with overlapping edges, acting as an external wall covering.

stylobate

voussoir

MELBOURNE ARCHITECTS

Melbourne's first architects were mainly in government service. Sent from Sydney, Robert Russell and Henry Ginn gave sober service to the modest settlement. These architects were invariably also surveyors and amateur artists, with an eye for the picturesque. While their buildings were few, their imprint on the future city was undeniable.

The discovery of gold in 1851 changed everything. Scores of highly trained and would-be architects arrived. Some, such as JJ Clark and William Wardell, had stunning careers in the Public Works Department, as newly rich Melbourne acquired some of the most gracious public buildings in the nation. Others, such as Leonard Terry, prospered privately, building banks and warehouses, and servicing powerful diocesan landowners. Joseph Reed, prolific and eclectic, was the outstanding private practitioner, designing many of Melbourne's most important public and religious buildings. In the 1880s, architects such as William Pitt consolidated, with unrivalled virtuosity, Melbourne's 19th-century architecture as writ equally through a public architecture of cultivated urbanity and a private architecture of the detached suburban villa.

From the 1890s, Arts and Crafts architects Ussher and Kemp, Robert Haddon and Harold Desbrowe-Annear ensured the ascendancy of the house as locus for aesthetic innovation. In the hands of these same architects, Federation Melbourne became dynamic. Since that time, the city's architectural fortunes have oscillated between the refined urbanism of Osborn McCutcheon, Percy Everett, Yuncken Freeman and Denton Corker Marshall, and the restless compositional energies of those working outside the city.

Bridging this polarity were architects whose work crossed between city and home, those blurring domestic and monumental themes: Walter Burley Griffin and Marion Mahony, Roy Grounds, Robin Boyd, Graeme Gunn, Edmond and Corrigan. Today's architects still work within that productive tension, between civic dignity and heroic individualism.

JOHN JAMES CLARK (1838–1915)

Former Royal Mint

Born in Liverpool, England, in 1838, John James Clark was the second son of George Clark, a farmer and tailor. With his parents and five siblings, Clark arrived in Melbourne in 1852. The family came as unassisted migrants, presumably in search of fortune after the 1851 discovery of gold in Victoria. Some of the family left for the goldfields, but 14-year-old James immediately became an acting draftsman on the staff of the colonial architect. By the time he was 19, JJ Clark was responsible for the design and supervision of Melbourne's most gracious public building, the new Treasury in Spring Street.

His precocious design facility meant that Clark's government income was enough to support his family during the mid-1850s. Clark worked as a public servant until 1878, when he was retrenched along with his superior William Wardell, in the so-called 'Black Wednesday' dismissals. Allowed limited rights to private practice, Clark worked nights with Smith and Pritchard, assisted Joseph Reed with several competitions, and successfully entered a number of competitions alone.

Clark's career within the Public Works Department (PWD) was a distinguished one, his name being associated with the urbane Renaissance Revival style associated with Melbourne's public buildings of the 1850s until the 1870s. The Treasury, Royal Mint, completion of the Customs House, and his involvement with Government House (under the direction of Wardell) are the legacy of Clark's 26 years in public service.

In 1865, Clark married Mary Taylor Watmuff (1845–1871). Their only child, Edward James, was born in 1868, and later became his father's partner in an Indian summer of architectural productivity for Clark senior.

Melbourne City Baths

Two years after his dismissal, JJ Clark began private practice in 1880. In 1881, he moved to Sydney where, with his engineer brother George, he formed a partnership. In 1883, JJ Clark was appointed colonial architect for Queensland and designed Brisbane's Treasury Building. From 1885 until 1889, he resumed private practice and then travelled to America and Europe with his son, who was then 21 years old. Clark returned to Australia with few commissions. Moving back first to Sydney and then to Perth, Clark designed hospitals and asylums for the Western Australian Works Department. In 1896, JJ and EJ Clark formed a partnership in Perth. After further competition wins there, they moved back to Brisbane to work for the Queensland railways, and their work included Central Station's tower design. The father-and-son team moved yet again in 1902, this time to Melbourne to design and oversee construction of the red brick Melbourne City Baths, yet another competition-winning commission.

A man who never created a large office, moved between states five times and made three overseas tours, JJ Clark was a devoted and tireless practitioner. He died in St Kilda in 1915 aged 77. He never retired.

Treasury Building

WILLIAM WILKINSON WARDELL (1823–1899)

Born in London in 1823, William Wilkinson Wardell was educated as an engineer. After serving articles in London and a short stint at sea, he began working for the commissioners of sewers and for architect WF ast. Influenced by the writings of Gothic polemicist AWN Pugin and the Oxford Movement under Cardinal John Henry Newman, Wardell, baptised in Anglican, converted to Catholicism in 1843.

The conversion initiated an entirely new circle of architectural patrons. Between 1846 and 1858, Wardell designed more than 30 Gothic Revival Catholic churches including numerous schools, convents and houses. In 1858, due to ill-health, Wardell sold his practice and emigrated to Australia with his wife, Lucy Ann Butler. By 1859, less than a year after his arrival in Melbourne, Wardell was designing the colossal St Patrick's Cathedral, Melbourne, and St John's College, Sydney (1859–1935). That same year, he was appointed Inspector-Clerk of Public Works and, in 1860, he was elevated to Inspector-General of Public Works in Victoria.

William Wilkinson Wardell

Given rights to private practice, Wardell managed to maintain a highly successful private office designing numerous buildings for the Catholic Church in Victoria and interstate, as well as being responsible for the construction of all public buildings in Victoria, including the lavish Italianate-styled Government House. Ignominy, however, came on 'Black Wednesday', 8 January 1878, when Wardell and other public servants were dismissed from government office in the midst of corruption allegations against the Governor, Sir George Bowen.

Wardell moved to Sydney and resumed private practice. One of his new clients was the English Scottish & Australian Banking Group and, ironically, Wardell was to design perhaps his most famous branch for them in Collins Street, Melbourne, in the city which had spurned him, but which, under his auspices, had gained some of the most accomplished examples of Gothic Revival architecture in Australia.

In 1884, Wardell was briefly in partnership with Walter Liberty Vernon, then, in the 1890s, with his own son Herbert. He died of heart failure and pleurisy in 1899.

St Patrick's Cathedral

JOSEPH REED (1823–1890)

Joseph Reed

Believed to have been born in Cornwall, England, in 1823, Joseph Reed arrived in Melbourne in 1853. Less than six months later, he won the competition to design the Public Library in Swanston Street. That same year, he produced designs for the Bank of NSW, Collins Street (now at the University of Melbourne), and Geelong Town Hall. It was an auspicious start to a prolific career that embraced all manner of architectural styles and building types. A dominant figure during Melbourne's period of greatest growth, Joseph Reed was a frequent competition winner and responsible for some of the largest and most important building commissions in the city. He arguably assisted in making Melbourne one of the great Victorian cities. An accomplished eclectic and a fine draftsman, his aptitude for skilful picturesque composition in virtually every stylistic idiom was matched by dogged professionalism. He established Melbourne's first major private office.

An active professional, in 1856, Reed became the first elected member of the Victorian Institute of Architects and later its president. In 1858, he became architect for the recently formed University of Melbourne and designed almost all of its 19th-century buildings. Commissions also soon came in for the Wesley Church, the Royal Society Building, Victoria Street and a new classical temple front for the Collins Street Baptist Church.

In 1862, Reed went into partnership with Frederick Barnes (1824–1884). A trip to Europe in 1863 engendered an enthusiam for the polychrome brick architecture of Lombardy and it found immediate results in Reed's Romanesque-inspired designs for the Independent Church, Collins Street, and Rippon Lea, FT Sargood's house at Elsternwick. For the Melbourne Town Hall and Menzies Hotel (1867, demolished), Reed & Barnes shifted to a grand Second Empire mode. The practice prospered with ever larger and more complex commissions, including the Gothic Revival Wilson Hall (1878–82) and the massively grand Exhibition Buildings, complete with Florentine dome. In 1883, on Barnes's retirement, Anketell Henderson and FJ Smart became Reed's new partners. In 1890, Henderson left, taking some of the firm's best clients with him and the practice became Reed Smart & Tappin. On Reed's death from 'inanition and exhaustion' that same year, the firm soon became Bates Peebles & Smart, eventually Bates Smart & McCutcheon and finally, today, Bates Smart.

Rippon Lea

LEONARD TERRY (1825–1884)

Born in 1825 in Scarborough, Yorkshire, Leonard Terry arrived in Melbourne in 1853. After working briefly for local architect Charles Laing, on Laing's death in 1857, he became the principal designer of banks in Victoria and of buildings for the Anglican Church, becoming diocesan architect in 1860.

Early commissions included a series of bluestone warehouses in central Melbourne and his most prestigious work before 1860 was the Melbourne Club (1858), which employed the Renaissance Revival style, an idiom much favoured at the time by Sir Charles Barry in England. It was this gracefully scaled and detailed Italian palazzo style that was to characterise Terry's conservative but competent designs for at least 50 branches of all the major banks in Victoria, Tasmania, Western Australia and New Zealand.

Terry's church designs by contrast were generally of bluestone and simply treated in Early English or Decorated Gothic style. For Trinity College at the University of Melbourne, he produced a medievalising Tudor design for the principal's house (Leeper Wing, 1869–72). In 1874, the former Ballarat architect Percy Oakden joined Terry as a junior partner and the firm's work expanded to include numerous non-conformist church and school commissions. Around 1879, as supervising architect to St Paul's Cathedral, Terry visited England to consult with the architect William Butterfield — although it was Oakden who supervised most of the work.

Married twice with a total of nine children, Terry died on 23 June 1884 of a thoracic tumour. Despite bequeathing an enormous number of politely urbane buildings for the new colony, Terry's passing went largely unnoticed.

NAHUM BARNET (1855–1931)

Born in Melbourne in 1855, Nahum Barnet was articled to Terry & Oakden. He was to become the city's most innovative producer of commercial buildings during the Federation period. A precocious designer, the young Barnet argued in 1882 for an Australian architecture based on Ruskinian ideas of Nature and functional adaptation to climate in an article entitled 'Climatic Architecture'.

Barnet's work in the central city was characterised by the tall red brick arches of the American Romanesque such as the Bedggood and Co. Building, 172 Flinders Lane (1901), and Auditorium Building, 167 Collins Street (1913); by dynamic asymmetrical compositons epitomised by the Young Women's Christian Association (YWCA) Building, Russell Street (1913, demolished 1976); and by the swirling Art Nouveau detail of his Paton Building, 115–117 Elizabeth Street (1905). His work indicated a Federation city that was picturesque and expressive rather than Melbourne's mannered urbanity of the 1870s. Barnet's other major work is Victoria's most important Jewish temple, the Baroque Classicist Melbourne Synagogue, 2–8 Toorak Road, South Yarra (1928–30).

Barnet died in 1931 aged 76.

Auditorium Building

WILLIAM PITT (1855-1918)

Born in 1855 in Melbourne, William Pitt was the son of artist William Pitt senior, who ran various Melbourne cafés and hotels, and sometimes decorated them, including a Neapolitan panorama for premises owned by theatrical entrepreneur George Coppin. Pitt junior served articles from 1875 with George Browne before commencing sole practice in 1879. That year, he won first prize for his design for the Melbourne Coffee Palace Bourke Street, Melbourne's first temperance hotel.

A different commission came in 1883 with another prize-winning design, Coppin's 'Our Lodgings' (now Gordon House) in Little Bourke Street, a philanthropic venture aimed at providing subsidised inner-city housing. During the 1880s, Pitt's practice boomed in parallel with the economy. He redesigned the Princess Theatre in French Second Empire style, complete with a sliding roof, and collaborated in 1887 with Ellerker & Kilburn to design the vast Boom style extravaganza of the 500-room Federal Coffee Palace in Collins Street. In the late 1880s, Pitt designed three distinguished Venetian Gothic Revival office blocks for Collins Street's west end: the Melbourne Stock Exchange; the Olderfleet Building and the Rialto Building.

Like many others, Pitt's rise to fame and fortune crashed in 1893. A parallel career in Victorian State Parliament (1891-1910) assisted his financial survival, as did partnership with Albion Walkley from 1900 when Pitt's expertise as a theatre architect guaranteed ongoing theatre design work in Melbourne, Adelaide, Sydney and New Zealand. Pitt's practice also included the design of St Kilda (1887) and Brunswick (c. 1889) town halls; the Victoria Brewery, East Melbourne (1896) grandstands for Flemington and Caulfield racecourses; and also the Melbourne Cricket Club (1905).

An avid sportsman, Pitt was an expert marksman and a Patron of the Collingwood Football Club for whom in 1892 he designed, without charge, their first grandstand at Victoria Park. He died of cancer at Mikado, his home at Abbotsford, in 1918.

Princess Theatre

USSHER & KEMP

The partnership of Beverley Ussher (1868–1908) and Henry Kemp (1859–1946) produced some of Melbourne's most distinctive domestic architecture of the Federation period. Their Arts and Crafts–inspired houses were exemplars of the so-called Queen Anne or Federation style which was characterised by Marseilles tiles, red bricks, turned timber veranda columns, casement windows, a dynamic picturesque roof form and a silhouette of tall chimneys, dormers and finials.

Born in Broughton in Lancashire, England, in 1859, Henry Hardie Kemp was articled first to Manchester architects Corsen & Aitken in 1875 and then, in London, to RW Edis and briefly Paull & Bonella before migrating to Melbourne in 1886. As with many of his English contemporaries such as E Nesfield and RN Shaw, Kemp was interested in the half-timbered medieval vernacular of Cheshire and Manchester. In Melbourne, Kemp joined the firm of Terry & Oakden, and, in 1887, the firm became Oakden, Addison & Kemp.

Before the 1892 crash, Kemp was involved in projects such as Queens College, University of Melbourne; the Australian Building, 49 Elizabeth Street (1887–88, then the tallest building in Melbourne); and North Park, Essendon (1888), for Alexander McCracken. After a brief stint in Sydney (c. 1895–97), Kemp joined Beverley Ussher in partnership in 1899.

Born in Melbourne in 1868, Beverley Ussher was articled to Alfred Dunn and later visited England and Europe in 1887–88. On returning to Melbourne, Ussher went into partnership with Arts and Crafts enthusiast and Englishman Walter Butler (1864–1949) whom he had met while in England. The partnership lasted until 1893.

Six years later, Ussher and Kemp became partners. The firm specialised in domestic architecture and their designs for Dalswraith (1906) for William Gibson of the drapery firm of Foy & Gibson and the A Norman house, Kew (1908), set the standard for arguably the first truly original Australian domestic style.

Tragically, Ussher died in 1908 aged 40, cutting short a productive and brilliant partnership. Kemp continued in sole practice until 1911, when he was joined by George Charles Inskip for two years. From 1918, Kemp practised with his nephew F Bruce Kemp before his retirement in 1929. He died at his house, Heald Lawn, Kew (1912), in 1946.

Dalswraith

HAROLD DESBROWE-ANNEAR
(1865–1933)

Caricature of Harold Desbrowe-Annear (SOURCE: Melbourne Punch, 1925)

Born near Bendigo in 1865, Harold Desbrowe-Annear was articled to Melbourne architect William Salway in 1883. By 1889, Annear had left to set up private practice. A prize-winning delineator, Annear also began to speak and write on the ideas of John Ruskin and HH Richardson (for Annear, 'the greatest modern architectural genius'), as well as methods of architectural criticism.

He was committed to the ideals of the Arts and Crafts movement and argued for the fellowship of artists, craftsmen and architects. His early designs were in a modified American Romanesque idiom and yet his most distinguished early work, the Springthorpe memorial, Kew cemetery (1897), was a masterful hybrid of classical invention, Secessionist detail in the tradition of Wagner and Plecnik, and moving picturesque sculptural tableau. In 1902–1903, Annear designed three houses at The Eyrie, Eaglemont, one of which was for himself and his wife. These houses, composed in a free interpretation of the so-called domestic Queen Anne, featured relatively open plans with sliding door panels, copious amounts of built-in timber furniture and windows whose sashes slid upwards into the wall cavity.

Springthorpe Memorial

With these houses and the later plain-surfaced Broceliande (later known as Troon) (1918) and Inglesby (1919) in South Yarra, Annear was for decades incorrectly viewed by later architectural historians as an early modernist architect in Melbourne. Overlooked in such a view were the diverse and changing sources of Annear's domestic work and his faith in the development of an Australian architecture that was intimately related to place, climate and occasion. After World War I, his 1920s work embraced themes of the Spanish Colonial Revival and American Colonial, and idiosyncratic versions of Georgian which resulted in townhouses that, in the manner of Edwin Lutyens, suggested an Antipodean 'Wrennaisance'.

Chadwick House

Annear also was vocal in urban design issues. He proposed a new plan for South Melbourne and designed the triumphal arch over Princes Bridge for the 1901 Royal visit, as well as the reinforced concrete Church Street bridge (1924). He was an architect who designed for wealthy Melbourne society, for some of the city's artists and also for the everyman, as evidenced by his house designs in his 1922 publication, For Every Man His Home.

A flamboyant figure committed to architecture as an art, the monocle-wearing Annear died in St Kilda in 1933.

Church Street Bridge

ROBERT JOSEPH HADDON (1866–1929)

Born in London in 1866, Robert Joseph Haddon was articled from 1881 until 1884 to architects F Templeton & Mew, and for four years he was assistant to TH Watson. In 1889, Haddon emigrated and, in Melbourne, he joined the firm of Sydney Smith & Ogg. Three years later he moved to Hobart where he taught at the Government Technical School before moving to Adelaide in 1894. After his marriage in 1896, Haddon moved to Perth working for two years with the Public Works Department. By 1899, he had returned to Melbourne.

Robert Joseph Haddon

Despite his peripatetic lifestyle, Haddon's reputation as an architectural artist was established with his distinctive Free Style formal inventions and deliciously sinuous Art Nouveau detailing. His new practice was known as the Central Drawing Office and Haddon advertised himself as a 'Consulting Architect'. Firms such as GB Leith; Sydney Smith & Ogg; and Laird & Barlow thus, at various times, employed Haddon as a specialist designer.

In 1902, Haddon became an influential teacher and Head of Architecture at the Working Men's College, later to become RMIT. In 1919, longtime employee WA Henderson became partner in the firm of Haddon & Henderson. An enthusiastic professional involved in institute affairs, Haddon also was a founding vice-president of the Arts & Crafts Society in 1908, the same year that he published *Australian Architecture,* in which he argued for originality in design through direct response to Australian conditions and local materials. His own house Anselm, Caulfield (1906), is testament to his design originality and skill in complex asymmetrical composition.

Compared with architects such as CFA Voysey and CR Mackintosh, Haddon remains one of Australian architecture's great originals. He died in 1929 aged 63.

MARCUS BARLOW (1890–1955)

Born in 1890, Marcus Barlow was one of Melbourne's most successful commercial architects of the first half of the twentieth century. An early and vocal promoter of the bungalow as a house type, Barlow championed in 1917 the new house form as 'A Servantless House'. The partnership of Grainger & Barlow (1914–1917), then Grainger, Little & Barlow (1917–22), and subsequently Grainger, Little, Barlow & Hawkins (1922–24), designed many such houses and had them published in the popular press.

Century Building

By the late 1920s, Barlow had shifted the focus of his practice to commercial office design. With FGB Hawkins as a partner (1924–27), he designed the highrise Renaissance palazzo of Temple Court, Collins Street. Barlow's masterpiece was the Manchester Unity Building (1929–32), a modern Gothic skyscraper completed during the Depression and an icon of limit height inter-war office building in central Melbourne. The vertically streamlined Century Building followed in 1938–40 and then, further up Swanston Street, the MU Oddfellows House (later Jensen House) of 1941.

A designer whose choice of style and construction followed a pragmatic reading of modernity and fashion, Barlow epitomised the commercially shrewd professional practitioner. He died in 1955 aged 65.

WALTER BURLEY GRIFFIN (1876–1937) AND MARION LUCY MAHONY (1871–1961)

Walter Burley Griffin and Marion Mahony

Detail of Capitol Theatre ceiling

Detail of Essendon Municipal Incinerator

American architects Walter Burley Griffin and Marion Mahony brought to Australia not just the design of Canberra, the nation's new capital city, but also a series of dramatic formal architectural inventions and a renewed appreciation for the Australian landscape.

Born in 1876 at Maywood, near Chicago, Walter Burley Griffin graduated in 1899 from the University of Illinois at Urbana Champaign, where under the direction of Nathan Ricker, architectural education centred around tectonic mastery and invention. Griffin was also a student of landscape architecture. While working with Chicago architect Frank Lloyd Wright between 1901 and 1906, Griffin carried out private commissions and landscape designs of his own, finally setting up his own practice in 1906.

Alongside Griffin in Wright's Oak Park office was Marion Lucy Mahony. Born in 1871, Mahony was, in 1894, the second woman to graduate in architecture from Massachusetts Institute of Technology. A brilliant draftsperson, illustrator and designer, Mahony was responsible for many of the exquisite drawings of Wright buildings published in the 1910 Wasmuth folio and which brought him international acclaim. In Wright's office from 1895 until 1909, Mahony completed several Wright commissions after he removed to Europe with a client's wife.

In 1911, Griffin and Mahony entered the international design competition for Canberra, the new Federal capital and shortly afterward, they married. In 1912, Griffin was announced as the winner. By 1914, Griffin, Mahony, Roy Lippincott (Griffin's brother-in-law) and George Elgh had moved to Australia, setting up office in Melbourne. While Griffin for seven years was Federal capital director of design and construction, he also maintained a private practice in Melbourne. Designs for the Summit and Glenard estates in Eaglemont were followed by Café Australia (1916, demolished) and Newman College (1915–18). The Griffins also built in Eaglemont their own tiny 'doll-house', Pholiota, from Knitlock, the precast concrete block and roof tile system which Griffin had patented in 1917. After Griffin's controversial resignation from his Canberra appointment, he continued to develop the Melbourne practice. The seven-storey office building Leonard House, Elizabeth Street (1922–23, demolished) had an innovative curtain wall facade. The Capitol Theatre (1924) contained an extraordinary atmospheric stepped ceiling with coloured concealed lighting, simultaneously expressionist and archetypal in its monumentality. It was the firm's most substantial commission.

In 1924, the Griffins left Melbourne to live at Castlecrag, an estate in Sydney which the firm had designed in 1921 and which contained several Griffin-designed rock and concrete houses. Through the 1920s and early 1930s, the Griffins designed more of these landscape-sensitive houses. After 1929, with partner Eric Nicholls, the Griffins designed over fifteen municipal incinerators for sites in Sydney, Melbourne, Adelaide and Ipswich, Queensland. After an invitation in 1935 to design buildings for the University of Lucknow, the Griffins briefly settled in India. They were entranced by Indian culture which they found had sympathy with their anthroposophical beliefs which had developed coincidentally with designing the incinerators. Tragically, Griffin died of peritonitis in Lucknow in February 1937. Mahony returned briefly to Castlecrag and then to Chicago in a bid to continue practising. Before she died in 1961, Mahony wrote The Magic of America, an unpublished account of her life with Griffin which included their efforts to forge a new and democratic architecture for Australia.

ARTHUR GEORGE STEPHENSON
(1890–1967)

Born in Melbourne in 1890, Arthur George Stephenson studied architecture at Melbourne and Sydney technical colleges, in addition to his articled training with several Melbourne architects, notably Alec S Eggleston. During World War I, he served with distinction and was awarded the Military Cross. After further study at the Architectural Association in London, Stephenson returned to Melbourne in the early 1920s and began what was to become Australia's largest architectural practice.

The firm of Stephenson & Meldrum, later Stephenson & Turner, specialised in hospital design. In the 1920s, their designs for St Vincent's Hospital, Frankston Hospital and Jesse McPherson Maternity Hospital, William Street, were thoroughly competent and eclectically styled. It was after an extended trip to the United States, Europe and the USSR in 1932, however, that Stephenson returned enthused by the new functionalist architecture of the latest European hospitals.

The Mercy, Freemasons' and Bethesda Hospitals became touchstones in Melbourne of a radically unadorned functional modern architecture. With Donald Turner in Sydney, Stephenson's firm designed the Sydney Dental Hospital (1936–38) and King George V Memorial Hospital (1938–41). The firm's most notable hospital in Victoria was the Royal Melbourne Hospital, which during World War II became a military hospital for the US Forces. With offices in New Zealand, the Middle East and virtually every Australian capital city, Stephenson & Turner became the model for corporate architectural practice.

Stephenson, a great facilitator and employer of young architectural talent, gained universal respect for his ability to nurture team design. He even sponsored staff to travel overseas. In 1953, Stephenson was awarded the RIBA Gold Medal, the first awarded to an Australian. In 1954, he was knighted for services to architecture. Sir Arthur Stephenson died on 18 November 1967.

Arthur George Stephenson

Mercy Hospital

PERCY EVERETT (1888–1967)

Percy Everett

Born in 1888, Percy Edgar Everett was the son of a coach-builder who built houses during the off season. Enrolled as the first student of architecture at the Gordon Technical College in Geelong, Everett was articled to the Geelong Harbor Trust for four years. In 1908, aged 19, he designed the Wool Dumping Shed on Yarra Pier. Two years later, he became junior partner in the Geelong firm of Seeley King & Everett, George R King being the Gordon's highly respected principal.

In 1914, after Laird & Buchan bought out the firm, Everett continued in sole practice as an architect in association with Laird & Buchan (1914–34). That same year, Everett's career took a disconcertingly different direction. In 1916, he became Principal of the Brunswick Technical School with rights to private practice. Around 1930, he transferred to Brighton Technical School after travelling to the USSR, the United States and the Middle East.

In 1934, he became Chief Architect of the Victorian Public Works Department (PWD). From this date, he completely transformed the department's output and insisted that he approve and sign every drawing. Instead of polite stylistic eclecticism, the PWD now produced resolutely Moderne designs. The most sophisticated examples – such as Essendon and Oakleigh technical schools, and Buildings 6,7 & 9 at RMIT – owe much to the work of Willem Dudok and the streamlining of Erich Mendelsohn. For the university and certain high schools, he developed a cream brick modernised collegiate Gothic style. A prolific designer of hospitals, sanatoria and schools, Everett's major postwar contribution was the development of a standard masonry veneer-clad school type which became the common model for all Victorian state and secondary schools well into the 1960s.

In 1953, Everett retired from the PWD and was awarded the Queen's Coronation Medal. While Everett's designs had been regarded by many as outdated, his vast output gave a distinctively progressive flavour to the image of interwar governance. Percy Everett died in 1967 aged 78.

*Caulfield Institute
of Technology*

WALTER OSBORN McCUTCHEON (1899-1981)

Born in Melbourne in 1899, Walter Osborn McCutcheon was articled to Bates Peebles & Smart before completing formal study in 1927 at the University of Melbourne Architectural Atelier. The year before he had entered into partnership with his employers and the firm became Bates Smart & McCutcheon (BSM). Already the oldest firm in Australia, BSM grew by the late 1960s to be one of the largest practices in the country and exists still today as Bates Smart.

Walter Osborn McCutcheon

During the 1930s, BSM prospered with their RVIA Street Architecture Medal-winning AMP Building (1929-31) and Buckley & Nunn's Mens' Store both authored by McCutcheon who was at the same time Director of the School of Architecture at RMIT (1935-42). Between 1942 and 1944, McCutcheon became Chief Architect of the Corps of Engineers of the US Army, South West Pacific Area (1942-1944). War was a time of revelation for McCutcheon, as the development of repetitive building systems and mobilisation programs were crucial to the efficiency of wartime enterprise. Methods of prefabrication, dry systems of construction and the coordination of specialist teams combined with efficient delivery systems inspired the structure of BSM's postwar practice.

In the 1950s, BSM became Australia's experts in highrise office building design. ICI House, Melbourne was McCutcheon's curtain-walled masterpiece, while Wilson Hall exemplified the firm's attention to craft and increasing expertise in university building and masterplanning. Under McCutcheon's leadership, the firm continued to expand and his system of office teams which included engineering and interior design sections continued to flourish well into the 1960s.

A major innovation instigated by McCutcheon was the entire reorganisation of office practices and it was his direct involvement in and sharing of this information with the wider profession that led to the formation of the practice group of the Royal Australian Institute of Architects.

Awarded the RAIA Gold Medal in 1965, McCutcheon was knighted in 1966. A distinguished contributor to the architectural profession, Sir Osborn McCutcheon died in 1981.

ICI House

GROUNDS ROMBERG AND BOYD

Roy Grounds

Frederick Romberg

Robin Boyd

Arguably the most important architecture firm in Melbourne in the 1950s, Grounds Romberg and Boyd, established in 1953 and dissolved in 1962, was the partnership of three different and extraordinary architectural talents.

Roy Burman Grounds (1905–1981), the oldest of the trio, was a graduate from the University of Melbourne Architectural Atelier. He was articled to Blackett Forster & Craig before travelling to the United States, working first in New York then in Los Angeles as a set designer. Returning to Melbourne in 1932, Grounds joined Geoffrey Mewton in partnership. Mewton and Grounds became known not just as designers of functionalist modern houses but also a series of regionally responsive open-planned houses. Grounds's own house Ranelagh, Mt. Eliza (1933–34) and Mewton's Stooke House, Brighton (1934) were the pacesetters of a new abstract idiom. Grounds in sole practice between 1939 and 1942 designed significant apartment blocks: Clendon (1939–40); Clendon Corner (1940); Moonbria (1940–41) and Quamby (1941). After World War II, he shifted design direction. Employing platonic geometries, a remarkable series of houses appeared with a circle (Henty), triangle (Leyser) and square (Grounds) as their plan.

Frederick Romberg (1910–1992) was born in Tsingtao, China. Educated at the ETH in Zurich under the tutelage of Otto Salvisberg, an expert in reinforced concrete, Romberg arriving in Melbourne in 1939 on a travelling scholarship. He worked briefly for Stephenson & Turner, then, with Mary Turner Shaw, he designed the seminal Newburn flats in Queens Road (1939–42). This off-form concrete block was followed by the expressionistic masterpiece Stanhill (1940–45) and site-sensitive Hilstan, Brighton (1950; demolished).

Robin Boyd (1919-1971) was born in Melbourne. While articled to A&K Henderson, Boyd became active in architectural writing, editing the student broadsheet *Smudges* before publishing after war service, *Victorian Modern* (1947), the state's first history of modern architecture. After a brief partnership with Kevin Pethebridge and Frank Bell (1945-47), Boyd began designing experimental and visually daring modern houses. He was the first director of the RVIA Small Homes Service (1947–53), writing weekly articles for the *Age* newspaper and through this, he became a household name in Victoria. In 1952, Boyd published his seminal modernist history *Australia's Home*.

Glenunga

When the three architects joined forces in 1953, it appeared that little would stand in their way. But the three tended to design separately within the office. Grounds continued to design assured but low key modern houses and explored new formal combinations with monumental implications. His Academy of Science, Canberra (1956–59), was an innovative mollusc-like concrete shell structure whose support legs sat in a moat. Boyd produced an extraordinary series of 'idea' houses daring in structure and form. His own house (1957) had a draped catenary curved roof. Boyd continued to write constantly, increasingly as an international commentator on contemporary architecture, but also producing his major arguments against visual pollution, *The Australian Ugliness* (1960). Romberg shouldered much of the administration within the office, but continued to demonstrate his design flair in the ETA factory and ongoing work for Ormond College.

In 1959, with the awarding of the National Gallery of Victoria and Cultural Centre to Roy Grounds, relations between the three partners became strained. In 1962, Grounds took the commission with him and devoted the next two decades of his life to its completion until his death in 1981. He also completed buildings at Monash and Melbourne universities, and at the Victorian College of the Arts. Romberg and Boyd continued in partnership until Boyd's premature death in 1971 at the age of 52. Romberg had become Professor of Architecture at the University of Newcastle while Boyd continued to write and design. Of the three, it was Boyd who, between 1947 and 1971, was Australia's most public architectural figure and advocate of modern architecture.

National Gallery of Victoria

YUNCKEN FREEMAN

The firm of Yuncken Freeman originated in 1933. Otto Yuncken and the Freeman brothers (John and Tom) had been working for establishment firm A & K Henderson and all three had been offered partnership. Instead of accepting, the three left and set up practice on their own. Yuncken Freeman and Freeman was established and shortly afterward W Balcombe Griffiths joined the firm, followed by Roy Simpson in 1938.

Yuncken Freeman Bros. Griffiths and Simpson became experts in hospital design and high quality neo-Georgian houses. In 1948, the firm was responsible for 'Operation Snail', a major state-sponsored project of imported pre-cut timber houses. In 1953, Barry Patten became a partner, followed soon after by John Gates. Between them, they designed eight major office towers in Melbourne between 1956 and 1976 – the first being Norwich Union Insurance, 53 Queen Street (1956–57); the last, Estates House, 114 William Street (1976), next door to the firm's most acclaimed work, BHP House (1967–72). All were designed with rigorous modular planning and structural innovations. The Sidney Myer Music Bowl, Canberra Civic Centre, the Victorian State Offices, and the masterplan and buildings of La Trobe University were other significant Yuncken Freeman projects.

With its commercial success, Yuncken Freeman became one of Australia's largest architecture firms and employed at its peak a staff of 200 in eight different offices, including a major branch office in Hong Kong and with projects in New Zealand, Japan, Hawaii and across Australia. Yuncken Freeman was dissolved in 1985.

GRAEME GUNN (1933 -)

Born in 1933, Graeme Gunn graduated in architecture from Royal Melbourne Institute of Technology. After working for Grounds Romberg and Boyd, he established his own practice in 1962. Innovative residential designs including the medal-winning Richardson House, Essendon (1963) were followed by a 1965 invitation from Merchant Builders to design their founding range of project houses. Accompanied by Ellis Stones's bush landscaping, Gunn's vocabulary of brick seconds, stained timbers, and easy-going open plans revolutionised the Melbourne speculative house market.

It was the beginning of an association that would last more than 20 years and include the important early cluster housing developments: Elliston, Rosanna (1969); Winter Park, Doncaster (1970); and Vermont Park, Vermont (1975). Gunn's non-residential designs were equally significant. His off-form concrete Plumbers and Gasfitters Union Building (1969) became a local Brutalist landmark, while later works (in partnership with Len Hayball and others) such as the Prahran Market Redevelopment (1971–81) and Melbourne City Baths (1980) were exemplars of sympathetic refurbishment and re-use of historic buildings. Gunn was also an influential teacher, playing a leading role at RMIT's Department of Architecture from 1972 until 1982.

Today, Gunn's practice continues to specialise in high-quality residential design.

DARYL JACKSON (1937–)

Born in Clunes, in rural Victoria, in 1937, Daryl Jackson graduated in architecture from the University of Melbourne in 1958. After working for Edwards Madigan and Torzillo in Sydney, and Don Hendry Fulton in Melbourne, Jackson went to London in 1961 to gain overseas experience, spending two years in the office of Chamberlin Powell & Bon. In 1963, he travelled to the United States, worked for Paul Rudolph in New Haven, Connecticut, and later for Skidmore Owings & Merrill in San Francisco.

On returning to Melbourne in 1965, Jackson went into partnership with Evan Walker, who had also spent time overseas gaining a masters degree at the University of Toronto. The new firm decided to specialise in school design and master planning, soon becoming the state's leading experts. Jackson also collaborated with Kevin Borland in the design of the Harold Holt Swimming Pool (1969) and this experience gave the firm a second speciality: sports structures.

The design philosophy of the office during the 1960s and 1970s was rigorous adherence to function, honest exposure of materials and structure, and a palette of colours sensitive to the Australian sunlight. It was an antipodean form of Brutalism, with concerns for placemaking and reducing buildings to more human-scale urban forms. Jackson/Walker designed major buildings in Fiji and Canberra, ACT, including the National Swimming Centre and Canberra School of Music.

In 1978, Walker decided to enter state politics as a Labor MLC. From 1979, Jackson continued in practice under his own name, expanding the firm's activities to include (in association with others) high-rise office towers such as 120 Collins Street and the award-winning Great Southern Stand at the Melbourne Cricket Ground, as well as completing work in Great Britain, Germany and the Middle East and with offices in most Australian capital cities. Jackson's designs of the 1980s and 1990s have been distinguished by a continuing interest in expressive structure for large span buildings and the inclusion of symbolism and formality, indicative of a more eclectic and inclusive approach to composition.

In 1990, Daryl Jacskon was awarded the Order of Australia for services to architecture.

Great Southern Stand, MCG

DENTON CORKER MARSHALL

John Denton, Bill Corker and Barrie Marshall

The firm of Denton Corker Marshall (DCM) was formed in 1975. John Denton (b. 1945 in Suva, Fiji), Bill Corker (b. 1945 in Melbourne) and Barrie Marshall (b. 1946 in Melbourne) all began architecture together at the University of Melbourne in 1963. After various incarnations with former partners prior to 1975 and the opening of a Canberra office in 1973, the firm gained direction with the competition-winning design for the Melbourne Civic Square (1976–80, demolished 1998). In 1980, the practice expanded again, this time in partnership with Yuncken Freeman Hong Kong.

Competition entries brought DCM a finalist's place in the design of Australia's new Parliament House and, in 1981, the commission for 1 Collins Street (in association with Robert Peck YFHK Pty Ltd), as well as the new Australian Embassy in Beijing. The firm's work has been characterised by careful contextual and programmatic responses – an architectural vocabulary that fosters the tradition of abstraction in modernism and bold architectonic formalism. DCM have also developed their firm's expertise to embrace landscape, interior and urban design.

Since 1985, DCM has operated alone, without architectural associations, subsequently opening offices in Sydney, Hong Kong, Jakarta and, more recently, Hanoi and Warsaw. It designed the Australian Embassy in Tokyo and, in Sydney, the Museum of Sydney and Governor Phillip and Macquarie towers. In Melbourne, DCM has been responsible for four major skyscrapers, the Adelphi Hotel, the Exhibition Centre, the Suprematist-styled gateway to Melbourne at the Flemington Road entry to Tullamarine Freeway and the new Museum of Victoria due for completion in 2000.

In 1996, in a rare departure from tradition, the RAIA Gold Medal was awarded not to one person, but the firm of Denton Corker Marshall.

Melbourne Exhibition Centre

EDMOND AND CORRIGAN

The partnership of Maggie Edmond (1946–) and Peter Corrigan (1939–) has been one of Melbourne's most influential firms since the mid-1970s. Their multi-award-winning buildings have challenged orthodox architectural taste and celebrated the humble architecture of the suburbs.

Born in 1939 in Daylesford, Victoria, Peter Corrigan graduated in architecture from the University of Melbourne in 1966 and completed further studies at Yale University in 1969 where he was deeply affected by the teaching and buildings of Robert Venturi. After working in several East Coast offices including Roche Dinkeloo and Paul Rudolph, he returned to Melbourne in 1974 to design sets and costumes for Don Giovanni at the Sydney Opera House. Design for theatre has been one of Corrigan's major preoccupations and an inspiration for his architecture for more than three decades. Corrigan has also been an influential teacher at RMIT since 1973 and, in 1989, he was awarded an honorary doctorate.

Maggie Edmond graduated from the University of Melbourne in 1969. After working in sole practice (1969–71) and later at Meldrum Burrows & Partners and Yuncken Freeman, she went into partnership to form Edmond and Corrigan in 1975. Their subsequent Resurrection Church and School, Keysborough (1974–78) and St Joseph's Chapel, Box Hill (1976–78) earned national notoriety for their exploration of the 'poor theatre' of the ordinary combined with vigourous expressionistic composition in the tradition of Hans Scharoun and Alvar Aalto. Subsequent buildings such as the St Francis Xavier School, Frankston (1984); Belconnen Community Centre, ACT (1985); Athan House, Monbulk (1986); and a series of fire stations across Melbourne have continued these themes.

The firm's largest work, RMIT Building 8 (1990–94) is also its most ambitious, bringing to central Melbourne a degree of complexity and material richness not seen since the 1880s. The work of Edmond and Corrigan has attracted international attention, been exhibited at the Belgrade (1991) and Venice (1992) biennales, and also the subject of a major monograph (1993), the title of which, *Cities of Hope*, characterises the architectural ideals of this once 'larrikin' firm.

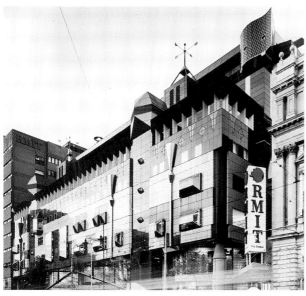

RMIT Building 8

TOURS

Melbourne began as a planned, privately developed city with satellite settlements such as Brighton, St Kilda, South Melbourne and Williamstown dotted around Port Phillip Bay. The area's relatively flat landscape was striated by orthogonal survey lines which then became major north–south and east–west roads. As a result, Melbourne is an easy city to negotiate by car. With an overlay of train and tram lines, and bus routes, all radiating from the Hoddle's central city grid, access to Melbourne's vast sprawl is guaranteed. The City Centre tour is done best, however, by simply walking.

The nine tour areas which follow have been chosen for their high concentrations or range of period styles, building types and even subdivisional character. Each tour lists the location of buildings and their architects. Some buildings may not be visible from the street and, where indicated, owners' privacy should always be respected.

These tours give an edited but rewarding snapshot of Melbourne's many characters. The City Centre has the densest and richest collection of buildings that reveal Melbourne's layers from pre-Gold Rush fragments of just two storeys, the Victorian city of six storeys, then after 1916, 12 storeys, the limit of fire ladders and City Beautiful taste, to the skyscraper city that bristled after 1955 when height controls were lifted; East Melbourne includes fine Victoriana and Melbourne's sporting stadia; South Melbourne is one of the city's Victorian 'villages'; Carlton and Fitzroy showcase terrace houses and the eclectic building styles of the University of Melbourne; South Yarra reveals houses and apartments of the genteel class; Toorak in leafier mode has the mansions of the wealthy; St Kilda shows off its colourful beachside past from the 1850s to the 1990s; Kew contains bourgeois villas and Melbourne's best collection of 1950s houses; and Eaglemont exemplifies the Griffins' sensitive landscape-inspired subdivisions coupled with innovative residential design.

1. CITY CENTRE

1. **Former Victorian Railways Administration Offices**
   67 Spencer Street
   Victorian Railways Engineering Office (116)
2. **Old Customs House**
   424 Flinders Street
   Knight Kemp & Kerr (35)
3. **Port Authority Building**
   29–31 Market Street
   Sydney Smith, Ogg & Serpell (230)
4. **Alkira House**
   17 Queen Street
   Hudson & Wardrop (265)
5. **Commercial Travellers Association Building**
   318–324 Flinders Street
   HW & FB Tompkins (158)
6. **Hosies Hotel**
   286 Flinders Street
   Mussen McKay & Potter (305)
7. **Degraves Street Underpass**
   Flinders Street/Degraves Street (306)
8. **Young & Jackson's Hotel**
   210–220 Flinders Street (25)
9. **Flinders Street Station**
   Flinders & Swanston Streets
   Fawcett & Ashworth (139)
10. **Princes Bridge**
    Yarra River at St Kilda Road
    Jenkins, D'Ebro & Grainger (100)
11. **St Paul's Cathedral**
    2 Swanston Street
    William Butterfield, Reed & Barnes;
    Joseph Barr (81)
12. **Federation Square 2001**
    Swanston & Flinders Streets
    LAB with Bates Smart
13. **Forum Cinema**
    150 Flinders Street
    Bohringer Taylor & Johnson (218)
14. **Former Herald & Weekly Times Building**
    44–74 Flinders Street
    HW & FB Tompkins (188)
15. **Shell House**
    1 Spring Street
    Harry Seidler & Associates (403)
16. **Milton House**
    25 Flinders Lane
    Sydney Smith & Ogg (144)
17. **Metcalfe & Barnard Office–Warehouse**
    145–149 Flinders Lane
    HW & FB Tompkins (143)
18. **Adelphi Hotel**
    187 Flinders Lane
    Denton Corker Marshall (411)
19. **Nicholas Building**
    27–41 Swanston Street
    Harry Norris (211)
20. **Royston House**
    247–251 Flinders Lane
    Sulman & Power (134)
21. **Majorca House**
    258–260 Flinders Lane
    Harry Norris (223)

22. **McPhersons Co. Ltd**
    546–566 Collins Street
    Reid & Pearson with SP Calder (240)
23. **Rialto Towers**
    525 Collins Street
    Gerard de Preu
    with Perrott Lyon Mathieson (401)
24. **Menzies at Rialto**
    497–503 Collins Street
    William Pitt (114)
25. **Olderfleet Building**
    477 Collins Street
    William Pitt; Robert Peck Von Hartel
    Trethowan with Denton Corker Marshall (113)
26. **Queensland Building**
    84 William Street
    Butler & Hall (181)
27. **National Mutual Life Centre**
    435–455 Collins Street
    Godfrey Spowers Hughes
    Mewton & Lobb (351)

28. **Royal Insurance Group Building**
    430–444 Collins Street
    Yuncken Freeman (339)
29. **Temple Court**
    422–428 Collins Street
    Grainger Little Barlow
    & Hawkins (194)
30. **FAI Insurance Building**
    412 Collins Street
    PWD (Percy Everett) (270)
31. **Former AMP Building (1931)**
    419–429 Collins Street
    Bates Smart & McCutcheon
32. **AC Goode House**
    389–399 Collins Street
    Wright, Reed & Beaver (103)

Melbourne's city centre is defined by Robert Hoddle's 1837 grid plan. While successive decades have alternately raised and erased subsequent layers of building types and styles, and urban spaces, the city's tartan grid of broad streets and minor east–west streets has been resilient to change. Containing Victoria's finest collection of 19th-century public buildings, and the most significant commercial architecture from every period, the city centre houses a rich architectural lode, from the tree-lined elegance of Collins Street to the intimate filigree of lanes and arcades which thread their way north from Flinders Street. Especially noteworthy in reading the city's vertical scale is the 132-foot (40-metre) height limit introduced in 1916 and broken only in 1955 by ICI House, ironically a building that lies outside the city grid.

33. **Former ES & A Bank**
390 Collins Street
William Wardell (92)
34. **Former Melbourne Stock Exchange**
376–380 Collins Street
William Pitt; Allom Lovell and Associates (107)
35. **333 Collins Street**
333 Collins Street
Nelsen Architects International with
Robert Peck von Hartel Trethowan (414)
36. **Paton Building**
115–117 Elizabeth Street
Nahum Barnet (149)
37. **Block Arcade**
282–284 Collins Street
Twentyman & Askew (111)
38. **Former Royal Banking Chambers**
287–301 Collins Street
Stephenson & Turner (268)
39. **Centreway**
259–263 Collins Street
HW & FB Tompkins (163)
40. **Newspaper House**
247–249 Collins Street
Stephenson & Meldrum (234)
41. **Kodak House**
252 Collins Street
Oakley & Parkes (241)
42. **Lyric House**
250 Collins Street
A & K Henderson (221)
43. **Manchester Unity**
91 Swanston Street
Marcus Barlow (351)
44. **Capitol Cinema**
109–117 Swanston Street
WB Griffin & Marion Mahony
with Peck & Kemter (183)
45. **Melbourne Town Hall and Offices**
90–130 Swanston Street
Reed and Barnes; Stephenson & Meldrum,
A & K Henderson (55)
46. **Regent Theatre**
191–197 Collins Street
Cedric H Ballantyne (224)
47. **Auditorium Building**
167–173 Collins Street
Nahum Barnet (177)
48. **Former T & G Building**
141 Collins Street
A & K Henderson; Metier III (203)
49. **Collins Street Baptist Church**
170–174 Collins Street
John Gill; Reed & Barnes (29)
50. **Georges**
162–168 Collins Street
Grainger & D'Ebro; Albert Purchas;
Daryl Jackson & Sir Terence Conran (91)
51. **Scots Church**
140–54 Collins Street
Reed & Barnes (75)
52. **St Michael's Church**
122–126 Collins Street
Reed & Barnes (58)
53. **120 Collins Street**
120 Collins Street
Daryl Jackson Pty Ltd with Hassell
Architects Pty Ltd (416)
54. **Professional Chambers**
110–114 Collins Street
Ussher & Kemp (152)

55. **Gilbert Court**
100–104 Collins Street
J A La Gerche (307)
56. **Austral Building**
115–119 Collins Street
Nahum Barnet (125)
57. **Francis House**
107 Collins Street
Blacket & Forster (215)
58. **101 Collins Street**
101 Collins Street
Denton Corker Marshall; Johnson Burgee (402)
59. **Collins Place**
Collins & Exhibition Streets
Harry Cobb (IM Pei) with Bates
Smart & McCutcheon (369)
60. **No. 1 Collins Street**
1 Collins Street
Denton Corker Marshall
with Robert Peck YFHK (395)
61. **House for Hon. William Campbell**
61 Spring Street
Leonard Terry; Robert Peck YFHK Pty Ltd (63)
62. **Melbourne Club**
36–50 Collins Street
Leonard Terry; Terry & Oakden (40)
63. **Alcaston House**
2 Collins Street
A & K Henderson (229)
64. **Windsor Hotel**
137 Spring Street
Charles Webb; Norris & Partners;
Allom Lovell Associates (90)
65. **Russell Street Telephone
Exchange & Post Office**
114–120 Russell Street
Commonwealth Dept. of Works (285)
66. **Century Building**
125–133 Swanston Street
Marcus Barlow (272)
67. **Yule House**
309–311 Little Collins Street
Oakley & Parkes (233)
68. **Former City of Melbourne Building**
112–118 Elizabeth Street
Ellerker & Kilburn (106)
69. **ACA Building**
118–126 Queen Street
Hennessy & Hennessy (256)
70. **Australian Club**
100–110 William Street
Lloyd Tayler; Wilson & Charlesworth (86)
71. **Melbourne & Metropolitan Board
of Works Head Office (1969–73)**
625 Little Collins Street
Perrott Lyon Timlock & Kesa
72. **General Post Office & Mail Exchange**
164–200 Spencer Street
John Smith Murdoch (179)
73. **AMP Tower & St James Building**
527–555 Bourke Street
Skidmore Owings & Merrill with
Bates Smart & McCutcheon (354)
74. **BHP House**
140 William Street
Yuncken Freeman (367)
75. **Former Goldsborough Mort Woolstore**
514–528 Bourke Street, 152–162 William Street
John Gill (30)
76. **London Assurance Building**
468–470 Bourke Street
Bernard Evans & Associates (329)
77. **Melbourne General Post Office**
Elizabeth & Bourke Streets

PWD (Smith & Johnson) (38)

78. **Myer Emporium**
314–336 Bourke Street
HW & FB Tompkins (242)

79. **Buckley & Nunn Department Store**
310 Bourke Street
Bates Peebles & Smart (173)

80. **Former Buckley & Nunn Men's Store**
294–296 Bourke Street
Bates Smart & McCutcheon (238)

81. **Royal Arcade**
331–339 Bourke Street
Charles Webb; Hyndman & Bates (57)

82. **Public Benefit Bootery**
323–325 Bourke Street
Grainger Little Barlow & Hawkins (210)

83. **David Jones**
299–307 Bourke Street
Harry Norris (227)

84. **The Leviathan Clothing Store**
271–281 Swanston & Bourke Streets
Bates Peebles & Smart (164)

85. **Hoyts Cinema Centre**
134–144 Bourke Street
Peter Muller (356)

86. **Former ES & A Bank**
88–90 Bourke Street
Leonard Terry (67)

87. **Crossley's Building**
54–62 Bourke Street (12)

88. **Princess Theatre**
163–181 Spring Street
William Pitt; Henry White (102)

89. **Sum Kum Lee General Store**
112–114 Little Bourke Street
George De Lacy Evans (105)

90. **Total Carpark**
170–190 Russell Street
Bogle & Banfield (349)

91. **Methodist Mission Church**
196 Little Bourke Street
Crouch & Wilson (65)

92. **Num Pon Soon Chinese Club**
200–202 Little Bourke Street
Peter Kerr (47)

93. **Myer Department Store Crossover**
at 290 Little Bourke Street
Tompkins Shaw & Evans (345)

94. **Warehouses**
23–31 Niagara Lane
George De Lacy Evans (99)

95. **Supreme Court**
228 William Street
Smith & Johnson (74)

96. **Seabrook House**
573–577 Lonsdale Street
Leonard Terry (39)

97. **Mitchell House**
352–362 Lonsdale Street
Harry Norris (39)

98. **St Francis Catholic Church**
Elizabeth & Lonsdale Sts
S Jackson; George & Schneider;
Reed & Barnes (2)

99. **Queen Victoria Women's Centre**
210 Lonsdale Street
JJ & EJ Clark (154)

100. **Wesley Church**
148 Lonsdale Street
Joseph Reed (28)

101. **Telstra Corporate Centre**
242 Exhibition Street
Perrott Lyon Mathieson (415)

102. **Royal Australasian College of Surgeons**

Lonsdale & Spring Streets
Irwin & Stevenson (255)

103. **State Library of Victoria**
304–328 Swanston Street
Joseph Reed and others (33)

104. **Brooks Building**
305–325 Swanston Street (6)

105. **Sniders & Abrahams Warehouse**
7 Drewery Lane
HR Crawford (160)

106. **Former John Smith House**
294–308 Queen Street
Charles Laing; David Ross (7)

107. **Records Office**
287–295 Queen Street
SE Bindley (138)

108. **Royal Mint**
280–318 William Street
PWD (JJ Clark) (54)

109. **Shop & Residence**
328–330 King Street (22)

110. **Argus Centre**
300 La Trobe Street
Katsalidis Architects with Axia Pty Ltd (418)

111. **RMIT Building No. 1**
124 La Trobe Street
Terry & Oakden, Nahum Barnet;
Oakden Addison & Kemp (95)

112. **City Law Courts**
Russell & La Trobe Streets
GBH Austin (162)

113. **Russell Street Police Headquarters**
Russell & La Trobe Streets
PWD (Percy Everett) (274)

114. **8 Hour Day Memorial**
Russell & Victoria Streets
Percy Bell (140)

115. **Old Melbourne Gaol**
Russell & Franklin Streets (42)

116. **Former Emily McPherson College
of Domestic Economy**
Russell & Franklin Streets
PWD (E Evan Smith) (204)

117. **RMIT Buildings 5, 6, 7 & 9**
Bowen Street
PWD (Percy Everett) (269)

118. **Storey Hall**
344–346 Swanston Street
Tappin Gilbert Dennehy; Ashton Raggatt
McDougall & others (429)

119. **RMIT Building 8**
Swanston Street
Edmond & Corrigan
with Demaine Partnership (419)

120. **Melbourne City Baths**
438 Swanston Street
JJ & EJ Clark; Kevin Greenhatch &
Gunn Williams Fender (142)

121. **Former ES & A Bank**
453–457 Elizabeth Street
Chancellor & Patrick (325)

122. **Melbourne Terraces**
Queen & Franklin Streets
Katsalidis Architects (430)

123. **Royal Melbourne Regiment,
6 Battalion Drill Hall**
49–53 Victoria Street
GH Hallendal (266)

124. **Queen Victoria Markets**
Elizabeth & Victoria Streets
William Salway (56)

125. **St James Old Cathedral**
419–435 King Street
Robert Russell; Charles Laing (4)

2. EAST MELBOURNE

Parliament House

Bounded by Spring Street, Victoria Parade (the northern boundary of the 1837 town reserve), Hoddle Street/Punt Road (the reserve's eastern boundary) and the Yarra River, the elevated area east of Melbourne's grid comprises Eastern Hill, which contains the state's largest cathedral, its parliamentary and public service precinct, and a host of other institutional and ecclesiastical establishments that date from the 1850s; the Treasury and Fitzroy Gardens (initially laid out by Edward La Trobe Bateman in 1857); and, further east, the suburb of East Melbourne which from the 1850s had always been a favoured residential location. Further east again, beyond Hoddle Street, private land speculation and relaxed subdivisional controls determined narrow streets and smaller sites. Workers' cottages and light industry prevailed in contrast to East Melbourne's broad streets, gentlemen's villas and iron-laced terraces.

Old Treasury Building

Bishopscourt

Eastern Hill Fire Station

ICI House

Townhouses, Cremorne Street

1. **ICI House**
    1 Nicholson Street
    Bates Smart & McCutcheon (314)
2. **Synagogue (Mickva Yisrael)**
    488 Albert Street
    Crouch & Wilson (73)
3. **Eastern Hill Fire Station**
    108-122 Victoria Parade
    Smith & Johnson, Lloyd Taylor & Fitts (137)
4. **St Peter's Eastern Hill**
    Gisborne & Albert Streets
    Charles Laing (3)
5. **Parliament House**
    Spring Street
    Knight & Kerr (36)
6. **Parliament Station**
    Spring Street
    McIntyre Partnership Pty Ltd (392)
7. **Old Treasury Building**
    Spring Street
    Public Works Department (JJ Clark) (31)
8. **Victorian State Offices**
    Treasury Place
    Yuncken Freeman (342)
9. **Commonwealth Offices**
    Treasury Place
    John Smith Murdoch (167)
10. **Tasma Terrace**
    2-12 Parliament Place
    Charles Webb (78)
11. **St Patrick's Roman Catholic Cathedral**
    5 Gisborne Street
    William Wardell; WP Connolly & GW Vanheems (37)
12. **Catholic Archdiocese of Melbourne**
    383 Albert Street
    Yuncken Freeman (368)
13. **Victorian Artists' Society Building**
    430 Albert Street
    Richard Speight & HW Tompkins (133)
14. **Conservatory**
    Fitzroy Gardens
    MCC City Engineer (225)
15. **Captain Cook's Cottage (1934; reconstructed)**
    Fitzroy Gardens

16. **St Hilda's (1907)**
    1–17 Clarendon Street
17. **Clarendon Terrace**
    208–212 Clarendon Street
    Osgood Pritchard (27)
18. **Freemasons Hospital (1936)**
    Albert & Clarendon Streets
    Stephenson & Meldrum
19. **Mercy Hospital**
    Grey & Clarendon Streets
    Stephenson & Meldrum (253)
20. **Bishopscourt**
    120 Clarendon Street
    Newson & Blackburn; Walter Butler (20)
21. **Little Parndon**
    159 Gipps Street (46)
22. **Former Clement Hodgkinson House**
    157 Hotham Street
    Joseph Reed (44)
23. **Eastbourne Terrace**
    62 Wellington Parade, 8–10 Simpson Street
    Sydney Smith & Ogg (142)

24. **Yarra Park Housing**
    Punt & Bridge Roads
    Perrott Lyon Mathieson (431)
25. **Wheeler House**
    41 Rowena Parade
    Robinson Chen (407)
26. **Townhouses**
    106–112 Cremorne Street
    Rossetti & Holmes (436)
27. **Great Southern Stand,**
    Melbourne Cricket Ground
    Brunton Avenue
    Daryl Jackson Pty Ltd and Tompkins
    Shaw & Evans (410)
28. **National Tennis Centre**
    Batman Avenue
    Philip Cox Richardson & Taylor
    and PeddleThorp & Learmonth (405)
29. **Former Olympic Swimming Stadium**
    Swan Street & Batman Avenue
    K Borland, P McIntyre, J & P Murphy;
    later Borland Brown (296)

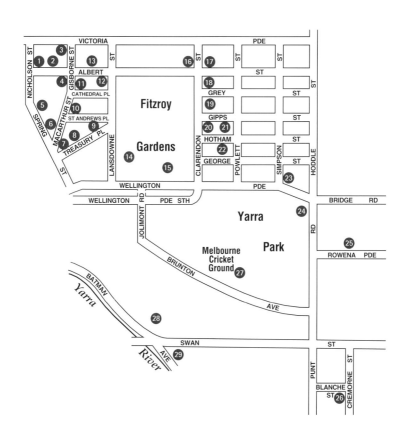

3. SOUTH MELBOURNE

National Gallery of Victoria

The Biltmore

Melbourne Exhibition Centre

Corrugated iron houses

Former South Melbourne Town Hall

Macrae & Wray Film Production

1. **Mission to Seamen**
   717 Flinders Street
   Walter Butler (165)
2. **Melbourne Exhibition Centre**
   2 Clarendon Street
   Denton Corker Marshall (440)
3. **Crown Casino**
   Queensbridge Street at Yarra River
   Bates Smart; Daryl Jackson Pty Ltd; Perrott Lyon Mathieson (439)
4. **Yarra Footbridge**
   Yarra River at Southbank
   Cocks Carmichael Whitford (409)
5. **Southgate**
   Southbank Promenade
   Buchan Laird & Bawden
6. **Victorian Arts Centre**
   100 St Kilda Road
   Roy Grounds; Suendermann Douglas McFall (370)
7. **National Gallery of Victoria**
   180 St Kilda Road
   Roy Grounds (332)
8. **Victoria Barracks**
   St Kilda Road & Coventry Street
   PWD (Gustav Joachimi); John Smith Murdoch (45)
9. **Fire Station No. 28**
   Moray Street, South Melbourne
   Simon Swaney Pty Ltd (421)
10. **First Church of Christ Scientist**
    336 St Kilda Road
    Bates Peebles & Smart; Bates Smart & McCutcheon (186)
11. **Former BP House**
    1 Albert Road
    Demaine Russell Trundle Armstrong & Orton (348)
12. **MacPherson Robertson Girls High School**
    350 Kings Way
    Seabrook & Fildes (252)
13. **City Edge Housing**
    Kings Way & Park Street
    Daryl Jackson Evan Walker (376)
14. **See Yup Temple**
    76 Raglan Street
    George Wharton; Harold Desbrowe-Annear (52)
15. **Court House and Police Station**
    209 & 211–213 Bank Street
    E Evan Smith (PWD) (197)
16. **Former South Melbourne Town Hall**
    208–220 Bank Street
    Charles Webb; Oakley and Parkes; Daryl Jackson Pty Ltd (82)
17. **Macrae & Way Film Production**
    3 Francis Street
    Biltmoderne (398)
18. **State School No. 1253**
    286 Dorcas Street
    Charles Webb (70)
19. **Corrugated iron houses**
    399 Coventry Street (21)
20. **Rochester Terrace**
    33–51 St Vincent Place
    Charles Boykett & Charles Bolton Boykett (62)
21. **The Biltmore, former Albert Park Coffee Palace**
    152–158 Bridport Street
    Walter Scott Law; Frederick de Garis & Son (96)

Emerald Hill (South Melbourne) is the slight rise lying south of the city centre and before Port Phillip Bay. The location originally for the Melbourne Orphanage, the surrounding area was one of Melbourne's very early subdivisions. Nearby, St Vincents Place was laid out in 1857 and is Melbourne's grandest residential square. Now almost entirely gentrified and trendy, South Melbourne retains its 19th-century character and many of its major public buildings. Since the 1980s and as part of a strategy that has been enacted since the master-planned placement of the National Gallery of Victoria and Victorian Arts Centre on their St Kilda Road site in 1960, the area immediately south of the Yarra River has been the focus of concerted development. The Melbourne Exhibition Centre and Crown Casino are the most recent additions in attempts to rid the area of its industrial past and revitalise the sunny side of the Yarra.

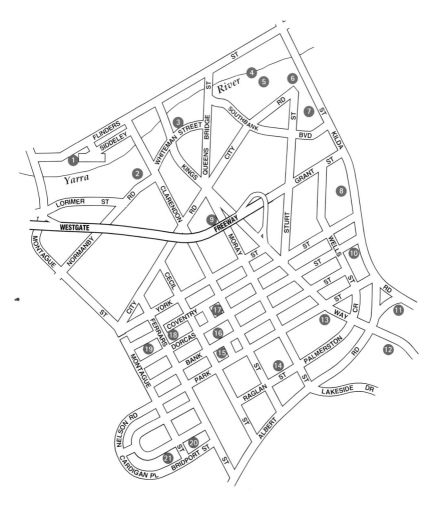

4. CARLTON/FITZROY

Lying north of the 1837 town reserve boundary of Victoria Parade, Carlton and Fitzroy were subdivided privately into the slim row and terrace house allotments which have given Melbourne's inner suburbs their distinctive spatial character. Some sites were reserved for public use, and the location of the University of Melbourne (from 1854), the Carlton Gardens (later the site of the Exhibition Buildings), Princes Park and the Melbourne General Cemetery derive from those original far-sighted decisions. Carlton was the beneficiary of a series of squares (University, Lincoln, Argyle, Murchison and Macarthur). From the 1950s, Carlton became known for its Italian migrant community, who transformed Lygon Street into Melbourne's premier street of cafés, pasticceria and gelateria. In the 1960s, the precinct became the target for slum demolition and high-rise towers on green-field sites. Today, Carlton and Fitzroy maintain a rich and urbane mix of people and functions, ranging from the gentrified and trendy to 19th-century Parkville; from down-at-heel lanescapes and estates to bohemian and café-ridden Brunswick Street.

1. **Whitley College**
   271 Royal Parade
   Mockridge Stahle & Mitchell (357)
2. **International House**
   231–241 Royal Parade
   Raymond Berg and Leighton Irwin & Co. (328)
3. **Wardlow**
   114 Park Drive (104)
4. **Saunders House**
   Gatehouse & Morrah Streets
   David Saunders (344)
5. **Royal Melbourne Hospital**
   Grattan Street, Parkville
   Stephenson & Turner; Daryl Jackson Pty Ltd (273)
6. **Meat Market Craft Centre**
   36 Courtney Street
   GR Johnson; Gibbs & Finlay (83)
7. **Queensberry Child Care Centre, former State School No. 2365**
   225 Queensberry Street
   Education Department Architects' Office (87)
8. **Former Ampol Building**
   792 Elizabeth Street
   Bernard Evans
   University of Melbourne
   Royal Parade, University of Melbourne
9. **Conservatorium of Music**
   Bates Peebles & Smart (166)
10. **Grainger Museum**
    Gawler & Drummond (252)
11. **Babel Building**
    Godfrey Spowers Hughes Mewton and Lobb (286)
12. **Cloisters, Law School**
    FM White et al. (41)
13. **South Lawn and Underground Carpark**
    Rayment & Stones; Loder & Bayley (372)
14. **Wilson Hall**
    Bates Smart & McCutcheon (295)
15. **School of Graduate Studies**
    Henry Bastow et al. (?)
16. **Traffic Entry & Security Office**
    Peter Elliott Architects Pty Ltd (434)
17. **Chemistry Building**
    Percy Everett (PWD) (278)
18. **Old Zoology Building, former**
    Reed Henderson & Smart (101)
19. **Beaurepaire Centre**
    Eggleston MacDonald & Secomb (302)
20. **Trinity College Chapel**
    North & Williams (174)
21. **Ormond College**
    Reed & Barnes and others (89)
22. **Newman College**
    WB Griffin & M Mahony and AA Fritsch (174)
23. **Kathleen Syme Education Centre**
    Faraday & Cardigan Streets
    Reed and Barnes (77)

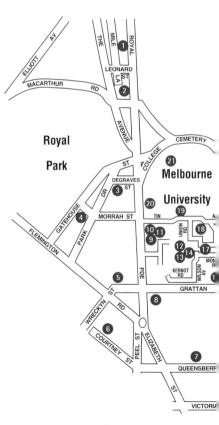

24. **Housing**
Tyne Street
Williams & Boag (426)

25. **Jimmy Watson's Wine Bar**
333 Lygon Street
Romberg & Boyd (338)

26. **Police Station and Lock-up**
330 Drummond Street
Public Works Department (80)

27. **Offices**
221 Drummond Street
Ashton & Raggatt (399)

28. **Sacred Heart Roman Catholic Church**
199 Rathdowne Street
Reed Smart & Tappin (132)

29. **Building 94 RMIT (1996)**
23–27 Cardigan Street
AC Powell and Pels Innes Neilson Kosloff

30. **Trades Hall**
Cnr Lygon & Victoria Streets
Reed & Barnes (69)

31. **Plumbers & Gasfitters Union Building**
52 Victoria Street
Graeme Gunn (375)

32. **Medley Hall, former Benvenuta**
48 Drummond Street
Walter S Law (115)

33. **Melbourne Exhibition Buildings**
Nicholson Street, Carlton Gardens
Reed & Barnes (85)

34. **Museum of Victoria**
Rathdowne Street, Carlton Gardens
Denton Corker Marshall (448)

35. **Fitzroy Cable Tram Engine House**
Gertrude & Nicholson Streets
Twentyman & Askew (112)

36. **Royal Terrace**
Nicholson & Gertrude Streets
attributed to John Gill (24)

37. **Cairo Flats**
98 Nicholson Street
Taylor Soilleux & Overend (249)

38. **Lyddy Polish Manufacturing Co. Building**
167–169 Fitzroy Street
EM Nicholls (189)

39. **Glass Terrace**
64–78 Gertrude Street
David Ross; Charles Webb (23)

40. **Former Devonshire Arms Hotel**
38 Fitzroy Street (5)

41. **Fitzroy Town Hall**
201 Napier Street
WJ Ellis; George Johnson (109)

42. **Collingwood Town Hall**
140 Hoddle Street
George R Johnson; AC Leith & Bartlett (98)

43. **Bendigo Hotel**
125 Johnston Street
Sydney Smith & Ogg (159)

44. **Workers' Cottages**
1–30 Greeves Street; 310, 311, 312 &
313 Fitzroy Street; 12 & 14 Mahony Street
Alfred Kursteiner (49)

45. **Office Building**
61 Victoria Street
Carter Couch (404)

46. **Kay Street Housing**
Station Street, Kay Street
G Burgess; Edmond & Corrigan;
Peter Crone (390)

47. **Carlton Baths**
Rathdowne Street
Peter Elliott Architects Pty Ltd (408)

48. **Primary School No. 1252**
Lee Street
WH Ellerker; Lindsay Holland Pty Ltd (79)

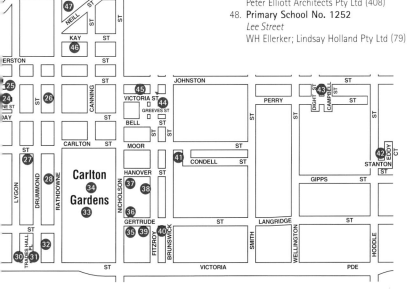

5. SOUTH YARRA

Myer Music Bowl

Government House

Church Street Bridge

Como

Domain Park

The expression 'South of the Yarra' has long connoted wealth and privilege in Melbourne. The area's elevation and its handsome prospects to the river valley to the north, and Port Phillip Bay to the south and west, the location of the Royal Botanic Gardens (sited in 1846 by Governor La Trobe and laid out by William Guilfoyle in 1873), the Kings Domain and Government House (1871–76)—all added to South Yarra's cachet as a desirable place to live. From the 1920s until the 1960s, South Yarra experienced extraordinary urban consolidation with the private development of walk-up apartments in every stylistic dress. By contrast, society architects such as Harold Desbrowe-Annear and Marcus Martin built elegant Georgian-inspired townhouses while architect/developer Howard Lawson designed virtually all the apartment blocks in the area bounded by Punt Road, Domain Road, Darling Street and Alexandra Avenue between 1920 and 1940. By the 1950s, architects had begun to experiment with ultra-modern variations on the single townhouse interspersed by faceless blocks of three- and four-storey flats and the occasional highrise apartment block which razed significant 19th- and early 20th-century houses. The retail spine of South Yarra is Toorak Road, the area's boutique shopping street which intersects with the fashionable and seemingly infinite Chapel Street. Today, South Yarra upholds its stylish and expensive image.

1. **Sidney Myer Music Bowl**
   The Kings Domain
   Yuncken Freeman Bros. Griffiths & Simpson (330)
2. **Government House**
   Government House Drive, The Kings Domain
   PWD (William Wardell) (66)
3. **Jolimont, La Trobe's Cottage**
   Dallas Brooks Drive, Kings Domain (1)
4. **Shrine of Remembrance**
   St Kilda Road, Birdwood Avenue
   Hudson & Wardrop; Ernest E Milston (217)
5. **Under Gardener's Cottage**
   Royal Botanic Gardens
   Henry Ginn (15)
6. **Melbourne Church of England Boy's Grammar School**
   Domain and St Kilda Roads
   Webb & Taylor ; AE Johnson (32)
7. **Classrooms, Melbourne Church of England Boys' Grammar School**
   Bromby Street
   Mockridge Stahle & Mitchell (303)
8. **Domain Park**
   193 Domain Road
   Romberg & Boyd (337)
9. **Kurneh Flats**
   206 Domain Road
   Bernard Joyce (359)
10. **Morell Bridge**
    Yarra River at Anderson Street
    John Monash (135)
11. **Robin Boyd House II**
    290 Walsh Street
    Grounds Romberg & Boyd (318)

12. **Fenner House**
    228 Domain Road
    Neil Clerehan (346)
13. **Amesbury House**
    237–239 Domain Road
    Walter Butler; Harold Desbrowe-Annear (187)
14. **Clerehan House II**
    90 Walsh Street
    Neil Clerehan (320)
15. **Offices**
    5 Avoca Street
    Guilford Bell & Graham Fisher (425)
16. **Maisonettes**
    Caroline Street and Domain Road
    Marcus Martin (198)
17. **Beverly Hills Flats**
    61-67 Darling Street
    Howard Lawson (248)

18. **Melbourne Boys' High School**
    Alexandra Avenue
    PWD (E Evan Smith) (196)
19. **Church Street Bridge**
    Yarra River at Church Street
    Harold Desbrowe-Annear (208)
20. **Scroggie House**
    52 Kensington Road
    Gunn Hayball (388)
21. **Como**
    Como Avenue
    others & later AE Johnson (11)
22. **Country Road**
    252 Toorak Rd
    Metier III (424)
23. **Former South Yarra Post Office**
    Toorak Road & Osborne Street
    AJ McDonald (131)
24. **Clerehan House I**
    18 Fawkner Street
    Neil Clerehan (320)

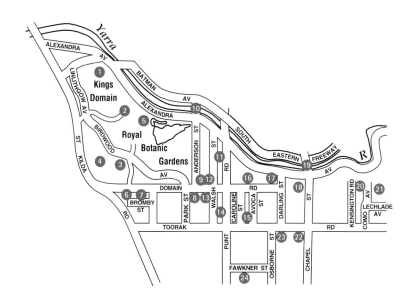

6. TOORAK

Mandeville Hall

Toorak House

By 1900, Toorak was a suburban Arcadia containing towered Italianate houses with formal gardens, fabulous 1880s Boom-style mansions with sweeping drives, and Arts and Crafts houses redolent of Kent and Surrey. The suburb's reputation had been boosted by being home twice to Government House. Toorak House had been leased as the governor's residence from 1854 until 1875. Stonington was vice-regal residence from 1901 until 1932. Today, Toorak and Malvern are experiencing increasing urban densities which threaten to diminish the precinct's long history as home to Melbourne's richest class and biggest houses. A by-product of these subdivisons has been the number of smaller, often extremely interesting houses in Toorak by architects such as Harold Desbrowe-Annear, Walter Burley Griffin and Marion Mahony, Roy Grounds and Robin Boyd, anomalies within the neo-Georgian stronghold that Toorak had become by the late 1940s. Today, however, Toorak still holds the sway of money; its tree-lined avenues and addresses such as St Georges, Lansell, Irving and Orrong roads continue to impress.

1. **Quamby (1941–42)**
   3 Glover Court
   Roy Grounds
2. **Brett House**
   3 Buddle Drive
   Grounds Romberg & Boyd (310)
3. **Grounds House and Flats**
   24 Hill Street
   Roy Grounds (300)
4. **Richardson House**
   10 Blackfriars Close
   Robin Boyd; Peter Crone (299)
5. **House**
   729 Orrong Road, Toorak
   Harold Desbrowe-Annear
6. **Trawalla**
   22 Lascelles Avenue
   Levi Powell; Powell and Whittaker (64)
7. **Moonbria Flats**
   * Mathoura Road
   Roy Grounds (276)
8. **Clendon Lodge (1923)**
   74 Clendon Road
   WB Griffin & Marion Mahony
9. **Mullion, Smith House**
   6 Stonehaven Court
   EM Nicholls (222)
10. **Cranlana**
    62–62a Clendon Road
    Harold Desbrowe-Annear; Yuncken
    Freeman Bros., Griffiths & Simpson (213)
11. **Mandeville Hall**
    10 Mandeville Crescent
    Charles Webb (88)
12. **Eulinya**
    Irving and Albany Roads
    W&R Butler (201)
13. **Langi Flats**
    579 Toorak Road
    WB Griffin & Marion
    Mahony (202)
14. **Toorak House**
    21 St Georges Road (14)
15. **Caringal Flats**
    3 Tahara Road
    JW Rivett (284)
16. **Illawarra**
    1 Illawarra Crescent
    James Birtwhistle (117)
17. **House**
    2 Glendye Court
    Holgar & Holgar
18. **Houses (1925, 1922)**
    1 and 4 Heyington Place
    Harold Desbrowe-Annear
19. **Glyn**
    224 Kooyong Road
    Klingender & Alsop (168)
20. **Broome**
    6 Glyndebourne Avenue
    Marcus Martin (199)
21. **Stanley R Salter House**
    16 Glyndebourne Avenue
    WB Griffin & Marion
    Mahony (190)
22. **Cloyne (1926)**
    609 Toorak Road
    Harold Desbrowe-Annear

23. **Redheath**
    202 Kooyong Road
    Yuncken Freeman Freeman & Griffiths (246)
24. **Little Milton**
    26 Albany Road
    Muriel Stott with Stephenson
    & Meldrum;
    Edna Walling (200)
25. **Former Dr Boyd Graham House**
    68 Hopetoun Road
    A Mortimer McMillan (258)
26. **Fuzzell House**
    15 Russell Street
    Max May (389)
27. **Stonington**
    336 Glenferrie Road
    Charles D'Ebro (119)
28. **Katanga (1932)**
    372 Glenferrie Road
    Harold Desbrowe-Annear
29. **Revell**
    9 Toorak Avenue
    Edward Fielder Billson (185)
30. **Denby Dale**
    424 Glenferrie Road
    RB Hamilton & Marcus Norris (263)
31. **Wyalla, later Thanes**
    13a Monaro Road
    Butler & Bradshaw (161)
32. **Littlejohn Memorial Chapel, Scotch College**
    Glenferrie Road
    Scarborough Robertson & Love (245)

33. **Atlas House**
    80 Kooyongkoot Road
    Tom Kovac (442)
34. **Former Warrington, then Kawarau**
    405 Tooronga Road
    Beswicke & Coote; Ussher & Kemp (122)
35. **St James's Anglican Church**
    Burke Road & High Street
    Bogle & Banfield (327)
36. **Harold Holt Memorial Swimming Pool**
    High Street
    Kevin Borland & Daryl Jackson (361)
37. **St Joseph's Church**
    47 Stanhope Street
    AA Fritsch (180)
38. **Former ES&A Bank**
    Cnr High Street & Glenferrie Road
    ES&A Architects' Branch
    (Stuart McIntosh) (322)
39. **Malvern/Glenferrie Tram Depot**
    Coldblo Road, Malvern (175)
40. **Mrs Craig Dixson House**
    23 Moorhouse Street, Armadale
    JFW Ballantyne (195)
41. **Glenunga**
    2 Horsburgh Grove
    Romberg and Shaw (277)
42. **Clendon; Clendon Corner (1940, 1941)**
    Malvern & Clendon Roads
    Roy Grounds

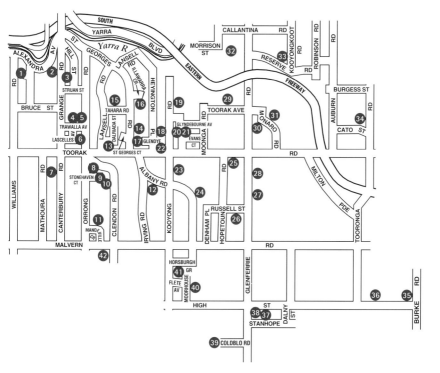

7. ST KILDA

St George's Church

Rippon Lea

Stanhill

St Kilda today sports many urban characters. Alternately seedy, trendy, bohemian and gentrified, the fortunes of this seaside suburb have risen, fallen and surged again over more than 140 years. St Kilda Hill contains significant churches, mansions and substantial homes that date from the 1850s to the 1870s. With the railway connection to the city centre (one of the city's oldest), the suburb had become a fashionable place to live and something of a summer resort. After World War I, many of St Kilda's grand houses became rooming and boarding houses, sometimes houses of ill-repute. Early apartment blocks were built in front gardens while the entertainment industry at beachside continued its peripatetic development. With Luna Park, the Palais Theatre, music and dance halls on the Upper Esplanade, and increasing numbers of apartment buildings, St Kilda by the 1920s was described as 'the Lido of the South'. From the 1940s through until the 1970s, St Kilda's reputation was at its lowest, the haunt of prostitutes, artists and rock bands whose debuts were made at the infamous Esplanade Hotel. But it was arguably a richer time. With Acland Street's links to central European and Russian migrants and East St Kilda's history as a centre of Jewish culture in Melbourne since the 1920s, the suburb was more diverse than sinister. Today, St Kilda is booming. Fitzroy Street and Acland Street are packed with cafés, bars and restaurants, apartments are being refurbished and innovative new blocks are springing up while battles rage over height controls and gentrification makes rapacious inroads into St Kilda's seamy past. Architecturally, however, St Kilda maintains its rich complexity and a wonderfully competitive layering of the tawdry and the stylish.

Palais Cinema

The Canterbury

2. **South African War Memorial**
   Alfred Square
   Peck & Kemter (169)
13. **Palais Cinema**
   Lower Esplanade
   Henry E White (207)
14. **Luna Park**
   Lower Esplanade & Cavell Street (176)
15. **Edgewater Towers**
   12 Marine Parade
   Mordecai Benshemesh (351)
16. **Woy Woy Flats**
   77 Marine Parade
   Mewton & Grounds (251)
17. **Hartpury Court**
   11 Milton Street
   Arthur W Plaisted (193)
18. **St Kilda Town Hall Redevelopment**
   Carlisle Street & Brighton Road
   Ashton Raggatt McDougall (432)

19. **St Kilda Public Library   (1969. 1994)**
   150 Carlisle Street
   Enrico Taglietti; Ashton Raggatt McDougall
20. **Rippon Lea**
   192 Hotham Street
   Reed & Barnes (61)
21. **Labassa**
   2 Manor Grove
   JAB Koch (121)
22. **Glenfern**
   Hotham & Inkerman Sts
   attr. Charles Laing (34)
23. **The Priory**
   61 Alma Road
   Ellerker & Kilburn (129)
24. **The Astor Theatre**
   1 Chapel Street
   R Morton Taylor (259)
25. **St George's Church**
   4 Chapel Street
   Albert Purchas (76)
26. **St Mary's Church   (1859–71)**
   208 Dandenong Road
   William Wardell
27. **Windsor Fire Station**
   Albert Street
   Edmond & Corrigan (441)

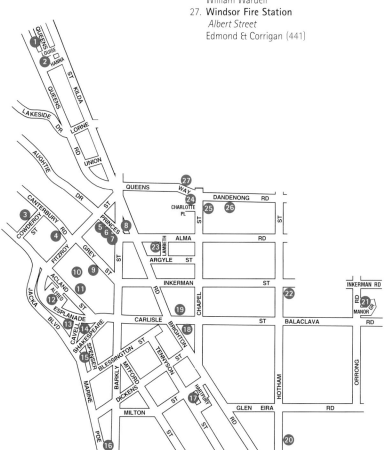

8. KEW

Trinity Grammar School Chapel

Villa Alba

Dalswraith

Godsell House

The Yarra River snaking its way north-east from the city centre and the native trees of Studley Park give the western portion of Kew much of its special character. The location for the Kew Lunatic Asylum (later Willsmere and now a housing estate) which dates from the 1860s and whose chateauesque towers appear above the trees, Kew was also home to substantial numbers of large Victorian houses and gardens that date from the 1870s through until the 1910s. Molesworth Street and Sackville Street still contain some of Melbourne's most elegant and imposing Italianate villas. Remarkably, many of the estates remained intact until the 1940s when subdividision began in earnest invariably when mansion ownership shifted from private to institutional hands. The sites that were sold in the 1950s were frequently the steeply sloping blocks on virtual cliff faces or in creek gullies with views west and north to the Yarra. For the adventurous postwar architect, it was heaven. Innovative responses to single house design with lightweight structure and new materials by architects like Robin Boyd, Peter McIntyre, Chancellor & Patrick, Anatol Kagan and McGlashan & Everist could be found in many of the newly created streets. As a result, the area bounded by The Yarra Boulevard, Studley Park Road, Princess Street and Wills Street contains one of the best concentrations of 1950s architect-designed houses in Melbourne. Elsewhere, Kew is quintessentially and comfortably suburban with an entire spectrum of detached house styles from Federation to the present day and complemented by some of Melbourne's oldest and established private schools.

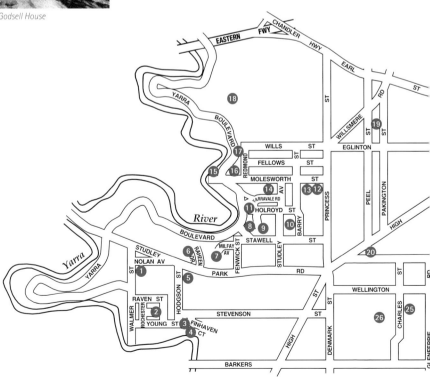

1. **Villa Alba**
   44 Walmer Street
   possibly William Greenlaw (94)
2. **Milston House**
   6 Reeves Court
   Ernest Milston (312)
3. **Godsell House**
   8 Hodgson Street
   Sean Godsell (444)
4. **McIntyre House**
   2 Hodgson Street
   Peter & Dione McIntyre (308)
5. **Dalswraith (Campion College)**
   99 Studley Park Rd
   Ussher & Kemp (147)
6. **Raheen**
   94 Studley Park Road
   William Salway; Glenn Murcutt
   with Bates Smart & McCutcheon (93)
7. **Clemson House**
   24 Milfay Avenue
   Grounds Romberg & Boyd (317)
8. **House (1963)**
   18 Yarra Street
   McGlashan & Everist
9. **House (1953)**
   14 Carnsworth Avenue
   Geoffrey Danne
10. **D'Estaville**
    7 Barry Street
    Knight & Kerr (43)

11. **House (1952)**
    Belvedere & Yarravale Roads
    Anatol Kagan
12. **House (1891)**
    3 Molesworth Street
    Beswicke & Coote
13. **Mynda (1885)**
    5 Molesworth Street
    Lloyd Tayler
14. **Freiberg House**
    26 Yarravale Road
    Chancellor & Patrick; Edna Walling (321)
15. **Haughton James House**
    82 Molesworth Street
    Grounds Romberg & Boyd (315)
16. **Townhouses**
    76 Molesworth Street
    Graeme Gunn (371)
17. **Pettigrew House**
    21 Redmond Street
    Boyd Pethebridge & Bell (281)
18. **Former Kew Asylum**
    Wiltshire Drive
    Public Works Department (53)
19. **Kitamura House**
    123 Pakington Street
    John Wardle (438)
20. **Former Kew Post Office, Court House, Police Station**
    190 High Street
    John Henry Harvey (124)
21. **Springthorpe Memorial**
    Booroondara Cemetery, Park Hill Rd
    Harold Desbrowe-Annear (136)
22. **Norman House**
    7 Adeney Avenue
    Ussher & Kemp (151)
23. **Preshil School**
    395 Barkers Road (Mount Street)
    Kevin Borland (341)
24. **MLC Resource Centre**
    Glenferrie Road
    Daryl Jackson Evan Walker
25. **Trinity Grammar School Chapel**
    Charles Street
    Crone Ross (423)
26. **Xavier College Chapel**
    Barkers Road
    Schreiber & Jörgensen (220)

9. EAGLEMONT/IVANHOE

Chadwick House

Delbridge House

Lippincott House

Heidelberg Town Hall

Since the 1840s, when a portion of the area had been reserved by the government as a site for a village and some very early buildings had been constructed (notably Banyule and St John's Anglican Church), Heidelberg had maintained its semi-rural/semi-suburban character for the greater part of the 19th century. The east-facing slopes of the Yarra River from the Darebin Creek to Salt Creek became favoured locations for views painted by *plein air* artists of the so-called Heidelberg School such as Tom Roberts, Arthur Streeton and Frederick McCubbin. By the 1890s, suburban development had begun to encroach. One could live at Heidelberg or Ivanhoe and commute to the city by train. From 1903, The Eyrie in Eaglemont was home to architect Harold Desbrowe-Annear and a number of his most important houses can be found nearby. In 1914, American architect and landscape architect Walter Burley Griffin designed the Summit Estate section of Mount Eagle (area bounded by Lower Heidelberg Road, The Eyrie, Glen Drive and Maltravers Road) and in 1916, the Glenard Estate (the area bounded by Lower Heidelberg Road, Banksia Street and the Boulevard). Located on either side of Lower Heidelberg Road, the two subdivisions featured roads which followed the gently curving contours of the hillside and shared green spaces at the rear of suburban lots which were linked by pedestrian footpaths to others to form landscaped spines between the houses. The intention was that the landscape be understood as common land and that these green spaces be located at the most advantageous landscape sites with distant views and planted with or retaining existing, indigenous trees. Griffin and his wife Marion lived in their tiny house Pholiota (1922) on the Glenard Estate and commuted daily to their city office. Sadly, a total of only three Griffin-designed houses were built on the two estates and one must now imagine the Griffins' ideal of a democratic and coherent visual suburban environment.

1. **McKenzie House (1987–89)**
   7 Roemer Crescent
   Ashton Raggatt McDougall
2. **Featherston House**
   22 The Boulevard, Ivanhoe
   Romberg & Boyd (362)
3. **MacGeorge House**
   25 Riverside Road
   Harold Desbrowe-Annear (170)
4. **St Stephen's Anglican Church**
   22-24 Merton Street
   Louis Williams (205)
5. **Heidelberg Town Hall**
   253-277 Upper Heidelberg Road
   Peck and Kemter with
   AC Leith & Associates (262)
6. **Beaumont Estate**
   Melcombe Road & Hampton, Tudor,
   Surrey & Lincoln Cts
   Edgar Gurney (250)
7. **Bell/Banksia Street Freeway Link**
   Bell & Banksia Streets
   Cocks Carmichael Whitford
8. **Fire Station No. 15 (1993)**
   Bell & Edwin Streets
   Edmond & Corrigan

9. **House (1903)**
   14 Martin Street
   Harold Desbrowe-Annear
10. **Vaughan G Griffin House (1924)**
    52 Darebin Street
    WB Griffin & Marion Mahony
11. **St John's Anglican Church**
    1 Burgundy Street
    John Gill (18)
12. **House (1910)**
    234 Rosanna Road
    Harold Desbrowe-Annear
13. **Banyule**
    60 Buckingham Drive
    John Gill (10)
14. **Heide Park & Art Gallery**
    7 Templestowe Road
    McGlashan & Everist (352)
15. **Lippincott House**
    21 Glenard Drive
    Roy Lippincott &
    WB Griffin (171)
    Pholiota
    23 Glenard Drive
    WB Griffin & Marion
    Mahony (172)

16. **Williams House**
    4 Glenard Drive
    Charles Duncan (336)
17. **Delbridge House**
    55 Carlsberg Road
    owner-designed
18. **Annear House** (1903)
    36–38 The Eyrie
    Harold Desbrowe-Annear
19. **Chadwick House**
    32–34 The Eyrie
    Harold Desbrowe-Annear (146)
20. **House** (1903)
    28–30 The Eyrie
    Harold Desbrowe-Annear
21. **Mervyn Skipper House**
    45 Outlook Drive
    WB Griffin & Marion Mahony (219)
22. **Kyritsis House** (1898–90)
    15 Outlook Drive
    Wood Marsh
23. **Snelleman House**
    40 Keam Street
    Peter McIntyre (298)

24. **Purcell House**
    17 Hartlands Road
    Guilford Bell (350)
25. **St George's Anglican Church** (1962)
    46 Warncliffe Road
    Romberg & Boyd
26. **Ravenswood** (1891)
    Beauview Parade & York Avenue
27. **Ashton House** (1957, 1997)
    262 The Boulevard
    Don Hendry Fulton; McBride Charles Ryan
28. **'Stargazer' (Castle) House**
    Aquila & Taurus Streets
    Peter McIntyre (297)
29. **Keith Mann House**
    39 Inverness Way
    Montgomery King & Trengove (309)

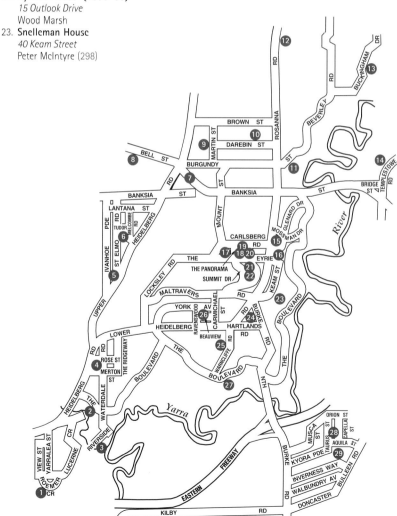

ACKNOWLEDGEMENTS

Our thanks extend to the following individuals and organisations for the provisions of materials, information and editorial assistance:

Bridget Dwyer; Ray Tonkin — Heritage Victoria; Miles Lewis, Greg Missingham, Terry Sawyer, Alex Selenitsch, George Tibbits, Catherine Townsend, Jeffrey Turnbull, Evan Walker, Julie Willis — University of Melbourne; Harriet Edquist, Peter Navaretti — RMIT; Robert Bruce — Bates Smart; Carlotta Kellaway; Ian and Ros Coleman; Vicki Johnson; John Statham; Richard Peterson; Graeme Butler; Sally Sagazio, Rohan Storey - National Trust of Australia (Victoria); Anne Neale; Kate Gray, Katrina Place, Simon Reeves, Robyn Riddett — Allom Lovell & Associates; Bryce Raworth; Barry Patten; Graeme Gunn; Maggie Edmond; Suzanne Dance; Lindsay Holland; Norman Day; Tim Black; Peter Elliott; Hamish Lyon.

Plans redrawn by: Como— Paul Porjazoski; Labassa—Paul Porjazoski; Banyule—Paul Porjazoski; Stonnington—Paul Porjazoski; Trawalla—Paul Porjazoski; Spurling House—John Statham; Chadwick House—John Statham; Anselm—John Statham; Wyalla—John Statham; Glyn—John Statham; McGeorge House—John Statham; Second Church of Christ Scientist—Paul Porjazoski; Haileybury College Chapel—Paul Porjazoski; Trinity Grammar School Chapel—Paul Porjazoski; Altona Meadows Uniting Church—Paul Porjazoski; St Faith's Anglican Church—Paul Porjazoski; Chapel of St Joseph —Paul Porjazoski; Richardson House—Jefa Greenaway; Gottlieb House—Jefa Greenaway; Purcell House—Jefa Greenaway; Alessio House—Jefa Greenaway; Atlas House—Jefa Greenaway; Seccull House—Jefa Greenaway; Athan House—Simon Perkins; Beach House, Rye—Simon Perkins; Carlton Baths—Simon Perkins; Brunswick Community Health Care Centre—Simon Perkins; Foy House—Brendan Jones; Boyd House—Brendan Jones; Featherston House—Brendan Jones; Kitamura House—Brendan Jones; Hildebrand House—Brendan Jones

Plan/illustration sources: *Architecture & Arts*; *RVIA Journal*; Cross Section Archive, thesis collection—Architecture Library, University of Melbourne; John Wardle Architects; Kai Chen.

NOTES ON CONTRIBUTORS

Neil Clerehan is a Principal of Clerehan Cran Architects. With a career that has spanned almost five decades, he is the recipient of numerous RAIA Awards.

Dr Philip Goad is Senior Lecturer in the Faculty of Architecture Building & Planning at the University of Melbourne where he teaches design and architectural history.

Dr Conrad Hamann is Associate Professor in Architectural History in the Department of Visual Culture at Monash University where he teaches art and architectural history.

Bryce Raworth is a well-known conservation consultant and architectural historian in Melbourne. He has a particular interest in early 20th-century architecture in Australia.

George Tibbits is a Senior Associate in The Australian Centre at the University of Melbourne. He is a notable architectural historian and composer.

Bruce Trethowan is an architect and Director of Robert Peck Von Hartel Trethowan in Melbourne. His firm has restored numerous significant and historic Melbourne buildings.

INDEX